D1529196

THE
ISLAM
BOOK

BIG IDEAS

THE ART BOOK

THE ASTRONOMY BOOK

THE BIBLE BOOK

THE BUSINESS BOOK

THE CLASSICAL MUSIC BOOK

THE CRIME BOOK

THE ECOLOGY BOOK

THE ECONOMICS BOOK

THE FEMINISM BOOK

THE HISTORY BOOK

THE ISLAM BOOK

THE LITERATURE BOOK

THE MATH BOOK

THE MOVIE BOOK

THE MYTHOLOGY BOOK

THE PHILOSOPHY BOOK

THE PHYSICS BOOK

THE POLITICS BOOK

THE PSYCHOLOGY BOOK

THE RELIGIONS BOOK

THE SCIENCE BOOK

THE SHAKESPEARE BOOK

THE SHERLOCK HOLMES BOOK

THE SOCIOLOGY BOOK

SIMPLY EXPLAINED

THE ISLAM BOOK

Penguin
Random
House

First American Edition, 2020
Published in the United States by DK Publishing
1450 Broadway, Suite 801, New York, NY 10018

Copyright © 2020 Dorling Kindersley Limited
DK, a Division of Penguin Random House LLC
20 21 22 23 24   10 9 8 7 6 5 4 3 2 1
001–316422–July/2020

THE KORAN translated with notes by N. J. Dawood
(Penguin Classics 1956, Fifth revised edition 1990).
Copyright © N. J. Dawood, 1956, 1959, 1966, 1968, 1974,
1990, 1993, 1997, 1999, 2003, 2006, 2014

A catalog record for this book is available
from the Library of Congress.
ISBN 978-1-4654-9148-0

DK books are available at special discounts when
purchased in bulk for sales promotions, premiums,
fund-raising, or educational use. For details, contact:
DK Publishing Special Markets, 1450 Broadway,
Suite 801, New York, NY 10018
SpecialSales@dk.com

Printed and bound in UAE

For the curious

www.dk.com

CONTRIBUTORS

RAGEH OMAAR, FOREWORD

Rageh Omaar made his name as the BBC correspondent reporting from Baghdad during the 2003 invasion of Iraq. He also reported from Afghanistan, the Middle East, and Africa for the BBC as a foreign correspondent. He later worked for Al Jazeera English, before, in January 2013, joining ITV News where he is International Affairs Editor and host of Britain's iconic News at Ten program. Rageh has also made numerous documentary series for British national television including BBC's *The Life of Muhammad*. He is also the author of *Revolution Day: The Real Story of the Battle for Iraq* (2005) and *Only Half of Me: Being a Muslim in Britain* (2006).

DR. FARHAD DAFTARY, CONSULTANT

Dr. Daftary is an authority in Shia studies, in particular the Ismaili tradition. He has written more than 200 articles and encyclopedia entries, and many acclaimed books, including *A History of Shi'i Islam* (2013). Books on which he has acted as editor include *Islam: An Illustrated Journey* (2018). He is co-director and head of the Department of Academic Research and Publications at The Institute of Ismaili Studies, in London.

AYA KHALIL, CONSULTANT

An American-Egyptian, Aya Khalil holds a master's degree in education and is the author of the picture book *The Arabic Quilt: An Immigrant Story*. As a journalist focusing on Muslim-related issues, her writing has been published in *The Huffington Post* and *The Christian Science Monitor*, and on the popular website MuslimGirl.com. She blogs regularly on Muslim-related issues, posting stories on topics such as "10 Words & Phrases to Avoid if You're #FlyingWhileMuslim."

IBRAHIM MOGRA, CONSULTANT

Ibrahim Mogra is an imam and the director of Mogra Faith & Culture Consultancy Limited, and a member of The Muslim Council of Britain. In 2016, he received the Hubert Walter Award for Reconciliation and Interfaith Cooperation from the Archbishop of Canterbury "for his sustained contribution to understanding between the Abrahamic faiths." He has edited and contributed to a number of religious education textbooks and has written a teachers' handbook on Islam.

SALMA HAIDRANI

A multi-award-winning freelance writer and journalist based in London, Salma Haidrani has written for *i-D, Vice, Dazed, HUNGER,* and *GQ* magazines on topics including contemporary faith and identity, women's rights, social issues, and marginalized communities. She is also a contributing author to the best-selling anthology *It's Not About the Burqa: Muslim Women on Faith, Feminism, Sexuality and Race* (2019).

ANDREW HAMMOND

A former journalist with BBC Arabic radio, and Reuters in Egypt, Saudi Arabia, and the United Arab Emirates, Andrew Hammond later became a Middle East policy analyst with the European Council on Foreign Relations (ECFR). He is also an Islamic historian, who studied Arabic at London's School of Oriental and African Studies, and Turkish and Ottoman at Oxford University, where he obtained his doctorate. His books include *The Islamic Utopia: The Illusion of Reform in Saudi Arabia* (2012) and *Popular Culture in North Africa and the Middle East* (2017).

ANDREW HUMPHREYS

Journalist, author, and editor Andrew Humphreys has worked in Egypt, Central Asia, India, Morocco, Syria, and Turkey. He was the cofounder and editor-in-chief of *The Cairo Times* newspaper, and his journalism has appeared in the UK's *Financial Times, The Sunday Times,* and *The Telegraph.* He is the author of two books on 19th-century Egypt, published by the American University in Cairo Press.

SHELINA JANMOHAMED

Shelina Janmohamed is the vice president of Islamic marketing at global advertising and marketing agency Ogilvy. She is the author of *Love in a Headscarf* (2009), a memoir of growing up as a British Muslim woman, and *Generation M: Young Muslims Changing the World* (2016), described as a defining text on a Muslim generation bringing faith and modernity together. In 2009, she was named one of the UK's 100 most powerful Muslim women by the Equality and Human Rights Commission (EHRC).

CHARLES TIESZEN

Charles Tieszen, PhD (University of Birmingham, 2010) is an historian of religious thought. A fellow of the Royal Historical Society, his work focuses on the historical development of Islamic thought and the history of relationships between Muslim and non-Muslim communities. His most recent book is called *The Christian Encounter with Muhammad.*

DR. COLIN TURNER

Dr. Colin Turner is director and chief executive officer of the International Foundation for Muslim Theology and was, until 2017, Reader in Islamic Thought at the University of Durham. A trained historian, his chief areas of interest are Muslim theology, Quranic interpretation, and the life and works of Bediuzzaman Said Nursi. He is the author of numerous books and articles, including the best-selling *Islam: The Basics* (2005) and *The Quran Revealed: A Critical Analysis of Said Nursi's Epistles of Light* (2013).

DR. MAHSHID TURNER

Director of the International Foundation for Muslim Theology, Dr. Mahshid Turner is a freelance researcher and lecturer. Trained in theology at the University of Durham, she publishes on Muslim theology, philosophy, and Quranic interpretation. She is the first female Muslim chaplain at a British university, having served at the University of Durham in that capacity since 2015.

CONTENTS

AN ISLAMIC IDENTITY
632–786

THE GOLDEN AGE OF ISLAM
756–1526

REFORM AND REVIVAL
1527–1979

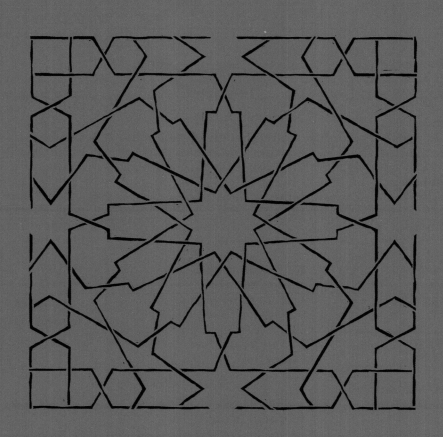

FOREWORD

At the start of the 7th century CE, a man who had just turned 40, a man who had grown up an orphan, clambered up a barren, rocky hillside to reach a cave in a valley near Mecca, an important city for trade and the worship of numerous deities in the Arabian desert. Such retreats were something he had often undertaken for contemplation and solitude. It was up here that, one day, he received his very first revelation from the angel Gabriel, known as Jibreel in Arabic—it was one simple word: "Read." Gripped by fear and overcome with emotion, he responded, saying, "But I don't know how to read." Again, the divine order came: "Read." Then, miraculously, having not thought himself capable, he began to recite the first words of a new holy book. That man, Muhammad, would go on to become the Prophet, and the revelation that started in the Cave of Hira would become known as the Quran, the holy book of Islam—the religion followed by an estimated 1.8 billion people across the world.

For me, one of the most profound and telling aspects of this moment of Islam's birth is that the very first word with which the religion was brought into being was "Read." I can think of no other word today that is as relevant and vital to the contemplation of Islam than "read." A huge part of my life over the last 25 years as an international news reporter has involved bearing witness to political upheaval, conflict, and humanitarian tragedies in Muslim countries—as someone who was himself raised as a Muslim. From Iraq to Indonesia, Somalia to Syria, Bosnia to Bangladesh, I have witnessed and tried to convey to viewers of all faiths—and those with none—conflict and misunderstanding between Muslims and the West, between Muslims and non-Muslims, and also among Muslims themselves. As I've done so, I have always traveled to my assignments carrying books. Books like this one, that you now hold in your hands. In my travels across the Islamic world during these turbulent decades, I have worked alongside diplomats, soldiers, and humanitarian relief workers who would often say how valuable it would be to have a reference book that gives a clear and accessible explanation about the principles of Islam and the rich, multilayered history of the religion and the ideas that have inspired it. The remarkable achievement of this book is that it provides an invaluable resource for Muslims and non-Muslims alike. Discussions of the flowering of Islam's scientific "Golden Age" and the uses of calligraphy, as well as questions about women's rights in Islam and the rise of extremism, help all of us, whether we call ourselves Muslim or not, to understand the faith better. The joy of this clearly written and cleverly illustrated book is that it starts from the premise that there are no questions too simple for this book to be of interest and value. The reverse is also true; however much you think you know about Islamic history and the Muslim world, this book will still delight and open doors to this faith for you.

Rageh Omaar

INTROD

UCTION

This book describes the foundational ideas not just of Islam, the religion, but also of many of the great Islamic civilizations, cultures, and political and social movements that the religion inspired, and continues to inspire.

Along with Judaism and Christianity, Islam is one of the world's three great monotheistic religions. It was founded in the early 7th century CE by Muhammad, a merchant from the city of Mecca (Makkah) on the Arabian Peninsula. He received from God the revelations contained in the Quran, the holy book of Islam, and preached them to a steadily increasing group of followers. Muhammad was not preaching a wholly new religion,

rather he was urging the primarily polytheist inhabitants of Arabia to return to the worship of the one true God. This was the same God of the Abrahamic tradition, whose past prophets included Ibrahim (Abraham), Musa (Moses), and Isa (Jesus)—who Muslims believe is not the son of God, but a prophet. For Muslims, Muhammad is the last in this line of prophets.

The three "religions of the Book" share a belief in the transience of earthly life, in the imperative of prayer and good deeds, in our accountability before God for our actions, and in the assurance of a return to God on the Day of Judgement. For Muslims, this is all described in the Quran, which, along with the sayings and examples set by the Prophet during his lifetime, laid the blueprint for a life in Islam.

The spread of Islam
Islam is a holistic religion that integrates all aspects of life. Traditionally in Islam there was no division between what the Western world terms Church and State. Muhammad and his immediate successors were religious, political, and military leaders in one office. The ideas enshrined in Islam were spread rapidly from Arabia and throughout what we now call the

Middle East and across North Africa. Islam advanced into Europe, taking root in southern Spain; it moved deeper into Africa, and through Central Asia, into India and east to China. Muslim traders took Islam to Southeast Asia, where it flourished on the islands and archipelagos of the Indian Ocean.

As the religion expanded, scholars, clerics, and legal minds took what were oral traditions and engaged in a process of verification and transcription—defining the Islamic identity. From this came a framework for Islamic law, or Sharia, new practices of Quranic interpretation, an Islamic calendar, and many of the traditions that define the faith.

There were those who objected to the codification of the religion and who pursued their own more personal version of Islam—they would be known as Sufis. There were disagreements, too, over who should succeed Muhammad as leader of the Muslims; one group split from the mainstream and became known as the Shia.

A golden age
Along the way, Islam created great centers of learning, which accommodated both theological study and the formulation of Islamic

You can't talk about Muslims or Islam if you don't know it.
Ghostface Killah
American rapper, 2015 interview with Vice magazine

law, as well as the pursuit of philosophy, medicine, astronomy, and the sciences. At a period in history when the knowledge of the ancient world—particularly of the Greeks—was about to be lost, Islamic scholars took on the task of preserving that knowledge and building on it. A succession of mighty Islamic empires emerged, first in Arab lands, centered on Damascus in Syria (Umayyad), then Baghdad in Iraq (Abbasid), and Cairo in Egypt (Fatimid and Mamluk), and then later among non-Arab peoples: in Turkey (Ottoman), Persia (Safavid), and India (Mughal).

Islam in modern times

It is only in recent history, from around the late 17th century, that the growth of Islam slowed. Around this time its global influence began to be eclipsed by the Christian empires of Europe. Those empires set about colonizing Muslim-majority countries, a situation that only came to an end midway through the 20th century. In many instances, Islam provided a focus for opposition to colonial powers and an inspiration for nationalist movements. In the latter part of the 20th century, Islam was resurgent, flourishing in every part of the world, meeting the challenges of modern times while remaining faithful to traditional values.

Today, the Islamic world spans the globe. The Pew Research Center, a US-based think tank that gathers data on global trends, estimated in 2015 that there were 1.8 billion Muslims around the world, making Islam the second-largest religion after Christianity. Islam is also the world's fastest growing religion. In 2020, almost one in four people globally was a Muslim. Looking ahead, the Pew Research Center estimates that by 2050 the number of Muslims will grow to 2.76 billion, or 29.7 percent of the entire global population—meaning almost one in three people in the world will be a Muslim.

Over the course of its roughly 1,400 years, Islam has massively shaped the history of the world, in all kinds of ways, from the political to the cultural and spiritual. In years to come, the influence of Islam will only grow, and it is beneficial to both non-Muslims and Muslims alike that its core ideals be better understood.

A note on spellings

Islam originated in an Arabic-speaking culture, and its terminology is permeated by Arabic words. The science of transliterating Arabic into English is imprecise; for instance, the Prophet's name can be written in English as Muhammad, Mohamed, Mohammed, Mahomat, and numerous other permutations. English does not have characters to represent exactly the same sounds as Arabic letters. In this book we have used spellings that are a comfortable read for English speakers. Similarly, for the benefit of English readers, we have used the word "God" throughout this book, rather than "Allah," the Arabic name for God. ■

Islam is misunderstood by many. The extremists grab the headlines; those of us who want to practise our religion and live under this country's laws do not make the news.
Sadiq Khan
Mayor of London since 2016

MUHAM
570–632

MAD

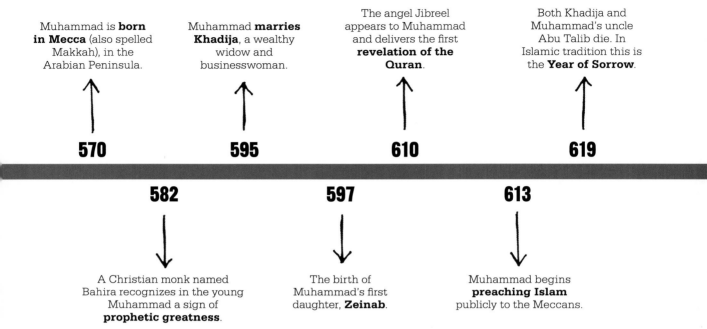

Muhammad is **born in Mecca** (also spelled Makkah), in the Arabian Peninsula.

Muhammad **marries Khadija**, a wealthy widow and businesswoman.

The angel Jibreel appears to Muhammad and delivers the first **revelation of the Quran**.

Both Khadija and Muhammad's uncle Abu Talib die. In Islamic tradition this is the **Year of Sorrow**.

570

595

610

619

582

597

613

A Christian monk named Bahira recognizes in the young Muhammad a sign of **prophetic greatness**.

The birth of Muhammad's first daughter, **Zeinab**.

Muhammad begins **preaching Islam** publicly to the Meccans.

In the 6th century BC, the fertile lands around the eastern Mediterranean were ruled by the powerful Byzantine Empire and the fertile plains of Mesopotamia to the east nurtured the Persian Sasanian civilization. The deserts of Arabia to the south were home to leaderless, seminomadic tribes. Vying for control of valuable trading routes, these tribes were constantly at war.

According to Islamic tradition, around 570, a boy was born in Mecca (Makkah), Arabia, into the Quraysh tribe. Named Muhammad, he was orphaned at the age of six, and grew up in the care of his uncle. He became a merchant, married, had children, and flourished in business. In later life, he often retreated to a remote cave, where he liked to meditate. On one such occasion he was visited by the angel Jibreel (Gabriel) who revealed to him the word of God.

Three years after receiving the first revelation, Muhammad—to whose name Muslims often add the phrase *Sallallahu alayhi wa sallam* ("Blessings of God and peace be upon him")—began preaching in his hometown of Mecca, slowly amassing a group of followers. However, his message of purity and justice, especially justice for the poor, and his condemnation of the idolatrous ways of the wealthy elite, earned him many enemies. Fleeing persecution, Muhammad led his community away from the city of his birth to settle in Medina, almost 210 miles (340 km) to the north, where his message had been more favorably received. This exodus is known as the *Hijra*.

Core of the faith
The religion Muhammad preached came to be known as "Islam" (from the Arabic word for "submission"), and its followers as "Muslims." It was in Medina that the faith's core beliefs and rituals were developed, based on the teachings of the Prophet Muhammad.

Central to the new faith was recognition that there was only one god—a radical claim in polytheistic 7th-century Arabia. Moreover, Muslims had to acknowledge that this one God, known in Arabic as Allah, had sent Muhammad as His Final Messenger. God had entrusted His message to earlier prophets, from Adam onward, but it was Muhammad who received the last divine revelation—over a period of 23 years—contained within the preachings known as the Quran.

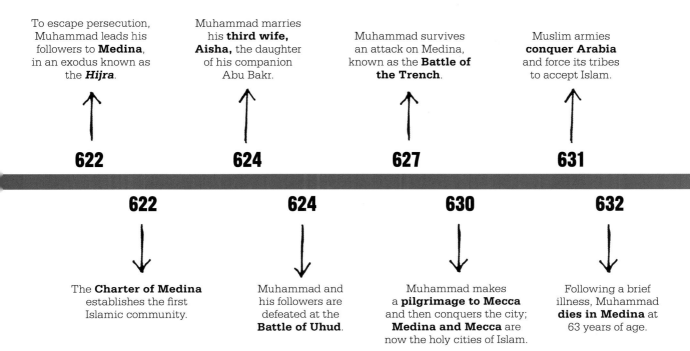

To escape persecution, Muhammad leads his followers to **Medina**, in an exodus known as the **Hijra**.

622

Muhammad marries his **third wife, Aisha,** the daughter of his companion Abu Bakr.

624

Muhammad survives an attack on Medina, known as the **Battle of the Trench**.

627

Muslim armies **conquer Arabia** and force its tribes to accept Islam.

631

622

The **Charter of Medina** establishes the first Islamic community.

624

Muhammad and his followers are defeated at the **Battle of Uhud**.

630

Muhammad makes a **pilgrimage to Mecca** and then conquers the city; **Medina and Mecca** are now the holy cities of Islam.

632

Following a brief illness, Muhammad **dies in Medina** at 63 years of age.

The examples set by Muhammad's life would provide his followers with the five pillars of their faith, starting with the recognition of one God and Muhammad as His messenger. The other pillars included regulated daily prayers, the importance of being charitable to others, and the obligations of fasting and pilgrimage to Mecca.

Fighting for survival

Pilgrimage was already common among the Arabs, who had a centuries-old tradition of journeying to the Kaaba, an ancient shrine in Mecca that was filled with statues of the many gods worshipped by the tribes. The threat Muhammad posed to the lucrative pilgrimage trade was one reason the Meccans had driven him out of their city. He remained a threat even from a

distance, and Medina's Muslims were obliged to take up arms against the Meccans to ensure their continued survival. After years of fighting, Muhammad and his followers captured Mecca.

On taking control of Mecca, Muhammad's first action was to clear the Kaaba of its idols and dedicate the shrine to the worship of the one God. Muhammad returned to Medina, but during the remaining years of his life he made several pilgrimages to the Kaaba—notably in 632, an occasion revered as the Farewell Pilgrimage. On this occasion, the Muslims who accompanied him observed every move, act, and gesture. The Prophet's actions set a precedent to be followed by Muslims around the world, enshrined as the Fifth Pillar of Islam, the Hajj.

Lasting legacy

When Muhammad had made the *Hijra* in 622, it was at the head of a small, outcast community. By the time of his unexpected death just 10 years later, the Muslims controlled much of the Arabian Peninsula. For the many tribes who had now accepted Islam, military success was a sign of the righteousness of the Prophet's message and of God's invisible presence in the Muslim community.

Many of the beliefs Muhammad preached were not new. They were beliefs that God had revealed through previous messengers, but it had taken a final prophet to renew the message. In this way, Islam could trace its roots all the way back to the first prophet, Adam, and it would live on long after the death of its last prophet, Muhammad. ∎

YOU KNEW NOTHING OF THE BOOK OR BELIEF
THE QURAN, 42:52

IN CONTEXT

THEME
Al-Jahiliya, the Time of Ignorance

WHEN AND WHERE
Pre-7th century CE, the Arabian Peninsula

BEFORE
1st century BCE Roman rule extends over the eastern Mediterranean, including the Arabian Peninsula.

3rd century CE The Middle East is dominated by the Byzantine and the Persian Sasanian Empires.

5th century The Quraysh tribe take control of Mecca and its shrine, the Kaaba, and turn the city into a thriving mercantile hub, attracting both pilgrims and traders.

AFTER
570 The birth of the Prophet Muhammad in Mecca; member of the Quraysh tribe. The Final Prophet who unites the Arab tribes under a single God.

The single most important concept in Islam is the indivisible oneness of God. In other words, monotheism. This is the concept upon which a Muslim's entire faith rests.

When Muhammad first began preaching the mission of Islam, in 613 CE, it was this central idea of oneness that served to bind his followers together. In stark contrast to this message, the Arab tribes at this time were divided, leaderless, weak, and worshipping multiple gods. In the words of the Quran, these were gods that could "create nothing and were themselves created; which can neither harm

The Arabian Peninsula in the era immediately before Islam was a political vacuum, flanked by two great warring empires, with the remains of a once great civilization to the south.

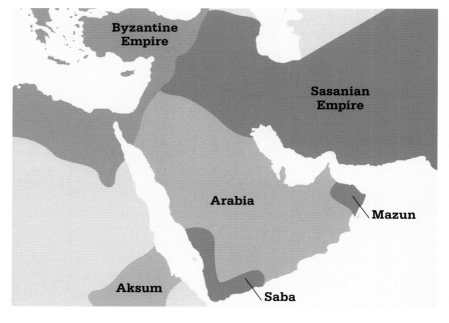

See also: The early life of Muhammad 22–27 ▪ The Kaaba at Mecca 34–35 ▪ The rise of political Islam 238–41

> The Prophet uprooted the practices of *jahiliya* one by one.
> **Abul Ala Mawdudi**

nor help themselves, and which have no power over death or life" (25:3). Before Islam, the Arabs were said to be living in *al-Jahiliya*, the "Time of Ignorance."

Pre-Islamic powers
In the centuries immediately prior to the birth of Muhammad, the Arabian Peninsula was surrounded by the Christian Byzantine Empire to the northwest and the Persian Sasanian Empire to the east. These two imperial titans were locked in a power struggle with each other.

In the south of the peninsula, rich and fertile Saba (Yemen) was one of the oldest centers of civilization in the region, with a complex history, but by the 6th century the once great kingdom had broken apart.

Between these three powers stretched the vast swathe of Central Arabia, which is predominantly harsh desert. Its sparse population was made up of nomadic Arab tribes who were constantly at war with one another and eked out a living by controlling the trade routes that crisscrossed the region.

Pre-Islamic religions
Communities of Christians, Jews, and Zoroastrians existed in Arabia prior to the 7th century, but the desert Arabs were generally mistrustful of these religions, which they associated with the imperial powers. While the Arabs had little time for formal religion of their own—their allegiances were to their individual tribes—there were places they considered holy. These were the sites of shrines, linked to particular deities. Among

This marble altar to the goddess al-Lat, depicted with her sacred lion, is dated to the 2nd century CE, from the temple of Bel (or Baal) in Palmyra, Syria.

the gods they worshipped were the high god al-Ilah, and his daughters, the goddesses al-Lat, al-Uzza, and Manat. One notable shrine devoted to al-Ilah was the Kaaba, near the well of Zamzam at Mecca.

By this time, many Arabs had given up the nomadic life. By the 4th century, for example, two tribes from Yemen had settled at the oasis of Yathrib, which would later become known as Medina, where they took up agriculture. A tribe known as the Quraysh had settled around Mecca by the end of the 5th century. They engaged in trading and stock-breeding and created a thriving city of great wealth. However, according to Islamic historians, what the tribes lacked was any real moral and ethical way of living. This would only change after Muhammad began receiving revelations in the early 7th century and undertook his mission of prophecy. ▪

Modern *jahiliya*

As a concept, *jahiliya* can be applied far beyond pre-Islamic Arabia. To label something as *jahiliya* was especially popular among Islamic reformers in the early and mid-20th century, who were angry at the predominance of Western influence and the ways many Muslims imitated and were captivated by it.

It was Islamist writer Abul Ala Mawdudi (1903–79) of Pakistan who coined the term "modern *jahiliya*," which he characterized as "the new barbarity," incompatible with Islam. Egyptian Islamic reformer Sayyid Qutb (1906–66) used the same term when he wrote in his commentary on the Quran that "People—in any time and any place—are either governed by God's law ... or they are governed by a law invented by humans. ... In that case they are in *jahiliya*." For Qutb, *jahiliya* was the "rule of humans by humans," making them servants of one another instead of servants of God.

MUHAMMAD IS GOD'S FINAL MESSENGER

THE QURAN, 33:40, AND VARIOUS HADITH

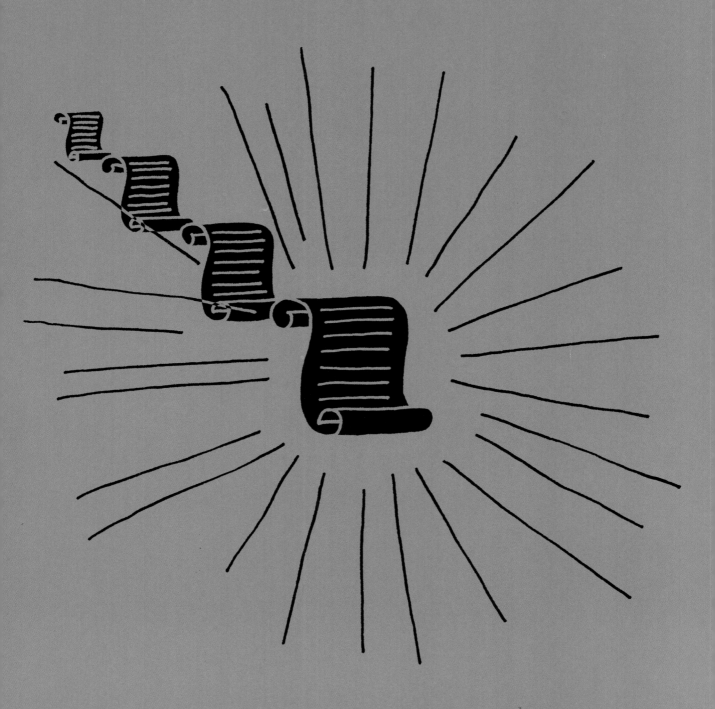

IN CONTEXT

THEME
The early life of Muhammad

WHEN AND WHERE
570–622 CE, Arabia

BEFORE
c. **2000–1500 BCE** In the Bible, God makes a covenant with the patriarch Abraham; Islam will recognize this figure (in Arabic, Ibrahim) as one of the first prophets.

c. **14th–13th century BCE** In Jewish, Christian, and Muslim tradition, the prophet Moses receives commandments from God on Mount Sinai.

c. **1st century CE** Jesus, later recognized by Muslims as a prophet, foretells the coming of a final messenger of God.

AFTER
19th century In India, Mirza Ghulam Ahmad claims to be a prophet bringing a new message that will reform Islam.

A ccording to Islamic tradition, in around 582 CE a Christian hermit, Bahira, was living in the Syrian desert when, one day, a boy passing by with a camel train caught his attention. After talking with him, Bahira concluded that the sign of prophecy was upon the boy. He was destined for greatness, Bahira told the boy's guardians, and should be cared for well. The young boy was Muhammad, who became the prophet of Islam and, according to Muslims, God's Final Messenger.

Muhammad was born in 570 in Mecca (Makkah) into the Banu Hashim clan of the Quraysh tribe. His father died before he was born and his mother when Muhammad was six. His grandfather, Abd al-Muttalib, took him into his care until he, too, died when Muhammad was eight. From this point, his uncle Abu Talib raised him. They lived in meager circumstances and Muhammad worked with his uncle as a traveling merchant. He later married and had children, and was known for his kindness to the poor, but otherwise Muhammad led an unexceptional life.

The angel Jibreel appeared to Muhammad to reveal verses of the Quran. Jibreel would sometimes take on the form of a man; at other times, he would share revelations by voice only.

The angel says "Read"
Muhammad often climbed to a cave on Jabal al-Nur (Mountain of Light) in the Meccan Valley to meditate for days at a time. In 610, on the 27th night of what is now Ramadan (the ninth month of the Islamic calendar), he was awoken from sleep in his cave by a divine presence. According to tradition, it was the angel Jibreel (the Arabic name for Gabriel) who appeared to him. The angel simply commanded Muhammad to "Read!"

Khadija

Khadija bint Khuwaylid was the Prophet Muhammad's first wife. She was born in Mecca between 555 and 567 CE. She was widowed, but became a successful and wealthy merchant, overseeing a large contingent of caravans that traded with Syria and Yemen. She hired Muhammad to accompany one of her caravans. She received good reports of the honourable way that Muhammad had conducted his business, and he brought back twice as much profit as Khadija had been expecting. She proposed marriage to him; according to most traditions, she was 40 and Muhammad was 15 years her junior, but he accepted the proposal.

Khadija was Muhammad's only wife until her death in 619 (her mausoleum, shown here, was in Mecca until 1925). The number of children they had together is disputed, but it is generally given as six to eight, only four of whom survived to adulthood. Although Muhammad would go on to remarry 10 times, he remained devoted to Khadija, and to this day she is often referred to by Muslims as "Mother of the Believers."

See also: *Al-Jahiliyya*, the Time of Ignorance 20–21 ▪ The Five Pillars of Islam: *sawm* 46–49 ▪ Compiling the Quran 64–69 ▪ The composition of the Quran 70–75 ▪ Tolerating the beliefs of others 80–81 ▪ Sayings and actions of the Prophet 118–23

A confused Muhammad replied, "I am not a reader." The angel embraced Muhammad and commanded him again to read. This happened three times before Muhammad asked, "What shall I read?" Jibreel responded with the very first revelation, what is now the first five verses of chapter 96 of the Quran:

*Read in the name of your Lord
    who created; created man
    from clots of blood.
Read! Your Lord is the Most
    Bountiful One, who by the
    pen taught man what he
    did not know.*

Another passage from the Quran (53:2–10) recounts Muhammad's encounter with the angel Jibreel and serves to affirm that the Prophet did not proclaim his own words, but only those given to him from God:

*He does not speak out of his
    own fancy. This is a revelation
    inspired. He is taught by one
    who is powerful and mighty.
He stood on the uppermost horizon;
    then, drawing near, he came
    down within two bows' length
    or even closer, and revealed
    to His servant that which
    He revealed.*

Fears of madness

Muhammad was terrified. He feared that he had been possessed by a *jinni*, an evil spirit. He began to climb further up the mountain, intending to fling himself to his death, but on the mountainside he had another vision. He became aware of an overwhelming and towering presence that filled the whole horizon. He heard a voice saying, "O Muhammad! You are the messenger of God and I am Jibreel."

Muhammad made his way home and, still in a state of terror, told his wife Khadija what had happened. She comforted him and took him to consult her cousin Waraka, who was a priest in the Christian Nestorian faith and was well versed in scripture. Waraka listened to Khadija and said, "If you have spoken the truth to me, O Khadija, there has come to him the greatest Law that came to Moses; surely he is the prophet of this people."

Islamic scholars believe that there were about 10 more revelations made to Muhammad »

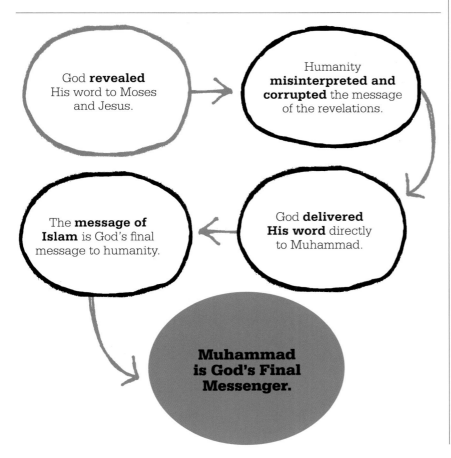

God **revealed** His word to Moses and Jesus.

Humanity **misinterpreted and corrupted** the message of the revelations.

God **delivered His word** directly to Muhammad.

The **message of Islam** is God's final message to humanity.

Muhammad is God's Final Messenger.

Thus have we sent forth a messenger of your own who will recite to you Our revelations and purify you of sin...
2:151

over the following two years, but these were not at first revealed in public. Instead, Islamic scholars characterize this time as one of great despair for Muhammad, during which his thoughts turned to ending his life.

The turning point eventually came in the form of another revelation, which seemed to offer him divine reassurance:

*By the light of day, and by the night
when she spreads her darkness,
your Lord has not forsaken you,
nor does He abhor you.
The life to come holds a richer
prize for you than this present life;
and you shall be gratified with
what your Lord will give you.
Did He not find you an orphan and
give you shelter?
And did He not find you in error
and guide you?
And did He not find you poor and
enrich you?
Therefore do not wrong the orphan,
nor chide away the beggar.
But proclaim the goodness
of your Lord.*

Muhammad is ... the Messenger of God and the Seal of the Prophets.
33:40

This revelation, which now forms chapter 93 of the Quran, is credited with giving Muhammad the belief that he had been divinely chosen to be the prophet of his people.

A religion called Islam
In approximately 613, Muhammad began to preach in public to the citizens of Mecca. These were largely members of his own tribe, the Quraysh. His initial message was simple. Based on the traditional Arab code of honor, the Prophet's preaching concentrated on clear

social messages: to live frugally, care for the poor, and be generous with sharing wealth for the good of the whole community.

Muhammad also wanted the Quraysh to be aware of God's goodness. God had created man and the universe and it was right that man should pray regularly to God to bring order. This God was identified as al-Ilah, the High God of the Arabs, who was worshipped at the Kaaba in Mecca. The Quraysh were to abandon worship of all other gods.

Eventually, the message that Muhammad preached became known as *Islam*, from the Arabic word for "submission," a reference to the act of submission that followers were expected to make to God. The followers of Islam became known as *Muslims*, meaning "those who submit."

The first Muslims
Muhammad's wife, Khadija, accepted the truth of the angel's revelations from the start and she is regarded as the first Muslim. His uncle Abu Talib rejected the new religion, but other members of the family became followers, including Muhammad's cousin Ali ibn Abi Talib. Another early convert was a family friend, Abu Bakr, a figure of influence in Mecca, who was able to bring many younger converts into the new religion. Both Ali and Abu Bakr would later have significant roles to play in the further development of Islam.

The revelations Muhammad received answered a need among the Arabs. God had sent the Jews

Muslim pilgrims visit the Cave of Hira on Jabal al-Nur in the Meccan Valley, in what is now Saudi Arabia, where Muhammad received his first revelation from the angel Jibreel.

In the Muslim's heart is the home of Muhammad.
Muhammad Iqbal
Indian philosopher (1877–1938)

and Christians their prophets and scriptures (the Bible and the Torah), but until now the Arabs had no prophet of their own. Muhammad brought a message from God delivered in the Arabic language for his people.

The final messenger

The revelations continued for the rest of Muhammad's life. They did not arrive with such spectacle as the visitation from Jibreel on Jabal al-Nur. More often they simply came over the Prophet, as if he was in a trance. Neither did the revelations always come in verbal form; Muhammad frequently received visions rather than words. According to the Prophet, it was not an easy process; he is reported to have once said, "Never once did I receive a revelation without thinking that my soul had been torn away from me."

The revelations varied widely in content, ranging from spiritual concerns to topics governing the establishment and propagation of a new community. Over time,

however, two crucial elements came to dominate the message. The first was that there is only one God. This monotheism (belief in one God) was in stark contrast to the polytheism common in Mecca, where hundreds of gods were worshipped. The second key element was that the revelations, which would become known as the Quran ("recitations"), were God's message sent to humanity through Muhammad.

In this way, Muhammad presented Islam not as a new religion with a new holy scripture, but instead as the continuation of the revelation of God. The Jews and Christians already had holy scriptures that were revealed to them, but they had corrupted these revelations. One final message was required. Muhammad is thus the Seal (the last) of the Prophets and the Final Messenger. ■

Historical sources on Muhammad

Although it is the foundation of Islam, the Quran does not reveal very much about its prophet— Muhammad is only mentioned by name four times—beyond his moral excellence. As a result, Muslims look to secondary texts: these include the *hadith*, which are accounts of his sayings and actions, given by those who were close to him, and *al-sira*, which are reports of historical events from Muhammad's life, such as military expeditions and political treaties.

Drawing from all these sources, four historians of the classical Islamic period wrote on the life of Muhammad. The earliest was Muhammad ibn Ishaq (704–68), who was writing less than a century after the death of the Prophet. Although the histories include stories of a miraculous nature, they are not uncritical. Records of Muhammad's outspoken third wife Aisha, for example, include sharp comments she made about her husband.

YOUR BLOOD WILL BE MY BLOOD

PROPHET MUHAMMAD, THE SECOND PLEDGE AT AQABA

IN CONTEXT

THEME
Hijra, the flight from Mecca

WHEN AND WHERE
622, Mecca

BEFORE
610 While on spiritual retreat on Jabal al-Nur, Muhammad receives a first revelation from the angel Jibreel.

613 Muhammad begins to preach the word of God to the people of Mecca, who are enraged and persecute the Prophet and his followers.

AFTER
630 After years of war, Mecca swears allegiance to its Muslim conquerors under Muhammad. Like Medina, Mecca too becomes a holy city of Islam. From here, Islam will spread to become the religion of the entire Arabian Peninsula.

By about 613, Muhammad claimed the authority of a prophet, or one sent by God. He was also God's Final Messenger—named in the Quran as "the Seal," or the last of those to whom God had given a divine revelation. His mission was to preach monotheism—the worship of the one true God—and to return those around him to what he articulated as correct belief.

Over time, a small group of supporters, who came to be known as Muslims, gathered around the Prophet to hear and recite the divine revelations given to him—the Quran—and to listen to the emerging message of Islam.

See also: The early life of Muhammad 22–27 ▪ The *umma,* the community of Islam 32–33 ▪ The Kaaba at Mecca 34–35 ▪ The Five Pillars of Islam: *salat* 42–43

In **Mecca**, Muhammad gains a **small group of supporters**, who become known as **Muslims** or "those submitted to God."

↓

Most Meccans are resentful of Muhammad and **persecute him and his followers**.

↓

A group from **Medina embraces Islam** and invites Muhammad to come to their city.

↓

Muhammad flees Mecca and, pursued by the Quraysh tribe, arrives at **Medina**.

↓

The *Hijra*—Muhammad's flight to Medina—marks the starting point of the Muslim calendar.

The Night Journey

Muhammad's famous Night Journey, which took place in about the same period as the *Hijra*, is briefly mentioned in the Quran: "Glory be to Him who made His servant go by night from the Sacred Temple to the farther Temple whose surroundings We have blessed, that We might show him some of Our signs" (17:1).

The Prophet's biographer Ibn Ishaq and various *hadith* provide more detail. They describe a miraculous night journey (the *Isra* in Arabic), when he rode a flying steed named Buraq from Mecca to Jerusalem. Once there, he ascended to heaven (the *Miraj*), where he met many of the great prophets. He was even granted a veiled vision of God, who commanded the Muslim community to pray 50 times a day. When the Prophet requested a more lenient obligation, the number was lowered to five daily prayers.

The story serves to ground the importance of Jerusalem in Islam's sacred geography, provide a basis for the five daily prayers required of Muslims, and affirm the nature of Muhammad as a spiritual guide.

Resistance to the message

Aside from this early community of believers, many in Mecca rejected Muhammad's message and bitterly resented his condemnations of their society's injustices. These centered on what Muhammad felt was a neglect of virtue and morality, particularly in regard to the poor and marginalized.

Muhammad also condemned the neglect of earlier prophets' teachings and the idolatry practiced at the Kaaba, and called Meccans back to pure worship of the one God. At this time, the Kaaba was the most important shrine in Arabia and a focus of pilgrimage from around the region.

As such, the Kaaba—and its polytheistic pantheon of gods—gave the city status and wealth derived from the fees that the Meccans charged the pilgrims. Muhammad's attack on Meccan polytheism was a threat to an important source of income.

Muhammad and his followers were looked upon by most Meccans with suspicion and even hatred. Muslims were persecuted for their beliefs. They found it difficult to survive, and were at times even killed. According to tradition, a group of Muslims left Mecca in 615 and sought refuge in the Christian kingdom of Aksum, across the Red Sea, in present-day Ethiopia. »

In Aksum, the Muslims were well received and given an audience with the king. When he asked whether the Muslims brought anything from God, one of them recited a passage from the Quran concerning Mary, mother of Jesus. Recognizing its parallels with the Gospels, the king wept. The Muslim refugees were granted safety in Aksum, though many later returned to rejoin Muhammad and the original Muslim community at Mecca in 622, followed by a second wave returning to Medina in 628.

A pact with Medina

Those Muslims who remained in Mecca continued to face persecution and threats to their lives. Refuge was first sought in the nearby town of Taif, but an invitation from the city of Medina proved more promising. Visiting Medina in 620, Muhammad had met with a small group who embraced Islam. These new Muslims returned to Mecca on pilgrimage in the following year, bringing with them additional converts who wanted to follow Muhammad and join his new community. They told Muhammad of their growing numbers in Medina and pledged to follow him and the message he preached. This agreement became known as the First Pledge of Aqaba, named after a hill to the north of the city where their meeting occurred.

In 622, a larger contingent of Muslims returned to Mecca on pilgrimage. This group also met with Muhammad, promised him their support, and invited him to seek refuge in Medina. This was no small decision. To go meant abandoning his own blood, the Quraysh tribe, and switching allegiance to a rival tribe, or tribes. To Arab sensibilities, this verged on treachery.

Muhammad sought assurance that he and his followers would be treated equally among the Medinans. They, in turn, asked what would happen if God granted Muhammad success after migrating to Medina: would he also remain true to them? As recorded by poet Kaab ibn Malik al-Ansari, one of his companions, Muhammad replied, "Your blood will be my blood. In life and death, I will be with you and you with me."

According to Islamic tradition, the subsequent pact the Medinans formed with Muhammad became known as the Second Pledge of Aqaba. The Medinans who formed the pact became known as the *ansar*, or the Helpers.

A failed assassination

With sympathetic followers in Medina, the guarantees agreed with them, and a divine revelation that permitted him to migrate to Medina, Muhammad could now make plans to flee Mecca. First to leave was a large group of about 70 Muslims and their families, who secretly made their way out of the city, toward Medina.

In Mecca, however, members of Muhammad's tribe, the Quraysh, were outraged by the alliance he had formed with the Muslim contingent from Medina. They planned an attack upon his home in order to assassinate him. Posted around the Prophet's house, the assailants watched during the night, waiting for their opportunity.

Fortunately, Muhammad had been warned of the plan to kill him. His cousin (and future son-in-law) Ali ibn Abi Talib took the Prophet's place in his bed, and Muhammad escaped through a window. It was only the next morning that the would-be assassins realized they had been tricked. Angry at the deception carried out by Muhammad and his followers, the Quraysh offered a bounty of 100 camels for anybody who could bring back the Prophet and his deputy Abu Bakr, dead or alive.

The *Hijra*

While the fugitives hid for three days in a cave before setting out for Medina, members of the Quraysh searched for them throughout Arabia. One pursuer, Suraqa bin Malik, tracked down Muhammad and Abu Bakr, but when he came close to them, his horse stumbled and fell. Suraqa remounted, but this time his horse's hoof got stuck in the sand. Close enough to shoot an arrow, Suraqa was nevertheless unable to do so. It occurred to him that God might actually be with Muhammad and Abu Bakr, and that no matter what he tried they would be victorious. Recognizing defeat, Suraqa gave up.

Meanwhile, the Muslims who had already migrated to Medina anxiously waited for Muhammad's arrival. According to *hadith* compiled by 9th-century scholar Muhammad al-Bukhari, a Jewish resident who had climbed to the roof of his home looked out across the desert and saw the Prophet and his companions in the distance. He shouted, "O you Arabs! Here is your great man whom you have been waiting for!" Muhammad remained camped on the edge of the Medinan oasis for three days, then entered the city.

Thus, in 622, Muhammad and his followers ended their journey to Medina. Such was the momentous importance of the transition from Mecca to Medina that for Muslims the *Hijra* marks year zero in the Islamic calendar. ∎

He that leaves his home in God's cause shall find many a refuge in the land and great abundance.
4:100

In 623, soon after the *Hijra*, under Muhammad's leadership the Muslims built their first great mosque at Medina, which is depicted in this 16th-century tile from Cairo, Egypt.

THE NOBLEST COMMUNITY EVER RAISED UP FOR MANKIND

THE QURAN, 3:110

IN CONTEXT

THEME
The *umma*, the community of Islam

WHEN AND WHERE
622–30, Medina

BEFORE
612–13 Muhammad begins preaching the word of God in Mecca, for which he and his followers suffer persecution.

622 Muhammad and his followers are invited to settle in Medina, where they are welcomed by Muslim converts.

AFTER
630 With Mecca now an Islamic city, Muhammad's armies embark upon conquest of the rest of Arabia.

632 Muhammad dies and his role as leader of the Islamic community is taken by his companion Abu Bakr. He and the subsequent Rashidun caliphs expand the reach of Islam around the eastern Mediterranean basin.

Initially the *umma* is **all people**, for whom God has sent His prophet Muhammad.

In Medina, the *umma* becomes the religious community that is made up of **the People of the Book**.

After Muhammad's return to Mecca, the *umma* evolves to refer specifically to **the Muslim community**.

Soon after settling in Medina, Muhammad began the task of consolidating rival tribes and asserting his authority. A distinct community formed, known as the *umma*, with Muhammad as its leader and the arbitrator of disputes. The *umma* initially included non-Muslims, and was more of a political entity than a strictly religious body. Later, the concept would be redefined to mean the Islamic community only.

Despite Muhammad's initial welcome in Medina and his demonstrable abilities as a leader, not all of the city's communities accepted his message or followed him as a leader. The Muslims also faced continual attacks from Meccan tribes.

Muhammad retaliated by organizing raids on Meccan camel caravans, a strategy that had the added benefit of providing funds for the fledgling Muslim community.

See also: *Hijra*, the flight from Mecca 28–31 ▪ The Five Pillars of Islam: Hajj 50–55 ▪ A successor to the Prophet 102–03 ▪ The rightly guided caliphs 104–07

> Whenever a dispute or controversy likely to cause trouble arises ... it shall be referred to God and to Muhammad.
> **Charter of Medina**

In 624, what began as an attack on caravans escalated into the Battle of Badr, from which Muhammad and his followers emerged victorious. The Quran attributes this success to divine favor: "God had already given you victory at Badr when you were helpless" (3:123). As verse 3:13 relates,

Indeed, there was a sign for you in the two armies which met on the battlefield.
One was fighting for the cause of God, the other being a host of unbelievers.
The faithful saw with their very eyes that they were twice their own number.
But God strengthens with His aid whom He will.

Later in 624, the Muslims fought with the Meccans again at the Battle of Uhud. When Muslim fighters broke ranks in order to pursue some of the Quraysh, this lack of discipline led to the Muslims becoming outflanked, and many were killed. Even Muhammad suffered serious injury and was forced to retreat with the other survivors.

A return to Mecca

In 628, after the Meccans had twice besieged Medina and been repelled, they signed the Treaty of Hudabiyya, which outlined a 10-year truce and allowed Muslims to enter Mecca on pilgrimage.

By 630, however, Muhammad's military power enabled him to return to Mecca and take it with ease. Muhammad had come not to punish the Quraysh but to abolish the worship of false gods. He rode to the Kaaba and circled it seven times, crying "Allahu akbar!" (God is great), and then he smashed every idol at the shrine.

This symbolized the final victory of Islam. From here, the Prophet's message of a return to monotheism, in a community set apart by God, would spread throughout the whole world. ▪

The Muslim community constructs a mosque at Medina. Built in 622, the Masjid Quba is still visited today by pilgrims at the end of the Hajj.

> O Quraysh, this is Muhammad who has come to you with a force that you cannot resist.
> **Abu Sufyan**
> *Quraysh leader at Mecca, 630*

The Charter of Medina

Soon after his arrival in Medina in 622, Muhammad strove to end the city's inter-tribal fighting and establish all his followers on an equal footing, under the Charter of Medina. The text declares the document to be "a book of the Prophet Muhammad to operate between the Muslims ... and those who may wage war in their company"— stating, for example, "To the Jew who follows us belongs help and equality." The nine tribes gathered under the charter would constitute "one *umma* separate from all peoples"—a community now thought to have had around 10,000 members.

According to the treaty, Muhammad's authority came directly from God, unlike others who might lay claim to power. He would arbitrate disputes among the groups covered by the treaty, and under his leadership many would later convert to Islam.

A BEACON FOR THE NATIONS

THE QURAN, 3:96

IN CONTEXT

SOURCE
The Kaaba at Mecca

WHEN AND WHERE
624–30, Mecca

BEFORE
c. **2000–1500 BCE** Ibrahim (Abraham in the Bible) is commanded by God to lay the foundations of a house of worship.

From 4th century BCE During the period of the Nabatean Empire, the Kaaba is dedicated to a deity from northern Arabia named Hubal.

5th century CE The Quraysh tribe control Mecca and the Kaaba is a site of pilgrimage for Arab tribes worshipping a multiplicity of gods.

AFTER
From 630 The Kaaba is the most holy shrine of Islam, to which all prayer is directed, and the focus of the annual Hajj pilgrimage.

The Quran reveals that it was Ibrahim (Abraham) and his son Ismail who were commanded by God to lay the foundations of the Kaaba and purify it as a house of worship (2:125–27). For this reason, it is also known in Arabic as the *Beit Allah*, or the House of God. However, besides passages in the Quran, there is very little historical evidence attesting to the Kaaba's origins.

Early commentators on the Quran suggested that the site was a place of worship for angels before the creation of man, and that later a house of worship was built there by Adam and Eve, which was lost

The first temple ever to be built for mankind was that at Mecca, a blessed site, a beacon for the nations.
3:96

during the flood in Noah's time. We do know that in the time before Islam, the Kaaba was held to be the most important of the many shrines at which the region's Arab tribes worshipped. The shrine was ringed by 360 idols, which may have represented the number of tribes that came there.

Reclaiming God's House

Embedded in the shrine's eastern corner was the sacred Black Stone, which was revered as heaven-sent. In 605, after a major fire, the Quraysh tribe who ruled Mecca rebuilt the Kaaba. When it came to putting back in position the Black Stone, the tribe's five clans could not agree who should have the honor. According to tradition, Muhammad was asked to arbitrate; he ordered the stone to be placed on a cloth and instructed the five clan leaders to take hold of the cloth and thus jointly position the stone.

After the Prophet returned to Mecca to clear the Kaaba of idols in 630, it could now serve as the focal point for Muslim worship. The Kaaba directed prayer to the one true God for whom it was originally intended, and grounded Islam in the sacred monotheism of Ibrahim.

See also: *Al-Jahiliya*, the Time of Ignorance 20–21 ▪ The *umma*, the community of Islam 32–33 ▪ The Five Pillars of Islam: Hajj 50–55 ▪ The birth of Saudi Arabia 232–37

> Ibrahim and Ismail laid the foundations of the House and dedicated it, saying 'Accept this from us, Lord. You are the One that hears and knows all.'
> **2:127**

The structure of the Kaaba

The Kaaba is made of granite and is roughly cube-shaped with walls of approximately 40 ft (12 m) in height and width. It has a gradually sloping roof that allows rainwater to drain from a waterspout. It has a door on its northeast façade through which members of the guardian Bani Shaiba tribe enter twice every year in order to ceremoniously clean the largely bare interior.

The Kaaba rests in the center of the Masjid al-Haram, the Holy Mosque built to enclose the shrine. In 624, a divine revelation ordered that the *qibla,* the direction to which Muslims face when they pray, be changed from the Noble Sanctuary in Jerusalem to the Kaaba. It takes on special meaning during the Hajj, the annual pilgrimage, since Muslims not only face it in prayer but also walk around it seven times in a ritual circumambulation to glorify God during their pilgrimage. For these reasons, the Kaaba and the city of Mecca are together considered the most sacred site in Islam. ▪

The *kiswa*

To honor the House of God, the stone structure of the Kaaba is covered with a cloth known in Arabic as the *kiswa*. It is a tradition that predates Islam and one that continued following the Muslim army's capture of Mecca in 630— Muhammad is said to have had the Kaaba draped with a white Yemeni cloth.

Today, 200 workers at a factory in Mecca create a new *kiswa* each year for the Hajj. Costing almost US$5 million, it is made from black silk lined with cotton and adorned with verses from the Quran stitched in gold and silver thread. Much of the work is still done by hand, but machines and computers also help speed up production.

The new *kiswa* is wrapped around the Kaaba on the second day of the Hajj, while pilgrims head out to Mount Arafat. At the end of the Hajj, the *kiswa* is removed and cut into pieces that are distributed among honored individuals and dignitaries.

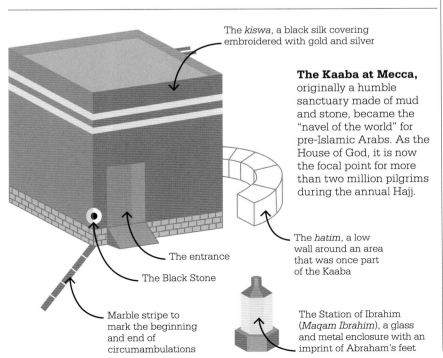

The *kiswa*, a black silk covering embroidered with gold and silver

The Kaaba at Mecca, originally a humble sanctuary made of mud and stone, became the "navel of the world" for pre-Islamic Arabs. As the House of God, it is now the focal point for more than two million pilgrims during the annual Hajj.

The entrance

The Black Stone

Marble stripe to mark the beginning and end of circumambulations

The *hatim*, a low wall around an area that was once part of the Kaaba

The Station of Ibrahim (*Maqam Ibrahim*), a glass and metal enclosure with an imprint of Abraham's feet

THERE IS NO GOD BUT GOD

PROPHET MUHAMMAD

IN CONTEXT

THEME
The Five Pillars of Islam:
Shahada

WHEN AND WHERE
610–32, Arabia

BEFORE
From 1000 BCE The Torah, then the Talmud, set down the rules for Jewish life that form part of God's covenants with Israel.

1st century CE Christianity incorporates the Judaic covenants, in particular the Ten Commandments.

610 The Prophet Muhammad starts to receive the revelations of the Quran.

AFTER
680 Shia Islam introduces additional "pillars" that guide faith and observance.

8th century Schools of Islamic law develop, offering further interpretations that guide Islamic life.

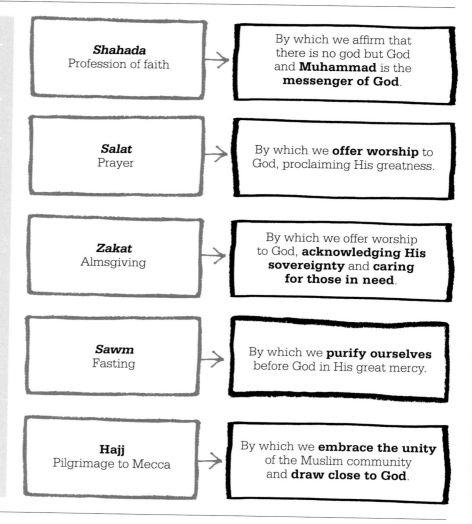

Shahada
Profession of faith → By which we affirm that there is no god but God and **Muhammad** is the **messenger of God**.

Salat
Prayer → By which we **offer worship** to God, proclaiming His greatness.

Zakat
Almsgiving → By which we offer worship to God, **acknowledging His sovereignty** and **caring for those in need**.

Sawm
Fasting → By which we **purify ourselves** before God in His great mercy.

Hajj
Pilgrimage to Mecca → By which we **embrace the unity** of the Muslim community and **draw close to God**.

According to several traditions in Muslim sources, the angel Jibreel asked Muhammad, "What is Islam?" In other words, what is the essence of the religion? What are the basic things one must do as a proper Muslim? Muhammad is said to have replied that Muslims must "worship God alone and none other, offer prayers to God, give to charity, and observe fasting during the month of Ramadan."

These core practices, along with the obligatory pilgrimage that each able Muslim must make to Mecca at least once in his or her lifetime, constitute the Five Pillars of Islam. In Arabic, they are *Shahada*, *salat*, *zakat*, *sawm*, and Hajj.

Ritual practice

All Muslims accept the Five Pillars, though various branches of Islam have their own unique additions. Known individually as *ibadat* (acts of worship), they have been the core practices of the faith ever since the Prophet introduced them. By taking part in these acts of worship within the overall framework of Islam, one is being a Muslim.

Although they are central to the belief system of Islam, the notion of the Five Pillars, and even the vocabulary of "pillar," emerged long after the time of the Prophet. The idea of the pillars was not defined until the 9th century, when the early scholars of Islam began collecting and publishing the words and actions of the Prophet, known as *hadith*. The account of Jibreel's questioning of Muhammad comes from the *Hadith of Jibreel*. This particular *hadith* is included in a collection made by the Persian scholar al-Bukhari

See also: The Five Pillars of Islam: *salat* 42–43 ▪ The Five Pillars of Islam: *zakat* 44–45 ▪ The Five Pillars of Islam: *sawm* 46–49 ▪ The Five Pillars of Islam: Hajj 50–55 ▪ The Six Pillars of Faith 86–87 ▪ The emergence of Shia Islam 108–15

(810–70), which is one of the earliest such works to list what he calls the five "principles."

These scholars were not imposing new forms of worship on believers, but simply reflecting what was already well established in the practice of Islam. Observant Muslims already proclaimed the oneness of God, prayed five times daily, committed regular acts of charity, undertook spiritually inspired fasts, and considered pilgrimage an act central to the religion of Islam. Each of the Five Pillars has its own unique history, development, and treatment in Muslim legal and spiritual works, beginning with the Quran.

The Pillars and the Quran

The Quran does not prescribe "Five Pillars of Islam," at least not as a collection of practices. Instead, it refers to them independently.

The *Shahada*, or profession of faith, does not occur in full in the Quran, but *sura* (chapter) 8:20, for example, commands those who have decided to follow Islam to

> Believers, obey God and His apostle, and do not forsake him, now that you have heard all.
> **8:20**

"obey God and His Prophet." The notion of prayer is found throughout the Quran: *sura* 20:130 advises, "Give glory to your Lord before sunrise and before sunset. Praise Him night and day, so that you may find comfort."

Meanwhile *sura* 48:29 describes the act of worship by the faithful: "You behold them worshipping on their knees, seeking the grace of God and His good will. Their marks are on their faces, the traces of their prostrations."

Sura 5:12 is one of many that describes charitable giving: "If you attend to your prayers and render the alms levy … I shall forgive you your sins." One passage from *sura* 2 gives details about fasting, another advises on proper pilgrimage: "Make the pilgrimage and visit the Sacred House for His sake" (2:196).

As the next few pages will describe, each of these acts has far more detailed requirements, variations, and considerations that have developed over time, according to a variety of needs. Today, however, the Five Pillars of Islam continue to function as a collective identity for what it means to be a Muslim. The Pillars serve as minimal obligations by which Muslims ought to abide. Their straightforwardness is intentional because Muslims are meant to follow God unencumbered by the clumsy burden of religious regulations. As the Quran explains to Muslims, God has "laid on you no burdens in the observance of your Religion" (22:78). »

Pillars of Shia Islam

The Five Pillars are practiced by Sunni and Shia Islam. While the Ismaili branch of Shia Islam has seven Pillars in all, mainstream Shia Islam has five "roots" or principles of faith (*usul al-din*) and ten "branches" or practices (*furu al-din*). The *furu al-din* are the Shia counterpart to the Sunni Five Pillars; they include *salat* (prayer), *sawm* (fasting), *zakat* (alms), and the Hajj (pilgrimage to Mecca), but to these four practices they add the following:

khums—A 20 percent capital gains tax. This is in addition to *zakat*.
jihad—The struggle to do good personally and socially, for example by not telling lies and by picking up litter.
amr bil-maaruf—Encouraging others to do good deeds.
nahi-anil-munkar—Forbidding what is evil and trying to stop others doing wrong.
tawalla—Expressing love toward the Prophet and those who follow the straight path.
tabarra—Disassociation from those who mock or insult God.

A Shia man prays at Kerbala, Iraq. Shia extend the *Shahada*—"There is no god except God, and Muhammad is the messenger of God"—with "Ali is the *wali* (friend) of God."

The profession of faith

While there is no prescribed order to the Five Pillars, the one that is often given first is the *Shahada*, or profession of faith, which forms the most basic element of Muslim belief. It is the combination of two basic phrases that Muslims say to honor God and bear witness to their submission to Him:

There is no god but God, and Muhammad is the messenger of God...

In Arabic it is *La ilaha illa llah, Muhammadun rasul Allah*. When saying the *Shahada*, Muslims will often begin it with *Ashadu ana*, or "I bear witness that...."

The word *shahada* is an Arabic verb that means to testify or bear witness. In this way, the words not only form a phrase of worship, but indicate a life that reflects submission to God.

While the Quran repeatedly highlights the *Shahada*'s two phrases, and others that are very similar, it does not link them together in any sort of profession of faith. For example, *sura* 47:19 reminds Muhammad, "Know that

Know that there is no god but God. Implore Him to forgive your sins and to forgive the true believers, men and women.
47:19

there is no god but God," while *sura* 48:29 states that "Muhammad is the messenger of God" (which some translations render as "Muhammad is God's apostle"). These passages, and others like them in the Quran, appear not as ritual utterances but as a part of wider contexts. The two phrases were linked later by Muslim scholars and made to serve as a succinct testimony of what it means to believe as a Muslim.

Evidence that the *Shahada* took time to become formulated exists on early Islamic coins of the late 7th

century. These bear the message "There is no god but God *alone,*" which is almost but not quite the *Shahada*. The same is true of the inscriptions on the Dome of the Rock (*Qubbat al-Sakhra*) in Jerusalem, Islam's oldest surving monument, which was originally completed in 691–92 CE; these refer to God and Muhammad but do not use the formula of the *Shahada* that is commonplace with inscriptions on later mosques.

Bearing witness

The first phrase of the *Shahada*— "There is no god but God" (*La ilaha illa llah*) — is, clearly, a reference to God as a monotheistic divinity and a denial of the pre-Islamic notion that there might be multiple gods. God's oneness is the single most significant religious component of Islam.

The *Shahada*'s second phrase— "Muhammad is the messenger of God" (*Muhammadun rasul Allah*)— acknowledges that Muhammad was granted revelation from God and that this is the final revelation to be sent to humankind. The statement further establishes Muhammad as the bearer of God's guidance and the supreme example of what it means to follow God.

At first sight, the *Shahada* stands out from the other pillars, in that it denotes correct belief as opposed to specific matters of action. It is said during each of the five daily Muslim prayers, but the *Shahada* also has various practical applications. For example, it is uttered by Muslims as notice of the intention to do an act for the sake of

This baby is celebrated at an *aqiqa* ceremony in the city of Mazar-i-Sharif in Afghanistan, when the *Shahada* is recited for the second time since his or her birth.

The *Shahada* is ever present in Muslim architecture, as seen here beneath the 230-ft (70-m) minaret at the Grand Mosque in Dubai, in the United Arab Emirates.

Muhammad is God's messenger. Those who are with him are strong against Unbelievers, but merciful to one another.
48:29

God, a concept known as *niyya*. The *niyya* can be either a verbal utterance or an inner attitude.

Most significantly, the *Shahada* is recited when someone becomes a Muslim. To simply pronounce the *Shahada* in the presence of two Muslim witnesses makes one a Muslim. Babies born to Muslims have the *adaan* (call to prayer) whispered in their ears at birth, of which the *Shahada* forms part, and this is recited again at the *aqiqa* ceremony seven days later that welcomes the baby into the family. At the other end of life, the *Shahada* is supposed to be the last words a Muslim hears at the moment of their death.

As well as being a verbal testimony, the *Shahada* also adorns many Islamic buildings, and is used as part of national symbols where it adorns flags and other emblems. On a personal level, it appears on clothing, jewelry, and other accessories.

Using the *Shahada* in this way is an expression of Islamic identity and helps to mark out public space as distinctly Islamic, just as its verbal usage helps to bear witness to Muslim identity and practice. ∎

Flying the *Shahada*

Owing to the centrality of the *Shahada* as an Islamic idea and as one of the Five Pillars of Islamic practice, the phrase appears in artistic representation in various national symbols. For example, the national flag of Saudi Arabia bears a white inscription of the *Shahada* in Arabic over a sword.

As the phrase is considered sacred, great care must be taken in how the flag is used and depicted. It is never lowered to half-mast, since this would dishonor the *Shahada*, and it is never hung vertically unless a special flag has been issued.

Controversy has erupted when the Saudi flag has been misused on merchandise, such as when it was printed on footballs that would then be kicked around, and on disposable drinking cups that would be tossed into garbage cans. A German brewer also inadvertently caused great offense to Muslims when it put the Saudi flag on beer bottle tops celebrating the 32 countries competing in soccer's 2018 FIFA World Cup, and a British chain of pubs had to remove the Saudi flag from its bunting for the same event.

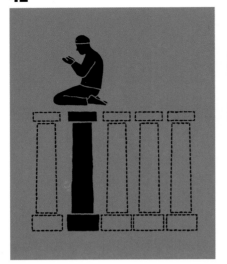

HURRY TO PRAYER, HURRY TO SALVATION
CALL TO PRAYER

IN CONTEXT

THEME
The Five Pillars of Islam: *salat*

WHEN AND WHERE
610–32, Arabia

BEFORE
5th–6th centuries BCE
Returning to Jerusalem from exile in Babylon, the prophet Ezekiel and the Men of the Great Assembly institute formal prayers and other ritual observances for the Jews.

1st century CE Throughout the Gospels, Jesus presents prayer as the way to receive God's blessings.

AFTER
2007 Muszaphar Shukar, a Muslim astronaut from Malaysia, prays from his post on board the International Space Station.

Today A global survey reports in 2017 that the majority of Muslims (two-thirds in the US, for example) pray daily.

The second pillar of Islam concerns daily prayers, known in Arabic as *salat*. Of course, Muslims might say any number of personal prayers to God, but the main prayers of Islam are prescribed, formal, and designated as a unique opportunity to worship God—as Muhammad did—by acknowledging Him and bearing witness to His oneness.

These formal prayers take place five times every day: at dawn (*fajr*), early afternoon (*zhuhr*), late afternoon (*asr*), sunset (*maghreb*), and evening (*isha*). Often the

When you are safe, attend to your prayers: for prayer is a duty incumbent on the faithful, to be conducted at appointed times.
4:103

muezzin calls Muslims to prayer. In earlier times, and sometimes still, the *muezzin* went up a tower, or minaret, connected to the local mosque and loudly chanted the call to prayer (*adaan*). Mostly, however, these calls are relayed by loudspeakers—or even by alarm clocks in the home.

Ritual ablutions
When called to prayer, Muslims are encouraged to go to the mosque, or, if not possible, to pray privately. Prayers are preceded by ritual ablutions (*wudu*), without which a Muslim would not be considered purified for proper worship. After making the intention (*niyya*) to perform *wudu*, a Muslim washes first the hands, mouth, and nostrils with clean water, and then the face followed by the forearms, wiping the head and ears, and washing feet and ankles, as these parts will touch the ground during prayers. The number of times this ritual is performed before prayer varies according to different traditions.

Having purified themselves, Muslims must also make sure the space in which they are praying is clean. If it is in a mosque, the space is already considered pure, but at

See also: The early life of Muhammad 22–27 ▪ The Five Pillars of Islam: *Shahada* 36–41 ▪ The Six Pillars of Faith 86–87 ▪ Rites of passage 256–59

A *rakat* is a sequence of prescribed movements that constitutes a single unit of Islamic prayer. Worshippers stand facing Mecca and begin with the invocation "God is great" to announce their intention to pray.

The worshipper begins prayer with a recital of verses from the Quran…

followed by bending low with hands on knees…

then standing, all the while reciting prayers…

before prostating themselves on the ground, forehead to the floor.

The worshipper then sits with feet folded under the body…

before making another prostration to complete the *rakat*.

home, at work, or in public, worshippers will use a prayer mat (*sajada*) to create a clean space.

Muslims then stand facing in the direction of Mecca. A niche (*mihrab*) marks this direction in mosques. Muslims praying elsewhere can simply face the general cardinal direction of Mecca (east, west, south, or north); as the Quran says, "To God belongs the East and the West. Whichever way you turn, there is the Face of God" (2:115). Or they can use an app or a specially marked compass to find the exact direction.

The act of prayer

The act of praying begins with the declaration, "God is great" (*Allahu akbar*). Then, a fixed set of prayers is recited that includes passages from the Quran. The *Shahada* is repeated and peace is offered to others. Prayers are said in Arabic and are accompanied by bows and prostrations (see above), together with raising and lowering of hands. The set ablutions, movements, and times of prayer give Muslims a shared sense of unity. Whether side-by-side at a mosque or in the privacy of their own home, they are praying at the same time as other Muslims around the world. This in itself is a reminder of God's greatness. ▪

Sunni Muslims are expected to pray five times a day. Shia Muslims combine the second and third prayers, as well as the fourth and fifth, so they pray three times a day.

Friday prayers

Observant Muslims pray five times a day every day, but the most important prayer of the week is *al-Juma*, which is the Friday congregational prayer. In a *hadith* Muhammad is quoted as saying, "The best day the sun rises over is Friday; on it God created Adam. On it, he was made to enter Paradise, on it he was expelled from it, and the Last Hour will take place on no other day than Friday." The Quran also establishes the importance of Friday as the sacred day of worship in a *sura* called *al-Juma*, which states, "Believers, when you are summoned to Friday prayers hasten to the remembrance of God and cease your trading. That would be best for you, if you but knew it" (62:9).

In addition to the prayers, Friday worship includes a sermon. Even if they do not regularly attend the mosque at other times, many Muslims will attend Friday prayers.

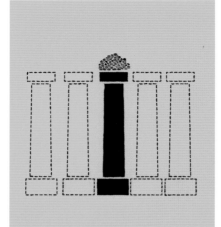

I SHOW [MERCY] TO THOSE THAT... GIVE ALMS

THE QURAN, 7:156

IN CONTEXT

SOURCE
**The Five Pillars of Islam:
*zakat***

WHEN AND WHERE
610–32, Arabia

BEFORE
1st century CE The Jews
codify the concept of *tzedakah*
to mean "doing what is right
and just." In practice, this
means a religious obligation
to give alms.

AFTER
632–34 Abu Bakr is the first
Muslim leader to institute a
statutory *zakat* system. Some
Arab tribes refuse to pay,
leading to the Ridda Wars.

717–20 Tradition relates that
during the reign of Caliph
Umar II *zakat* is not collected
because no one needs it.

2020 Islamic financial analysts
estimate that annual *zakat*
spending is anywhere
between US$200 billion
and $1 trillion per year.

The third pillar of Islam is almsgiving, known in Arabic as *zakat*. One of the chief concerns in the Quran, and one of the main components of Muhammad's preaching, was the treatment of the poor, marginalized, and disadvantaged. As the Quran reveals, "Show kindness to parents and to kin, to orphans and to the destitute, to near and distant neighbors, to those who keep company with you, to the traveler in need, and to the slaves you own" (4:36).

The Quran also makes clear that someone is righteous not only because of what he or she believes but also in the manner in which they treat the needy (2:177).

In this way, the Quran indicates that a love of God is demonstrated by a love for the most vulnerable in society. *Zakat* is the primary means by which Muslims demonstrate this kind of love.

From a theological standpoint, if everything that a Muslim receives comes as a blessing from God, then it is right that they return some of that abundance to God by giving to those who have received less. In this sense, *zakat* can be seen as a sort of purifying tax—just as ablutions purify the body, and *salat* (prayer) purifies the heart and soul, *zakat* purifies the wealth, property, and possessions of Muslims and makes them pleasing to God.

All the wealth that a Muslim receives comes from God.

It is right that **Muslims should return to God a portion of that wealth** by giving to those who are in need.

See also: The Five Pillars of Islam: *Shahada* 36–41 ▪ The Five Pillars of Islam: *sawm* 46–49 ▪ Sayings and actions of the Prophet 118–23

To be charitable in public is good, but to give alms to the poor in private is better for you.
2:271

In its purest observance, *zakat* should be paid to the needy in a person's own neighborhood. A Muslim should have knowledge of their own community in order to identify those in need of charity. In this way, *zakat* encourages social engagement and responsibility. In practice, however, it is more common for Muslims to pay to one of a variety of different institutions, either governmental or non-governmental, depending on the country a person lives in, or on their tradition of Islam.

Those who fail to give during their lifetime will subsequently be held accountable on the Day of Judgment.

Payment of *zakat*

Except for the poorest, every man and woman is expected to give *zakat* annually. Before being required to pay *zakat*, a person must have a minimum amount of wealth, known as *nisab*—this is calculated as the value of 87.48 grams of gold or 612.36 grams of silver. *Zakat* is due on any wealth over *nisab*. This includes savings, shares, stocks, and the cash value of any gold, silver, and jewelry.

The percentage at which *zakat* has traditionally been set is 2.5 percent, or one-fortieth.

In many Islamic communities, *zakat* is discretionary. Whether an individual actually gives or not is largely enforced by peer pressure or an individual's own personal sense of obligation. There are countries, however, such as Saudi Arabia, in which *zakat* is mandatory and is collected by the state.

Zakat al-Fitr

Zakat al-Fitr is another, lesser Islamic charitable obligation that falls at the end of Ramadan. This is money given to the poor so that they can partake in *Eid al-Fitr*, the major feast that marks the end of the month of fasting. It is traditionally given well in advance of the actual feast days.

This also dates back to the time of the Prophet—Muhammad determined the amount to be donated as one *saa* of food, which is about four double handfuls of grain, rice, or dates. These days, cash is given rather than food. Charitable websites set a value based on the price of staple food, typically about $15 per family member. ▪

The poor have a right to a small percentage of the riches of the wealthy.
Prophet Muhammad

Types of *zakat*

There are eight categories of eligible recipients of *zakat*, derived from the Quran.

Al-fuqara ("the poor")—*zakat* is collected to provide social welfare services or a public safety net for people in need.
Al-masakin ("the needy")— anyone in need of assistance in the aftermath of a crisis or natural disaster.
Al-gharimin—this relates to people burdened with debt.
Al-muallafati qulubuhum ("the reconciliation of hearts")—this relates to promoting the image of Islam.
Fi sabilillah ("those in the path of God")—promoting the Islamic value system.
Ibn al-sabil ("wayfarers")— refugees and internally displaced people.
Fir riqab—people in bondage or slavery, so people who are wrongly imprisoned or victims of trafficking.
Al-amilina alayha—the collectors and administrators of *zakat*, and a part of what is given can be used to cover administrative costs.

BELIEVERS, FASTING IS DECREED FOR YOU

THE QURAN, 2:183

IN CONTEXT

THEME
The Five Pillars of Islam: *sawm*

WHEN AND WHERE
622, Arabia

BEFORE
5th century BCE The Torah specifies 25 hours of fasting on Yom Kippur, the Jewish Day of Atonement.

1st century CE According to the Gospels, after his baptism, Jesus fasts for 40 days to prepare himself to do God's will (Luke 4:1).

AFTER
1918–47 Activist Mahatma Gandhi undertakes 17 fasts during the struggle for Indian independence: his longest fast lasts 21 days. For Gandhi, fasting is not only a spiritual practice but also a nonviolent weapon of protest.

The fourth pillar of Islam is fasting, known in Arabic as *sawm*. Muslims might fast on any number of occasions as a spiritual detoxification or as a penance for sins. Fasting can also function as a replacement for other ritual obligations that a Muslim might have been unable to fulfill. For example, *sura* 2:196 reveals that "if any of you is ill [and cannot complete the Hajj], he must do penance either by fasting or by almsgiving."

Observing Ramadan

Sawm has special relevance as a fast related to Ramadan, which is the ninth lunar month in the Islamic calendar. It was during this month

See also: The early life of Muhammad 22–27 ▪ *Hijra*, the flight from Mecca 28–31 ▪ The Five Pillars of Islam: *Shahada* 36–41 ▪ The Islamic calendar 116–17

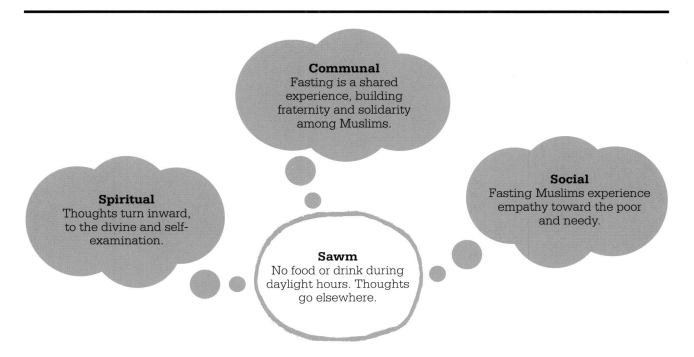

Communal
Fasting is a shared experience, building fraternity and solidarity among Muslims.

Spiritual
Thoughts turn inward, to the divine and self-examination.

Social
Fasting Muslims experience empathy toward the poor and needy.

Sawm
No food or drink during daylight hours. Thoughts go elsewhere.

that the Quran began to be revealed to Muhammad in 610, while he was meditating on Jabal al-Nur. The first command for Muslims to fast was given during the *Hijra*, when the Prophet and his followers fled Mecca to seek refuge in Medina.

During Ramadan's 30-day fast, all Muslims past the age of puberty are obliged to abstain from all food and drink (water included) during daylight hours. As no material substance should enter the body, smoking and sexual intercourse are also prohibited.

In the same pursuit of spiritual virtue, Muslims should also refrain from cursing, fighting, or gossiping during Ramadan. In general, however, the fast is not intended to be more than a person could reasonably bear ("God desires your well-being, not your discomfort," advises *sura* 2:185 of the Quran).

The elderly or people who are ill, pregnant, or traveling, for example, are not expected to fast—although they are expected to make it up at a later date.

Muslims and even non-Muslims who eat, drink, or smoke in public can be fined or even jailed in some Muslim-majority countries. In other

Fasting is a shield with which a servant protects himself from the fire.
Prophet Muhammad

Muslim countries, attitudes are more relaxed, and some locals will continue to frequent coffee shops and cafés throughout Ramadan.

The Night of Power
In ceasing to satisfy regular human appetites, the fasting person is encouraged to look inward and reflect upon spiritual matters—including revisiting any wrongs they may have done and giving thought to the suffering of those less fortunate. An especially pious act is to read the Quran in its entirety. This activity fits well in the month of Ramadan since the text can be divided into 30 sections of equal length (known as *juz*), one of which is read on each of the days of the fasting month.

The 27th night of Ramadan commemorates the occasion of Muhammad receiving the first »

revelation of the Quran and is known as the Night of Power (*Leilat al-Qadr*). This is considered the holiest night of the year, when, according to the Quran, a single act of worship is better rewarded than 1,000 months of prayer (*sura* 97).

Celebrating Ramadan

According to the Quran, Muslims are allowed to eat and drink in Ramadan "until you can tell a white thread from a black one in the light of the coming dawn" (2:187). Shortly before then, just before daybreak, Muslim families will gather

Better is the Night of Qadr than a thousand months.
97:3

together for a small breakfast, known as *suhur*, that must sustain them throughout the entire day. At sunset, heralded by the evening prayers, Muslims traditionally end the fast, as the Prophet did some 1,400 years ago, with a sip of water and some dates. This is followed by the evening meal, known as *iftar*. This is a time for families to visit and take part in a large communal meal that usually includes foods prepared especially for Ramadan.

Across the Islamic world, mosques, aid organizations, and wealthy individuals set up tents and tables for the public to eat free *iftar* meals every night of Ramadan. In the Arabian Gulf countries, sheikhs hold *majalis*, where they open their doors to people for free food and drink. For those who can afford it, five-star hotels host Ramadan tents offering lavish and pricey meals. At the same time, Ramadan evenings are filled with shopping and television. Many television companies launch their biggest shows during Ramadan, including

The Ramadan meal of *iftar* is a communal affair, shared with families or at vast public gatherings, as seen here at al-Satwa bus station in Dubai.

month-long soap operas and live game shows with large cash prizes. Orthodox Muslims often complain that the holy month is becoming commercialized.

The end of the month-long fast is commemorated with *Eid al-Fitr*, or the Feast of Breaking the Fast, which is a three-day national holiday—in Muslim countries. It is

There are people who fast and get nothing from their fast except hunger.
Prophet Muhammad

a huge social occasion, complete with large meals and gift giving. Children, in particular, often receive new clothes and presents. In places with majority Muslim populations, *Eid* celebrations are large affairs that spread across cities and public spaces, with more eating, only now it occurs during the day rather than at night.

The origins of Ramadan

Although many of Ramadan's customs have developed over time, its origins lie in the Quran. The second *sura* describes some of the basic elements of the communal fast observed by early Muslims onward:

Believers, fasting is decreed for
you as it was decreed for
those before you…
Fast a certain number of days, but
if any one among you is ill or on
a journey, let him fast a similar
number of days later;
and for those that cannot endure it,
there is a penance ordained:
the feeding of a poor man.
He that does good of his own accord
shall be well rewarded;
but to fast is better for you,
if you but knew it. (2:184)

The sense gathered from this passage is that Ramadan and its related activities link Islam to its monotheistic cousins, Judaism and Christianity, which also incorporate fasting and its associated festivals. Yet despite the links between Ramadan and the fasts undertaken by other People of the Book (both Jews and Christians), the event is intended to have a truly Islamic flavor. Ramadan is not the somber Lent of Christianity or Yom Kippur of Judaism. Although it is certainly a period of spiritual discipline, personal introspection, and purification, it is also meant to be joyful. This is why Muslims break the fast each evening with communal meals.

Ramadan also serves another purpose. Not only was the first revelation of the Quran given during this month, but also the Battle of Badr was fought, Ali and his son Hussein were born, the Prophet's first wife Khadija died, and Mecca was finally conquered in 630—all during this month. The sense of communal spirit engendered during Ramadan also reinforces Muslim identity by reminding participants of their history and formation. ∎

Ramadan lanterns, known as *fanous*, became popular in Fatimid-era Cairo and are now a tradition widely adopted throughout the Muslim world.

Ramadan specialities vary from country to country, but many include a type of biscuit made with dates known as *kahk* eaten during the *Eid*.

Flexible hours of fasting

Since Islam follows a lunar calendar, Ramadan moves 11 days back in relation to the Gregorian calendar each year. In some years—for example when Ramadan coincides with the heat and long days of July—fasting is more arduous than others. (The Arabic root *al-ramad* means "scorching heat.")

The length of dawn to sunset also varies in different parts of the world. While most Muslims will typically fast for 11 to 16 hours, in polar regions the period between dawn and sunset can exceed 22 hours. Until recently, there were no Muslim communities in the Arctic, but global migration has changed that. Faced with the impossibility of adhering to a strict sunrise-to-sunset rule, Muslims have had to find other ways of determining the hours of fasting—such as fasting during the hours corresponding to the closest Islamic country, or synchronizing fasting times with Mecca.

I AM HERE O LORD, I AM HERE

THE TALBIYYA (PILGRIM'S PRAYER)

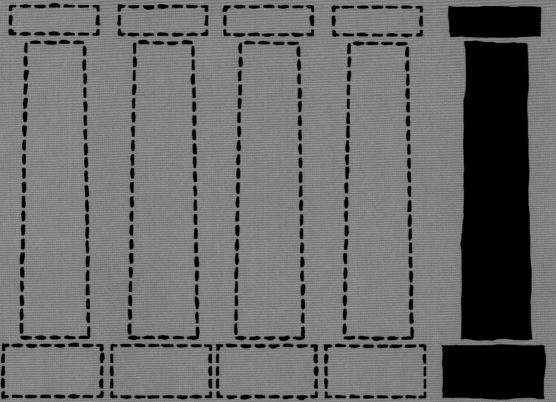

IN CONTEXT

SOURCE
The Five Pillars of Islam: Hajj

WHEN AND WHERE
630, Mecca

BEFORE
5th century The Quraysh tribe control Mecca and the Kaaba is the site of pilgrimage for Arab tribes worshipping a number of gods.

AFTER
After 631 The Hajj is made compulsory after Muhammad captures Mecca. Future Muslim rulers in Syria, Egypt, and Iraq will provide state patronage for organizing large pilgrimage caravans.

2012 The number of pilgrims partaking in the annual Hajj hits an all-time high of 3,161,573. The numbers have since declined as Mecca undergoes expansion work.

The fifth pillar of Islam is the Hajj, or the pilgrimage to the sacred city of Mecca. Its origins lie in Muhammad's journey from Medina to Mecca and his cleansing of the Kaaba, making it once again the center of worship of the one God. By participating in the Hajj, Muslims are leaving behind their daily, earthly bonds and physically returning to the spiritual center of Islam. It is both a voyage inward to one's self and a way of getting closer to God.

The prehistory of the Hajj

Many elements of the pilgrimage predate the time of Muhammad, and are intimately linked to the story of Ibrahim (the Abraham of the Book of Genesis). It tells how he left his wife Hajar (Hagar) and their infant son Ismail alone in the desert near Mecca. Having run out of water, and concerned that she would not be able to continue to nurse her baby, Hajar ran back and forth seven times between the two hills of Safa and Marwa, looking for someone who might be able to help them. Her search is echoed in the rituals performed by pilgrims to Mecca today.

Islamic tradition also holds that it was Ibrahim who first built what is now the Kaaba. He incorporated a black stone into the structure, which had been given to him by the angel Jibreel (Gabriel). This remains set into a corner of the Kaaba, and pilgrims attempt to kiss it or gesture toward it as they circumambulate during their Hajj pilgrimage.

Preparing for the Hajj

Hajj begins two months after the end of Ramadan. It is considered obligatory for every adult Muslim, who is physically able and has the financial means, to make the pilgrimage at least once in his or her lifetime. To make the pilgrimage, Muslims travel to Saudi Arabia by whatever means possible. Numerous Muslim travel agencies exist that offer special Hajj packages to groups and individuals, and work to make sure pilgrims have a memorable and enjoyable journey. Some governments even subsidize the cost of making the pilgrimage, and charities exist that help to support those unable to cover the financial expense.

A Muslim-only city

While Muslims and non-Muslims alike may enter the country of Saudi Arabia, only Muslims can enter the sacred city of Mecca. This prohibition is specified in the Quran (9:28). (Non-Muslims may visit the country's other holy city, Medina, but not the vicinity of the Prophet's Mosque.) Drivers approaching the holy city by car are met with road signs directing "Muslims only" toward Mecca, while steering non-Muslims away toward the city of Jeddah.

Similarly, signs at Jeddah's main airport directing travelers to the special Hajj terminal for onward travel to Mecca also include the message "Muslims only." Attempts to travel to the sacred city by non-Muslims will result in a fine, while non-Muslims discovered in the city will be taken before a judge and most probably deported. Discerning religious identity can be difficult, but entrance into the city is monitored and controlled by religious police.

The Great Mosque at Mecca is the focus of the Hajj. In Muhammad's time it was no more than a walled courtyard around the Kaaba; now it can hold up to 1.5 million worshippers.

Completing the Hajj typically takes about a week. Pilgrims follow a prescribed set of rituals, most of which relate to episodes in the life of the early prophet Ibrahim (Abraham). At the end of the Hajj, many pilgrims go on to Medina to visit the Mosque of the Prophet Muhammad.

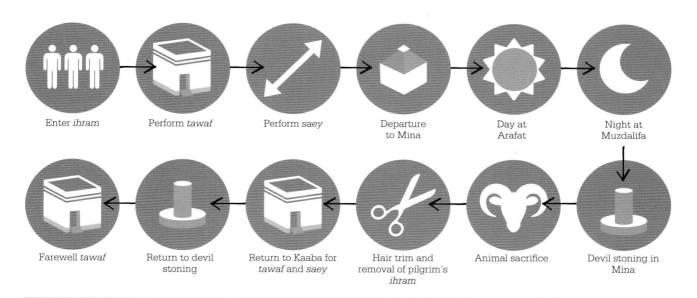

Enter *ihram* → Perform *tawaf* → Perform *saey* → Departure to Mina → Day at Arafat → Night at Muzdalifa

Farewell *tawaf* ← Return to devil stoning ← Return to Kaaba for *tawaf* and *saey* ← Hair trim and removal of pilgrim's *ihram* ← Animal sacrifice ← Devil stoning in Mina

Before embarking on the Hajj, a number of preparations must be made. Perhaps the most important is that all prospective pilgrims must ritually cleanse and purify themselves. In order to do this they don the *ihram*, or pilgrims' garb. For men this is typically two white unhemmed sheets: one wrapped around the waist, one thrown over the shoulder. Likewise, many women wear white robes, though others choose to wear simple clothing that reflects their countries of origin. Faces must be uncovered, so no *niqab* (face veil) can be worn.

Once in this state of purity (also called the *ihram*), pilgrims must stop bathing and not wear any ornamentation, such as jewelry and perfume. They must abstain from sexual activity and from engaging in any activity that might be considered sinful. The intention is to create a sense of communality and unity. Women and men of all nations, colors, and social levels are rendered indistinguishable and equal before God.

Make the sacred pilgrimage and visit the Sacred House for His sake.
2:196

Performing the Hajj

As pilgrims near the city of Mecca, they often shout, "I am here, O Lord, I am here!" Once inside the Great Mosque (which is also called the Holy or Sacred Mosque, or *al-Masjid al-Haram* in Arabic), they perform the *tawaf*, the circumambulation of the Kaaba in a counterclockwise direction. They do this seven times, trying each time to get as close as they can to the Kaaba. Pilgrims who make it nearest to the structure will kiss or touch the Black Stone that remains exposed in the Kaaba's eastern corner. The tawaf will be completed on three occasions during the Hajj.

Throughout the weeklong pilgrimage, Muslims will pray in the Great Mosque and participate in a variety of rites that can be » completed within its precincts. For example, they will drink water piped from the Zamzam well that lies just 65 ft (20 m) to the east of the Kaaba. According to Islamic tradition, God miraculously created this well in order to provide water for the baby Ismail when he and his mother Hajar were stranded in the desert; Ismail lived to be a great prophet, and Muhammad's forebear.

> Then let the pilgrims tidy themselves, make their vows, and circle the Ancient House.
> **22:28**

Many pilgrims will also perform the *saey*, the ritual walk or run between the Safa and Marwa hills in order to commemorate Hajar's search for help. These hills, like the Zamzam well, now fall within the precincts of the Great Mosque. The distance between the two hills is about 500 yd (450 m), and a covered walkway shelters pilgrims from the heat and sun. It has four one-way lanes, with the center lanes reserved for slow walkers.

Rituals outside Mecca

The Hajj can also include rites that take place outside of Mecca. For example, all pilgrims travel 5 miles (8 km) outside the city to Mina and then a further 9 miles (14.5 km) to Mount Arafat. According to Islamic tradition, Arafat is where Muhammad delivered his Farewell Sermon to those who went with him to Mecca on what would be his final pilgrimage. The mountain is

also known as the Mount of Mercy, as it is also where Adam, Islam's first prophet, was forgiven by God. Muslim pilgrims spend much of their time here praying for God's forgiveness for their sins and those of the entire Muslim community.

In Mina, pilgrims participate in the Stoning of the Devil. According to tradition, it was in Mina that Ibrahim was tempted to ignore God's command and reject his son Ismail. The Devil appeared three times and, each time, Ibrahim threw seven stones to drive him off. Pilgrims reenact this event in Mina by throwing pebbles, which they aim at high walls (until 2004 it was three pillars), in order to avoid hitting those on the other

Pilgrims perform *tawaf*, which entails walking seven times counterclockwise around the Kaaba. Three circuits should be done at a fast pace, then more slowly for the next four.

Muslim pilgrims throw pebbles as part of the symbolic Stoning of the Devil ritual at Mina, near Mecca. Many choose to gather their pebbles at Muzdalifa, between Arafat and Mina.

side, who are also throwing pebbles. The rites at Mina are so popular that a tent city springs up, with well over 100,000 air-conditioned tents sheltering pilgrims who arrive from Arafat after sunset to pray and collect their pebbles on the plain of Muzdalifa before going to Mina.

Eid al-Adha

The high point of Hajj is a three-day feast known as *Eid al-Adha*. This sacred feast commemorates Ibrahim's devotion to God, when he agreed to sacrifice his son Ismail but was spared; God provided a lamb to sacrifice instead, in a story that is also common to the Hebrew and Christian bibles. This feast is celebrated by all Muslims, wherever they are, not just those who are on pilgrimage, and it is considered the most sacred time of the year.

Muslims typically celebrate *Eid al-Adha* by carrying out a sacrifice. Traditionally the animal is slaughtered by the man of the house, but many these days prefer to have a professional butcher come and do it instead. The animal that is sacrificed—usually a goat, sheep, cow, or camel, depending on the family's wealt—is then divided into three parts. At least one third of the meat is donated to the poor, and a third to relatives. Some Muslims now choose a vegan *eid*; concerns about animal welfare and the need to consume less meat lead them to donate a fee to charity instead of making a sacrifice.

Muslims who celebrate *Eid al-Adha* in Mecca will often end their pilgrimage by visiting the city of Medina to see the Prophet's Mosque, Islam's second holiest site, which holds Muhammad's grave.

The *Umra*

There is a second pilgrimage to Mecca, the *Umra*. It is a "lesser pilgrimage" that can be undertaken at any time of the year, in contrast to the Hajj, which has specific dates according to the Islamic lunar calendar. The *Umra* is not a substitute for the Hajj, and is not mandatory. It includes only the first two rites of the Hajj—circling the Kaaba and hastening between the hills of Safa and Marwa—and ends with the ritual of shaving the head for male pilgrims. While it requires pilgrims to attain the same state of purity, it can be done in a few hours rather than days.

Of course, there will be many Muslims who will never be able to visit the holy city of Mecca and take part in the rites and festivities of either the Hajj or the *Umra*.

Exemptions of various kinds are made for those who are ill or infirm, or who cannot afford to go. For those who do make it, the Hajj (and, to a lesser extent, the *Umra*) are an important goal and experience for Muslims, helping to solidify and invigorate their identities as followers of Muhammad and of monotheistic worship. ∎

Safa and Marwa are two of God's beacons. It shall be no offense for the pilgrim or the visitor to the Sacred House to walk around them both.
2:158

MUHAMMAD IS NO MORE THAN A MESSENGER: OTHER MESSENGERS HAVE PASSED AWAY BEFORE HIM

THE QURAN, 3:144

IN CONTEXT

THEME
The death of the Prophet

WHEN AND WHERE
632, Medina

BEFORE
632 Muhammad delivers his Final Sermon at Arafat, reminding his followers to treat one another kindly and to abandon all blood feuds.

AFTER
632 The *umma* elects the Prophet's companion and father-in-law, Abu Bakr, to be the first caliph, or leader of the Islamic community.

634–56 Abu Bakr is succeeded as caliph by Umar and Uthman, and then finally by Ali, who is the cousin and son-in-law of Muhammad.

661 Ali, the last of the four Rashidun ("rightly guided") caliphs, is assassinated. The resulting rift will split Islam into Sunni and Shia factions.

ollowing the conquest of Mecca in 630, Muhammad returned to Medina. There, he spent much of his time trying to consolidate his power in Arabia by creating alliances and increasing the number of followers of Islam. In 632, the Prophet completed what would be his farewell pilgrimage to Mecca, setting a precedent for what would later became known as the Hajj. That March, he delivered his Final Sermon, in which he urged Muslims to follow the teachings contained in the Quran. A short time later, he returned to Medina for the last time. In the summer of 632, he fell ill and retired

If anyone worships Muhammad, Muhammad is dead. If anyone worships God, God is alive.
Abu Bakr

to the house he shared with his favorite wife, Aisha. Tradition has it that, feverish and weak, he rested his head on her lap and died.

Umar ibn al-Khattab, one of Muhammad's closest companions, was so shocked that he refused to believe the Prophet had died, and claimed that he would return after 40 days, just as the prophet Moses had gone to visit God and later returned to his people. Abu Bakr, Muhammad's close companion and father-in-law, reminded Umar that Muhammad had constantly warned them against honoring him in the way that Christians honored Jesus; he was not divine, but a mortal like themselves. To deny that he had died was to deny a basic truth.

From denial to acceptance
Abu Bakr spoke to the Muslim community in the mosque next to Aisha's house, and assured them that the Prophet had indeed passed. "Oh men, if anyone worships Muhammad, Muhammad is dead. If anyone worships God, God is alive." He then recited verse 3:144 from the Quran, which had been revealed to the Prophet after the Battle of Uhud. The Muslims

See also: The early life of Muhammad 22–27 ▪ A successor to the Prophet 102–103 ▪ The rightly guided caliphs 104–107 ▪ The Umayyad and Abbasid caliphates 136–39

Prophet Muhammad's tomb at his mosque in Medina lies behind multiple screens. Millions of Muslim pilgrims visit the shine each year, often as a part of the Hajj.

had suffered such heavy losses at Uhud that it was rumored that Muhammad too had been killed. But verse 3:144 insists:

*Muhammad is no more than
    a messenger: other messengers
    have passed away before him.
If he die or be slain, will you recant?
He that recants will do no harm
    to God, but God will
    recompense the thankful.*

On hearing these words, Umar finally accepted that the Prophet was dead, and mourned.

Islam after Muhammad

The shock of Muhammad's death was profound. He had guided every step taken by the followers of Islam. However, he had not just left a set of guidelines by which individual followers could live their lives, but a politically strong and stable society bound by a shared faith. After the *Hijra*, the community Muhammad formed in Medina had grown to dominate almost all of Arabia and brought peace and stability in place of intertribal warfare.

Not everyone was committed to the Prophet's religious vision, but he had established a large enough core of dedicated Muslims that could now preserve and build on his legacy.

While there were divergences of opinion on what to do next— and on who should succeed Muhammad—the *umma* remained strong and powerful. This was largely because the Prophet's goal had not been his personal political power but the creation of a just society. Being a man rather than a divine figure, Muhammad had provided a role model all Muslims could attempt to emulate. ▪

The green dome

After Muhammad died, there was disagreement about where he should be buried. Some suggested that he should be buried in his hometown of Mecca, where his relatives were. Others suggested he be buried in Jerusalem, where preceding prophets had been interred. Eventually, it was agreed he should be buried in Medina, although the exact location of a burial site had yet to be settled. Some thought he should be buried in the mosque where he preached, but Abu Bakr said he had heard Muhammad say that prophets should be buried where they die.

So Muhammad was buried beneath his bed in Aisha's house, next to the mosque.

Later, during the reign of Caliph Walid (r.705–15), the mosque, which is known as al-Masjid an-Nabawi (the Mosque of the Prophet), was expanded to include the tomb. It has been further expanded and rebuilt on many occasions, most notably during the reign of the Mamluk Sultan Qaitbay (r.1468–96). Today, a green dome within the mosque complex marks the site of the Prophet's final resting place.

WHAT ARE THESE IMAGES TO WHICH YOU ARE SO DEVOTED?

THE QURAN, 21:52

IN CONTEXT

THEME
Depicting the Prophet

WHEN AND WHERE
630, Mecca

BEFORE
From 500 BCE In Judaism, the only image of God is man. As God has no visible shape, it is absurd to make or worship images of Him. Man must only worship the invisible God.

3rd–4th centuries CE
Although the Bible forbids idols or "any graven image," frescoes and mosaics in early Christian churches begin to depict the life of Jesus and the saints with figures instead of symbols.

AFTER
Today Even in the age of mass media and streaming across multiple formats, most Muslims continue to maintain the prohibition on depicting God or Prophet Muhammad.

A key tenet of Islam is that there is only one God. Violating this belief— whether by worshipping another god, claiming God is not one, or creating something to represent Him—constitutes the greatest sin. Nothing should come between man and God. So while nothing in the Quran strictly bans portrayals of God, Islam discourages any image-making to avoid the temptation toward idol worship.

This prohibition extends to Muhammad and all the prophets of Islam. Here, early Muslims were reacting to Christianity, which they believed had been led astray by conceiving of Christ not only as a man but as a divine being. The Prophet himself was aware that if people saw images of his face, there was a risk that they would soon start worshipping him.

The text most often cited in defence of this ban is a *hadith*, words reportedly spoken by the Prophet, in which he is said to have warned, "Whoever makes a picture will be punished by Allah till he puts life in it, and he will never be able to put life in it" (*Sahih Bukhari* 3:428). This is taken to mean that for a human, to try making a new being is usurping God's role and is in any case doomed to fail.

Sometimes this concern can take extreme forms, as in the case of the Buddhas of Bamiyan. These colossal statues of Gautama Buddha were carved into a cliff in Afghanistan in the 6th to 7th century CE, the biggest one standing 180 ft (55 m) tall. After centuries untouched under Muslim rule, they were dynamited by the Taliban in 2001. In one account, Mullah Omar, the former Taliban leader, claimed he ordered their destruction in protest to a lack of global concern for Afghan humanitarian welfare, but in other sources he praised the act as a destruction of idols.

The Apostle of God, may God bless him, is neither too short nor too tall.
Ali ibn Abi Talib
Muhammad's cousin and son-in-law

See also: The emergence of Shia Islam 108–15 ▪ The divine art of Islamic calligraphy 190–91 ▪ Islamic art and architecture 194–201

Islamic buildings are often decorated with intricate patterning and religious calligraphy in place of other imagery, as here in a mosque in Istanbul, Turkey.

Those who make these images will be punished on the Day of Resurrection.
Prophet Muhammad

A veiled or flaming face

The views of the Taliban are shared by the so-called Islamic State, whose destruction of ancient monuments in Syria, for example, shocked the world, including many Muslims. Such views are far from representative of the whole of Islam.

Even in Muhammad's lifetime, attitudes to imagery were less than clear. According to one tradition, the Prophet criticized a tapestry that his wife Aisha had hung in their home, because it had images sewn into it; but when she turned the tapestry into pillow covers, he made no complaint.

Similarly, during the conquest of Mecca in 630, all idols and images were removed from the Kaaba and destroyed. But when a painting of Mary and Christ was brought out, Muhammad ordered that it should not be destroyed, recognizing their value to the Christian community.

Although there are many examples of Islam's aversion to religious imagery, there are also examples of Muslim devotion to such images, along with arguments made for how such devotion may not constitute idolatry. As with other world religions, Islam has a complex and varying theology of religious art.

Shia Islam, in particular, has always been much more open to the depiction of human figures, up to and including Muhammad. He featured as a central figure in many Persian miniatures, under both Sunni and Shia rulers. With rare exceptions, the Prophet's face is usually veiled in these depictions, or symbolically represented as a flame as a way of honoring him. Even today, Muslims generally take care to honor the Prophet by not depicting his face. For this reason, non-Muslim attempts to render his figure in art are frequently perceived by Muslims as disrespectful. ■

The *Jyllands-Posten* affair

In 2005, the Danish newspaper *Jyllands-Posten* published 12 cartoons under the title *Muhammads ansigt* (The Face of Muhammad). Almost all of the drawings were caricatures of Muhammad, and some were highly provocative. As the newspaper's editor made clear, the caricatures were intended as a critique of alleged Muslim hyper-sensitivity and resistance to criticism. Faith leaders called on the newspaper to issue an apology, as reactions to the cartoons spread across global Muslim communities, leading to protests, riots, and—a decade later—terrorist attacks in Paris and Copenhagen.

Muslim commentators at the time compared the cartoons to the issue of flag-burning in the United States, noting that many Americans favor a legal ban on flag-burning, which they see as an attack on their cultural identity, or even on America itself. Muslims view disrespect of the Prophet in the same way.

THE QUR

The opening *sura* of the Quran, **al-Fatiha**, is a key text of Islam. It is recited as part of daily prayers and its first verse begins every other *sura* in the Quran, bar one.

THE OPENING

The fourth *sura*, **al-Nisa**, contains a number of legislative verses regulating interpersonal relations and marriage.

WOMEN

The 12th *sura*, **Yusuf**, retells the story of the Prophet Joseph's mistreatment at the hands of his brothers and his subsequent life in Egypt.

JOSEPH

Sura 36, **Ya Sin**, is named for the two letters with which it begins: Y (Ya) and S (Sin). It establishes the Quran as a divine source.

YA SIN

THE COW

Sura 2, **al-Baqara**, is the longest, with 286 verses. It includes the story of the calf (or cow) that God told His people to sacrifice when Moses led them out of Egypt.

REPENTANCE

The ninth *sura*, **al-Tawba**, is the only *sura* in the Quran not prefixed by the verse, "In the Name of God, the Most Compassionate, the Most Merciful."

THE CAVE

The 18th *sura*, **al-Kahf**, includes the story of the Sleepers in the Cave, in which a group sleeps in a cave for 300 years to avoid religious persecution.

ORNAMENTS

The 43rd *sura*, **al-Zukhruf**, reminds believers that the goodness of God does not lie in material wealth, and to value instead their faith and love of God.

Muhammad began receiving the revelations that form the Quran from the angel Jibreel in 610, and continued receiving them at intervals for 23 years. During this period, Muhammad fled from Mecca on the *Hijra*, or migration, to Medina, then returned to conquer Mecca in 630, before finally ending his days back in Medina—all while continuing to receive God's divine message. The revelations were passed to Muhammad verse by verse, chapter by chapter, and relayed by the Prophet to his small group of followers.

A book like no other

The Quran is hard to describe, because it functions on many different levels. Foremost, it is an account of God, who is believed to be the source of all creation. But it is also filled with narratives about the patriarchs and prophets who can be found in the Hebrew Bible and the Old Testament of the Christian Bible. In addition, it contains rules on how to regulate social life as well as prayers to God, and a description of how the universe was created.

This was a scripture for the Arabs in their own language and the text in Arabic is elegant and poetic, affecting the reader with its beauty. The speaker throughout is God, who addresses the reader directly, showing His mercy but also His harsh punishment for those who stray from the straight path of faith.

As the verses were revealed to the Prophet, they were memorized and written down by his followers, recorded on whatever came to hand—palm fronds, scraps of parchment, even camel bone. Shortly after the Prophet's death, the fragments of the Quran were collected together and codified into the Holy Book that we know today. Handwritten copies of this book were then sent out across the rapidly expanding Islamic empire. In the space of no more than 120 years since the first verse was revealed, the Quran had become the cultural, intellectual, emotional, and sociopolitical point of reference for a civilization that stretched from the Iberian peninsula in the west to the Indian subcontinent in the east.

Core message

Despite the differences in approach and ritual that can be found among the world's Muslims, the one thing on which all subsets in Islam agree

Al-Rahman, the 55th *sura*, chastises man for his lack of gratitude toward God, who has showered him with an abundance of blessings.

Sura 80, **Abasa**, was given to the Prophet after he was said to have frowned and turned away from a blind man who interrupted his preaching.

The dramatic 99th *sura*, **al-Zalzala**, deals with the Day of Judgement, when Earth will suffer a terrible earthquake and other calamities.

The 113th *sura*, **al-Falaq**, is a short chapter that is recited (often with the 114th *sura*) to invoke God's protection against human and other kinds of evil.

THE MERCIFUL HE FROWNED THE EARTHQUAKE DAYBREAK

THAT WHICH IS COMING CLOTS OF BLOOD ONENESS MANKIND

The ominously named 56th *sura*, **al-Waqia**, contains indications of the inevitability of the end of the world.

The first five verses of **al-Alaq**, which is the 96th *sura*, were the first ever to be revealed to Muhammad, signaling the start of his prophetic mission.

The 112th *sura*, **al-Ikhlas**, is one with which most Muslims are familiar. Its four verses are profound statements of Divine unity and oneness (*tawhid*).

Al-Nas is the 114th and last *sura* in the Quran. It asks God for protection from evil spirits and the evil among mankind.

---

is the Quran's central message of divine unity, or *tawhid*. The Quran introduces itself as a book that is intended for those who "believe in the unseen." As such, its central message is not that God exists, but that only one God exists: its mission is not to prove the existence of the Creator, but to show that the Creator has no peers involved in His creation of the cosmos or in His constant support and renewal of the world and all the creatures in it.

The message of divine oneness, and the repudiation of the idea that nature, chance, or any other cause has any part in creation, is key to understanding the revelations that came to Muhammad and that form the Quran. All other teachings in the Holy Book—such as Muslim law, theology, philosophy, and political theory—are informed by and imbued with the spirit of divine oneness that runs through the Quran.

Social justice is also at the heart of the message. Followers are urged to help the poor, treating them fairly and with compassion, giving alms to those in need, and fasting in solidarity with the hungry. These practices would help ensure a stable society that would endure. Muhammad did not set out to found a new religion. Instead he sought to remind the Arabs of the old faith—the time when society had one God and everyone was treated fairly and equally.

Living word of God

The Quran is at the center of Islam, occupying for Muslims a position that is similar in significance to that of Jesus Christ for Christians. In the Christian faith, Jesus Christ is described in the Bible as "the Word made flesh." For Muslims, the Quran is the everlasting word of God, revealed not only between the covers of a book but also in the nature and structure of the physical universe itself, which the Holy Book is said to mirror.

Muslims believe that the Quran was revealed to Muhammad in order to clarify for all humanity our position and role on Earth and to help us understand why we are here. In short, the Quran is seen as a divine aid that has been sent to help mankind solve the riddle of human existence. As such, it was received as the word of God by one man in Arabia some 1,400 years ago and by almost a third of humanity today. ∎

THIS BOOK IS NOT TO BE DOUBTED

THE QURAN, 2:1

IN CONTEXT

THEME
Compiling the Quran

MORE ON THIS THEME
Sura 2 "The Cow" (*al-Baqara*) declares unequivocally "This Book is not to be doubted." It sets out the idea that the Quran is constant, immaculate, unalterable, and inimitable.

Sura 10 "Jonah" (*Yunus*) opens with an argument between Islam and its disbelievers, who say "Give us a Quran different from this, or change it," implying that the revelations are a product of Muhammad's own mind. The scripture responds by stating this is the word of God, there is no altering it.

Sura 25 "Salvation" (*al-Furqan*) has the unbelievers ask why the Quran was not handed down in a single revelation; the answer is given, "We have revealed it thus so that We may sustain your heart."

For Muslims there is no question that the Quran was delivered to the Prophet Muhammad in a series of divine revelations. These began when he was 40 years old and continued until the end of his life, 23 years later. What is less certain is when those divine revelations were written down and collected together to form the book we know as the Quran.

The majority of Muslim scholars believe that the Quran was copied during the lifetime of the Prophet. They claim that as verses were revealed, Muhammad would recite them in the presence of his followers, one of whom would transcribe the words. Muhammad could not write them himself because, as the Quran tells us, he was illiterate—several verses refer to the Prophet as "unlettered," for example 7:157 and 7:158. Some scholars also point to the fact that toward the end of his life the Prophet declared, "I leave among you two things of high estimation: the Book of God and my *sunna*." This leads them to suggest that the Quran existed in book form while Muhammad was alive. However,

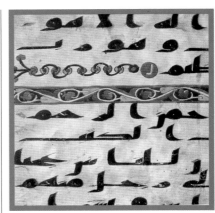

Early fragments from the Quran, such as this one discovered at Sanaa in Yemen, which dates back to the 8th century, are identical in content to the Quran as it is today.

this should not be taken in a literal sense; the likelihood is that the "book" existed only in the sense of a body of revelations, delivered but not yet collected together.

This view is corroborated by the scribe Zayd ibn Thabit. According to Islamic tradition, Ibn Thabit was a young follower of Muhammad and one of those chosen by the Prophet to write down the revelations, which he would also learn by heart. Ibn Thabit confirmed that at the

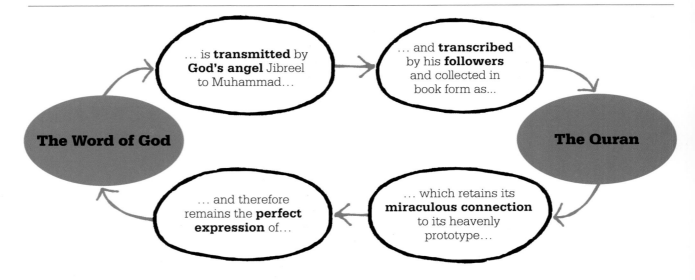

The Word of God … is **transmitted** by **God's angel** Jibreel to Muhammad… … and **transcribed** by his **followers** and collected in book form as… The Quran … which retains its **miraculous connection** to its heavenly prototype… … and therefore remains the **perfect expression** of…

See also: The early life of Muhammad 22–27 ▪ The death of the Prophet 56–57 ▪ The composition of the Quran 70–75 ▪ The rightly guided caliphs 104–07

time of Muhammad's death the Quran had not yet been "gathered together into a thing." The fact that the verb "gathered" was used, rather than "written," suggests that the elements of the Quran existed in written form but they had not yet been arranged chapter by chapter into a physical book. It is possible that while the Prophet was alive, the Quran was seen as a work in progress. Verses, and even whole chapters, were continually being revealed to Muhammad and he would not have known when his prophetic mission was to come to an end.

Collection and compilation
The catalyst for the decision to compile the Quran was the Battle of Yamama, which took place in 632, just a few months after Muhammad had died. Yamama saw the Muslims triumph over the Bani Hanifa tribe, whose leader, looking to emulate Muhammad, had also declared himself a new prophet. However, large numbers of the Prophet's Companions were slain. Many of these were "reciters" (*qurra*) who had committed the entire revelations to memory and whose job it was to transmit the Quran to others.

The Muslims feared that the loss of so many *qurra* put the survival of the Quran in jeopardy. The leadership of the *umma* (Islamic community) decided that the Quran needed to be collected and written down. Different historical sources provide varying accounts of how this was done and under whose direction. One of the widows of the Prophet, Hafsa, is said in one account to have had in her possession a great many loose

This Quran could not have been devised by any but God.
10:37

leaves of Quranic scripture. The Muslim leaders also made appeals to anyone who might possess additional verses to bring them forward. Texts were collected that were written on clay tablets, palm fronds, and even animal bones. All of this material was handed to a compilation committee of four— some sources say five—senior Companions, who were instructed to copy all the texts, comparing them against the recitations of

the *qurra* as they worked. Each verse was validated by the oral testimony of at least two *qurra*. Verses that existed in oral form only with no written version were subject to particular scrutiny.

The order of the texts was set by the Prophet. Islamic traditions say that with each new revelation, Muhammad always indicated its place in relation to previous revelations. This order was always maintained in prayers during the Prophet's lifetime, and was later adhered to by those who compiled the Quran.

The codex
Once complete, the codex (a book constructed of a number of loose sheets) was put in the safekeeping of Abu Bakr, the first leader, or caliph, of the Islamic community following the death of the Prophet. From Abu Bakr the codex was passed to his successor, Umar. During Umar's 10-year rule, Islam spread well beyond the confines of the Arabian Peninsula, carried by a wave of Arab expansion. »

The word "Quran"
The exact linguistic meaning of the word "Quran" (or Koran, as it is sometimes written) is unclear. It has four possible origins. One is the root word *qaraa*, which means "to collect" or "to compile." In this respect, the Quran is a book which was collected and compiled under the protection of God. The second root word is *qarana*, which means a "union" or "conjunction," and indicates the joining of letters to form words, words to form verses, verses to

form chapters, and so on. The third root word is *qarain*, which means "symbol," "evidence," or "argument." In the context of the Quran, this is taken as signifying the fact that one verse interprets, elaborates upon, and gives arguments and evidence for other verses. The fourth possible root word, and the one that is most commonly cited as the correct root, is *qiraat*, which means "reading" or "recitation," which makes sense because the Quran originally existed as a series of recited verses.

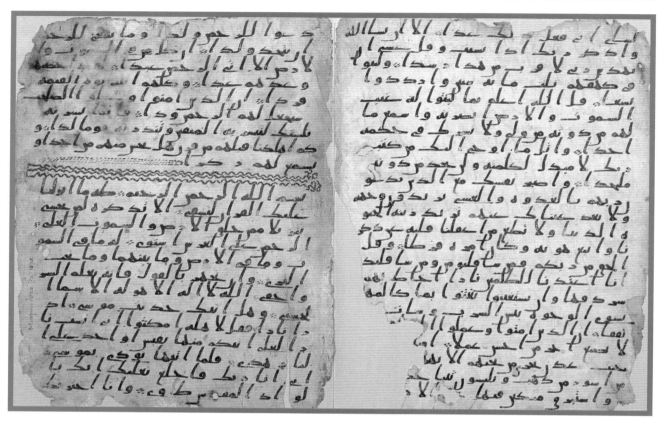

The Birmingham Quran is not a complete book but two leaves of a manuscript containing Quranic text. It has been radiocarbon dated to roughly the time Muhammad was alive.

We have sent you forth... with a Quran that We divided into sections, that you may read it to the people with deliberation.
17:106

As new territories were conquered, Umar dispatched Companions well versed in the Quran to spread the word. Ten Companions were sent to Basra in Iraq, for example, while a senior Companion named Ibn Masud was sent to Kufa, also in Iraq. Others went to Damascus, Syria. One tradition says that Companions were also sent to Yemen and Bahrain.

The Uthmanic recension
Under the next caliph, Uthman, there were more territorial gains. By this time, the Muslim nation was much more diverse than just the tribes of the Arabian Peninsula. In the new territories, many became converts to Islam, and they came from a multitude of different provinces, peoples, and tribes. They recited the Quran in either their own dialects (if they were Arabic speakers) or in badly learned Arabic if it was not their native language. As a result, differences in pronunciation began to creep into the recitations, and even disagreements over the correct meaning of the text.

The Muslim elders realized that these discrepancies would only increase over time to threaten the unity of the Islamic community. Reportedly in the year 653, Uthman resolved to remedy the problem before it got out of hand. Tradition relates that Uthman had multiple copies made from the original codex that had been compiled during the time of Abu Bakr. These were copied in the dialect of the Quraysh, the main Meccan tribe. One copy of what came to be known as the Uthmanic recension ("revised edition") was kept in Medina, while others were sent out to every corner of the Muslim empire, along with orders that all other manuscripts and fragments of prophetic revelations be burned.

The Eternal Book

That Abu Bakr compiled the Quran and Uthman turned it into one authoritative book is accepted by the vast majority of scholars and historians, certainly in the Islamic world. Some scholars, mostly in the West, have proposed that the final standardization of the Quran might have taken place at a much later date than Islamic tradition claims. In the mid-1970s, Professor John Wansbrough at London's School of Oriental and African Studies (SOAS) argued that the Quran was written and collected not at the time of the Prophet but over a period of 200 years. Historians Michael Cook and Patricia Crone echoed this theory in their

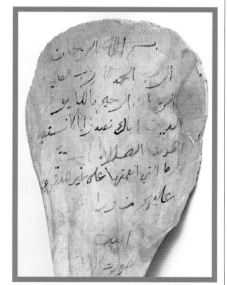

In the absence of paper, parts of the Quran were inscribed on all kinds of other materials, such as these lines from the *Fatiha*, written on the shoulder blade of a camel.

We have revealed it an Arabic Quran, that perchance you may understand it. It is a transcript of the Eternal Book in Our keeping, sublime, and full of wisdom.
43:1

Hagarism: The Making of the Islamic World (1977), in which they questioned the authenticity of Muslim accounts of the rise of Islam. However, in the 21st century, the carbon dating of a number of early Quranic fragments appears to back up the traditional view that the Quran was in existence within about 20 years following the Prophet's death. Radiocarbon analysis of Quranic texts held by the University of Birmingham in the UK has dated the parchment on which the text is written to the period between 568 and 645, with 95 percent accuracy. This coincides with the lifetime of Muhammad. This dating is supported by the fact the Quran makes no mention of any notable events in Islamic history beyond the Prophet's death.

The Uthmanic Quran is thus almost universally accepted as the collected revelations of the Prophet Muhammad, as received from God. The Quran consists always and everywhere of the same 114 chapters and the same 6,200 verses, presented in the same order. It has remained this way, with not a word changed or modified, for almost 1,400 years. ∎

The Companions of the Prophet

Known in Arabic as the *Sahaba*, the Companions in the strictest sense are those who were alive at the time of the Prophet Muhammad and had personal contact with him, however slight. They are key figures in the history of Islam because after the Prophet's death it was the testimony of the *Sahaba*, passed down through trusted chains of narrators, that provided the knowledge of the life and sayings of Muhammad (*hadith*). These form the basis for the Muslim way of life (*sunna*), and its code of conduct and law (Sharia).

There are a number of different categories of *Sahaba*: for example, the *muhajirun* ("immigrants") are those who followed the Prophet from Mecca to Medina on the *Hijra*; the *ansar* ("helpers") are the people of Medina who took in the Prophet and his followers.

The names and brief biographies of some of the most prominent Companions are recorded in several early works of Islamic scholarship— one of these includes more than 3,000 entries.

A GUIDE FOR THE RIGHTEOUS

THE QURAN, 2:1

IN CONTEXT

THEME
**The composition of
the Quran**

MORE ON THIS THEME
Sura 39 "The Throngs"
(*al-Zumar*) is a good example
of a Meccan *sura*. Relatively
short, it begins by restating
the authority of the Quran
("The Revelation of the Book is
from God") and continues to
talk about Creation and the
role of the Quran ("We have
given mankind in this Quran
all manner of parables" 39:27).

Sura 5 "The Table"
(*al-Maida*) is a prime example
of a Medinan *sura*. Running
to 120 verses, it touches on a
multitude of topics, including
forbidden foods, ritual hygiene,
the correct punishment for
theft, the penance for breaking
an oath, the making of wills,
and many other issues of a
practical nature.

A common criticism of
the Quran concerns its
form and structure. The
"chapters" and "verses" that make
up the Quran seem at first glance
to have been put together in an
arbitrary manner. There is no
sense of linearity in the Quran,
with no real beginning, middle,
and end. Scenes, themes, and
protagonists seem to change with
confusing frequency, making it
difficult for the reader to follow
the narrative. The first revelation
appears as verses one to five of
the 96th *sura*—the other 14 verses
of the *sura* were revealed later.

However, most of the criticisms
leveled at the Quran come from
those who read it in translation.
By contrast, the vast majority of
Arabic-reading Muslims view the
Quran as a miracle both of language
and of style. They consider it a work
of sheer inimitability—that is, a
work so uniquely extraordinary
that it can never be equaled.

Chapter and verse

The Quran is a relatively brief read,
shorter than the New Testament
of the Christian Bible. If the Quran
sometimes appears bulky on library

> But those that deny and reject
> Our revelations shall be the
> inmates of the Fire, wherein
> shall they abide forever.
> **2:39**

shelves, it is because most editions
also include copious explanatory
footnotes, which are frequently
longer than the text itself. Within
its text, the Quran covers a vast
range of topics, providing guidance
on worship, the afterlife, marriage
and family life, care for the needy
and disadvantaged, and even
matters of hygiene, community
affairs, politics, and economics.
It constitutes a complete guide
to life and beyond.

In presenting this information,
there are two principal internal
divisions in the book, known in
Arabic as the *sura* and the *aya*.

Rote and recitation

Western scholarship has added
numbers to the chapters and
verses of the Quran for ease of
reference, but Muslims prefer
to use the names of the *suras*,
or quote the beginning of the
particular passage under
discussion. This method
requires not only considerable
familiarity with the complete
text of the Quran but also
considerable skills of memory.

Nonetheless, many Muslims
memorize large portions of the
Quran, and some are even able
to commit the entire book to
memory. To learn the entire
Quran by heart brings great
prestige and blessing, and
a Muslim who has achieved
this is known as a *hafiz* or a
"guardian" of the Quran.

A *hafiz* keeps God's holy
book alive and is given great
respect. They often become
reciters of the Quran at daily
prayers in the mosque and at
other important rituals and
ceremonies. This skill is so
highly prized that auditoriums
are often filled to capacity for
recitation contests.

Young Afghans read from the Quran
at a mosque. Some parents recite
the Quran to their children instead of
nursery rhymes, and have them learn
to recite verses from the age of three.

See also: The early life of Muhammad 22–27 ▪ Compiling the Quran 64–69 ▪ The *Fatiha*: the first *sura* 76–77 ▪ What the Quran says about God 78–79 ▪ The physical form of the Quran 88–89 ▪ *Tafsir*, or the art of interpreting the Quran 90–91

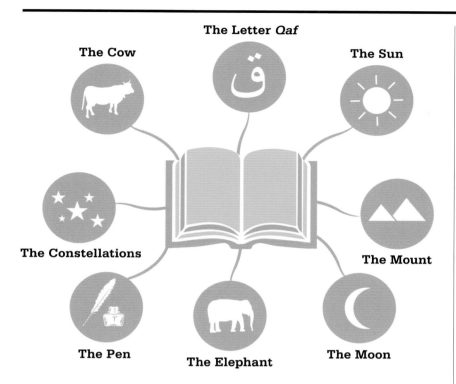

The Cow

The Letter *Qaf*

The Sun

The Constellations

The Mount

The Pen

The Elephant

The Moon

Chapters or *suras* of the Quran often take their name from a story or theme contained within them. They are not arranged in any narrative or chronological order. Opened at any point, they will offer reassurance of God's will to the reader.

These are usually translated into English as "chapter" and "verse," respectively. While not perfect, these translations are adequate in the sense that the *sura* and the *aya* function more or less in the same way as the chapters and verses of the Bible.

The *sura*

The word *sura* actually means a "row" or "fence"—or anything that is used to section off one thing from another. There are 114 *suras* in the Quran, all differing in length. They are not arranged chronologically or according to topic but, broadly, by length. The longer chapters are found at the beginning of the Quran, with the shorter chapters toward the end. The exception to this ordering is the short *sura* known as the *Fatiha*, which opens the Quran.

All the *suras* have a title. Generally speaking, these titles reflect the main theme, or one of the main themes of the *sura*. They function as a kind of thematic abstract. For example, the second *sura* of the Quran—"The Cow" (*al-Baqara*)—is a reference to the golden calf that was fashioned by Aaron and worshipped by the Israelites while Moses was on Mount Sinai. But while the *sura* spans 286 verses, there are fewer than a dozen explicit references to the calf after which the *sura* is named. The novice cannot necessarily tell from the title of a *sura* what the main theme will be. Significant exceptions include *sura* 4, Women (*al-Nisa*), which has a lot to say on wives, and *sura* 12, entitled Joseph (*Yusuf*), which tells the story of the patriarch-prophet Joseph. This *sura* is also notable for having a distinct beginning, middle, and end.

The *aya*

That the word *aya* has traditionally been translated as "verse" reflects only the role it plays as the shortest unit of division in the Quran. But the Arabic word really means "clear sign" or "evidence." This reflects the Islamic belief that the Quran presents the whole universe and so its constituent parts are all signs or evidence of the existence of God.

Each of the numbered sections below is an *aya*:

[1] *When Earth is rocked in her last convulsion;*
[2] *when Earth shakes off her burdens*
[3] *and Man says: "What may this mean?"—*
[4] *on that day she will proclaim her tidings,*
[5] *for your Lord will have inspired her.*
[6] *On that day mankind will come out in broken bands to be shown their labors.*
[7] *Whoever did an atom's weight of good shall see it,*
[8] *and whoever did an atom's weight of evil shall also see it.* »

Together, these eight *ayat* (the plural of *aya*) make up the whole of *sura* 99 of the Quran, called "The Earthquake" (*al-Zalzala*). The *ayat* do not necessarily each constitute a self-contained sentence; in this particular example, a single sentence straddles the first five *ayat*. Other *ayat*, however, may be no more than a few words.

In most Arabic-language Qurans, readers can see the number of *ayat* because each one is followed by a small rosette, and each rosette contains the number of that verse. In English-language translations of the Quran, the verse numbers are more usually noted in the margins. While the habit of dividing the verses and marking

Historical Qurans are often lavishly decorated with beautiful framing devices. In this 14th-century example from Cairo you can see the rosettes marking the verses of the *Fatiha*.

the divisions is an age-old practice, numbering the verses is a habit adopted later, but one that is more or less standard now in the Muslim world.

Given that the *suras* come in different lengths, it follows that they also have a widely varying number of verses. For example, *sura* 108, "Abundance" (*al-Kawthar*), has only three *ayat*. The longest of the *suras*, "The Cow" (*al-Baqara*), has 286 *ayat*.

Beginning the *sura*

Each *sura* begins with the *Bismillah*: in Arabic, *Bismillahi l-rahmani l-rahim* ("In the Name of God, the Compassionate, the Merciful"), which is also the first line of the *Fatiha*, the first *sura* in the Quran. The exception to this is *sura* 9, "Repentance" (*al-Tawba*). This is an ultimatum from God to the nonbelievers in the recently captured city of

> We have sent down to you clear revelations; none will deny them except the ungodly.
> **2:99**

Mecca, who remained opposed to Islam. The mercy of God is withdrawn from them.

Following the *Bismillah*, 29 of the Quran's *suras* are then prefaced with a combination of letters. These letters are written combined, but each of the letters is supposed to be pronounced separately. For example, *The Cow* (*sura* 2) begins

and full of imagery. Many begin with oaths. For example, *sura* 95 is introduced with, "By the fig and by the olive! By Mount Sinai and by this inviolate city..." Later Meccan chapters are more serene and contain frequent illustrations of the truth of God's message drawn from nature and history. They are more formal than other *suras* and often discuss matters of doctrine. God is frequently referred to in these chapters as "the Merciful."

Medinan *suras*

The Medinan chapters are quite different from the Meccan ones because, by this time, Muhammad was no longer leading a fledgling group of followers, but had become the head of a large, independent community of Muslims. As a result, the Medinan *suras* are less about establishing the credentials of the Prophet and the evidence of God's signs. Instead, they focus on the duties and norms of behavior, through discussion of legal and social matters, with advice on how such rulings should be applied in order to regulate life within the growing Muslim community.

An example is in *sura* 24, where Muslims are told to gather four witnesses in order to corroborate any accusation of adultery. This was an important safeguard for women in a society in which even the sight of an unrelated man and woman together might be cause for suspicion. Accusations by those who do not supply four witnesses should be rejected and such persons dealt with harshly, according to this Medinan chapter of the Quran. ∎

with the letters *alif*, *lam*, *meem*, or A, L, M. Several chapters are actually named after the letters with which they begin, such as *sura* 20, which is called *Ta Ha*, or "T H." The meaning of these letters is unknown, which has sparked considerable speculation and many different interpretations. Classical Quranic commentators tend to take the view that these letters stand for words and phrases related to God's various names or attributes. Others are not overly concerned by explanations and are content with the general claim that God alone knows what the letters mean.

Meccan *suras*

Another important Quranic division may be of less significance to the ordinary worshipper than to Islamic scholars and historians. Scholars will distinguish between those *suras* revealed to Muhammad during the years he lived in Mecca—early in his prophetic career—and those revealed to him later, when he was based in Medina. The Meccan *suras* are generally shorter than

their Medinan counterparts. They tend to deal with subjects connected to the fundamentals of faith, and communities and events of the past. So if a *sura* seems to focus more on metaphysical issues, on God's oneness, on stories of the patriarchs and prophets of old, or on heaven, hell, and the hereafter, it is likely to have been revealed in Mecca. The earliest of these revelations are often very rhythmic

With measured tone recite the Quran, for we are about to address to you words of surpassing gravity.
73:4

IN THE NAME OF GOD, THE MERCIFUL, THE COMPASSIONATE

THE QURAN, 1:1

IN CONTEXT

THEME
The *Fatiha*, the first *sura*

MORE ON THIS THEME
***Sura* 16** "The Bee" (*an-Nahl*) warns against worshipping gods other than God. It speaks of the favored and those who have gone astray. "Had God pleased, He would have united you into one community. But He confounds whom He will and gives guidance to whom He pleases."

***Sura* 36** "*Ya Sin*", sometimes called the "heart of the Quran," emphasizes the oneness of God and reminds Muslims, it is "by the Wise Quran, you are surely one sent forth on a straight path".

***Sura* 55** "The Merciful" (*al-Rahman*) describes some of the resources that God has provided for man and chastises him for his lack of gratitude toward God.

The **one and only God** exists on a cosmic scale as **Lord of the Universe**.

God relates strongly toward mankind, to whom he is **merciful and compassionate**.

God can also display **anger** (wrath) toward mankind.

There are **two kinds of people**: those on the **straight path** and those who have gone **astray**.

Both kinds of people will be called to account before God on the Day of Judgment.

The opening *sura* (chapter) of the Quran, prosaically entitled "The Opener" (*al-Fatiha*), is arguably the best known of all Quranic narratives and occupies a special place in Islamic liturgy and Muslim faith. As well as serving as an introduction to the Quran—despite the fact that it was not the first chapter to be revealed—the *Fatiha* is also an invocation that is an integral part of everyday prayer. It is usually recited silently—either individually or in a group —whenever believers feel the need

See also: The Five Pillars of Islam: *Shahada* 36–41 ▪ The Five Pillars of Islam: *salat* 42–43 ▪ The divine art of Islamic calligraphy 190–91

to praise or thank God. The seven verses that comprise the *Fatiha* may be translated as follows:

In the Name of God, the
*   Merciful, the Compassionate.*
Praise be to God, Lord of the
*   Universe,*
The Merciful, the Compassionate,
Sovereign of the Day of Judgment!
You alone we worship, and to You
*   alone we turn for help.*
Guide us to the straight path,
The path of those whom You have
*   favored, not of those who have*
*   provoked Your ire, nor of*
*   those who have lost their way.*

The *Fatiha* is a declaration of divine oneness, and it is an acknowledgement of God's "beautiful names" and attributes of perfection. It can be used as a petition for guidance, help, and mercy. It also serves as an affirmation of divine power and lordship, and an admission of humankind's absolute dependence on God for succor and salvation.

Whoever does not recite the *Fatiha* in his prayer, his prayer is invalid.
Prophet Muhammad

The *Bismillah*

The opening *aya*, or verse ("In the Name of God, the Merciful, the Compassionate"), appears at the beginning of every Quranic *sura* except one. Referred to commonly as the *Bismillah* (literally, "in the name of God"), the *aya* is a formulaic utterance that is spoken before any significant undertaking. While it is heard most commonly at the start of a meal, believers utter it before they leave the house, before they go on a journey, before

they embark on any particularly difficult task, and even—because it is encouraged in a *hadith*—before sexual intercourse. In the Indian subcontinent, a *Bismillah* ceremony is held to mark a child's initiation into Islam.

Compassion and mercy

The *Fatiha* is significant on account of its emphasis on an aspect of the divine that is often overlooked, namely the compassion and mercy of God. To describe the Creator as compassionate (*rahman*) is to underscore the mercy that God shows to creation as a whole. To describe the Creator as merciful (*rahim*), however, is to emphasize the compassion that God shows to each and every created being, separately and uniquely. The fact that the *Bismillah* should precede every *sura* except one demonstrates the importance given by the Quran to divine compassion. This finds an echo in the later Quranic verse that hails Muhammad and his message "as a blessing to mankind" (21:107). ▪

The *Fatiha* encapsulates much of Islam's core message. As such, it is frequently rendered in decorative calligraphy, as here, on the dome of the Hagia Sophia in Istanbul.

The Mother of the Book

The *Fatiha* goes by many alternative names. According to Islamic tradition it is *Um al-Quran*, or the "Mother of the Quran", or *Um al-Kitab*, the "Mother of the Book"—Arabic speakers tend to add the qualifier "Mother of …" to anything that summarizes something or comprises its most important part. It is also named Mother of the Book because it is the first chapter written in the Quran and the recitation in the canonical prayer begins with it. The *Fatiha*

is called *al-Saba al-Mathani* or the "Seven Oft-Repeated Verses" and the "Great Quran". The historian al-Tabari said that this is because the meaning of the entire Quran is summarized in the seven verses that make up the *Fatiha*.

The *Fatiha* is occasionally referred to as *al-Shifa* or "the Cure" because, according to Islamic tradition, Muhammad said "The opening of the Book [meaning the Quran] is a cure for every ailment and every poison."

THE LORD OF ALL BEING
THE QURAN 1:1–7

IN CONTEXT

THEME
What the Quran says about God

MORE ON THIS THEME
Sura 23 "The Believers" (*al-Muminun*) tells of God's role in the creation of humankind: "We first created man from an essence of clay" (23:12–14). It also confirms God's creation of the heavens and earth.

Sura 24 "Light" (*al-Nur*) contains the *ayat al-nur*, a lyrical—verging on mystical—group of lines on the nature of God: "God is the light of the heavens and the earth. His light may be compared to a niche that enshrines a lamp, the lamp within a crystal of starlike brilliance" (24:35).

Sura 25 "Salvation" (*al-Furqan*) says that it is God "who has created all things and ordained them in due proportion" (25:2).

Humankind is told that **all bounty is in the hand of God**.

→

We do not know how, or in what sense, this is true.

↓

We must just **believe and accept it**.

←

We can think about God, but we cannot comprehend Him.

The overarching emphasis of the Quran is that God is transcendent, or beyond human comprehension. He is remote in the sense of being completely unlike anything that He has created. However, He is at the same time, in the words of the Quran, closer to man "than his jugular vein" (50:16). In stressing God's presence in the physical world, the Quran also reveals that God is constantly and continuously engaged in the creative act. The God portrayed by the Quran is in a sense a "hands-on" creator, and not one who created the heavens and the earth in six days before "resting" on the seventh. God, according to the Quran, is engaged in an act of "continuous creation."

No need for proof
The Quran does not attempt to use any strong rational or philosophical arguments to prove the existence of God. In fact, the Quran does not really attempt to prove the existence of God at all. In keeping with the mission of the patriarchs and prophets who preceded Muhammad, the Quran sets out to prove not that there is a God, but that God is one.

See also: Compiling the Quran 64–69 ▪ The *Fatiha*, the first *sura* 76–77 ▪ The Six Pillars of Faith 86–87

The word "Allah" is made up of the Arabic letters *alif*, (1), *lam* (2 and 3) and *ha* (4), read right to left. The diacritical marks above modify the sounds, but they are not always written.

The Quran stresses the unity of God—He is indivisible, and so cannot have any kind of body, made up of parts as humans have. The Quran reveals those aspects of the divine "character" that are accessible to the human intellect and power of reason. For instance, on the subject of oneness, the Quran explicitly states that God "has begotten no children and has no partner" (25:1–2). *Sura* 2:255 tells us, "Neither slumber nor sleep overtakes Him", while *sura* 6:59 emphasises His omniscience: "He knows all that land and sea contain: every leaf that falls is known to Him."

Yet there are passages in the Quran that specifically refer, for example to God's hands and eyes—"The Hand of God is above their hands" (48:10), for example. Most Muslims consider this allegorical. In fact, to take descriptions such as these literally would lead to anthropomorphism (attributing human characteristics to God) and might be seen as comparing God with the beings He created, which is a great sin. At the same time, there are literalists who refuse any interpretations of the Quran and insist it be taken at face value.

While God in His absolute essence is unfathomable, He can be seen, as it were, through the

Beware, for God cannot be described with any attribute.
Ali ibn Abi Talib
Son-in-law of Prophet Muhammad

The names of God

"Allah" is a universal name for God and does not refer to an exclusively Islamic God. Allah is the same God that appears in the Christian Bible and Jewish Torah.

Philologists believe the word Allah is derived from a contraction of *al-ilah*, which means "the god" in Arabic. It is etymologically related to the Aramaic and Hebrew names for God, *Allaha* and *Elohim*. The word "God"—or Allah—appears more than three thousand times in the Quran, and there are countless passages where He is described in terms of various "attributes of perfection," including *al-Rahman* ("the Compassionate"); *al-Rahim* ("the Merciful"); *al-Malik* ("the Sovereign"); *al-Qudus* ("the Holy"); *al-Salaam* ("the Source of Peace"); and so on. Contrary to popular opinion, the divine names do not number 99, but are in fact innumerable: wherever perfection exists, such as beauty, wisdom, or power, God possesses that attribute absolutely. Thus, the Quran asserts, He is omniscient, omnipotent, and omnipresent.

"veil" of His creations, which are deemed to be "signs" (*ayat*) that point to Him. The Quran's exhortations to meditate upon the countless creational signs that make up the universe are not made merely so that humankind might acquire knowledge of His universe for the sake of knowledge alone. Instead, humankind is encouraged to study itself and the world in order to better know and understand the Creator. ▪

THERE SHALL BE NO COMPULSION IN RELIGION
THE QURAN, 2:256

IN CONTEXT

THEME
Tolerating the beliefs of others

MORE ON THIS THEME
Sura 22 "The Pilgrimage" (*al-Hajj*) says, "For every community, We have ordained a ritual which they observe. Let them not dispute with you concerning this. Call them to the path of your Lord: you are rightly guided. If they argue with you, say: 'God knows best all that you do. On the Day of Resurrection, God will judge your differences.'"

Sura 109 "The Unbelievers" (*al-Kafirun*) is a short *sura* that argues against religious intolerance, it states: "Say: 'You blasphemers! I do not worship what you worship, nor do you worship what I worship. I shall never worship what you worship, nor will you ever worship what I worship. You have your religion, and I have mine.'"

While Islam does not accept the Christian Bible in its entirety as a divinely revealed scripture, certain key parts of it are revered: these are the first five books of the Old Testament, the Psalms of David, and the Gospels. Many of the patriarchs of the Old Testament, such as Noah, Abraham, Job, and Moses, appear in the Quran, where they are lauded as prophets and messengers. Jesus, too, is revered as a prophet, but not as the son of God, an idea the Quran rejects. Biblical figures such as Joseph, for

Comparing the Abrahamic religions

	Moses 1391–1271 BCE	Jesus 3 BC–33 CE	Muhammad 570–632 CE
Judaism believes in Moses but deny the prophethood of Jesus and Muhammad.	✡ (filled)	✡ (outline)	✡ (outline)
Christianity believes in Jesus as the son of God and revere Moses as a prophet, but do not recognize Muhammad.	✝ (filled)	✝ (filled)	✝ (outline)
Islam honours Moses, Jesus, and Muhammad as prophets sent with the message of monotheism.	☪ (filled)	☪ (filled)	☪ (filled)

See also: The *umma*, the community of Islam 32–33 ▪ The example of Islamic Spain 166–71 ▪ The Crusades through Muslim eyes 180–81 ▪ Islam in Europe 210–15

> Believers, those who follow the Jewish Faith, Sabaeans, and Christians—whoever believes in God …—shall have nothing to fear or to regret.
> **5:69**

example, to whom a whole *sura* is dedicated, are mentioned far more in the Quran than Muhammad.

The general perception among Muslims is that the scriptures revealed to the Jews and Christians (known as the "People of the Book") have somehow been corrupted—hence the need for an incorruptible, and final, revelation, namely the Quran. While there are clear doctrinal and theological differences between Islam and Christianity, as far as the stories of Jesus and the Old Testament patriarchs are concerned the Quran is full of references and allusions to the Christian texts. This suggests that its original readers were, like Muhammad himself, very familiar with the Bible.

The protected peoples

The Quranic verses, "There shall be no compulsion in religion" (2:256) and "You have your religion, and I have my religion" (109:6) would appear to guarantee every human being's right to adhere to the practices of their own faith—or even to not believe in any god at all.

These verses would also appear to sanction the peaceable existence of minority faith communities within Islam. However, other verses in the Quran present more ambivalent attitudes toward Jews and Christians. Christians are said to be "nearest in affection" to Muslims (5:82), and yet Muslims are not to take Jews or Christians as "friends" (5:51). This reflects the varied experience of Muhammad and the early Muslim community. Initially, Muhammad sought the acceptance of Christians and Jews, but when their leaders rejected him as a false prophet, he received revelations that commanded him to distance himself from them. In the Constitution of Medina, which Muhammad negotiated with the Jews of that city, Jews were included in the *umma*.

As the Muslim armies encountered more communities of Jews and Christians, they were accorded the status of *ahl al-dhimma*, or "protected peoples." What this meant in practice varied with time and place, but typically *dhimmi* were allowed to practice their religions, even if they enjoyed fewer privileges than Muslims. They were subject to a special tax known as *jizya*. The largely harmonious coexistence of Muslims and the so-called People of the Book in Medina at the time of the Prophet, in Muslim Spain, and in the Ottoman Empire, is reflective of the Quranic ideal. ▪

The Quran and the Bible

Readers of the Quran and the Hebrew and Christian Bibles will find many characters and stories in common. The words of the Quran appear to assume familiarity with Jewish and Christian texts, while offering some gentle correctives in certain details. In the Quran, for example, Adam and Hawwa (Eve) are forgiven by God before being sent from Paradise, because they begged for His mercy, rather than cast out and cursed as in the Bible. Infant Jesus, in a miracle unreported in the Bible, speaks up from the crib to defend his mother's honor when ill-wishers accuse her of fornication. The Quran also says that the Jews did not kill or crucify Jesus—it only appeared to them as if they had. Instead, Jesus was raised up by God to heaven, which Muslims believe he entered alive. They believe he will return in a Second Coming to fight the False Messiah and establish peace on earth.

> The Jews say the Christians are misguided, and the Christians say it is the Jews who are misguided. God will on the Day of Resurrection judge what they disagreed about.
> **2:112**

AND ALL THINGS WE HAVE MADE IN PAIRS

THE QURAN, 51:49

IN CONTEXT

THEME
Women in the Quran

MORE ON THIS THEME
Sura 4 "Women" (*al-Nisa*) is the most quoted chapter regarding women and Islam. It addresses mothers, sisters, daughters, wives, divorcées, widows, orphan girls, slave girls, and women accused of adultery, and sets out legal frameworks for matters such as inheritance and marriage.

Sura 24 "Light" (*al-Nur*) concerns female modesty: "Enjoin believing women… to preserve their chastity; not to display their adornments (except such as are normally revealed); to draw their veils over their bosoms…." Some have translated this as "let their headscarves fall over… and cover their necklines."

The fourth *sura* of the Quran is called *al-Nisa*, or "Women." It begins: "You people! Fear your Lord, who created you from a single soul. From that soul He created its spouse, and through them He bestrewed the earth with countless men and women."

This single verse embodies a basic and important theme of the Quran's teachings on the subject of men and women, which is that the sexes are complementary—they are created "from a single soul." The idea is reinforced in *sura* 51: "The heaven We built with mighty hands… And all things We have made in pairs" (51:49).

See also: Compiling the Quran 64–69 ▪ The modern Sharia state 266–69 ▪ A feminist Islam? 292–99 ▪ The *hijab* and *niqab* 300–03

At times in Islamic history, women have been encouraged to pray at home, but in most mosques today they pray in a designated space, as here at al-Barka Mosque in Bekasi, Indonesia.

The Quran also reveals that reward in the hereafter awaits believing men and women alike: "Be they men or women, those who are Muslims and have faith; who are devout, sincere, patient, humble, charitable, and chaste; who fast and are ever mindful of God—on these God will bestow forgiveness and a rich recompense" (33:35).

It is clear that, according to the Quran, men and women are two equal elements in the eyes of God.

Protected rights

The Quran was compiled in 7th-century tribal Arabia—a society in which women were seen very much as possessions, with few formal rights. In this cultural context, the Quran's teachings on equality were unprecedented, and heralded a marked improvement in the position of women in Arab society.

The Quran prohibited outright certain practices that were common at the time, such as female infanticide and sexual abuse of slave girls. It also gave women marriage, divorce, inheritance, property, and custody rights that they were unlikely to have enjoyed prior to the advent of Islam. While the Quran permits a man to take multiple wives ("you may marry other women who seem good to you: two, three, or four"), it goes on to stipulate that they must be properly and equally supported, and that any man who cannot do this must "marry one only" (4:3).

These and other teachings guarantee the financial security of divorced women: the second *sura*, called "The Cow," explicitly states that it is unlawful for any man to take from a divorced wife anything that he has given her, and adds that she should be treated with kindness, with no harm or wrong done to her. Nor are former wives to be prevented from remarrying: "These are the bounds set by God; »

The true believers, both men and women, are friends to one another.
9:71

Maryam, the Arabic name for Mary, is held in high honor in the Quran, and the 19th *sura* bears her name. This 17th-century Persian painting is thought to show her with her son Jesus (Isa).

Maryam, mother of Jesus

The Quran mentions about 25 female characters, but only Mary (Maryam in Arabic), the mother of Jesus (Isa), is identified by name. The name "Maryam" occurs more times in the Quran than the name "Mary" in the New Testament of the Christian Bible. The Quran even names *sura* 19 after her. While Muslims revere Maryam, scholars have stopped short of recognizing her as a prophet, although some medieval Muslim writers did so.

Other female figures in the Quran include the Queen of Sheba, the mother of Moses, the wives and daughters of Muhammad, the daughters of Lot, and the wife of the Prophet Joseph's master in Egypt. Of these, the Queen of Sheba stands out as the only woman whose primary role is not that of wife or daughter. In fact, she is often cited by feminists as a historical example of female leadership and of the entitlement of women to political rule.

do not transgress them" (2:229). The same *sura* enjoins: "Those of you who die leaving wives behind shall bequeath their widows a year's maintenance without causing them to leave their homes" (2:240). It also states that a wife shall inherit one-quarter of her husband's estate.

There are, however, two areas in which the Quran may appear to favor men over women. One is that of legal witness. In some legal situations where witnesses are required, the gender of the witness is immaterial, but where witnesses are needed for financial contracts, the Quran stipulates that one male witness is equal to two females. Some scholars suggest this merely reflects the fact that women in 7th-century Arabia were less experienced in financial matters—although the Prophet's first wife Khadija, a respected merchant, is a notable exception.

The other area of seeming inequality is inheritance, with daughters receiving only half what their brothers inherit. The usual explanation for this is that men had the extra burden of supporting the women in their household. As progressive as the Quran may have been, it also reflects the reality of its time, acknowledging the different roles of the sexes in the family.

Patriarchal authority
One of the most contentious passages in the Quran is the 34th verse of *sura* 4, "Women". These few lines are some of the most debated in Muslim scripture, and are often held responsible for the patriarchal nature of many

> The man and the woman are both from God's creation and God … never intends to oppress anyone from His creation.
> **Sayyid Qutb**
> *Egyptian thinker*

Islamic societies and for the restrictions imposed on many Muslim women:

"Men have authority over women because God has made the one superior to the other, and because they spend their wealth to maintain them. Good women are obedient. They guard their unseen parts because God has guarded them. As for those from whom you fear disobedience, admonish them, and forsake them in beds apart, and beat them. Then if they obey you, take no further action against them. Surely God is high, supreme."

The first phrase is often presented as a definitive statement that men are superior to women. However, this is at odds with the message of the Quran as a whole, which, for the most part, presents men and women as equals. Modern theorists question the interpretation of superiority more closely. Do all men have authority over all women? Is it restricted to the head male of the family? Is it just the husband who has authority over a wife?

Opinion leans toward the latter, arguing that the sentence should be understood as conditional—the only basis for a husband's authority is his provision of financial support. Scholars also note that the verse as a whole deals specifically with matters between husband and wife rather than all men and women.

The latter part of the verse, describing increasingly punitive sanctions to be taken against a "disobedient" wife, is even more controversial—especially with regard to its final instruction. In Arabic, this sanction is described by the verb *daraba*, which means, among other things, "to strike" or "to beat." Many Muslims over the ages have found this verse difficult to reconcile with the overall message of the Quran, and indeed with the actions of the Prophet, who is quoted in a *hadith* as saying "The best among you is the one who is best toward his wife."

Then and now

While the disciplining advised in *sura* 4:34 reflects a vast improvement on the pre-Islamic situation, modern translations have striven to suggest less sexist meanings. In 2007, Iranian–American Muslim author Laleh Bakhtiar completed the first feminist translation of the Quran. In this, she challenges the perceived permission for beating wives by offering an alternative meaning of the verb *daraba*, which is "to go away from," not to strike. More conservative scholars continue to take the verse at face value, but with reservations, saying that it condones striking a wife only as a last resort in order to preserve a marriage, and it is not a license for domestic abuse.

Scriptures such as these are ultimately hostage to those who would interpret them. What is clear is that if women in Muslim societies have historically been

Moroccan Asma Lamrabet is an Islamic feminist who challenges the dominance of men in interpreting religious texts. She argues for the right of women to be religious authorities.

oppressed, disempowered, or disenfranchised—and if they continue to be so today—it is as a result of the persistence of problematic cultural traditions, or the misinterpretation of Quranic precepts by jurists, or an unfortunate amalgam of both.

In essence, the Quran treats women as the social, political, and metaphysical equals of men, considering them to be differently fashioned beings who originate from the same source—God. Notwithstanding their different roles over time, it teaches that men and women were created to supplement and complement each other, to give each other ease, happiness, and repose, and to aid each other in cultivating this world and bringing about salvation and everlasting bliss in the next. ∎

BELIEVERS, HAVE FAITH IN GOD
THE QURAN, 4:136

THEME
The Six Pillars of Faith

MORE ON THIS THEME
***Sura* 4** "Women" (*an-Nisa*)
is a long *sura* that aims at
protecting the newly formed
Muslim community by stating
what is acceptable behavior
for Muslims. This includes the
articles of faith (4:136).

***Sura* 50** "The Letter Qaf"
deals with Resurrection and
the Day of Judgment. It also
includes mention of the "twin
keepers" (50:16–18), or *kiraman
katibin*, the angels believed
by Muslims to record a
person's every action.

***Sura* 112** "Oneness"
(*al-Ikhlas*) is a short declaration
of *tawhid*, God's absolute
oneness. It is made up of
just four *ayat*, or verses.

The creed (*aqida*) and ritual practices of Islam are clearly identified in the Quran and *hadith*.

The **Five Pillars of Islam** (*arkan al-islam*) relate to **ritual actions**.

The **Six Pillars of Faith** (*arkan al-iman*) relate to **indisputable beliefs**.

Taken with the social obligations and prohibitions described in the Quran and *hadith*, **these pillars define Islam as a religion and way of life**.

In addition to the Five Pillars of Islam, observant Muslims also accept six fundamental "Pillars of Faith." While the Five Pillars of Islam are largely concerned with everyday ritual practices, the Pillars of Faith are more intangible and, as the term suggests, deal with matters of belief, serving to define the religion. Five of these Pillars of Faith are mentioned together in one key verse in the Quran (4:136), namely belief in: the one God; His angels; His scriptures; His apostles; and the Last Day. The remaining pillar of the core articles of faith is "divine destiny" (*qadar*), which is sometimes translated as "fate" or "predestination."

There are differences between Sunni and Shia, and within other schools, concerning the finer points of interpretation, notably regarding

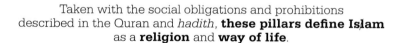

See also: *Hijra*, the flight from Mecca 28–29 ▪ The Five Pillars of Islam: *Shahada* 36–41 ▪ The Five Pillars of Islam: *salat* 42–43 ▪ The Five Pillars of Islam: *zakat* 44–45 ▪ The Five Pillars of Islam: *sawm* 46–49 ▪ The Five Pillars of Islam: Hajj 50–55

Say: 'God is One, the Eternal God. He begot none, nor was he begotten. And none is equal to Him'.
112

qadar, but the six articles are not disputed. The belief that God is the sole divinity, a concept in Arabic called *tawhid*, is the main focal point in the Quran, and is a principle on which all else depends. He is unique, has no associates, and neither begets nor was begotten. The supreme sin, which stands counter to *tawhid*, is the deification or worship of anyone or anything besides God; in other words, practicing idolatory or polytheism, which is known in Arabic as *shirk*. The Quran states that God will forgive everything else except "those who serve other deities besides Him" (4:48).

Angels and prophets

The Quran refers frequently to angels. They are invisible beings of a higher order, which, according to a *hadith*, were created from light. The role of the angels is to transmit messages from the Creator of the universe to His servants. The most obvious example of this is the archangel Jibreel (Gabriel), who delivered the revelation of the Quran to Muhammad. The Arabic word for angel, *malak*, carries this idea of communication, as it is said to be derived from *laaka*, which means "to send on a mission."

Muslims are called not just to believe in the final revelation— the Quran—but also to recognize the texts that preceded it: notably the Torah and the Gospels. This recognition of earlier texts demonstrates that God has never abandoned humanity but has sent messengers at irregular intervals. According to Muslim tradition, there have been about 124,000 of these messengers or prophets, each giving the same message of divine unity according to their context and situation. Twenty-five messengers are mentioned in the Quran, but scriptures were revealed to only five of these: Noah, Ibrahim (Abraham), Moses, Jesus, and Muhammad.

The Last Day

About a quarter of the Quran is devoted to life after death and matters of the soul, as belief in God necessitates belief in the hereafter. On the Last Day, also known as the Day of Judgment (*Yom al-Din*), the universe will be destroyed. After this the dead will be resurrected to face God and account for their actions. The righteous will be rewarded with a place in Paradise, while unbelievers and sinners will go to Hell.

The sixth pillar, which is *qadar*, acknowledges God's omniscience. He knows everything that has happened and everything that is to come. This knowledge is preserved on an "imperishable tablet" (*al-lawh al-mahfouz*). A person's actions are not set by being in the book—man has free will, but God knows his actions beforehand. ▪

During the *Miraj* (ascension to Heaven), Muhammad, on board his mount Buraq, was among the angels, who are shown in this 17th century Persian miniature.

NONE MAY TOUCH EXCEPT THE PURIFIED

THE QURAN, 56:79

Muslims believe that the Quran is based on a heavenly prototype, a book written in Arabic and existing with God in heaven. It was given to Muhammad in the form of revelations and only later was it written down. The belief that the holy scripture exists in heaven makes the handling of its earthly representations a matter of great care and delicacy.

The Quran portrays itself as a "noble" book, which "none may touch except the purified" (56:79). More esoteric interpretations of the Quran favor a metaphorical reading of this verse, claiming that

It is a fearful offence for a man to sit, even unwittingly, on the Quran.
Ogier Ghiselin de Busbecq,
16th-century Flemish diplomat

what it is trying to say is that only those who are spiritually purified will be able to "touch"—in other words, access and understand—the true meanings of the book. The more popular and literalist approach takes the verse at face value, though the two readings are not mutually exclusive.

A book above all others

In accordance with the "none may touch" verse, the majority of Muslims treat the Quran as a sacred object. Consequently, those who are in a state of ritual impurity due to not having made their ablutions, or women who are menstruating, are barred from physical contact with the pages of the Quran.

In many Muslim households, the Quran occupies an elevated position in the literal as well as the metaphorical sense, often being stored on the highest bookshelf in the house, a veritable "book above all other books." Although the Quran is a message from God that was revealed in order to be read and pondered at all opportunities, in some households the bookshelf is often where the Quran remains. It is taken down and read only on

See also: The Five Pillars of Islam: *Salat* 42–43 ▪ Compiling the Quran 64–69 ▪ The composition of the Quran 70–75

To pay respect to the Quran, readers will often use a *rehal*, which is an X-shaped foldable stand that cradles the holy book. The Quran should never be placed on the floor.

This Quran could not have been devised by any but God.
10:37

special occasions such as births, deaths, and marriages, or, in one particular cultural custom, as a charmlike object that travelers pass under when they leave the house on a long journey.

Muslims also believe the Quran should also be transported very carefully, preferably in a bag to avoid damage. If it should accidentally fall, then it is honored, sometimes with a kiss. Some Muslims will make a charitable donation in cases where they have handled a Quran carelessly.

Disposing of a holy book

The respect shown toward the Quran is maintained for old and worn-out copies as well. These may not be thrown away, but instead should be wrapped in cloth and buried in a place where people would not normally walk. Typically, this is often on the grounds of a mosque or even a graveyard. Some Muslims accept burning or shredding as an acceptable alternative disposal method, or fastening the Quran to a stone and placing it in flowing water.

Understandably, not all Muslims treat the Quran in this way. Many see it very much as a "working book," one that is to be read, recited, and studied assiduously, but without the need for it to be treated like some untouchable object. For such Muslims, the Quran may well be a book that must be revered, but first and foremost it is a book that is to be lived. ▪

Created or uncreated?

The notion of the "createdness" or "uncreatedness" of the Quran was a theological issue hotly debated in the early centuries of Islam, with repercussions that are still felt today. Clearly the ink and paper with which the Quran is written, together with the sounds of the words with which it is recited, are all created. But what about the word of God that is reflected in the Quran's message? Was that "created," or has it always existed and is therefore "uncreated?"

Those who asserted the eternity of the Quran believed that denying its eternity would mean denying the divinity of the revelation and its eternal validity. If the Quran was created, some theologists argued, it must be the product of a particular historical context, and when that context changes, the validity of the Quran disappears. They saw the notion of the createdness of the Quran as compromising the very foundations of belief and ultimately corroding the authority of Islam.

NEW IN EVERY AGE, FRESH FOR EVERY PEOPLE
JAFAR AL-SADIQ (8TH CENTURY)

IN CONTEXT

THEME
***Tafsir*, or the art of interpreting the Quran**

WHEN AND WHERE
883, Baghdad

BEFORE
610–32 Muhammad receives a series of revelations from God, which are committed to memory by his companions.

632 After Muhammad dies, his successor Abu Bakr has the revelations gathered into a single volume—the Quran.

7th–8th centuries Muslim scholars begin collecting oral anecdotes of the Prophet's sayings (*hadith*), including his comments on Quranic verses.

AFTER
1972 Abul Ala Mawdudi completes his six-volume *Tafhim-ul-Quran* (*Toward Understanding the Quran*), a highly influential combination of orthodox and modernist interpretations of the Quran.

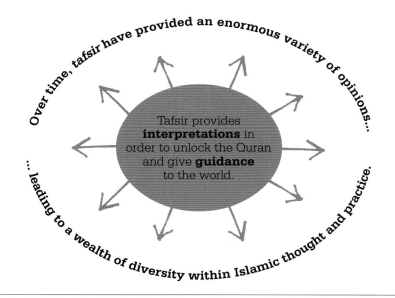

Over time, tafsir have provided an enormous variety of opinions...

Tafsir provides **interpretations** in order to unlock the Quran and give **guidance** to the world.

... leading to a wealth of diversity within Islamic thought and practice.

The Quran can be read and understood on many levels. Certain verses are relatively straightforward in their message and are accessible to a general reader. But the text was written down a long time ago, and now contains much that is unclear and obscure. Sometimes this is because words have multiple meanings and the true meaning may have been lost. Sometimes a verse is rooted in historical circumstance, such as *sura* 111, which begins "May the hands of Abu-Lahab perish!" and threatens his wife, who is "laden with firewood," and shall have "a rope of fiber round her neck!" Here, context is everything.

To fully understand the layers and nuances of meaning in the Quran, a reader has to be familiar with the historical context of when and where the text was revealed, written down, and passed on. A field of scholarship developed, starting not long after Prophet Muhammad's death, which is

See also: The early life of Muhammad 22–27 ▪ Compiling the Quran 64–69 ▪ Sayings and actions of the Prophet 118–23 ▪ The creation of Pakistan 242–47

Muslims read the Quran and may even learn it by heart, but the meaning of many verses can be unclear because of arcane language and references. *Tafsir* offers guidance to meaning.

dedicated to interpreting and commenting on meanings of verses within the Quran. This practice is known as *tafsir*.

Scholars of meaning

The word *tafsir* comes from the Arabic root *fassara* (to interpret). In the formative years of Islam, in the 7th and 8th centuries, Quranic interpretation was based mainly on the explanations found in the many *hadith*, which cited the comments made on the Quran by the Prophet and his Companions. But early followers soon realized there was a need for a more detailed verse-by-verse explanation of ambiguities in the Quran, and this in turn gave rise to the wider scope of *tafsir*—covering linguistics, jurisprudence, and theology—and the emergence of a body of dedicated scholars known as the *mufassirun*.

Schools of *tafsir* emerged in various scholastic centers, from Medina and Mecca to Baghdad, for example. Their commentaries came to cover the entire Quran and were published in books containing grammatical explanations and historical context, as well as personal opinions. Well-known *mufassirun* from the classical period include al-Tabari (839–923), whose comprehensive *tafsir* of 883 is the earliest major commentary on the Quran to have survived.

According to Sufi historian and theologian al-Suyuti (1445–1505), who came from Cairo and produced more than 500 works, a *mufassir* must possess a mastery of classical Arabic, expertise in no fewer than 15 fields of study—such as theology, jurisprudence, and linguistics—and knowledge of the historical context in which the verses were revealed. Only a *mufassir* who met these and a host of other essential requirements could be trusted to avoid misinterpretation or a too literal reading of Quranic text.

An ongoing process

The fact that *tafsir* is an ongoing process, never producing one authoritative commentary, was explained by the 8th-century scholar and sixth Shia Imam Jafar al-Sadiq: "God did not make [the Quran] for one specific time or one specific people, so it is new in every age, fresh for every people, until the Day of Judgment."

The tradition of *tafsir* continues to this day. Eminent *mufassirun* of the modern era include Abul Ala Mawdudi (1903–79), better known as the founder of Pakistan's Islamic revivalist party Jamaat-e-Islami, who spent 30 years producing his six-volume translation and commentary, and Iranian Shia scholar Allama Tabatabai (1904–81), who began his 27-volume work of Quranic commentaries in 1954 and completed it in 1972. ▪

Al-Tabari

Born in 839 in Tabiristan, Iran, Abu Jafar Muhammad ibn Jarir al-Tabari spent most of his life as a scholar in Baghdad, where he died in 923. A prolific author, his reputation rests on two epic works in particular: an 8,000-page history of prophets and kings from the Creation until about 914–15; and his commentary of the Quran.

Completed in 883, the *Tafsir al-Tabari* is the earliest surviving work to attempt a comprehensive understanding of the Quranic text. In more than 30 volumes, it condenses the vast wealth of *hadith* and commentaries of earlier Muslim scholars and classifies them according to their compatibility with one another. It also gives lexical meanings of words and examines their use in Arabic culture. Both al-Tabari's history and his *tafsir* are considered the greatest examples of their genre.

He who says [something] concerning the Quran without knowledge has taken his seat of fire.
Prophet Muhammad

ENTER PARADISE AND ABIDE THEREIN FOR EVER

THE QURAN, 39:73

IN CONTEXT

THEME
The Quranic concept of Heaven

MORE ON THIS THEME
Sura 9 "Repentence" (*al-Tawba*) includes one of many instances in which Paradise is described as a garden: "God has promised the men and women who believe in Him Gardens watered by running brooks, wherein they shall abide forever: goodly mansions in the Gardens of Eden: and, what is more, they shall have grace in God's sight" (9:72).

Sura 47 "Muhammad," which relates to the Battle of Badr, describes Paradise as having "rivers of water undefiled, and rivers of milk forever fresh; rivers of wine delectable to those that drink it, and rivers of clarified honey" (47:15).

According to the Quran, all people shall die at their appointed time and return to God (6:60). After death, Muslims are buried: cremation is forbidden in Islam. At some point, the world will end, with the annihilation of all life, an event that is known as the Day of Judgment (in Arabic, *Yom al-Din*). On this day, the fate of every person will be determined by reference to the Book of Deeds, in which every action, small or great, is recorded. Those whose good deeds on Earth outweigh their bad will proceed to Paradise (*Janna*).

The Quran offers a number of descriptions of Paradise, including *sura* 55, which speaks of well-watered gardens and the life of bliss believers will spend there, reclining on "couches lined with rich brocade" (55:56) with all kinds of fruit in easy reach, and many virgins "chaste and fair" (55:69).

According to *hadith*, there are eight gates to Paradise, each of which equates to a virtuous practice of Islam; so, for example, there is the Bab al-Salah, for those who were punctual in prayer; the Bab al-Rayyan, for those who fasted; and the Bab al-Hajj for those who went on the pilgrimage.

Opinions vary on whether non-Muslims may enter Paradise. *Sura* 2:62—"whoever believes in God and the Last Day and does what is right"—suggests they might. ∎

Paradise, depicted here in a Persian miniature, is described as a series of levels guarded by angels. The highest level is known as *firdaus*.

See also: The Six Pillars of Faith 86–87 ∎ Paradise on Earth 202–03 ∎ Rites of passage 256–59

CURSED BE THE INMATES OF THE CONFLAGRATION
THE QURAN, 67:11

IN CONTEXT

THEME
The Quranic concept of Hell

MORE ON THIS THEME
Sura 4 "Women" (*al-Nisa*) makes several references to hell and its punishments, such as, "Those that deny Our revelations We will burn in fire. No sooner will their skins be consumed than We shall give them other skins, so that they may taste the torment" (4:56).

Sura 37 "The Ranks" (*al-Saffat*) introduces the Zaqqum Tree, which "grows in the nethermost part of Hell, bearing fruit like demons' heads" (37:62).

Sura 78 "The Tidings" (*al-Naba*) reveals that "Hell will lie in ambush, a home for the transgressors. Therein shall they abide long ages; therein they shall taste neither refreshment nor any drink, save scalding water and decaying filth..." (78:21).

O n the Day of Judgment, those whose bad deeds outweigh their good deeds will be relegated to the torments of *Jahannam*, or Hell. The Quran contains countless descriptions of what sinners will encounter there, with fire and flames being a constant motif.

The Holy Book is also specific in identifying the sins that will lead to Hell: these include dying as a disbeliever ("Such shall be the tenants of the Fire, wherein shall they abide for ever"—2:218); killing a believer (4:93); hypocrisy (4:145); and blasphemy (39:60), among others. The Quran reveals that there will be different grades of Hell according to a sinner's deeds (6:132), with the hypocrites being cast into the lowest depths. The *hadith* introduce further sins and punishments, and more information about Hell not found in the Quran —for example, the *Sunan al-Nasai* reports Muhammad as saying there are seven sins that doom someone to Hell, including fleeing from battle and slandering a chaste woman.

Paradise is an uphill climb, whereas Hell is downhill. Hence, there is a struggle to Paradise and not to Hell.
Al-Ghazali
Persian scholar (1056–1111)

While a number of verses in the Quran refer to sinners' time in Hell as eternal, some Muslim scholars have argued that Hell is not only a punishment; it offers the chance for redemption, as revealed in *sura* 6:128, which says "The Fire shall be your home, therein to abide for ever: unless God ordain otherwise." There is also a *hadith* that has Muhammad expressing the wish that, "Verily a day would come over Hell when there shall not be a single human being in it." ∎

See also: *Hijra*, the flight from Mecca 28–31 ▪ The Six Pillars of Faith 86–87

AN ISLAMIC IDENTITY

632–786

MIC

Y

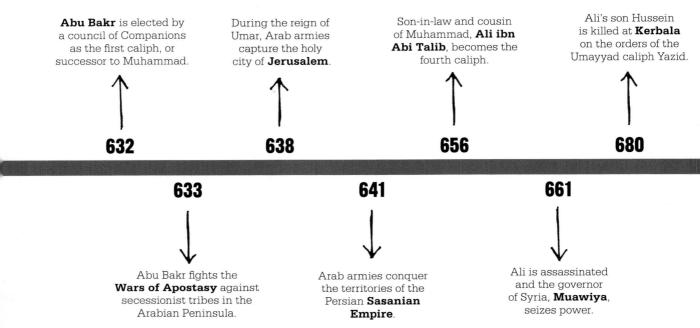

Abu Bakr is elected by a council of Companions as the first caliph, or successor to Muhammad.

During the reign of Umar, Arab armies capture the holy city of **Jerusalem**.

Son-in-law and cousin of Muhammad, **Ali ibn Abi Talib**, becomes the fourth caliph.

Ali's son Hussein is killed at **Kerbala** on the orders of the Umayyad caliph Yazid.

632

638

656

680

633

641

661

Abu Bakr fights the **Wars of Apostasy** against secessionist tribes in the Arabian Peninsula.

Arab armies conquer the territories of the Persian **Sasanian Empire**.

Ali is assassinated and the governor of Syria, **Muawiya**, seizes power.

T he Prophet Muhammad achieved remarkable things. As conduit for the word of God, he spread the message of the Quran initially to just a handful of followers—mostly his family—which eventually grew into a community of believers, the *umma*, that numbered at least 10,000 by the year 630.

Muhammad transformed himself into a political leader who united people of different faiths in Medina, and by necessity became a military leader who then led those communities to war against the powerful merchant clans of Mecca, and prevailed. He offered his followers a vision of a fairer, more charitable, more spiritually fulfilling way of living, and he presented himself as the model for Muslims to follow. Then, in 632, he died.

After Muhammad
The first 30 years after the death of the Prophet were spent ensuring that the community he had built did not disintegrate, and the lessons he had taught were not forgotten. When the Muslim council selected a successor to Muhammad—his close friend and father-in-law Abu Bakr (r. 632–34)—the new leader was immediately faced with revolt by Arab tribes who considered the death of the Prophet to have severed their ties to Islam. In the Wars of Apostasy, Abu Bakr quashed the rebels and brought the Arabian Peninsula under Muslim rule.

Abu Bakr's successors, Umar (r. 634–44) and Uthman (r. 644–56), who had also been among the close Companions of the Prophet, continued the expansion far beyond Arabia. Within a decade of the

death of the Prophet, Arab armies had taken Damascus, Jerusalem, Egypt, and much of the old Persian Sasanian Empire.

Beyond the zeal and ferocity of the Arab armies, the conquests were successful for other reasons. The Muslims left intact most of the bureaucracy they inherited in the Byzantine and Persian territories, and were content for business to continue mostly as it had before. They also pursued a policy of religious freedom, and did not seek to impose Islam on vanquished peoples. Instead, they imposed a tax on non-Muslims, which served to keep the Islamic war coffers full.

A lasting split
The choice of who should succeed Muhammad had not been wholly unanimous. Some championed the

A Muslim army led by Tarek ibn Ziad **crosses the Mediterranean** from North Africa to defeat a Visigoth army in Spain.

Spanish Muslim armies **advance northward into France** until defeated between Tours and Poitiers by Frankish leader Charles Martel.

Surviving Umayyad Abd al-Rahman establishes a new caliphate in al-Andalus (Spain) with a **capital at Cordoba** and secedes from the Abbasid caliphate.

711   **732**   **756**

692   **717**   **750**   **786**

Completion of the **Dome of the Rock** in Jerusalem, the earliest surviving example of Muslim architecture.

The start of the caliphate of Umayyad Umar II, the first caliph to encourage **conversion to Islam**.

Caliph al-Saffa, first of the **Abbasid caliphs**, massacres almost all the members of the Umayyad family.

Harun al-Rashid becomes caliph and the Abbasid dynasty reaches its zenith.

candidacy of the Prophet's cousin and son-in-law, Ali, who was passed over on three occasions. He eventually became the fourth caliph, but was killed by fanatics in 661. Leadership was seized by the governor of Damascus, who passed it to his son. This was challenged by the family of Ali, leading to the battle of Kerbala, where Ali's son Hussein was killed. The death entrenched the split between the supporters of Ali, known as Shia, and the greater Sunni community.

Codifying Islam

The schism between Sunni and Shia Islam was no impediment to continued expansion under the new, Damascus-based Umayyad dynasty. Hand in hand with expansion went consolidation. Since Muslims could no longer look

to Muhammad to provide answers to their questions on all matters Islamic, the caliph Uthman had already overseen the standardizing of the text of the Quran. Now, under the Umayyad caliphs, scholars pored over the reported words and deeds of the Prophet, together known as *hadith*, and collected them into authorized volumes. These became a source for Islamic law (Sharia) and a key for further interpretation of the Quran (*tafsir*).

It is at this time that much of what we understand as Islam was codified. Islamic scholars established correct procedures for such matters as how and when Muslims should pray, and the obligatory giving of charity (*zakat*). They pronounced on rules regarding issues such as the consumption of alcohol, gambling,

and dietary restrictions. They formulated a lunar calendar and fixed dates for Islamic festivals. Institutions of Islamic law proliferated, eventually producing four main schools of jurisprudence —Hanafi, Maliki, Shafii, and Hanbali—that are named after their founders.

Some Muslims reacted against this codification of the faith and sought to return to what they saw as Islam's more spiritual roots. These esoteric Muslims became known as Sufis. Frequently outlawed and persecuted, they would prove surprisingly resilient.

Meanwhile, the Umayyads who rose by the sword died by it too, slaughtered by the Abbasid clan, who afterward sheathed their weapons and ushered in a golden period of Muslim civilization. ∎

98

ALL THE EARTH IS A MOSQUE

PROPHET MUHAMMAD

IN CONTEXT

THEME
**An Islamic place
of worship**

WHEN AND WHERE
c. **622, Medina**

BEFORE
Pre-Islam No one knows the
origins of the Kaaba at Mecca,
but it is likely that it is in use
as a shrine from the earliest
era of civilization in Arabia.

AFTER
715 Umayyad caliph Walid I
builds one of the earliest of
grand mosques on the location
of a Christian cathedral in
Damascus, Syria.

1575 Mimar Sinan, Islam's
greatest architect, completes
his masterpiece, the Selimiye
Mosque in Edirne, Turkey, for
Ottoman sultan Selim II.

Muslims are permitted
to perform their five
daily prayers almost
anywhere, as long as the place
where they pray is clean, or at least
can be made clean by laying out a
prayer mat. Just a few places are
named where they are not allowed
to pray—these include the roof of
the Kaaba at Mecca, graveyards,
garbage dumps, slaughterhouses,
bathrooms, the areas where camels
rest, and main roads. These places
aside, more than one *hadith* states
that the whole world is a *masjid*, or
"place of prostration." It is from this
word, *masjid*, that we get the English
term "mosque," possibly via the
Spanish word *mesquita* (mosque).

See also: The early life of Muhammad 22–27 ▪ The Umayyad and Abbasid caliphates 136–39 ▪ The caliphate of the Ottoman Empire 186–89 ▪ Islamic art and architecture 194–201

The mosque has very few essentials, the main ones being a clean space in which to pray, a *mihrab* to indicate the direction of prayer, and a source of clean water so that worshippers can perform their ablutions. Other elements are optional or symbolic.

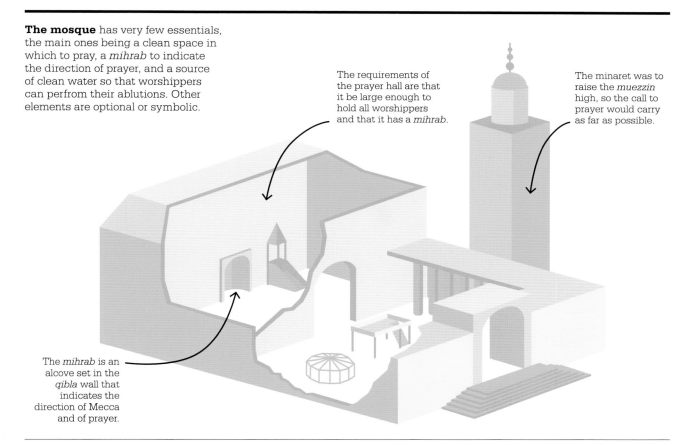

The requirements of the prayer hall are that it be large enough to hold all worshippers and that it has a *mihrab*.

The minaret was to raise the *muezzin* high, so the call to prayer would carry as far as possible.

The *mihrab* is an alcove set in the *qibla* wall that indicates the direction of Mecca and of prayer.

Because almost anywhere can be a place of prostration, the mosque in Islam is not considered a sacred space in the way that a Christian church is. For example, when a mosque is built there is no need to consecrate the ground.

The mosque has become the central symbol of Islam in the wider world. Though it is not essential for prayer, it provides a place where Muslims can come together as a community, and it provides a source of Islamic identity. In this way, the mosque serves the cause of Islam, which is why another *hadith* says, "Whoever builds a mosque for God, God will build for him a house in paradise."

The first mosques

During the Meccan phase of the Prophet's mission, the area around the Kaaba was often referred to as the *masjid*. However, for reasons of safety Muhammad and his followers performed their prayers in one another's houses.

The first proper mosque is traditionally said to be the Masjid al-Taqwa, or Mosque of Piety, constructed by the Prophet and his followers when they reached Medina, in 622, after fleeing persecution in Mecca. On arrival in the oasis just south of Medina, the Prophet untethered his camel and allowed it to wander, saying that wherever the camel stopped would

be the place where the mosque would be constructed. The Prophet settled in a house near the new mosque for a little while, moving later when a larger and more permanent mosque could be built in the center of Medina.

That larger mosque was the Masjid al-Nabawi, or Mosque of the Prophet. It took the form of an open courtyard, large enough so that the ever-growing community could meet in one place, and simple enough in construction that it could easily be expanded as the number of worshippers grew. The walls were made of mud-brick; palm-tree trunks were used for the columns, and palm leaves for » the roof of a covered area that protected worshippers from the midday sun. The direction of prayer—known as the *qibla*—was indicated by a large stone. At this early stage of the Prophet's time in Medina, the *qibla* pointed to Jerusalem, until 624, when it was changed to Mecca.

The Prophet and his followers spent most of their time at the mosque, and not necessarily in prayer. Muhammad was not only a Prophet and a preacher; he was also the political leader of the Medinans and his fellow Meccans-in-exile, and he conducted the running of the city from the mosque. It was as much a city hall and place of political administration as it was a place of worship.

Mosque basics

As Islam expanded throughout the Arabian Peninsula and then quickly beyond, many more mosques were built to emulate the mosque of the Prophet in Medina. While form and styles varied—and still vary—according to local building traditions and materials, the majority of mosques were united by a number of fixed elements and characteristics that have remained constant even into the modern era.

Since prayer must be performed facing Mecca, mosques must have some obvious way of indicating its direction. This is the *mihrab*, which typically takes the form of a recessed alcove in the *qibla* wall of the main prayer hall. In larger mosques, next to the *mihrab*, there is a pulpit, or *minbar*, a flight of steps leading up to a platform where the *imam* (leader of Friday prayers) delivers his weekly sermon. A second platform, called the *dikka*, can sometimes be found at the rear of the prayer hall, or in the courtyard; this is where another cleric stands to repeat the sermon and lead those worshippers too far from the *minbar* to hear.

All mosques must have a place for worshippers to make their pre-prayer ablutions; these wash areas are sometimes located in a covered area adjacent to the main prayer area, or might take the form of a courtyard fountain. Most larger mosques provide a designated space for women to pray. While layouts differ, the usual setup for mixed-sex prayer is that men stand in rows at the front with women behind. Another option is for men to stand on one side of the prayer area and women on the other, divided by a partition in the form of curtains or screens. However, in some of the smaller mosques, particularly in rural areas throughout the Muslim world, adequate facilities for women wanting to pray in the mosque are sadly lacking.

Mosques in Saharan Africa, such as this one in Diafarabé in Mali, seem to rise up out of the muddy earth as though they are part of it. Decoration is similarly simple and austere.

The Dome of the Rock

One of the earliest surviving mosques, the Dome of the Rock (Qubbat al-Sakhra) is completely unlike any other Muslim building. It was built in 688–92 over the rock on Temple Mount, in Jerusalem, from which the Prophet Muhammad is said to have ascended to the heavens on his miraculous Night Journey. Before then, the site was part of the Temple of Solomon, a structure of immense religious significance to Jews. Ownership of this piece of ground remains a source of bitter conflict to this day, contested by Jews and Muslims.

It was the Umayyad caliph Abd al-Malik who ordered the building of the Dome. With no established tradition of mosque design as yet, the Dome was built by Syrian craftsmen trained in the Byzantine style—its architecture and decoration owe much to the building traditions of the Eastern Christians. Modest in size with no room for worshippers inside, the Dome was never intended to host congregational prayers—it was raised as a symbol of Muslim dominance in newly conquered Jerusalem.

> Keep your infants, your insane, and your evil ones away from your mosque.
> **Prophet Muhammad**

> When anyone of you enters the mosque, let him send peace upon the Prophet.
> **Prophet Muhammad**

It is also essential that people should never enter the mosque with shoes and defile the prayer area, so there is always an area for worshippers to leave their footwear.

Minarets and domes

Asked to define what a mosque is, most people's answer might include a minaret and a dome, but neither of these is obligatory, certainly not in modern times. The minaret evolved from the raised platform on which the *muezzin*, who calls the faithful to prayer, would stand to better project his voice. Over time, these platforms turned into towers, or minarets, which the *muezzin* could climb in order to make his voice carry even further.

As the most visible element of the mosque, the minaret became a sort of flagpost marking the physical presence of Islam. They were often beautifully decorated with tiling or carved stonework, and climbed ever higher. Currently the world's tallest minaret belongs to the Djemaa al-Djazaïr in Algiers,

Abu Dhabi's Sheikh Zayed Mosque holds more than 50,000 worshippers. It boasts the world's largest handwoven carpet, as well as one of the world's largest chandeliers.

which stands at 870 ft (265 m). A familiar sight across the Muslim world, the dome is simply an architectural choice. Dating back to ancient Mesopotamia and Rome, it is used not only for its structural strength but because to stand under it is to be reminded of the soaring heavens.

Modern mosques

The technology of microphones and loudspeakers has made the minaret redundant, while modern building technologies mean there are many more options available to architects than the dome with which to roof large spaces. The modern mosque can be as humble as a repurposed apartment with a loudspeaker on the roof or it can be as dazzling as Abu Dhabi's Sheikh Zayed Mosque, which combines the traditional and modern, and took 11 years to build (it was completed in 2007) at a cost of around $545 million. However, this is not even close to the most expensive mosque ever built—this is the Great Mosque of Mecca in Saudi Arabia, also known as the Masjid al-Haram, which was reconstructed in 2016 at a cost estimated at more than $100 billion.

Although not as essential to Islamic worship as many might assume, the mosque serves an important role as the focus and public face of any Muslim community, however small or large. Accordingly, mosques can range from lavish statements of national pride to humble but welcoming neighborhood centers. ■

HE WAS SUPERIOR TO US AS A MUSLIM
TARIKH AL-TABARI BY AL-TABARI (c. 915)

With the death of the Prophet after a short illness in 632, the Muslim community was plunged into crisis. Muhammad was gone forever and the Quran made it clear that no other messenger would come after him. As God's final revelation, the Quran was to suffice mankind until the end of time. But who was to succeed Muhammad as leader of the community and how was this person to be selected? Just as significantly, what would be the nature of their authority?

Most of his followers believed that Muhammad, like the Quran, had remained silent on the subject,

Abu Bakr is elected leader of the early Muslim community following Muhammad's death.

He believed that religious and **political leadership** of Muslims was the **right of the Meccan Companions** of Muhammad, rather than Muhammad's family.

He **warred against** the Muslims who **refused to pay** *zakat* …

… and returned **peace and stability** to the Arabian Peninsula.

See also: The *umma*: the community of Islam 32–33 ▪ The death of the Prophet 56–57 ▪ The rightly guided caliphs 104–07 ▪ The emergence of Shia Islam 108–15 ▪ Sunni and Shia in the modern Middle East 270–71

neither appointing a successor nor proposing any particular election process. Some, however, claimed that the Prophet had chosen his son-in-law, cousin, and closest male relative Ali to succeed him: Ali's supporters were known as the *shia* or "party" of Ali. They evolved into the Shia—the schism that emerged between the Shia and the majority of the Muslims, later to be known as the Sunnis (those who adhere to the Prophet's path, or *sunna*) has continued until today.

The first caliph

Despite the claims in his support, Ali was not to succeed Muhammad and become the new leader of the Muslim community. The title of caliph (from the Arabic *khalifa*, meaning "successor") went instead to Muhammad's father-in-law and close companion, Abu Bakr. He was nominated and elected by a small committee of elders, who considered Ali too inexperienced for the responsibility of leadership.

During the 10 years leading up to the Prophet's death, Abu Bakr had been Muhammad's chief adviser, but had held no prominent

I have been given the authority over you. If I do well, help me; and if I do wrong, set me right.
Abu Bakr

public positions apart from leading the annual pilgrimage to Mecca in 631 and deputizing for Muhammad as prayer leader at public prayers in Medina during the Prophet's final illness.

The Persian historian al-Tabari (839–923) quotes a Companion of the Prophet named Muhammad bin Saad bin Abi Waqqas, as saying, "I asked my father if Abu Bakr was the first Muslim. He said, 'No, more than fifty embraced Islam before Abu Bakr; but he was superior to us as a Muslim.'"

The wars of *Ridda*

On becoming caliph, Abu Bakr's immediate challenge was to put down tribal insurrections that sprang up after the death of the Prophet. During Muhammad's lifetime, many of the Bedouin tribes had pledged allegiance to him as the Messenger of God, and most had agreed to pay an alms tax (*zakat*). With the Prophet's death, many of them repudiated the agreements made, arguing that their allegiance was to Muhammad, not to his successors. Some said they would continue as Muslims but not pay taxes, while others claimed prophets and Quranic-style revelations of their own.

Fearing a collapse of the *umma* and a return to the fragmentation that existed before the coming of Islam, Abu Bakr launched a series of military campaigns against the tribes. Known as the wars of *ridda* (apostasy), they were largely executed on behalf of the caliphate by the general Khalid ibn al-Walid (585–642). By the time Abu Bakr died, peacefully in his sleep, the tribes were back under the control of Medina. ▪

Abu Bakr

Abu Bakr, also called al-Siddiq ("the Upright"), was born in 573 in Mecca into a minor clan of the ruling Quraysh tribe. He was a fabric merchant, often visiting Yemen and Syria, and was relatively wealthy. When he heard of a man called Muhammad preaching a new faith, he paid him a visit and became an early convert.

Abu Bakr is said to have worked hard proselytizing on behalf of Islam, and bought a number of slaves who had converted to Islam and freed them. He acted as treasurer and advised Muhammad on his relations with the various clans. His prominence among early Muslims was also enhanced by Muhammad's marriage to Abu Bakr's daughter Aisha.

In Muhammad's last days, he asked Abu Bakr to lead the prayers at the mosque, which was considered a signal for his succeeding the Prophet. He was only caliph for two years, two months, and 15 days before he succumbed to illness and died in 634.

I AM PLACING ON THE EARTH ONE THAT SHALL RULE AS MY DEPUTY

THE QURAN, 2:30

IN CONTEXT

THEME
The rightly guided caliphs

WHEN AND WHERE
634–61, Arabia and Iraq

BEFORE
c. **570–634**
Prophet Muhammad is
the first leader of the Islamic
community. On his death, he
is succeeded by Abu Bakr, the
first of the Islamic caliphs.

AFTER
661 The governor of Syria,
Muawiya, succeeds Ali as
caliph and makes the position
hereditary. His Umayyad
dynasty will rule the Islamic
world for 89 years before
making way for the Abbasids.

1258 The last ruling Abbasid
caliph is killed when the
Mongols sack Baghdad,
bringing to an end the rule
of the caliphs.

bu Bakr was succeeded
as caliph by Umar ibn
al-Khattab (r. 634–44),
Uthman ibn Affan (r. 644–56),
and Ali ibn Abi Talib (r. 656–61).
Together these four are described
in Arabic sources as the *Rashidun*,
or "Rightly Guided" caliphs. After
Muhammad, they are viewed as
the four caliphs who were guided
by God and justly led the *umma*, or
Islamic community. Their rule was
brought to an end by civil war, with
the caliphate going to the victor.

Commander of the Faithful

Abu Bakr designated Umar as
caliph-in-waiting shortly before his
death. Although Umar was a close

See also: The death of the Prophet 56–57 ▪ Compiling the Quran 64–69 ▪ A successor to the Prophet 102–03 ▪ The emergence of Shia Islam 108–15 ▪ The Umayyad and Abbasid caliphates 136–39

Over every dishonest man there are two watchmen: one is his possessions and the other is his way of life.
Umar ibn al-Khattab

Companion of the Prophet, his accession to the caliphate was opposed by the supporters of Ali, who were dismayed that their candidate had been passed over again, as he had been when Abu Bakr became caliph. Yet Umar, to whom Ali would act as advisor, faced minimal internal resistance during his eventful ten-year reign.

One of the first things Umar did on becoming caliph was to add the epithet *amir al-muminin* ("Commander of the Faithful") to his title, highlighting the fact that his leadership was spiritual as well as political. Umar made no claims of emulating the prophetic role of Muhammad's original mission, but he was emphasizing the caliph's status as the overall leader of the Muslim people.

It was during Umar's reign that the first great Arab conquests were carried out. They began as a continuation of the wars of *Ridda* waged against the rebel tribes in Arabia by Abu Bakr. From their homelands in Arabia Muslim armies then rapidly swept north: most of the territory that is now Iraq fell in 633, and the city of Damascus followed in 634. At the Battle of Yarmuk in 636, the Arabs defeated a Byzantine army, bringing to an end 1,000 years of Greek-speaking rule in the eastern Mediterranean. That same year, the Muslims also defeated the Persian Sasanians at the Battle of Qadisiyya, near the Euphrates.

The first four caliphs of Islam (Abu Bakr, Umar, Uthman, and Ali, depicted in this Turkish miniature) were all personally known to Muhammad, which gave them an exalted status.

Continued conquests

In 638, the Muslims captured Jerusalem. Caliph Umar personally received the city's submission. The following year the Muslims crossed into Egypt. In 640, they captured the Byzantine fortress of Babylon, on the site of what would later become Cairo; in 641, they captured Egypt's capital of Alexandria. This marked the end of the first wave of Muslim conquests. In just seven years, Umar's armies had amassed a vast swath of territories, to bring into being what was at the time an empire second only in size to that of the Chinese. »

The **vicegerent of God on Earth** and the highest religious authority in Islam.

Caliph

A **political leader and warrior** who can protect the Islamic peoples and extend their rule in the world.

Another of Umar's triumphs was in the area of administration. Realizing that the loyalty of the vanquished was crucial to the growing Islamic empire's success, Umar made sure that those whose lands had been taken should not suffer too much social upheaval. To this end, he left the administrative structure of his new territories very much as it had been prior to their conquest. A good example is Syria, where the old civil service of the Byzantines was left intact. A similar situation occurred in Persia, where Persian remained as the main language and the old structures were kept as they had been. The conquered populations were also free to continue to practice their own religions, with no forced imposition of Islam.

Seeds of discontent

Umar died in 644, assassinated by a Persian slave. His legacy as the great Arab conqueror is bolstered

Absorption in worldly affairs breeds darkness in the heart, and absorption in affairs of the world to come enkindles light in the heart.
Uthman ibn Affan

by a reputation for modesty in his personal habits; he is reputed to have regularly slept in the corner of a mosque wrapped in his cloak. The caliphate passed to Uthman, who was chosen by an advisory council, or *shura*, made up of the Prophet's Companions. Uthman was a pious man, and one of Muhammad's first followers, but,

again, his appointment caused resentment among the supporters of Ali ibn Abi Talib.

Under Uthman, the empire continued to expand, but at a slower pace. Uthman's military campaigns added Cyprus to the Muslim domains in 649 and brought about the end of the Sasanians and the death of their last shah. His main legacy was his project to establish the definitive version of the Quran.

Uthman's reign was blighted by fiscal problems—a result, critics said, of lavish overspending. More injurious to his reputation were accusations of nepotism, with Uthman promoting members of his own Umayyad clan to positions of power and influence. There were revolts in Egypt and Iraq, and one party of complainants made their way to the capital of the caliphate, Medina. There they found Uthman abandoned by his former colleagues and they assassinated him. He was reputedly reading the Quran when he was killed and it was splattered with his blood. Centuries later, the "Quran of Uthman," a copy of the Holy Book allegedly stained with the martyred caliph's blood, was displayed on ceremonial occasions by the Abbasid caliphs.

The first Muslim civil war

With Uthman dead, the caliphate finally passed to Ali, cousin and son-in-law of Muhammad, and one of the earliest converts to Islam. Despite his credentials, and the time he had spent in waiting, he was not a universally popular choice. His appointment was

The Battle of the Camel saw Ali ibn Abi Talib defeat an army that was partially led by Aisha, a widow of the Prophet Muhammad, who directed the action while riding a camel.

The Great Mosque of Kufa is said by some to have been built by the Caliph Umar, but the city is most closely connected with Ali, who is believed to have been killed on this site in 661.

656, Ali met the armies of Zubeir near Basra, in what is now Iraq, in the Battle of the Camel, named for Aisha's mount, from which she directed her forces. Ali won the day; Zubeir was killed, and Aisha retreated to Medina.

The end of the *Rashidun*

Ali did not return to Medina, but instead made his capital in Kufa, Iraq, among his allies. For the first time since Muhammad's death, the seat of the caliphate moved away from Arabia. Zubeir was defeated but the threat from Muawiya remained. Muawiya ruled Syria as an autonomous province and commanded a large army. He made no claims to the caliphate but still insisted Ali punish the murderers of Uthman—who happened to be Ali's allies in Iraq.

In 657, Ali led his Iraqi army up the Euphrates Valley, where he met Muawiya's Syrian army. The two forces faced each other at Siffin, near modern-day Raqqa. For weeks they only skirmished, but when an all-out battle seemed likely, the Syrian forces tore leaves from their Qurans and impaled them on the tips of their spears, demanding that there be an arbitration according to the book of God. Ali agreed and it was decided that representatives of the opposing factions would meet the next year.

Many of Ali's supporters were dismayed by his decision and believed he had made a mistake. These dissenters became known as the Kharijites ("those who secede"), and had their own theology and distinct political strategy. Ali later

dealt these secessionists a heavy blow at the battle of Nahrawan in 658, but the Kharijites would have the last word. Three years later, a Kharijite broke into the caliph's private apartment, found Ali at prayer, and assassinated him.

Despite the problems that beset the reigns of Uthman and Ali, the period of the *Rashidun* caliphs is still seen by most Muslims as the purest expression of Islamic society. It was the era in which God's final revelation to mankind was given outward expression in the construction of an empire bound by the glue of religious faith. It was also a 30-year period in which the definite form of the Quran was established, ensuring that the revelation would be recorded for future generations. ∎

The Kharijites

After the Kharijites killed Ali, they remained a minor but disruptive force, leading rebellions against the Umayyad regime that followed the *Rashidun*. Known for their puritanism and fanaticism, the Kharijites considered any Muslim who committed a major sin to be an apostate. They abhorred intermarriage and relations with other Muslims, and insisted on a literal interpretation of the Quran. One 14th-century scholar wrote of the Kharijites, "If they ever gained strength, they would surely corrupt the whole of the Earth … they would not leave a baby, male or female, neither a man nor a woman, because as far as they are concerned the people have caused a corruption that cannot be rectified except by mass killing."

challenged by a group of prominent Muslims, who included a close Companion named Zubeir ibn al-Awwam, and Aisha, a widow of the Prophet. Ali also found himself under pressure from the Umayyads, clan of the martyred Uthman. While nobody accused Ali of being involved in the assassination, the Umayyads demanded that he punish the killers of their kinsman. Until Ali dispatched this duty, the Syrian-based leader of the large and powerful Umayyad clan, Muawiya ibn Abi Sufyan, refused to take an oath of allegiance to the new caliph.

In the very first year of Ali's rule, the Muslims became embroiled in their first civil war. In December

Never explain yourself to anyone because those who like you will not need it, and those who don't like you will never believe it.
Ali ibn Abi Talib

THE IMAM IS GOD'S CHOSEN LEADER

ALI IBN ABI TALIB (601–61)

IN CONTEXT

THEME
**The emergence of
Shia Islam**

WHEN AND WHERE
c. 680, Iraq

BEFORE
632 Prophet Muhammad dies
leaving no named successor.

AFTER
909–1171 The Fatimids,
who claim descent from the
Prophet's daughter Fatima,
become the first major Shia
dynasty. They establish a
new capital at al-Qahira (later
known as Cairo) from where
they rule large parts of North
Africa and western Arabia.

c. **1501** The Persian Safavid
dynasty converts the empire
from Sunni to Shia. To this
day, Iran (formerly Persia)
remains the main bastion of
Shiism in an Islamic world
that is predominantly Sunni.

Roughly 12 to 15 percent
of all Muslims belong to
Shia Islam, which is often
described as either a sect or a
denomination. It is neither: the
Shia tradition of Islam, or Shiism,
is a doctrinal, theological, and
juridical subset of Islam.

The term Shia comes from the
Arabic *shia*, meaning "group" or
"party." The party in this case was
made up of those who supported
the candidacy of Ali ibn Abi Talib,
the Prophet's cousin and son-in-
law, to be the leader of the Muslims
after the death of Muhammad.
The succession crisis that was an
ongoing feature of the era of the
Rashidun caliphs eventually gave
birth to Shiism as a distinct, if
minority, interpretation of Islam.
Nothing has created a more
profound division among Muslims
than this long-standing schism,
and Muslims all over the world are
still living this unresolved quarrel
in the 21st century.

The claims of Ali

When Muhammad died without—
as many claimed—nominating a
successor, the majority of Muslims
believed that choosing a leader by

It is the law of nature
that the trees with
the sweetest fruits are
beaten the most.
Ali ibn Abi Talib

consensus aligned best with the
ideas of the *sunna*, the example of
the Prophet's life and teachings.

There was, however, a group
who believed that Muhammad
had chosen the man who would
continue his role as leader and
guide to the Islamic community.
This was Ali ibn Abi Talib, who,
in addition to being the Prophet's
cousin (and one of the first converts
to Islam) was married to his
daughter, Fatima. Ali and Fatima
were frequently in the company
of Muhammad, and they were
collectively refered to as the *ahl
al-beit* ("People of the House"), in

Following the death of Muhammad, many
followers believe that **electing a leader** is in
accordance with the *Sunna*—the teachings
and sayings of the Prophet.

Following the death of Muhammad,
the party of Ali (the *shia*) believe that God has
indicated **a line of rightful succession**
within the Family of the Prophet.

Sunni Islam is therefore
headed by a **leader
chosen by consensus**.

Shia Islam is therefore
headed by an **Imam who
has been chosen by God**.

See also: The rightly guided caliphs 104–07 ▪ The Safavid Empire 192–93 ▪ The rise of Islamic modernism 222–23 ▪ The Iranian revolution 248–51 ▪ Sunni and Shia in the modern Middle East 270–71

other words the people of the Prophet's household. Ali was also widely regarded as trustworthy, loyal, and fearless. At the time of the Prophet's death, however, he was 28, and the elders charged with appointing the caliph considered him too young to lead.

Ali's supporters pointed to certain Quranic verses which, they insisted, supported their claim that it was only members of the Prophet's family who should lead the Muslim community. They also cited a sermon Muhammad gave as he was returning from his last pilgrimage to Mecca, shortly before he died. He halted the caravan at a place called Ghadir Khumm, where he addressed his followers. He is claimed to have taken Ali by the hand and declared, "He of whom I am the master, of him Ali is also the master."

Ali was eventually elected to lead the Islamic community in 656, after the death of the third caliph, Uthman, but Muslims remained divided. Ali was forced to take military action in defense of his rule, and he was assassinated after just five years as caliph. Ironically, his killers were not his enemies but former supporters who felt he had failed to act decisively enough to punish Uthman's killers and protect his own position as caliph.

Massacre at Kerbala
Upon Ali's death, many expected that the caliphate would pass to his eldest son, Hassan. However, Muawiya, the powerful governor of Syria, challenged Hassan and advised him to avoid bloodshed by giving up any claims to the caliphate. Hassan agreed, on certain conditions: these included

Shia pilgrims at the Imam Hussein Shrine in Kerbala, Iraq, commemorate the martyrdom of the grandson of the Prophet Muhammad, who was killed on the 10th of Muharram, 680.

that Muawiya never use the title of *amir al-muminin* ("Commander of the Faithful") and that he not nominate any successor. Hassan then retired to Medina, where, in 669 or 670, he was reputedly poisoned by his wife, most likely at the instigation of Muawiya.

From his power base in Damascus, Muawiya ruled as caliph for 20 years. When he became seriously ill in 680, rather than honor his pledge to Hassan, he declared his son Yazid as his

A single tear shed for Hussein washes away a hundred sins.
Popular Shia saying

successor, and wrote letters to the regional governors ordering them to give allegiance to the new caliph.

Many balked, particularly in Iraq, where support for the family of the Prophet was strong. Letters were sent to Medina, urging Hassan's younger brother Hussein to come to Iraq, where his supporters promised to drive out the Syrians and "reclaim the soul of Islam." Hussein left Medina with 18 members of his family in a group that totaled just over 70 people. Three weeks later, they were approaching Kufa, in Iraq, when they were met by an Umayyad army, which ordered them to return to Medina. Instead, Hussein led his party to the Euphrates river, where they camped on a plain called Kerbala (now a major Iraqi city). Here, they were overtaken and »

Sunni

The Prophet Muhammad did not appoint a successor.

Leaders of the Islamic community (caliphs) are **chosen by council** based on a number of criteria, including suitability to rule and piety.

Caliphs are political and spiritual leaders but they are **not prophets**.

No statues or paintings are permitted to be involved in worship.

Mecca, **Medina**, and **Jerusalem** are the centers of faith.

The only place of **pilgrimage** is **Mecca**.

About **85 percent** of the world's Muslims are Sunnis.

All Muslims follow the Quran, the *sunna*, and the Five Pillars of Islam.

Shia

The Prophet Muhammad chose Ali as his successor.

Direct descendants of the Prophet are the only true leaders (Imams) of Islam.

Imams are political and spiritual leaders, and **infallible guides**.

Representations of Ali and other Imams are **objects of veneration**.

Mecca, Medina, Jerusalem, **Najaf**, and **Kerbala** are the centers of faith.

The **Imams are revered as saints** and Shia perform pilgrimages to their shrines, as well as Mecca.

About **15 percent** of the world's Muslims are Shia.

Differences between Sunni and Shia are few; both believe in the same fundamentals of Islam. They diverge on the matter of the succession of leadership following the death of the Prophet, and their different historical experiences since that time.

---

encircled by an army of 4,000, who attempted to starve Hussein and his followers into submission. On the seventh day, Hussein and a small band of his warriors charged the enemy and were cut down. The Prophet's grandson was reputedly the last to die. His head was cut off, impaled on a spear, and sent to Yazid.

Referred to by Shia Muslims as the Massacre of Kerbala, this battle became a symbol for the supporters of Ali to rally around. It galvanized their development into a distinct religious community with its own rituals and account of events.

Twelvers

The fundamental idea to which all Shia subscribe was that the family of the Prophet had a special status within Islam. Sunni Muslims also venerated the Prophet's family, but what distinguished the Shia was that they believed only the family of the Prophet were properly qualified to lead the *umma* (Islamic community) and to be the caliph, or in the Shia's chosen terminology, the Imam.

Even this basic tenet, however, led to many questions. For example, who belonged to the family of the Prophet? Was it all the offspring of

Ali's sons Hassan and Hussein? And what of their children? Very quickly there could be a huge number of candidates for the position of Imam. Should it only be the eldest? Such questions had major implications for the Shia leadership and, unsurprisingly, there was disagreement and Shia Islam rapidly splintered into a number of different strands.

After Hussein was killed, his son Ali Zayn al-Abidin became Imam (spiritual leader) of the Shia. The title continued to pass from father to son until the 12th Imam. This last Imam, Muhammad ibn

Hassan, did not actually die but went into a hidden existence in 874, known as occultation, and he will eventually return as the messianic figure known as the Imam al-Mahdi. His reappearance will signal the beginning of the ultimate struggle for good that in Islam marks the end of the world. Shia who subscribe to this belief are known as Twelvers, or Imamis. They represent the majority of Shia. Most of the population of modern Iran are Twelvers; former president of Iran Mahmud Ahmadinejad would keep an empty chair in cabinet meetings for the Imam al-Mahdi.

Ismailis and Zaydis

The second major branch of the Shia, which emerged in the 8th century, is the Ismailis, also known as the Seveners. They trace the Imamate line from Jafar al-Sadiq to

> To God we belong and to God is our return.
> **Imam Hussein**
> *Spoken at Kerbala, 680CE*

his second son Ismail, who was designated Imam but who died before his father. They do not recognize the legitimacy of Ismail's younger half-brother, Musa al-Kazim, as the Twelvers do. Instead they recognize Muhammad ibn Ismail ("son of Ismail") as their Seventh Imam. Some Ismailis believe he

was the last Imam, hence their later designation as the "Seveners." Other Ismailis believe that the line of Imamate in hereditary succession has continued from Muhammad ibn Ismail to their present, 49th Imam, who maintains direct lineal descent from Prophet Muhammad. Since the 19th century, the Ismaili Imam has been known by the honorific of Aga Khan—the current Imam, Prince Shah Karim Al Husseini, is Aga Khan IV. Ismailis exist today in a worldwide diaspora guided by the Aga Khan.

For another subgroup of the Shia, the line of Imams passes from Ali Zayn al-Abidin, not to the »

Recently, the Ismailis have become known for the cultural, philanthropic, and educational efforts of their leader, exemplified in the Aga Khan Museum in Toronto, Canada.

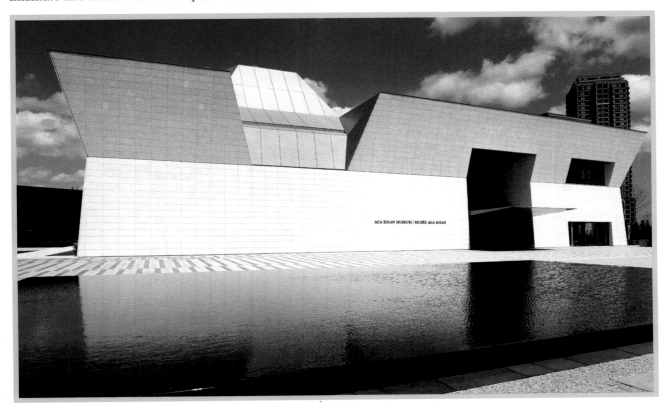

AGA KHAN MUSEUM | MUSÉE AGA KHAN

elder son Muhammad al-Baqir, but to the younger Zayd—hence their name, the Zaydis. The Zaydis only exist today in northern Yemen.

What Shia believe

The different Shia traditions all share with Sunnis a belief in divine unity (*tawhid*), prophethood, and resurrection and the hereafter. To these strands all Shia add two extra principles, which are divine justice (*adl*) and the Imamate (*imama*), to make up their five "articles of faith." On the first three elements, Sunni and Shia hardly differ. On divine justice, both believe that humans know the difference between good and evil, and that we have complete free will. Sunnis, however, believe that God already has knowledge of our decisions before we make them, and that fate is predestined.

The most marked difference in belief between Sunni and Shia relates to the Imamate. For the Shia, the Imams of the "House of Ali" continue the prophetic mission of Muhammad. They believe the Imams to be divinely inspired spiritual and political successors to the Prophet, possessed of infallible, God-given knowledge. Sunnis find this particular element of Shia belief not just questionable, but doctrinally unacceptable.

Devotionally, too, there are significant differences between Sunni and Shia. Shia often make pilgrimages to the shrines of the Imams and their descendants, known in Persian as *imamzadeh*. At these shrines they appeal to the Imams to intercede with God on their behalf, a practice known as *tawassul*. Sunnis view this as highly unorthodox. Shia also place emphasis on celebrating the traditions of the Imams and events related to them, such as Ashura, which commemorates the death of Hussein at Kerbala.

In terms of law and everyday practice, there is very little that separates Shia from Sunni. However, while Sunnis depend on the *sunna* of the Prophet, the Shia include the Twelve Imams as sources of spiritual inspiration, and of social and political guidance. Shiism is a highly structured tradition, unlike Sunnism, which has no organized clergy. Shiism also places a greater emphasis on the esoteric meanings and interpretations of the Quran.

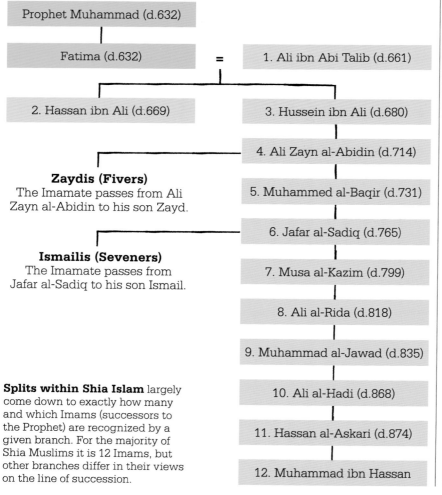

Prophet Muhammad (d.632)

Fatima (d.632) = 1. Ali ibn Abi Talib (d.661)

2. Hassan ibn Ali (d.669)   3. Hussein ibn Ali (d.680)

4. Ali Zayn al-Abidin (d.714)

Zaydis (Fivers)
The Imamate passes from Ali Zayn al-Abidin to his son Zayd.

5. Muhammed al-Baqir (d.731)

6. Jafar al-Sadiq (d.765)

Ismailis (Seveners)
The Imamate passes from Jafar al-Sadiq to his son Ismail.

7. Musa al-Kazim (d.799)

8. Ali al-Rida (d.818)

9. Muhammad al-Jawad (d.835)

10. Ali al-Hadi (d.868)

11. Hassan al-Askari (d.874)

12. Muhammad ibn Hassan

Splits within Shia Islam largely come down to exactly how many and which Imams (successors to the Prophet) are recognized by a given branch. For the majority of Shia Muslims it is 12 Imams, but other branches differ in their views on the line of succession.

This religion [Islam] will remain standing until 12 caliphs, all of them Qurayshi, rule over you.
Prophet Muhammad

Shia and Sunni can coexist and cooperate, true to their own interpretations of Islam but confederates in faith.
Shah Karim al-Husseini
Current Aga Khan (b.1936)

Rise to power

After Ali, none of the Shia Imams attained any significant political power. The most notable of them was the Sixth Imam, Jafar al-Sadiq (702–765), who distinguished himself as a dispenser of legal rulings and was a significant figure in the formulation of Shia doctrine. The Eighth Imam, Ali al-Rida, also known as Imam Reza, came close to power when he was adopted as heir by Abbasid Caliph al-Mamun, as a way of reuniting Islam, but he died before the caliph—possibly from poisoning. His tomb at Mashhad in Iran remains a major pilgrimage site.

The first occasion on which the Shia were able to establish themselves in power anywhere in the Islamic world came in the 10th century, when Shia refugees from the Abbasid caliphate founded a new political dynasty in Tunisia. Known as the Fatimids (after Fatima, daughter of the Prophet and wife of Ali), they took control of Egypt, founding a new capital, Cairo, where they ruled for more than 200 years. Shiism next rose to prominence with the creation of the Safavid empire in the 16th century. Its rulers transformed Iran into a

Shia nation—and Shiism has remained the official religion of the Iranian state ever since.

A modern Shia state

The Shias' reputation for radicalism is a modern phenomenon. The politicization of the Shia clergy, for example, was caused largely by a new generation of Shia theorists of the 19th century. This culminated in the 1979 revolution in Iran, when supporters of Ayatollah Khomeini brought to an end to the monarchical regime of Muhammad Reza Shah Pahlavi, ushering in the world's first modern Islamic republic. Since then, Iran has been ruled in accordance with a specific Shia theory of government known as the

Imam Ali, the first Shia Imam, is a popular subject for portraiture, particularly in Muharram, the month of his son Hussein's martyrdom, as seen here in Kashan, a city in Iran.

"guardianship of the jurist," with a Supreme Leader "deputizing" for the Imam al-Mahdi.

The example of Khomeini and Iran serves to highlight the critical difference between Sunni and Shia, which is not about theology, but the issue of leadership. Remove the almost 1,400-year-old dispute over succession and there are arguably more differences, in respect to Islamic law, at least, between the different Sunni groups than there are between Sunni and Shia. ∎

AND FOR THE MOON, WE HAVE ORDAINED PHASES

THE QURAN, 36:39

IN CONTEXT

THEME
The Islamic calendar

WHEN AND WHERE
c. 638 CE, Arabia

BEFORE
8000 BCE Prehistoric people in Scotland create the oldest known lunar calendar in the form of 12 pits that correlate with phases of the Moon.

46 BCE Julius Caesar proposes the Julian calendar, a revised lunar calendar that predominates in the Roman world and most of Europe.

c. **442 CE** The Meccan calendar changes from a lunar calendar to a lunisolar calendar, with an additional month added from time to time to regulate pilgrimage trade.

AFTER
1582 The Catholic countries of Europe adopt the Gregorian calendar, which corrects the Julian calendar with a new calculation of leap years.

I n 638 CE, six years after the Prophet Muhammad's death, an administrator in the civil service of the caliph Umar made a complaint about the lack of dates on official correspondence. This made it impossible, he said, to determine which instructions were the most recent. Court officials decided that the Muslims should

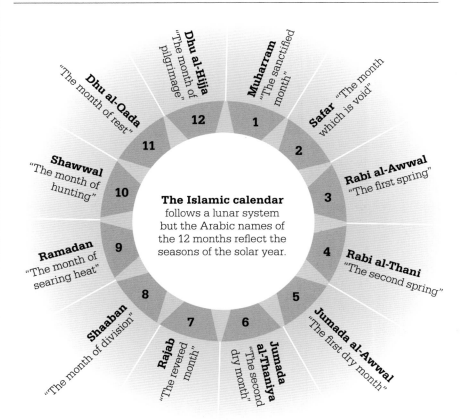

The Islamic calendar follows a lunar system but the Arabic names of the 12 months reflect the seasons of the solar year.

Dhu al-Hijja "The month of pilgrimage" — 12
Muharram "The sanctified month" — 1
Safar "The month which is void" — 2
Rabi al-Awwal "The first spring" — 3
Rabi al-Thani "The second spring" — 4
Jumada al-Awwal "The first dry month" — 5
Jumada al-Thaniya "The second dry month" — 6
Rajab "The revered month" — 7
Shaaban "The month of division" — 8
Ramadan "The month of searing heat" — 9
Shawwal "The month of hunting" — 10
Dhu al-Qada "The month of rest" — 11

See also: *Hijra*, the flight from Mecca 28–31 ▪ The Five Pillars of Islam: *sawm* 46–49 ▪ The Five Pillars of Islam: Hajj 50–55 ▪ The uses of astronomy 162–63

have a calendar system of their own. They determined that the year of Muhammad's arrival at Medina and the subsequent founding of the *umma*—622 CE in the Gregorian, or Western, calendar—should be year 1. As the foundation of the *umma* stems from the Prophet's *Hijra*, or migration to Mecca, the new calendar was known as the *Hijra* calendar. Its dates carry the suffix AH, Latin for *anno Hegirae*, or "in the year of the *Hijra*." Years before the *Hijra* are indicated by BH, for "before the *Hijra*."

A difference of 11 days

The *Hijra* is a lunar calendar, based on the monthly cycles of the moon. Although in theory a lunar month runs from the physical sighting of one new crescent moon to the next, in practice sighting is no longer used as a method. Instead, calendar days run in accordance with astronomy's more precise calculations based on the orbit of the moon. Some schools of Muslim law make an exception for

God ordained the months 12 in number when He created the heavens and the earth.
9:36

the first day of Ramadan, which is traditionally based on the sighting of the new crescent moon. This is why the exact starting date of Ramadan is often not known until shortly beforehand.

The months of the year alternate between 29 and 30 days so the monthly average is 29.5 days, adding up to a 12-month lunar year that is only 354 or 355 days long. In contrast, the Gregorian calendar follows a solar year, lasting 365 or 366 days. The Islamic calendar does not have leap years.

Because of this disparity, the Islamic year cannot be calculated by simply subtracting 622 from the Gregorian year, because every 33 years the *Hijra* calendar gains a year on the Gregorian. The position of the Islamic months relative to those of the Gregorian calendar also moves "backward" by 11 days a year. For example, if Ramadan starts on or around April 12 one year, it will start on or around April 1 the next.

Everyday use

Most Muslim countries use two or more calendar systems. Iran, for example, uses three: the *Hijra* calendar to identify Islamic feast and fast days; a solar calendar, which also calculates its year 1 from the date of the Prophet's migration to Medina (the official calendar in Iran); and the Gregorian calendar. In fact, the Gregorian calendar is arguably the system most in use among Muslim communities, particularly in businesses where frequent contact with overseas clients and partners occurs. ▪

Key dates in the Islamic calendar

In addition to Ramadan and the major feasts of *Eid al-Fitr* and *Eid al-Adha* (when communal meals are cooked, see left) there are a number of other calendar dates of importance to Muslims. The first of Muharram is Islamic New Year (*Ras as-Sana al-Hijriya*) and is a worldwide holiday in Muslim countries. The 10th of Muharram is Ashura, when Shia communities commemorate the martyrdom of Hussein, the Prophet's grandson, at the Battle of Kerbala. The 12th of Rabi al-Awwal is the *Mawlid al-Nabi*, or Prophet Muhammad's Birthday. This is celebrated across the Islamic world, except in Qatar and Saudi Arabia, where the interpretation of Islam forbids *mawlids*, celebrations of the birthdays of holy figures.

The 12th of Rajab marks *Leilat al-Miraj*, the Night Journey of the Prophet to Jerusalem and Heaven. Some Muslims make special prayers on this night and light candles or display illuminations. The 15th of Shaaban is *Leilat al-Baraat* (Night of Salvation), a night on which God may forgive sinners. Twelver Shia also celebrate the birthday of the 12th Imam on this date.

WHOEVER TURNS FROM MY WAY IS NOT FROM ME

PROPHET MUHAMMAD

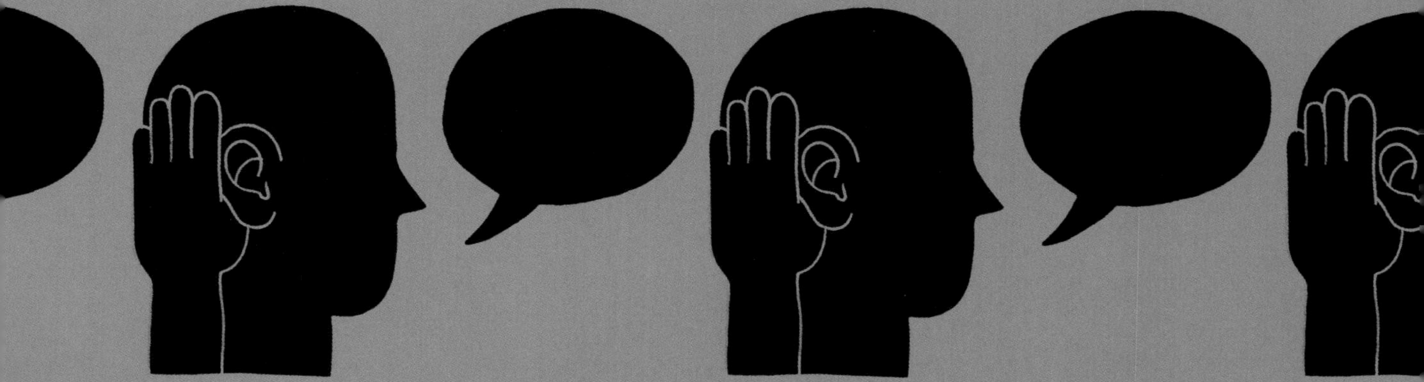

IN CONTEXT

THEME
Sayings and actions of the Prophet

WHEN AND WHERE
9th century, Arabia

BEFORE
***c.* 570–632** During the Prophet's life, his words and actions are observed by his followers and taken as an example of a correct way of Muslim living.

AFTER
***c.* 767–820** Islamic jurist al-Shafii rules on the authority of a *hadith* of Muhammad, so that even the Quran is "to be interpreted in the light of *hadith*, and not vice versa."

19th century So-called Quranists reject the authority of the *hadith*, believing that Islamic law and guidance should only be based on the Quran.

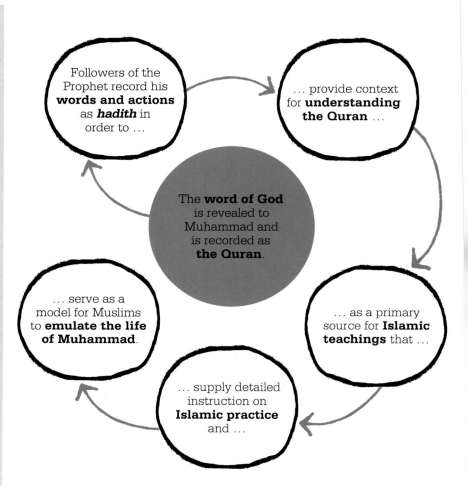

Followers of the Prophet record his **words and actions** as *hadith* in order to …

… provide context for **understanding the Quran** …

The **word of God** is revealed to Muhammad and is recorded as **the Quran**.

… as a primary source for **Islamic teachings** that …

… supply detailed instruction on **Islamic practice** and …

… serve as a model for Muslims to **emulate the life of Muhammad**.

I slam is based on two bodies of scripture. The core of the religion is the Quran, which Muslims believe to be the word of God as revealed to the Prophet Muhammad. Supplementing this are the teachings of Muhammad. Known as *hadith*, these are oral anecdotes recalling the words and deeds of the Prophet, and the actions of his Companions that he endorsed. The distinction is that while the Quran is the word of God, *hadith* are the words and actions of Muhammad and do not have the status of divine revelations.

The precise number of *hadith* is debated but, excluding those of uncertain authenticity, they run into the thousands. From the *hadith*, Muslims know about almost every facet of Muhammad's personal life and his prophetic mission. If an answer to a question about Islam and Muslim life cannot be found in the Quran, then guidance will be found in a *hadith*.

Taken as whole, the *hadith* constitute the *sunna* ("the way"), which is the example provided by the life of Muhammad that every Muslim attempts to emulate.

Uses of *hadith*
Much of the everyday practice of Islam comes not from the Quran but from the *hadith*. Many of the verses in the Quran are very general in their nature, and the *hadith* are used to add detail. For example, the Quran tells Muslims to pray, but it is the *hadith* that describe the exact words to be recited and the actions to be followed when a Muslim prays. Similarly, the *hadith* explain how to correctly observe other pillars of Islam, such as the amount of alms to be given, how and when to fast, and rituals

See also: The early life of Muhammad 22–27 ▪ The Five Pillars of Islam: *Shahada* 36–41 ▪ The death of the Prophet 56–57 ▪ God's guidance through Sharia 128–33

involved in completing the Hajj. Covering almost every conceivable subject—from legal proclamations (on apostasy, usury, and criminal punishments) to the treatment of women—*hadith* were a prime source for the formulation of Sharia, or Islamic law. Other *hadith* instruct Muslims on etiquette (how to receive guests, what to do if a fly lands in your drink), while some are more esoteric: one *hadith*, for example, gives the height of Adam as 60 arms, while another promises the often-quoted figure of 72 *houris* (virgins) that await a martyr in heaven.

Often, statements that have been attributed to the Quran turn out to actually be *hadith*. Then there are other alleged *hadith*—for example, those condemning Jews, Christians, or homosexuality; or those that prescribe stoning as the punishment for adultery, or death as the penalty for apostasy —for which the authenticity is considered somewhat questionable by some scholars.

God Almighty said busy yourself with my worship and I will fill your heart with riches.
Prophet Muhammad

Collecting the *hadith*

As far as historians can ascertain, the main collections of these sayings and actions of the Prophet did not emerge until about 200 years after his death. It was only in the 9th century that books of *hadith* were known to be in circulation. This presents a big gap between when the Prophet spoke and acted, and when his words and actions were recorded.

There are several possible explanations for this. One is that while the accounts were recorded during the Prophet's lifetime, they were not collated until much later. Another is that the accounts were initially transmitted orally from one generation to the next, and it was only when there was a risk of them being forgotten that they were committed to paper. Some historians suggest that the *hadith* may not have been written down until later because the early caliphs forbade it, fearing that Muslims would equate the Prophet with God and the *hadith* with the revelations of the Quran.

The long gap between Muhammad's death and the writing down of the *hadith* allowed an almost limitless number to proliferate throughout the Muslim world. Many of these had probably been fabricated by individuals looking to advance their own particular beliefs or interests. By the 9th century, the situation had become so out of hand that a group of legal scholars, working independently of each other, began compiling the most reliable *hadith* into authoritative collections.

Key compilations

As far as Sunni Islam is concerned, the two main collections of *hadith* are the *Sahih al-Bukhari* and the *Sahih Muslim*, compiled by Muhammad al-Bukhari (810–70) and Muslim ibn al-Hajjaj (*c.* 815–74) respectively—*sahih* means »

Shia Muslims pray in Karachi, Pakistan. According to a *hadith*, all Muslims will be held accountable on the Day of Resurrection for how well they observed daily prayers.

A couple marries in Shkodra, Albania. A *hadith* says that a woman is married for her wealth, lineage, beauty, or piety —the *hadith* advises the latter as the best reason for marrying.

"authentic." Al-Bukhari's work is, for most Sunnis, the single most authoritative religious text after the Quran. It contains no fewer than 7,275 *hadith*, spread over several volumes. It is arranged thematically, with 93 chapters covering topics such as belief, prayer, ablution, alms, fasting, commerce, inheritance, crime, punishment, wills, oaths, war, food and drink, marriage, hunting, and bathroom etiquette. Muslim's collection contains 4,000 *hadith*, and is also arranged by theme.

Both al-Bukhari and Muslim were known for their meticulousness in attempting to ascertain the authenticity of the *hadith* by documenting the chain of transmission. Al-Bukhari, in particular, is regarded as the founder of a discipline known as *ilm al-rijal* ("the science of learned men"), or the detailed study of the individuals who passed along the *hadith*.

Not one of you can truly believe if you do not want for your brother believer what you want for yourself.
Prophet Muhammad

Chains of authenticity

In any book of *hadith*, each entry is presented in two parts: a main body of text, known as the *matn*, which includes the actual record of what the Prophet said or did, and an *isnad*, or "chain of transmission." The *isnad* takes the form of a long line of attribution that ideally links the *hadith* back to the Prophet. As the 9th-century Islamic scholar and expert in Islamic law al-Shafii explained it, "If a trustworthy person transmits [a *hadith*] from another trustworthy person until the chain ends with the Messenger of God, then it is established as being from the Messenger of God."

At the time the main collections of *hadith* were collated, which was the mid-9th century, these chains usually stretched five or

Sunni and Shia *hadith*

Hadith have frequently proven divisive within Islam. What one camp considers authentic, another may claim is a forgery. Among Sunni Muslims, there are six books of *hadith* held to contain the most authentic texts. In addition to the *Sahih al-Bukhari* and the *Sahih Muslim*, Sunnis also regard collections by Abu Dawud (*c.* 817–89), Tirmidhi (824–92), Ibn Maja (824–*c.* 887), and al-Nasai (*c.* 829–915) in high esteem. These collections share many of the same *hadith* but there are differences of opinion and interpretation among them.

Shia Muslims have their own distinct body of *hadith* material, with their own four canonical books of *hadith*, which they refer to as the "Four Principles"—none of which are used by the Sunnis. In general, Shia Muslims give priority to *hadith* that were transmitted from the Prophet through the *ahl al-beit* (the 12 Imams and the Prophet's daughter Fatima).

> He who has not thanked humans has not thanked God.
> **Prophet Muhammad**

six people, or more, back to Muhammad. A typical *hadith* would read as follows: "X said that Y said that W said that V said that he heard the Prophet say …". In the case of an action of the Prophet, a *hadith* would read: "X said that Y said that W said that V said that the Prophet was seen to …". A break in the chain, such as a person not remembering who told them a *hadith*, or quoting someone they had never met, would make the *hadith* unreliable. Specialists in the study of *hadith*—known as *al-muhadithun* —recognize more than 40 classifications of *hadith*, from the completely authenticated (*sahih*), to the weak (*daif*) but still acceptable to some, and the outright forgeries (*mawdu*).

In addition to verifying the chain of transmission, specialists also studied the relation of each *hadith* to the Quran. This two-tier approach led to differences in the content of the compilations, in their classifications of which *hadith* were authentic and which not, and in their interpretation.

The *hijab*, or headscarf, like the one worn by this woman reading the Quran in a Damascus mosque, is not described by the Quran but comes from a *hadith* on modesty.

Quran Only movement

While *hadith* remain extremely popular with many Muslims, and are used widely as citations in books, sermons, and other religious material, there is a minority of Muslims who reject all *hadith* as fabrications. Emerging in the 19th century and known as Quranists or the "Quran Only" movement, adherents claim that the Holy Book alone is sufficient for human guidance and that the body of *hadith* is fatally unreliable. This was one of the platforms of the Partisans of the Quran (*ahl-e Quran*), a group of Indian Muslim intellectuals that formed in the Punjab region of India in the 1890s. This line of thinking has also had a strong influence in Turkey.

The majority of Muslims acknowledge the problems that beset the *hadith* on the issue of authenticity, but point out that if

> He that obeys the Messenger has assuredly obeyed God.
> **4:80**

the *hadith* are rejected, much of Islam goes with them—the *sunna*, which guides the lives of most of the world's Muslims, the Sunnis, is derived from the *hadith*. The fact is that the Quran, like the *hadith*, was transmitted orally, and if the Quran is authentic, they say, we should at least give the *hadith* the benefit of the doubt. ∎

HE HAS FORBIDDEN YOU... THE FLESH OF SWINE

THE QURAN, 16:115

IN CONTEXT

THEME
Muslim dietary laws

WHEN AND WHERE
7th century CE, Arabia

BEFORE
Pre-Islamic era The Torah and the Bible both include prohibitions on foodstuffs, characterizing certain foods as either "clean" or "unclean."

AFTER
8th century CE As Islam spreads beyond Arabia and Muslims incorporate different peoples into their fold, scholars systematize food rules beyond the instructions in the Quran.

Today Since the late 20th century, manufacturers and marketers have targeted a booming Muslim population with halal products that extend beyond food to embrace cosmetics, clothing, finance, and travel.

All foods are **halal (lawful)** unless specifically forbidden.

The Quran names a handful of foodstuffs as **haram (unlawful)**, notably pork.

Certain other foodstuffs are considered **makruh ("detestable but not forbidden absolutely")**, including horsemeat, shrimp, and other shellfish.

For Muslim believers, food and drink are seen as gifts from God and prime examples of His compassion, provision, and generosity. It is for this reason that many observant Muslims preface all meals with the words, *Bismillah wa barakati Allah* ("In the name of God, and with the blessing of God").

Strictly speaking, there is no such thing as Islamic cuisine; Muslims eat whatever is customary in their own familial or cultural tradition. There are, however, strict dietary laws that determine what an observant Muslim may and may not eat and drink.

Halal and *haram*
The Quran says surprisingly little on the issue of food and drink; there is nothing in the text, for example, like the very detailed dietary code that we find in the Old Testament of the Bible. The

See also: The Six Pillars of Faith 86–87 ▪ Islam and alcohol, gambling, and drugs 126 ▪ The global business of halal 292

Quran says that Muslim believers are allowed to consume what is "good and pure"—food that, presumably, is clean, fresh, and wholesome. The general rule of thumb is that everything is lawful (halal) unless specifically forbidden as unlawful (*haram*), and even then one may, in extenuating circumstances, consume that which is unlawful if there is absolutely no other option.

The Quran also says little on the issue of outlawed food and drink. There is a clear ban on all intoxicating drinks, and foods that contain alcohol are also prohibited by default. Also deemed *haram* are the following: carrion, which is understood to mean the meat of an animal not slaughtered by the Islamically prescribed method; blood; the meat of an animal sacrificed to idols; the meat of an animal that has died from strangulation or blunt force; meat from which wild animals have already eaten; and the flesh of swine, in other words pork and other meats from pigs.

Eat of the good and lawful things which God bestowed on you...
16:114

Making meat halal

While the word halal simply means "lawful," when used in the phrase "halal meat," it refers to meat taken from animals that have been slaughtered in accordance with doctrinally prescribed methods. This entails slitting the animal's throat as swiftly and mercifully as possible while reciting the name of God to acknowledge that an animal can only be killed with God's permission. The knife must be as sharp as possible and the carotid artery, jugular vein, and windpipe must be severed in one stroke, before the blood is drained out of the carcass.

A more detailed treatment of prohibited foods can be found in the many *hadith*, which broaden the base of forbidden foods to include items not mentioned in the Quran. Among the prohibited items in the *haram* category are predatory animals with fangs, for example cats, dogs, lions, bears, and so on; birds with talons, for example owls; mice and rats; snakes, scorpions, and other animals that are traditionally considered to be vermin.

A third legal category, *makruh*, which means "detestable but not forbidden", covers things such as horsemeat and shellfish. There are further gradations, including *mubah* (neutral) and *mustahab* (recommended), that lie in between halal and *haram*, although these are not necessarily applied to food. Schools of law are unanimous on what is halal and *haram*, but there are many differences of opinion with regard to what is *makruh*. ▪

Dining etiquette

While the Quran is silent on the specific issue of table manners and etiquette, many *hadith* outline what is praiseworthy and blameworthy when it comes to eating. When eating with your hands, for example, food should be taken with the right hand rather than the left—the left being used traditionally to clean oneself after using the bathroom. Overeating is discouraged; a *hadith* advises that Muslims should finish eating before they feel full, with "a third of the stomach for food; a third for drink; and a third for air". Eating etiquette includes eating in company rather than alone, thus sharing the bounties God has provided. And if you do not like a food you have been given, then you should refrain from eating rather than criticizing it.

Most Muslims fast during the month of Ramadan, but they are also encouraged to do so for six days of the following month, for two days around the 10th of Muharram, and on the ninth day of the month of Hajj.

All meat sold in Muslim countries is halal. Increasingly, many shops and food outlets in Muslim-minority countries also cater to Muslim consumers with halal offerings.

WINE AND GAMES OF CHANCE... ARE ABOMINATIONS
THE QURAN, 5:90

IN CONTEXT

THEME
Islam and alcohol, gambling, and drugs

WHEN AND WHERE
7th century, Arabia

BEFORE
Pre-Islamic era Although both Christians and Jews use wine in their ceremonies, the holy scriptures of both religions include warnings on the destructive nature of alcohol and intoxication. For example, "Wine is a mocker, strong drink a brawler, and whoever is led astray by it is not wise" —Proverbs 20:1.

AFTER
The modern era Alcohol is completely banned in some Muslim countries. Other Muslim countries permit it to some degree, to sell to non-Muslims for example, but ban it completely for the duration of Ramadan.

All intoxicating drinks are forbidden by Islamic law, together with all other substances that impact negatively upon consciousness and are taken recreationally. The medicinal use of drugs such as opioids is conditionally permitted. The Quran makes three specific references to alcohol, two of which seem only slightly censorious, with just one, *sura* 5:90, outright condemning it. According to traditionalist scholars, this reflects the pragmatic nature of Islamic law. The desert Arabs were so used to inebriation that prohibition could not have been brought in overnight. Instead, alcohol was abolished gradually, with two warnings about its ill effects followed later by an outright ban. Despite the prohibition, in all Muslim-majority countries today there are some Muslims who drink alcohol and indulge in drug use—even though it is forbidden.

Gambling is often condemned by the Quran in the same verses that outlaw alcohol—"They ask you about drinking and gambling. Say: 'There is great harm in both'" (2:219). Both are seen as addictions with the potential to destroy lives and place strain on the social fabric. Betting on sports is also forbidden, as are any forms of lottery or games of chance played for money. The various schools of law disagree on whether or not raffles should be included in the definition of gambling. Similarly, games of chance, even when not played for money—cards, for instance—are also the subject of continued debate. ∎

Believers, do not approach your prayers when you are drunk …
4:43

See also: Muslim dietary laws 124–25

GOD HAS LAID HIS CURSE ON USURY
THE QURAN, 2:276

IN CONTEXT

THEME
Moneylending in Islam

WHEN AND WHERE
7th century, Arabia

BEFORE
2000–1400 BCE The Vedic texts of ancient India mention usury but express no opinion. The later Buddhist *Jatakas* (600–400 BCE) specifically condemn its practice.

***c.*600 BCE** In Judaism, several biblical passages scorn the charging of interest. The Hebrew word for interest is *neshekh*, meaning "a bite."

AFTER
634–44 CE Under the caliph Umar the charging of interest is prohibited by law.

19th century Indian Islamic reformist Sayyid Ahmad Khan argues for a differentiation between usury and interest on commercial investment.

The Arabic word *riba* is a noun derived from a root meaning an "increase" or a "growth." It is usually translated as "usury"—charging excessive interest (or any interest at all) when lending money. In several different verses, the Quran cautions believers not to deal in usury in any shape or form, and claims that God will act against those who do: "Believers, fear God and waive what is still due to you from usury, if your faith be true; or war shall be declared against you by God and His Messenger" (2:278–79).

Muslim scholars offer various suggestions as to why usury has been declared *haram*, or unlawful, so forcefully. The answer lies with the merchants of Mecca. Some verses that mention usury date from early in the Prophet's career, when he was addressing his message to the citizens of Mecca, urging them to change their ways. We know that there was great inequality of wealth between the city's merchants and the underclasses. Muhammad would

Those that devour usury shall rise up before God like him that Satan has demented by his touch…
2:275

have seen that through usury the rich were being rewarded for being wealthy and the poor penalized for being poor. This ran counter to the spirit of brotherhood that formed part of the Prophet's message of Islam.

In most Muslim-majority countries, there is disagreement over what exactly constitutes *riba*, and institutions still deal in interest, often through the use of legal loopholes that turn interest into "commission." ∎

See also: God's guidance through Sharia 128–33 ▪ Islamic banking 293

WE HAVE ORDAINED A LAW AND ASSIGNED A PATH

THE QURAN, 5:49

IN CONTEXT

THEME
God's guidance through Sharia

WHEN AND WHERE
8th century, Arabia

BEFORE
c. 1500 BCE The Torah records the Ten Commandments—religious and ethical laws given to Moses by God.

610–632 CE The Prophet Muhammad receives the revelation of the Quran, and his followers begin to circulate his words and actions.

AFTER
c. 14th century Ibn Taymiyya, an Islamic scholar, issues a *fatwa* (legal ruling) against the Mongols for not basing their laws on Sharia.

1997 The European Council for Fatwa and Research is founded to assist European Muslims in interpreting Sharia.

The Arabic word *sharia* means "path." More specifically, in a historical context, it means "the path to the watering place." In the Arabian Peninsula, which is largely desert, a path to water is a route to survival. Similarly, in the Islamic sense, Sharia is the pathway, by God's law, to spiritual salvation. It is a system of ethics and law (*fiqh*) that is meant to govern humankind and guide everything people do. As is often said, Islam is not just a statement of faith; it is one's whole way of life.

At first, Muslims relied on God's revelations (the Quran) and the example of the Prophet's life (*sunna*) for direction. With Muhammad's death, however, this guidance ceased. Over the next 100 years, the Islamic community rapidly expanded from a following limited to the cities of Medina and Mecca to an empire stretching from Spain to Central Asia. The question of how to apply the Quranic revelations to everyday life, across the various cultures of the growing Muslim community, was becoming ever more complex. Despite the emergence of Islamic judges, who

We then set for you a law to the right path. Follow it and do not yield to the desires of those devoid of knowledge...
45:18

could rule on public and private concerns, there was a call for a more uniform and clearly defined form of guidance—Sharia.

Defining Islamic law

Scholars eager to standardize Islamic jurisprudence emerged in many Muslim communities, leading to disagreements over how to apply the law. Should its scope be restricted to the teachings of the Quran and the *sunna*, or could jurists incorporate their own analysis and reason?

By the 8th century, Muslims differed widely on the application of Sharia. One scholar, Abu Abdullah Muhammad ibn Idris al-Shafii, came to the fore to offer unifying thought on the legal concerns of the day. According to al-Shafii, there were four sources of law: the Quran, the *sunna*, the consensus of the community (*ijma*), and "analogical" reasoning (*qiyas*).

The main source of Sharia is the Quran itself. In many passages, it directly addresses matters such as exploitation of the poor, usury, theft, and adultery—all of which it explicitly condemns. The Quran also guides Muslims in personal and community affairs. It has plenty to say on issues related to women's rights, including on

Abu Abdullah Muhammad ibn Idris al-Shafii

The life of the great scholar al-Shafii is rich in legends. Details of his early life are unclear, but according to the oldest surviving accounts he was born into a Qurayshi family in Gaza in 767. When he was young, his family moved to Mecca, where he studied *hadith*. He is said to have memorized the Quran by the time he was 10 years old. He later moved to Medina, where he studied under Malik ibn Anas, the founder of the Maliki school of Islamic law.

He served as a governor in Yemen, taught in Baghdad, and finally settled in Egypt.

From his travels, al-Shafii could see that the application of Islamic law across the Muslim world was highly idiosyncratic. He resolved to "take law from the source" by which he meant a return to the Quran and *hadith*. Through his teachings and writings he is credited with creating the essentials of *fiqh* (Islamic jurisprudence). He died in 820 and was buried in Cairo.

See also: The early life of Muhammad 22–27 ■ Sayings and actions of the Prophet 118–23 ■ The quest to make God's word supreme 134–35

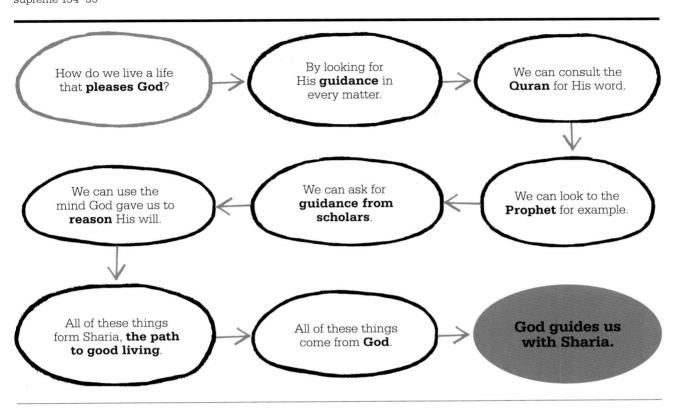

How do we live a life that **pleases God**? → By looking for His **guidance** in every matter. → We can consult the **Quran** for His word.

We can use the mind God gave us to **reason** His will. ← We can ask for **guidance from scholars**. ← We can look to the **Prophet** for example.

All of these things form Sharia, **the path to good living**. → All of these things come from **God**. → **God guides us with Sharia.**

divorce, custody of children, and rights of inheritance. However, much of its treatment of legal concerns is generic. For example, "He that kills a believer by design shall burn in Hell for ever" (4:93) is

Do not live in a land in which there is neither a scholar to inform you about your religion, nor a doctor to tell you about your body.
Al-Shafii

fine in a theological sense, but it offers no advice on the murderer's punishment on Earth. For this reason, the word of the Quran is supplemented by the example of Muhammad, derived from the *sunna*—the scholarly collections of the reported sayings and actions of the Prophet known as *hadith*.

The third source of law is the consensus of the community, or *ijma*. Muhammad is reported to have said that his community would never agree on an error. Al-Shafii therefore gave authority to legal rulings reached by consensus among the Muslims. Over time "the community" came to be defined in legal terms as a body of legal scholars and religious authorities whose decisions would be made on behalf of wider Muslim society. »

"The path to the watering place" (the literal translation of "Sharia") was a concept that had resonance for believers who came from the harsh desert lands of the Arabian Peninsula.

Analogical reasoning can be used to determine acceptable behavior.

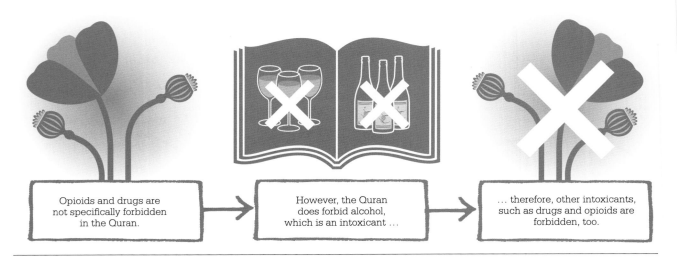

Opioids and drugs are not specifically forbidden in the Quran.

However, the Quran does forbid alcohol, which is an intoxicant ...

... therefore, other intoxicants, such as drugs and opioids are forbidden, too.

Intellectual striving

Muadh ibn Jabal was a Companion of the Prophet. He was sent to Yemen to teach its people about Islam. Before he set off, Muhammad asked him how he would settle any disputes among the Yemenis. "By referring to the Quran," Ibn Jabal replied.

"And what if the answer is not in the Quran?" Muhammad asked.

"By following your ways," replied Ibn Jabal.

A light has surely come to you from God and a veritable Book, with which God will guide to the paths of peace those who seek to please Him ...
5:15–16

"And if there is no precedent for your question?" asked Muhammad.

"Then I will exercise my own reason and judgement," responded Ibn Jabal.

In situations where the Quran and *sunna* provided no answers, and where no consensus could be reached, jurists would follow Ibn Jabal's example and use their own judgment to arbitrate new legal concerns. This was known as *ijtihad*, a word that means "striving intellectually."

Al-Shafii restricted the role of personal reasoning in *ijtihad* to the analogical, or *qiyas*. This involves deriving a conclusion from one's experience in one or more similar situations. This, the fourth base source of Sharia law, involved finding analogous situations in the Quran or *sunna* from which new legal rulings could be derived. For example, the Quran prohibits making a sale or a purchase during the call to Friday prayers: Muslims are instead urged to cease trading so that they may gather for worship (62:9–10). What about other contracts that might be made during the call to prayer? Should a marriage, for example, be arranged during this time? The Quran is silent on the matter, but analogical reasoning can be used to derive a legal opinion. If the aim of the Quran is to discourage actions preventing Muslims from worship, then, likewise, restrictions on business can be applied to other contracts, such as a marriage.

Closing the gate

From the 10th century, some scholars began to criticize the use of independent judgement to derive new rulings, believing this encouraged the placing of too much confidence in the power of human reason. The principle of consensus of the community was also jettisoned. The idea evolved that the "gate of independent reasoning" was now closed, and that jurists should busy themselves with the study and reinterpretation of old laws, imitating their predecessors rather than forging ahead with legal innovations of their own.

Islamic scholars continue to play a major role in Muslim political life, like here, where religious leaders attend a peace conference in Baghdad, Iraq.

Four schools

In time, a number of distinct schools of law emerged in different parts of the empire. From the 13th century, four schools in particular came to predominate in Sunni Islam. Each is named for the individual who framed its main concerns: Hanafi, Hanbali, Maliki, and Shafii.

The most widespread of the four is the Hanafi school, named after the legal expert Abu Hanifa (699–767), a native of Kufa in Iraq. Both it and the Maliki school, founded by Malik ibn Anas (711–95), encourage use of all four sources of law. The Shafii and Hanbali schools focus on the Quran and *sunna* alone— al-Shafii rejected rulings based on juristic discretion and public interest altogether. Adherents of the Shafii school predominate in India and Southeast Asia. The fourth and smallest Sunni school of law, named after Ahmed ibn Hanbal (780–855), is seen as the most conservative of the schools.

Hanbalism is the official school of law in Saudi Arabia and Qatar. Shia Islam has its own schools, notably the Jaafari, which is recognized as the fifth school of Islamic law alongside the four Sunni schools.

Sharia today

In the modern era, statutes, many of which come from European legal systems introduced during the colonial period, have replaced traditional laws in much of the Islamic world. However, most Muslim-majority countries incorporate Sharia at some level within their legal framework, mainly in regard to civil laws, covering things like marriage and inheritance. Muslims with questions on the best way to live according to Islam will often address them to a learned sheikh for authoritative advice.

The rise of modern Islamism in the late 20th century has seen Sharia become associated with an extreme form of prohibitive law that cuts off the hands of thieves, stones adulterers, and engages in public beheadings. Most Muslims view this with horror. They are more inclined to the vision of Sharia described by the Syrian jurist al-Jawzi (d. 1350), who wrote, "The foundation of the Sharia is wisdom and the safeguarding of people's welfare in this life and the next… Every ruling that replaces justice with injustice, mercy with its opposite … is a ruling that does not belong to the Sharia." ∎

The issuing of *fatwas*

A *fatwa* is simply a religious edict, or judgement. It can only be pronounced by a qualified scholar of Islam, known as a *mufti*, who has reached his (only occasionally her) ruling by considering the four sources of Sharia law. In the modern era, *fatwas* serve to expand on and update aspects of Sharia law to keep pace with changing social and economic circumstances. *Fatwas* are issued on every topic imaginable. There are websites that provide databases of rulings, which run to tens of thousands of entries. If a specific *fatwa* cannot be found in the database, the website can connect the user to a "cyber-*mufti*" who will issue a *fatwa* in less than 24 hours.

Fatwas sometimes spark controversy. For example, in the aftermath of the 9/11 attacks, Saudi Arabia's highest religious authorities issued a *fatwa* sanctioning a holy war against Saddam Hussein by all Muslims to evict his forces from Kuwait.

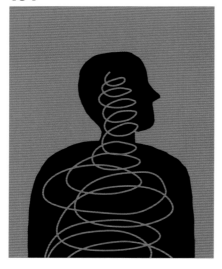

THE SUPREME JIHAD IS AGAINST ONESELF

THE HISTORY OF BAGHDAD BY AL-KHATIB AL-BAGHDADI (11TH CENTURY)

IN CONTEXT

THEME
The quest to make God's word supreme

WHEN AND WHERE
7th–8th century, Arabia

BEFORE
7th century Muhammad and his followers suffer persecution by the Meccans and are forced to take up arms.

661–750 The Umayyad caliphate undertakes expansion of the Islamic empire by conquest.

AFTER
12th century Muslim Andalusian philosopher Ibn Rushd divides jihad into four types: jihad by the heart, by the tongue, by the hand, and by the sword.

c. 1964 Egyptian thinker Sayyid Qutb argues for jihad as the mission to make Islam dominant in the world.

The word **"jihad"** is derived from a root shared with words that relate to **striving, struggle, and resistance**.

According to the Prophet, the **"greater jihad"** is the struggle that all Muslims wage **within and against themselves**.

The **"lesser jihad"** relates to the struggle **with others**, which can take **the form of war**.

Jihadism is a modern term wrongly used in the West to denote a **violent and extremist Islamist worldview** that has nothing to do with the Quranic jihad. Many Muslims regard the term as Islamophobic.

T he word "jihad" is typically mistranslated as "holy war," either through lack of understanding or, in some cases, deliberate misinterpretation. The narrowing down and reduction of the meaning of this word has led to misconceptions and negative reactions on the part of Muslims and non-Muslims alike.

See also: *Hijra*: the flight from Mecca 28–31 ▪ The rightly guided caliphs 104–107 ▪ The Umayyad and Abbasid caliphates 136–39 ▪ The rise of political Islam 238–41 ▪ The new extremists 272–77

The meaning of jihad

Jihad is one of a number of words sharing the same root letters j–h–d, all of which pertain to striving, struggle, and resistance. The concept of *ijtihad*, which refers to intellectual reasoning, comes from the same root. In the Quran, the term "jihad" is used in the general sense of the exertion of willpower and energy for a particular cause, and always "in the name of God" (*fi sabil Allah*). The struggle against the whims and demands of the lower self, or *nafs*, is said to have been referred to by the Prophet Muhammad as the "greater jihad" (*jihad al-akbar*). The Quran is quite explicit that the most fulfilling form of jihad is the struggle that all Muslims wage within and against themselves: "Blessed shall be he that has kept [himself] pure, and ruined he that has corrupted [himself]" (91:7).

Jihad may also take the form of armed struggle. This is known as the "lesser jihad" and it has its own Arabic term, *qital* ("combat"). While the greater jihad is a continuous

Permission to take up arms is hereby granted to those who are attacked, because they have been wronged.
22:39

inner, spiritual struggle to remain on the straight path of correct belief and practice, the lesser jihad is temporary and a response to a specific set of circumstances.

Jihad through the ages

How jihad has been interpreted and implemented has been influenced to a large extent by the politics of the time. In the early days of Islam, jihad often took the form of armed struggle. From the outset, the Prophet was forced to defend

himself and his followers from the Meccans, who first persecuted the Muslims and then tried to eliminate them altogether. But in taking up arms, Muhammad adhered to the lessons of the Quran: "If you punish, let your punishment be commensurate with the wrong that has been done you. But it shall be best for you to endure with patience" (16:126). Armed jihad occurred under the Umayyads when the caliphate—and, by extension, Islam—was expanding its territory. In the more peaceable Abbasid period that followed, jihad became more linked to personal inner struggle.

In the recent era, the almost exclusive use of jihad to mean "holy war" has been employed by critics to suggest Muslims are on a mission to Islamicize the world. Conversely, some Muslims have reacted by denying any connection between jihad and warfare. Both positions are flawed. The Quran is clear that the meaning of jihad is far broader than—but does not exclude—fighting an enemy. ▪

What is jihadism?

The word "jihad," as found in the Quran, can have a variety of meanings, the purest of which is an internal struggle of the spirit. "Jihadism" (and the related "jihadi" and "jihadist") is a relatively recent term used mostly in the West to describe extreme Islamist militant movements who employ violence to achieve their ends.

Jihadists are defined as those who consider violent struggle necessary to eradicate obstacles to restoring God's rule on Earth, and defending the Muslim community, or *umma*, against infidels. Such groups believe that jihad is a collective obligation that must be fulfilled by every able Muslim. Those Muslims who do not share this world view are typically labeled "deviants" and are considered legitimate targets.

In the modern era, the term jihadism is particularly linked with militant groups such as al-Qaeda and Islamic State. The word is not used by most Muslims because they see it as associating a noble concept with illegitimate violence.

You have come from the Lesser Jihad to the Greater Jihad—the striving of a servant (of God) against his desires.
Al-Khatib al-Baghdadi
Islamic scholar 1002–71

PART OF THE COMPLETION OF ISLAM

CALIPH WALID II (r. 743–44)

IN CONTEXT

THEME
The Umayyad and Abbasid caliphates

WHEN AND WHERE
661–1258, Damascus and Baghdad

BEFORE
634 Ali ibn Abi Talib becomes the fourth caliph to be elected following the death of the Prophet Muhammad.

AFTER
1258 With the destruction of Baghdad by the Mongols, there is no longer a single dominant power in the Islamic world. Rival dynasties carve up the territories that were once ruled by the Umayyad and Abbasid caliphates.

1517 After seizing Egypt, Syria, and Arabia, the Turkish Ottoman dynasty proclaims itself the new caliphate, which lasts until 1924.

With the death of Ali ibn Abi Talib in 661, his rival Muawiya, the governor of Syria, became the first caliph who was not chosen by a council of the Companions of the Prophet, but relied on his military might to seize power. Muawiya was the first of what would be known as the Umayyad caliphs, named for the Umayya tribe of Mecca, to which he belonged. Their caliphate was to last for less than 90 years, but in that time the boundaries of the Islamic world were extended to create an empire that would not be equaled in size until the peak of the Ottoman Empire some 900 years later.

See also: An Islamic place of worship 98–99 ▪ The rightly guided caliphs 104–07 ▪ The House of Wisdom 150–51 ▪ The caliphate of the Ottoman Empire 186–89 ▪ Islamic art and architecture 194–201

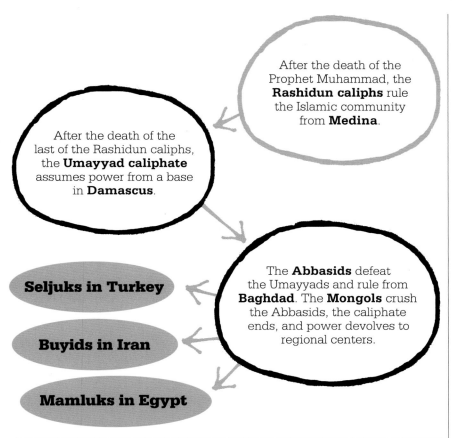

After the death of the Prophet Muhammad, the **Rashidun caliphs** rule the Islamic community from **Medina**.

After the death of the last of the Rashidun caliphs, the **Umayyad caliphate** assumes power from a base in **Damascus**.

The **Abbasids** defeat the Umayyads and rule from **Baghdad**. The **Mongols** crush the Abbasids, the caliphate ends, and power devolves to regional centers.

Seljuks in Turkey

Buyids in Iran

Mamluks in Egypt

considered to be hereditary, many clans refused to pay their respects. Instead, some of the old families of Medina rallied around Abdullah ibn Zubeir, son of one of Muhammad's closest Companions, who called for a council to choose a new caliph. From the Prophet's family, Ali's younger son Hussein gave his support to the dissenters. Yazid dealt brutally with the threat, sending 4,000 soldiers to massacre Hussein's group of 70 followers and family on the plains of Kerbala in Iraq in 680.

Empire building

Yazid left no natural successor and the position of caliph was filled by a candidate from another branch of the Umayyad clan. On taking power, Abd al-Malik (r. 685–705) was obliged to quash an attempted coup in Damascus, conquer rivals in Iraq, and eliminate the threat of Abdullah ibn Zubeir in Mecca, all in the cause of reuniting the caliphate. Once that was achieved he took the war to the Byzantine Empire, advancing into Turkey and the Caucasus, and sweeping across North Africa. »

He [Muawiya] placed his throne in Damascus and refused to go to Muhammad's throne [Medina].
The Maronite Chronicle
7th-century Syrian manuscript

Even more significantly, when Muawiya named his own son as his successor, it marked the beginning of a new era of rule in Islam, based not on suitability or piety, but on lineage.

Hereditary rule

Under the Rashidun caliphs, faith had been the chief social unifier. For the Damascus-based Umayyads, however, faith often appeared to count for little. Blood and tribal relations now became the chief motivating principle. Under Muawiya's rule, the army was modernized and the empire continued to expand outward.

To govern these far-flung lands, he returned to a more tribal style of leadership, reviving the old practices such as *wufud*, which involved tribes sending delegations to keep the caliph informed of their interests. The reintroduction of such practices led many of Muawiya's critics to describe him not as a caliph but as a *malik*, or secular king, in the style of the pre-Islamic rulers of Arabia.

Evidence that Muawiya saw himself more as king than caliph came when he named his ineffectual son, Yazid, as heir to the caliphate. Offended by the idea that the caliphate was now

Under Abd al-Malik, Arabic was made the language of government administration. New coins were minted and the old Byzantine and Persian currencies were replaced by a single, centralized system of gold dinars and silver dirhams across the entire expanding empire. The latter part of the Umayyad era was also marked by impressive building projects. These included desert palaces constructed for the wealthy elite, but also places of worship, most notably the magnificent Dome of the Rock in Jerusalem (688–92).

Abd al-Malik was succeeded by his son Walid I (r. 705–15), under whose leadership a second wave of expansionist conquests took place, with Muslim rule crossing the Mediterranean into the Iberian Peninsula and spreading to the Indian subcontinent. During Walid's reign, the caliphate was expanded to its largest territorial extent, although in 732 Arab armies pushed up through Spain into the Loire in France, until they were halted at the Battle of Tours by the Frankish king Charles Martel.

By this time, the practice of the caliph nominating his heir was the accepted way of things. A letter written by a later Umayyad caliph illustrates the entitlement that came with the position: in it, Walid II (r. 743–44) states that the caliphate is "part of the completion of Islam and the perfection of those mighty favors by which God makes His people obliged to Him."

Festering inequality

Beneath all this progress festered serious ills. Under the Umayyads, many pre-Islamic traditions were revived, with old Arab clans reestablishing themselves as the landholding elite. The caliphate was beleaguered by bloody power struggles. Just as pernicious was the emergence of Arabism. Being an Arab was frequently given more significance than being a Muslim. This gave rise to a stratified society, with Arab Muslims at the top, then the non-Arab converts to Islam, with Jews and Christians next, and slaves at the bottom. The discontent of the non-Arab Muslims would be the undoing of the Umayyads.

Claiming descent from the Prophet's uncle, Abbas ibn Abd al-Muttalib, the Abbasids of northern Arabia had long been rivals of the Umayyads. They shrewdly cultivated the support of the disaffected non-Arabs on the fringes of the Umayyad empire to foment rebellion. With their help, Abbasid agents seized power first in north-east Iran, after which their armies engaged the Umayyads in a series of battles that ended with the death of the last Umayyad caliph at the Battle of the Great Zab River (750).

Damascus to Baghdad

At his inauguration, the first Abbasid caliph, al-Saffa (r. 750–54), gave a sermon to justify the new caliphate. In it, he established that the Abbasids were "the kin of God's messenger" and created "from the ancestors of the Prophet, causing us to grow from his tree."

The second Abbasid caliph, Mansur (r. 754–75), began the construction of a new dynastic capital in central Iraq, on the site of

The Great Mosque at Damascus was built during the reign of Walid I. Byzantine artisans were used to create the mosaics, shown here, that cover the facades around the courtyard.

The Great Mosque of Samarra in Iraq was, for a while, the largest mosque in the world. Built by the Abbasids in the ninth century, it has a highly unusual spiraling cone for a minaret.

a small village called Baghdad, on the banks of the Tigris River. He created a magnificent round city, wrapped with high walls, and pierced by four great gates. It symbolized the centralization of power in the hands of the caliph. Enthroned in their new citadel, the early Abbasids were firmly autocratic, keeping power within the family, and always quick to dispatch potential rivals into the hands of the executioner.

The fifth Abbasid caliph, Harun al-Rashid (r. 786–809), grandson of Mansur, is often regarded as the greatest of the caliphs. His reign launched a golden age of Islamic culture and science, which was continued by his son Mamun. Father and son also did a lot to promote Islamic scholarship, with their caliphal patronage resulting in advances in the fields of Muslim jurisprudence, philosophy, and theology, as well as in mathematics, medicine, and the sciences.

Decline and fall

The remaining 300 years of the Abbasid era were less successful. Of the dozen caliphs who ruled between 860 and 934, half were murdered. One of the later caliphs, Mustaqfi (r. 944–46), was forced to cede control of Baghdad to a dynasty of military leaders, the Buyids, in order to hold onto the caliphate. Meanwhile, other power-hungry dynasties took advantage of a weak caliphate to proclaim themselves as governors or sultans in other parts of the empire. The Abbasids were frequently forced to allow these regional rulers to establish power bases in return for money. When the Mongol armies swept in from the east to attack Baghdad in 1258, the empire had already been splintered. Even so, the demise of the Abbasids was vicious. Baghdad was ransacked and its palaces and places of learning razed to the ground. Almost a million people were slaughtered. The 37th and last Abbasid caliph was rolled in a carpet and trampled to death. The caliphate, which had been the most important Islamic political and spiritual institution since the time of Muhammad, was extinguished. ■

These people [the Umayyads] have acted as unbelievers, by God, in the most blatant fashion. So curse them, may God curse them!
Abu Hamza the Kharijite
8th century

The lives of the Abbasid caliphs

Muhammad ibn Ali al-Abdi was a caliphal courtier. In 932, he was asked to write a chronicle of the Abbasid caliphs. His sketches of the rulers were not always flattering. On the contrary, he tells us that the first Abbasid caliph, al-Saffa, was "quick to spill blood." His successor, Mansur, was "the first to sow discord between the family of Abbas and the family of Ali who until then had made common cause." In contrast, al-Abdi has nothing but praise for Harun al-Rashid. This caliph was "scrupulous in fulfilling his role as a pilgrim in waging holy wars." He was also said to have undertaken many public works on the road to Mecca and at Mina and Arafat, both important stops on the Hajj. He scattered his wealth and the treasure of his justice on all his subjects. "Error," wrote al-Abdi, "was repressed, the truth reappeared and Islam, shining with new splendor, eclipsed all."

GRANT ME THEN THE BEAUTY OF YOUR FACE

RABIA AL-ADAWIYYA (*c.* 714–801)

IN CONTEXT

THEME
Sufism and the mystic tradition

WHEN AND WHERE
8th–9th century, Syria and Iraq

BEFORE
c. 610–32 Prophet Muhammad establishes Islam and sets an example by living a life of piety, simplicity, and charity.

AFTER
13th century Some Sufi practices, such as reciting God's names, are incorporated into Jewish worship.

1830–47 Emir Abdelkader, a Sufi scholar, leads the struggle against the French invasion of Algeria.

1925 Turkey's new republic abolishes Sufi orders.

21st century
More than 100 Sufi orders exist worldwide.

The origins of Sufism— or Muslim mysticism as some prefer to call it—date back to the earliest days of Islam. Under the rule of the Umayyad caliphate, which began less than 30 years after the death of the Prophet, some Muslims had already grown disenchanted with the self-indulgence of the ruling elite. They wanted to return to what they felt was the simplicity of Islam during the time of Muhammad. There was also an aversion to the ongoing codification of Islamic law, which seemed to be reducing the faith to the minutiae of rules and rituals. While the scholars of the Sharia were concerned about where Muslims prayed and the correct sequence of actions to be performed, certain other Muslims were concerned with the state of the worshipper's heart and mind. They wanted to reproduce within themselves the state of mind that made it possible for Muhammad to receive the revelations of the Quran.

Thought and practice
The term "Sufi" came into use in the mid-9th century, and comes from the coarse woollen cloth,

Exist in this world as if you had never set foot here, and in the next world as if you had never left it.
Hassan al-Basri

known as *suf*, from which the garments of the early mystics were woven. Early or classical Sufism, which spans the first three centuries of the Islamic era, centered on the individual's sincere attempt to commune with God directly. Sufi teachings are diverse but the ultimate goal is to attain the state of *ihsan*—worshipping God as if you could see Him.

Achieving this involves erasing any bad character traits in order to attain a state of "unification." There are further stages beyond this, all of which have the goal of shedding the self until nothing remains except God. The process is often presented as a journey, similar to an act of pilgrimage.

In order to make this journey, Sufis broke ties to the material world through poverty, fasting, silence, or celibacy. Over time, they developed various techniques to concentrate their minds, such as night vigils, the chanted repetition of the divine names of God, or meditative breathing exercises.

The tomb of Sheikh Salim Chishti (d. 1572) at Fatehpur Sikri in India. Chishti was the founder of a Sufi order. The tomb was built by Emperor Akbar as a sign of his respect for the sheikh.

See also: The Five Pillars of Islam: *Shahada* 36–41 ▪ God's guidance through Sharia 128–33 ▪ The writings of Jalal al-Din Muhammad Rumi 174–75 ▪ Spreading Islam through trade 182–85

Later, groups of Sufis would add music and ecstatic dancing to help induce a trancelike state.

Founding figures

Despite the emphasis on personal dialogue with God, there were several major figures of influence in early Sufism. Hassan al-Basri (642–728) was one of those who preached against worldliness and materialism during the early days of the Umayyad caliphate. He taught generations of students and because of this some historians refer to him as the "great patriarch" of early Sufism. Al-Basri is said to have gained much of his own knowledge from Ali ibn Abi Talib, which is why many of the Sufi orders trace their spiritual descent back to this fourth caliph.

A rare example of a woman recorded in early Islamic history, Rabia al-Adawiyya (*c.* 714–801) lived a life of seclusion in the deserts of Iraq, where she practiced intense self-denial and devotion to God. She is credited with being the person who introduced the doctrine of divine love, which is the belief that only God is worth loving and He is the only one who can return

He that knoweth God loveth Him, and he that knoweth the world abstaineth from it.
Hassan al-Basri

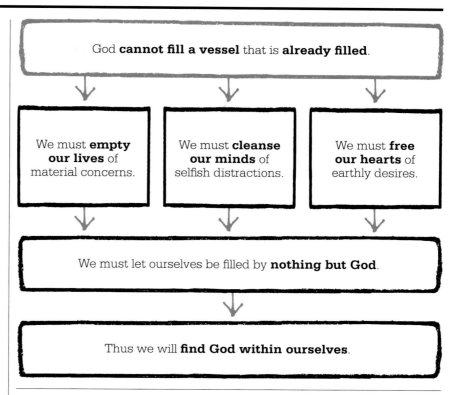

God **cannot fill a vessel** that is **already filled**.

We must **empty our lives** of material concerns.

We must **cleanse our minds** of selfish distractions.

We must **free our hearts** of earthly desires.

We must let ourselves be filled by **nothing but God**.

Thus we will **find God within ourselves**.

that love. An example of this outlook is revealed in a saying that is attributed to her: "O my Lord, if I worship You from fear of hell, burn me in hell. If I worship You from hope of Paradise, bar me from its gates. But if I worship You for Yourself alone, grant me then the beauty of Your face."

Hussein al-Mansur, also known as al-Hallaj (858–922), once spent a whole year in the courtyard of the Kaaba in Mecca fasting and in total silence. He is known for his saying "I am the truth," which caused outrage because it seemed to claim divinity. He was jailed but refused to repent. However, ultimately it was his claim that it was possible to make a valid spiritual Hajj while staying at home that brought about his reincarceration and execution.

The way

The early Sufis were highly mobile, traveling throughout the Islamic lands. Lodges were established in major cities where the Sufis could stay and exchange knowledge. In time, these lodges grew into schools or orders of Sufic thought, known as *tarika*—from the Arabic word meaning "path" or "road," signifying the spiritual journeying toward God. The orders would center on a Sufi master, or sheikh, who would act as spiritual guide or guru to the lodge's disciples (*murid*). Each *tarika* developed its own methodology, with its own set of stages and levels of attainment on the path to a purified soul. Most generally emphasized traits such as generosity, humility, and oneness with God. When a sheikh died, **»**

Whirling is a form of meditation practiced by the Mevlevi order of Sufis in Turkey. It takes place within the *sema*, or worship ceremony, during which Sufis aim to reach oneness with God.

one of his disciples would take charge of the *tarika*, leading the next generation. In this way, each *tarika* claimed legitimacy through a chain (*silsila*) of spiritual authority that inevitably would be traced all the way back to the Prophet. Some of the more influential *tarika* developed multiple branches, some of them spreading across the Islamic world.

Sufi orders and devotions
One of the earliest and most influential of the orders dates back to 12th-century Baghdad. Named for the respected preacher Abdul Qadir Jilani (1077–1166), the Qadiri Order had extended to Morocco and Spain, Turkey

and India, and east and west Africa by the end of the 15th century. Sufis often traveled in response to dreams in which they saw the Prophet instructing them to call people to God in far-flung places. Sufism's message of love, its esoteric teachings, and the highly

Yesterday I was clever, so I wanted to change the world. Today I am wise, so I am changing myself.
Rumi

visible piety of its devotees all helped the spread of Islam into new lands.

Qadiri devotees are known for focusing their devotional acts (*dhikr*) on repetitive chanting of the *Shahada*, faster and faster until the phrase breaks down. Disciples of the Naqshbandi Order, which has its origins in the early 14th century, in Bukhara in Central Asia, employ what is known as the "silent *dhikr*," in which the names of God are repeated inwardly in an act of meditation rather than spoken aloud in an invocation. The order spread across the Indian subcontinent in the 16th century and it remains hugely influential, with a reported 60 million disciples in countries all over the world.

The best known of all Sufi orders is undoubtedly the Mevlevi. It was founded in Konya, Anatolia (modern-day Turkey) by the followers of 13th-century mystic and poet Jalal al-Din Muhammad Rumi. The Mevlevis' unique form of *dhikr* is a slowly spinning dance, hence their alternative name of the "Whirling Dervishes."

The Chishti Order, which is popular on the Indian sub-continent, employs music and poetry, but other Sufi orders have more esoteric forms of *dhikr*. The Rifai Order of Macedonia is famous for disciples who pierce themselves with spikes while in a trancelike state, while in parts of Morocco there are Sufis who practice *dhikr* through great feats of strength.

Omar Khayyam

In the view of many Muslims, Sufis have always pressed the boundaries of Islamic orthodoxy. This is certainly an accusation that could be leveled at one of the best known Sufis, Persian Omar Khayyam (1048–1131). The son of a tentmaker (the meaning of the Arabic word *khayyam*), he grew up to be a brilliant astronomer, mathematician, and, most notably, a poet. His *Rubaiyat*—quatrains, or poems of four lines—are still in print today. Many of these verses are odes to wine and drunkenness,

> Drink wine and look at the moon, and think of all the civilizations the moon has seen passing by.
> **Omar Khayyam**

something that the Quran forbids, although the very fact Khayyam writes so much about wine suggests drinking alcohol was anything but uncommon in 12th-century Persia. He remains widely read in Persian, and in English, thanks to a highly interpretative translation by English poet Edward FitzGerald, issued in 1868.

Sufism today

Although the Sufis have rarely been interested in political power, they have often drawn the ire of authorities. Islam is a communal religion and it does not encourage radicalism or individualism. For a Muslim, or group of Muslims, to withdraw from the community in pursuit of a personal relationship with God is counter to the spirit of Islam. Throughout history, Sufis have regularly been persecuted—including in Safavid Iran in the 16th century, 19th-century Mecca and Medina, Turkey following the founding of the republic in 1923, and Pakistan today.

Nevertheless, Sufism has hundreds of millions of followers around the world, and many of its ideas and forms have entered mainstream global culture. Examples range from the poetry of Rumi and the *Qawwali* music of Pakistan—which became internationally popular thanks to artists such as Nusrat Fateh Ali Khan—to pop videos by Madonna and the best-selling novels by Brazilian author Paulo Coelho.

Whether directly or indirectly, Sufism's missionary work continues to this day, following—in the words of Andalusian scholar and mystic poet Ibn Arabi—"the religion of love wherever its camels turn." ∎

The Conference of the Birds

The Sufi tradition has produced some of the most memorable poetry and prose in Islamic history. One of the masterpieces is *The Conference of the Birds* by Persian Sufi poet Farid al-Din Attar (*c.* 1145–*c.* 1221 or 1230). In it, the birds of the world gather around the *hoopoe*, who has been chosen to lead them on a journey to see the *simurgh*, or King of the Birds. To reach their goal the birds have to traverse seven treacherous valleys, each representing a station on the way. At the end of the journey, only after the birds have learned to "destroy the mountain of the self" are they allowed to approach the throne of the *simurgh*. Of the thousands of birds who began the journey, only 30 make it to the end. Yet when they finally lay their eyes on him, they see not the King of Birds but themselves. Although the birds have traveled far and overcome many struggles, it is themselves they sought all along. It is the essence of Sufism.

Qawwali is a form of Sufi devotional music popular in parts of Pakistan. It gained international exposure through the concerts and recordings of Nusrat Fateh Ali Khan.

THE GOL
AGE OF
756–1526

DEN
SLAM

A Muslim army conquers the Visigothic kingdom of Spain, which becomes known to the Arabs as **al-Andalus**.

↑

Umayyad prince Abdul Rahman I establishes a court at **Cordoba** in Spain.

↑

Persian physician-philosopher **Ibn Sina (Avicenna)** completes his five-volume encyclopedic *The Canon of Medicine*.

↑

Ayyubid sultan **Salah al-Din takes Jerusalem** from the Christian Crusaders.

↑

711 **756** **1025** **1187**

750 **813–833** **1138–54**

↓

The **Abbasid dynasty** comes to power. It founds a new capital at Baghdad in 762.

↓

The Abbasid caliph al-Mamun establishes the **House of Wisdom** as a repository of all the world's knowledge.

↓

Muslim scholar **al-Idrisi compiles a world map** for Roger II of Sicily.

In 762, the second ruler of the Abbasid dynasty moved the capital of the Islamic caliphate from Damascus to the newly founded city of Baghdad. The move is often seen as marking the beginning of a golden age in which science, art, and culture flourished.

Islamic civilization now encompassed many diverse cultures and intellectual traditions. Abbasid nobles sponsored scholars to explore the knowledge gained from foreign territories. These scholars translated the works of other civilizations, particularly the Greeks, and used this knowledge to further their own discoveries. Certain advances made by Muslim astronomers, geographers, and mathematicians were motivated by problems presented in Islamic traditions, such as al-Khwarizmi's

development of algebra in order to solve Islamic inheritance laws, and developments in astronomy and geometry in order to determine the direction of Mecca.

In 802, when Caliph Harun al-Rashid dispatched an embassy to the Frankish ruler Charlemagne, it included the gift of a water clock that chimed the hours by dropping brass balls onto cymbals. This sophisticated timepiece was just one example of Arab advances that were far ahead of their European counterparts.

A golden age

With Arabic as the lingua franca, learning spread across the Islamic world—even if a person's mother tongue were Persian, Syriac, or Berber, if they were a Muslim, a rudimentary knowledge of Arabic

was necessary to read the Quran. Rulers at the courts of the great Muslim cities competed to attract the best scholars for the prestige they would bring. As far afield as Cordoba, for example, in Islamic Spain, a court established by a refugee Umayyad prince became a magnet for scholars from the East.

Historians point to the 10th and 11th centuries CE as the height of this golden age, when a pantheon of Muslim scholars and scientists made significant advances in a multitude of fields. Ibn al-Haytham experimented with light and vision, laying the foundation for modern optics. Al-Biruni toyed with a heliocentric system that had the sun at the center of the universe. Al-Razi produced the earliest descriptions of smallpox and measles, while Ibn Sina (known in

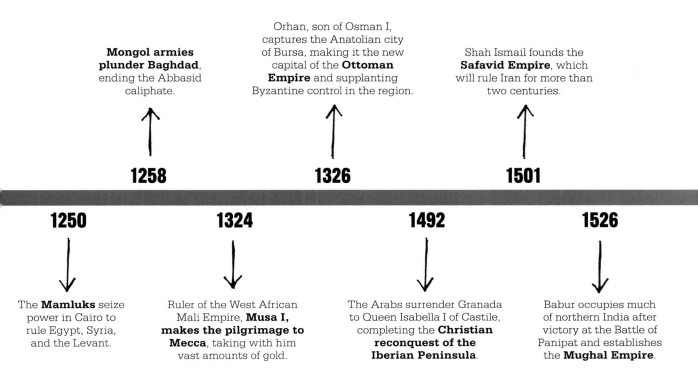

Mongol armies plunder Baghdad, ending the Abbasid caliphate.

Orhan, son of Osman I, captures the Anatolian city of Bursa, making it the new capital of the **Ottoman Empire** and supplanting Byzantine control in the region.

Shah Ismail founds the **Safavid Empire**, which will rule Iran for more than two centuries.

1258   **1326**   **1501**

1250   **1324**   **1492**   **1526**

The **Mamluks** seize power in Cairo to rule Egypt, Syria, and the Levant.

Ruler of the West African Mali Empire, **Musa I, makes the pilgrimage to Mecca**, taking with him vast amounts of gold.

The Arabs surrender Granada to Queen Isabella I of Castile, completing the **Christian reconquest of the Iberian Peninsula**.

Babur occupies much of northern India after victory at the Battle of Panipat and establishes the **Mughal Empire**.

---

the West as Avicenna) compiled a million-word medical encyclopedia that was used as a textbook in Europe until the 17th century.

The global spread of Islam

While the Abbasids were less expansion-minded than their predecessors, the religion spread nevertheless. It was carried along with goods on camel caravans across deserts into East and West Africa, and through Central Asia as far as China. It traveled aboard ships to ports on Indian Ocean islands and archipelagos in the Southeast Asian seas. When the great Arab traveler Ibn Battuta spent almost 30 years traveling in the first half of the 14th century, most of the lands he visited were Islamic. The knowledge that was gained from merchants and

travelers, backed by observations from scientists, enabled Muslims to become for a time the world's greatest cartographers, and some of its first ethnographers and travel writers. The far-reaching influence of Muslim trade and commerce can be seen in the number of related Arabic words that have passed into European languages, including *al-kohl* (alcohol), *laymun* (lemon), *naranj* (orange), *qahwa* (coffee), *qairawan* (caravan), *sukkar* (sugar), and *qutun* (cotton).

Three great empires

From the 10th to the 13th centuries, the Arab Muslim world was under almost constant attack. Mongols from the East stormed through the Abbasid Empire, plundering Baghdad. Christian armies were in the process of reconquering Spain,

and Crusaders invaded the Eastern Mediterranean. Power shifted from the Abbasids to other dynasties—including the Mamluks who, from a stronghold in Cairo, presided over a 250-year flourishing of the arts and architecture. By this time, Europeans had rediscovered classical Greek learning through the medium of Arabic texts. Their interest in these manuscripts would spark the Renaissance in Italy and beyond.

Meanwhile, Islam would revive and expand once more in the shape of three powerful empires. These new empires would not be Arab: the Ottomans were Turks, the Safavids were Persians, and the Mughals were Indians descended from the Mongols. Between them, these empires would control half of the known world. ∎

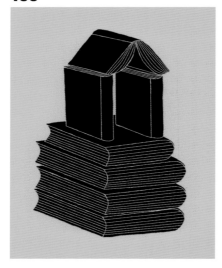

SEEKING KNOWLEDGE IS OBLIGATORY FOR EVERY MUSLIM
PROPHET MUHAMMAD

Greek texts by Aristotle, Euclid, Galen, Plato, Ptolemy, and others are **translated into Persian** by the Sasanians.

The Abbasids conquer the Sasanians and their texts are **translated into Arabic** in Baghdad.

Arab manuscripts are seized when the Christians expel the Arabs from Spain and **translated into Latin**.

The Latin texts are **translated into European languages**, spreading the lost classical texts throughout the Western world.

The search for knowledge and enlightenment is enshrined in Islam. "Read" was the first word God spoke to Muhammad in the cave of Hira, commencing the revelation of the Quran. Compilers of *hadith* credit Muhammad with saying, "Seeking knowledge is obligatory for every Muslim" and "Whoever follows a path seeking knowledge, God will make his path to paradise easy."

Translation project
The earliest Islamic scholars devoted themselves to transcribing and interpreting the Quran. This

changed under the Abbasids, who sponsored scholars to explore knowledge gained from foreign works rather than relying solely on the guidance found in the Quran. The Abbasids occupied lands formerly ruled by the Sasanians (an empire that ruled from 224–651) and translators undertook to transfer Sasanian texts into Arabic. The translation project was then extended to the learned texts of earlier civilizations, notably the Greeks and Indians. Scholars took the works of philosophers such as Aristotle and Plato, medical tomes by Galen, and treatises on geometry

See also: The Umayyad and Abbasid caliphates 136–39 ▪ The first modern scientists 152–55 ▪ The beginnings of Islamic philosophy 156–57 ▪ Arabic numerals and *al-jabr* 158–61 ▪ The uses of astronomy 162–63

> The ink of the scholar is more holy than the blood of the martyr.
> **Prophet Muhammad**

by Euclid and astronomy by Ptolemy, and through translation introduced their ideas into the Arabic-speaking Islamic world.

Paper and penmanship

The preservation and spread of knowledge was aided by the Arab replacement of costly parchment with paper, which had been invented by their trading partners, the Chinese. A paper mill was established in Baghdad in 795. At the same time, a new Arabic script was developed that was more fluid and faster to write than older forms. As a result, in Baghdad in the 8th century it became possible to write a book and sell it in the marketplace for the first time in human history.

The House of Wisdom

The translation movement reached a peak during the 20-year reign of the dynasty's seventh ruler, Caliph al-Mamun (r. 813–833). Half Arab, half Persian, al-Mamun promoted an openness toward other religions and cultures that attracted scholars in every field from all over the empire to gravitate to Baghdad.

This environment encouraged free thinking and led to an increasing amount of original writing in astronomy, mathematics, medicine, philosophy, and the various branches of science. Often, foreign rulers defeated in battle would be required to hand over books as part of the terms of surrender. Al-Mamun reputedly sought to bring together all of the world's knowledge under one roof; and the institution he created to

The House of Wisdom played host to scholars who translated Greek works into Arabic. They built upon classical knowledge to make breakthroughs in fields such as astronomy, as seen here.

accommodate this became known as the House of Wisdom, or *Beit al-Hikma* in Arabic.

No one knows what form the House of Wisdom took because no exact written description or archaeological evidence survives, but it was probably more than just a library. Written evidence suggests it also fulfilled the function of an academy, attracting many of the outstanding figures in Islam's golden age of learning. The translation movement lasted approximately two hundred years. During that time, Abbasid Baghdad became a center for learning that would not be equaled until the Renaissance in Italy in the 15th and 16th centuries. ▪

The oldest universities

Baghdad was far from being the sole example of an early Islamic city of learning. The world's oldest continually operating university was established in Fez, Morocco, in 859. Called al-Kairouan, it was founded by a woman named Fatima al-Fihri, whose family were originally of the Quraysh tribe from Mecca.

In 972, the Ismaili Shia Fatimid dynasty founded al-Azhar Mosque in Cairo, which began accepting students three years later. Classes were given in Islamic law, astronomy, philosophy, and logic. During the reign of Sultan Salah al-Din (r. 1174–93) the university became a Sunni institution, and it remains the leading university of Sunni Islamic learning today. It stands for a more moderate form of Islam than that promoted by the likes of Saudi Arabia. The Grand Sheikh of al-Azhar is considered by some Muslims to be the highest authority in Sunni Islamic jurisprudence and thought.

THERE IS NO CONFLICT BETWEEN ISLAM AND SCIENCE

DR. OSMAN BAKAR OF THE CENTER FOR MUSLIM-CHRISTIAN UNDERSTANDING

IN CONTEXT

THEME
The first modern scientists

WHEN AND WHERE
10th–11th centuries, across the Islamic world

BEFORE
5th and 4th centuries BCE
The leading figures of classical Greece produce great works on many scientific subjects. However, these remain almost purely theoretical.

762 CE The fledgling Abbasid caliphate founds a new capital in Baghdad, where it sponsors scholarship and research.

AFTER
1543 Andreas Vesalius publishes *On the Fabric of the Human Body* and Nicolaus Copernicus publishes *On the Revolutions of the Heavenly Spheres.*

There is a fringe view held by some Muslims that the texts of the Quran and the *hadith* contain everything that anyone would ever need to know about the world. It follows from this that there is no point in scientific enquiry—some even consider the pursuit of science un-Islamic.

Such thinking has always existed in Islam but it has always been the view of a small minority. Most Muslims see science as a means of increasing knowledge, which is something that is explicitly encouraged by the Quran. Numerous Quranic verses instruct followers to observe and reflect upon natural phenomena,

See also: The House of Wisdom 150–51 ▪ Arabic numerals and *al-jabr* 158–61 ▪ The uses of astronomy 162–63 ▪ The example of Islamic Spain 166–71 ▪ Ibn Sina and the *Canon of Medicine* 172–73

Some Muslims believe that **pursuing scientific studies is a collective duty** of the Muslim community. Many verses of the Quran specifically ask Muslims to observe and study the world.

Some Muslims believe that the **Quran contains the answers** to all the questions about our world that any believer could wish to know.

something that has usually been interpreted as encouragement for scientific enquiry.

The correct way of seeing

Abu Ali al-Hassan ibn al-Haytham, better known simply as Ibn al-Haytham (or Alhazen in the West), was born in Basra, in what is now southern Iraq, around 965. In his early years he worked as a civil servant for the Abbasid rulers in his hometown, but he soon abandoned the post to pursue an intellectual career in Cairo, the capital of the rival Fatimid dynasty. He caught the attention of the Fatimid caliph with a proposal for a dam. While he ultimately failed in his dam-building attempts, Ibn al-Haytham did produce a vast body of other valuable work, writing more than 200 manuscripts in fields including astronomy, engineering, ethics, mathematics, music, politics, and theology. However, his most influential thinking was compiled in the *Kitab al-Manazir*

Ibn al-Haytham's *Book of Optics* describes how he thought the eye was anatomically constructed and then considers how this anatomy might function as an optical system.

(*Book of Optics*), a revolutionary seven-volume treatise on the mathematical theory of vision, published in 1021.

The basic principles of geometric optics had been laid down in ancient Greece by Plato and Euclid, including such ideas as light traveling in straight lines and the laws of reflection. Where Ibn al-Haytham differed was that rather than dealing in the purely theoretical, his *Book of Optics* was a true science book, with detailed

descriptions of experiments, including the apparatus required and how it was to be used. The results of the experiments were presented in support of his theories.

Ibn al-Haytham's most important theory related to how we see. The Greeks believed that we see because rays of light are emitted from our eyes that illuminate objects. Ibn al-Haytham was the first to deduce that the reverse is true and that vision works through the refraction of light through the eye's lens. He also deduced that refraction is correctly explained by light moving more slowly in denser mediums, such as the eye's lens, because more particles get in its way. He also investigated meteorological aspects related to the rainbow, as well as exploring the nature of celestial phenomena such as eclipses and moonlight.

The Latin translation of Ibn al-Haytham's book on optics was to have a wide influence on »

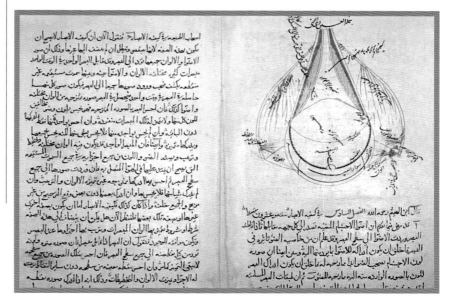

> The extremist among them would stamp the sciences as atheistic.
> **Al-Biruni**

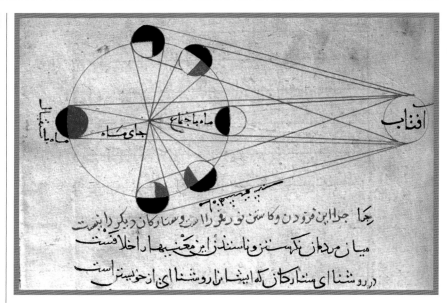

medieval European scientists and philosophers and, thanks to an edition published in Basel in 1572, on mathematicians such as Johannes Kepler (1571–1630), René Descartes (1596–1650), and Christiaan Huygens (1629–95).

How high is the sky?

Another 11th-century Arab physicist, Ibn Muadh al-Jayyani (989–1079) of Cordoba, also worked in the field of optics and celestial phenomena. He recognized that twilight following a sunset must be due to illuminated water vapor high in the upper atmosphere reflecting light after the sun has

set. From this, using geometry and a value for the size of Earth provided by astronomers in Baghdad, al-Jayyani deduced the height of Earth's atmosphere to be 52 miles (84 km). In the 20th century with the aid of jet aircraft, geophysicists determined that the border between Earth's atmosphere and space is actually about 62 miles (100 km). The Islamic scientist, who lived 900 years ago, was just 10 miles (16 km) out.

Al-Biruni studied almost all fields of science and wrote treatises related to most of them. This illustration, from one of his astronomical works, explains the different phases of the moon.

The supreme polymath

While it is possible to determine the key achievements of Ibn al-Haytham and Ibn Muadh, the output of Abu Rayhan Muhammad al-Biruni (973–1050) is so exceptional in so many areas it is difficult to know where to begin.

Born in Central Asia, al-Biruni spent most of his adult life in Ghazni, in Afghanistan, serving as a scholar and advisor at the court of the Ghaznavid sultan. There was almost nothing he saw that did not attract his interest. He wrote a book on determining the coordinates of cities, which provided crucial assistance in determining the direction of Mecca for prayer. He also produced a major study of India, the first work of its kind, which included analyses of the relationships between Greek civilization and that of the Hindus, and between Islam and Hinduism.

What happened to Muslim science?

Science in the Islamic world flourished from about 700 to the 11th century, then went into decline. By contrast, European scientific activity was negligible until about the 15th century, when it suddenly burst into life and quickly overtook the Islamic world. So what happened to Islamic science?

Some historians suggest that when the Mongols razed Baghdad and the Christians reconquered Spain, the two poles of Islamic learning were lost. The new Islamic empires that emerged were Turkish, Persian, and Indian and lacked a spirit of cooperation. There is also a view that the Islamic orthodoxy movement gained the upper hand over the rationalists and succeeded to some extent in "re-Islamicizing" science by portraying the Quran as the sole source of knowledge.

In the modern era, science in the Islamic world is resurgent, with three recent Muslim Nobel Prize winners in science.

In other fields, al-Biruni compiled a pharmacopoeia that described all the medicines known at the time, listing the names for drugs in multiple languages. He was also an outstanding mathematician who used calculus to describe the motion of heavenly bodies, laying the groundwork for Isaac Newton's laws of motion more than 600 years later. In physics, al-Biruni came up with a variety of methods for exploring densities, weight, and even gravity.

Scientific method

In common with the recorded practices of Ibn al-Haytham, al-Biruni's approach to scientific discovery was very similar to the modern scientific method. It consisted of a repeating cycle of observation, hypothesis, and experimentation, backed by independent verification. When al-Biruni could not find definitive evidence for a theory he remained neutral—even over the question that vexed some of the greatest minds of the era. This question was whether the sun and planets orbited Earth (following Ptolemy's geocentric theory), or whether Earth and the other planets orbited the sun (this was the heliocentric theory). In this neutral stance al-Biruni was acting in accordance with the Quran, which states in *sura* 17:36, "Do not follow what you know not."

Historians sometimes claim that modern science began in 1543, which saw the publication of both *On the Fabric of the Human Body* by Italian anatomist Andreas

Vesalius and *On the Revolutions of the Heavenly Spheres* (with its thesis that Earth moves round the sun) by Polish astronomer Nicolaus Copernicus. But there is no doubt that Ibn al-Haytham and al-Biruni were "modern scientists" 500 years before. Both embodied the spirit of the experimental method in science. While we do not know Ibn al-Haytham's views on theology, al-Biruni was quite clear when he stated that the Quran "does not interfere with the business of science nor does it infringe on the realm of science."

Modern renaissance

Pakistani Muhammad Abdus Salam (1926–96) was a corecipient of the 1979 Nobel Prize in Physics for his contribution in the field of particle physics. In his acceptance speech he quoted from the Quran to the effect that the deeper we seek, the more our wonder is excited. Salam was the first Muslim scientist to be honored with a Nobel Prize since the awards began in 1901. But, as on occasion he pointed out, he was following in a highly distinguished and venerable tradition of ground-breaking Islamic scientists. ∎

Typifying Islam's genius for applied science, engineer al-Jazari (1136–1206) invented various clocks, including this "elephant clock" which operated via hydraulics in the animal's belly.

WE SHOULD NOT BE ASHAMED TO ACKNOWLEDGE TRUTH

ON FIRST PHILOSOPHY BY AL-KINDI (9TH CENTURY)

IN CONTEXT

THEME
The beginnings of Islamic philosophy

WHEN AND WHERE
9th century, across the Islamic world

BEFORE
pre-9th century
Knowledge of Greek learning declines in the West with the fall of the Byzantine Empire. Many Greek texts, however, are translated by the Sasanians, and preserved.

AFTER
11th century Ibn Sina (Avicenna) further attempts to reconcile rational philosophy with Islamic theology.

11th century Al-Ghazali writes *The Incoherence of the Philosophers*, attacking the use of philosophy in theology.

12th century Ibn Rushd publishes *The Incoherence of "the Incoherence,"* refuting al-Ghazali's work.

Baghdad's House of Wisdom produced a number of celebrated scholars, many of them polymaths excelling in a wide range of fields. The first of these Abbasid polymaths was al-Kindi (Latinized as Alkindus in the West), who is best known for introducing the philosophy of Aristotle to the Arabic-speaking world in the 9th century. He made the Greek philosopher's work not only accessible but acceptable, by fusing Aristotelian philosophy with Islamic theology.

Al-Kindi (*c.* 800–73) was a follower of a doctrine known as Mutazilism (literally, "those who separate themselves"), which believed in a spirit of rational enquiry and opposed the literal interpretation of the Quran. The Mutazilites believed that it was the human intellect that guided mankind toward a true knowledge of God and a clearer understanding of the words of the Quran. Their opponents, however, maintained that secular philosophy was un-Islamic.

On First Philosophy

Of the many works written by al-Kindi, the most famous is called *On First Philosophy*. It begins with an invitation to the reader to honor ancient Greek philosophical wisdom. Al-Kindi argues that no one should ignore the achievements of past scholars on the basis that they are of a different race, culture, or creed. He accuses those who fail to appreciate the contribution of the Greeks of being narrow-minded and lacking in faith in Islam.

On First Philosophy includes a celebrated discussion of the eternity of the world. Aristotle believed that the universe has

Introducing God into Aristotle

Aristotle believed that the universe had existed forever, **hence no creator**.

Al-Kindi argued that the universe had a starting point and was brought into being by a **creator**.

See also: Sufism and the mystic tradtion 140–45 ▪ The House of Wisdom 150–51 ▪ Arabic numerals and *al-jabr* 158–61 ▪ The example of Islamic Spain 166–71 ▪ Ibn Sina and *The Canon of Medicine* 172–73

Ignorance leads to fear, fear leads to hatred, and hatred leads to violence.
Ibn Rushd

existed forever. But if the universe is eternal then there is no creator and therefore no God. For al-Kindi, a devout Muslim, the problem was how to fit God and Creation, as described in the Quran, into this view of the cosmos.

Al-Kindi came up with a strongly reasoned argument to refute the idea of an eternal universe, which he was able to express in mathematical terms. His reasoning led him to believe that time could not have existed before the creation of the universe and must have come into being together with the universe. This finiteness of the universe allowed al-Kindi to identify God as creator of the world, who brought it into being out of nothing.

Ibn Sina and Ibn Rushd

In the 10th century, a scholar named al-Farabi (*c.*872–950), known in the West as Alpharabius, continued to explore the intersection of Islam and classical philosophy. Al-Farabi wrote commentaries on the works of the Greeks, with an emphasis on central Islamic themes, such as law, prophecy, political succession, and jurisprudence.

Ibn Sina (980–1037), better known in the West as Avicenna, was a devout Muslim from Central Asia, who sought to reconcile rational philosophy with Islamic theology. He came up with a formal argument for proving the existence of God, known as the "Proof of the Truthful." It has been called one of the most influential medieval arguments for God's existence. Ibn Rushd (1126–98), known in

Al-Farabi founded his own school of philosophy known as "Farabism." He aimed at synthesizing philosophy and Sufism. He is featured on this stamp from Kazakhstan, his presumed birthplace.

the West as Averroes, was an Andalusian who argued that philosophy cannot contradict revelations in Islam because they are just two different methods of reaching the truth, and "truth cannot contradict truth." ▪

Al-Kindi

We know little about the life of Yaqub ibn Ishaq al-Kindi, better known simply as al-Kindi. He was born around the year 800 into pure-blooded aristocratic Arab lineage. He was a member of the powerful Kinda tribe, originally from Yemen but influential in Arabia since before the time of Islam. He was born in Kufa, in present-day Iraq, but probably moved to Baghdad early in life and received his education there.

He showed great early promise as a scholar and was recruited to work under the patronage of Caliph al-Mamun (r. 813–33).

As well as supervising the translation of Greek texts, al-Kindi produced more than 200 works of his own. He wrote on an astonishing range of subjects from ethics to music, and from the workings of the human eye to swordmaking. He played an important role in introducing Indian numerals to the Islamic world, and subsequently Arabic numerals to the Christian world. However, he is best known for founding an entire philosophical tradition on which Islamic thinkers were able to build for centuries. He died in 873.

THE REUNION OF BROKEN PARTS

THE COMPENDIUM ON CALCULATING BY REJOINING AND BALANCING BY AL-KHWARIZMI (8TH CENTURY)

S ome time around 830,
House of Wisdom scholar
Muhammad ibn Musa
al-Khwarizmi completed a
work that would revolutionize
mathematics. Its opening pages
include a dedication that explicitly
delineates the link between Islamic
faith and intellectual endeavor:
"That fondness for science, by
which God has distinguished the
Imam al-Mamun, the Commander
of the Faithful ... has encouraged
me to compose a short work
on calculating by (the rules
of) completion and reduction."

This book, *The Compendium
on Calculating by Rejoining and
Balancing* (in Arabic, *Kitab*

See also: The House of Wisdom 150–51 ▪ The beginnings of Islamic philosophy 156–57 ▪ The uses of astronomy 162–63 ▪ Jalal al-Din Muhammad Rumi 174–75

al-Mukhtasar fi Hisab al-Jabr w'al-Muqabala) laid out the principles that are the foundation of modern algebra, which in itself is the unifying thread of almost all of mathematics.

Al-jabr equals algebra

Al-Khwarizmi introduced some fundamental operations, which he described as reduction, rejoining, and balancing. The process of reduction (which we now call simplifying an equation) could be done by rejoining (in Arabic, *al-jabr*, from where we get the word algebra)—in other words, moving subtracted terms to the other side of an equation—and then balancing the equation.

Al-Khwarizmi did not invent these processes, but he brought together obscure mathematical rules, known only to a few at the time, and turned them into an instruction manual for solving mathematical problems that might occur in everyday situations. At the start of the book, he describes

Algebra deals with numbers and **quantities that are unknown**.

They are **related** to things that are **known**.

Unknown quantities can be determined by **examining the things that are known**.

The determination of the unknown quantities is possible.

numerous instances in which these mathematical formulas could be of use: "in cases of inheritance, legacies, partition, lawsuits, and trade ... or where the measuring of lands, the digging of canals, geometrical computations, and other objects of various sorts and kinds are concerned."

The Compendium on Calculating is divided into two halves. In the first, al-Khwarizmi lays down the rules of algebra and the sequences necessary to solve different problems. The second part of the book is full of examples of his methods as applied to a wide range of everyday problems. »

Al-Khwarizmi

Little is known about the life of al-Khwarizmi. Historians think that he was born around 780 in Khwarizm—then part of the Persian Empire, now Khiva in Uzbekistan—from which he took his name. At some point he moved to Baghdad, where he worked at the court of Caliph al-Mamun. Such was the respect in which he was held, he was appointed chief astronomer and head of the library of the celebrated House of Wisdom.

While probably Persian, al-Khwarizmi is usually described as an Arab mathematician because he wrote in Arabic and did all his work in the context of Arab Abbasid culture. As well as his work on algebra, he made important contributions to trigonometry, advocated the use of Hindi numerals, revised Ptolemy's *Geography*, oversaw the drafting of a new world map, took part in a project to determine the circumference of Earth, and compiled a set of astronomical tables for the movements of the sun, the moon, and the five planets known at the time. Al-Khwarizmi died around 850.

Instead of the mathematical symbols we use today, al-Khwarizmi wrote his equations entirely in words, supported by diagrams. For example, he wrote out the equation $(x/3 + 1)(x/4 + 1) = 20$ as "A quantity: I multiplied a third of it and a dirham by a fourth of it and a dirham; it becomes twenty." The dirham was a coin, which was used by al-Khwarizmi to signify a single unit.

The "Egyptian reckoner"

Al-Khwarizmi's text inspired countless mathematicians throughout the Islamic world. The Egyptian mathematician Abu Kamil (*c.* 850–930) wrote the *Book of Algebra* (*Kitab fi al-Jabr w'al-Muqabala*), which was designed to be an academic treatise for other mathematicians. In another book, *Rare Things in the Art of Calculation* (*Kitab al-Taraif fi al-Hisab*), the man nicknamed

> When I consider what people generally want in calculating, I found that it always is a number.
> **Al-Khwarizmi**

the "Egyptian reckoner" attempted to solve indeterminate equations (those with more than one solution). He further explored this topic in his *Book of Birds* (*Kitab al-Tair*), in which he posed a miscellany of bird-related algebra problems, including: "How many ways can one buy 100 birds in the market with 100 dirhams?".

Although better known for his poetry, the Persian Omar Khayyam (1048–1131) was also a highly accomplished mathematician. His *Treatise on Demonstration of Problems of Algebra* (1070) dealt with cubic equations.

Arabic numerals

Among the lasting contributions made by Islamic mathematicians was the popularization of the decimal system that is used throughout the world today. This has its origins in India, where the use of nine symbols along with zero was developed in the 1st to 4th centuries CE to allow any number to be written efficiently. The system was adopted and refined by mathematicians in Baghdad—hence the name, the Hindi-Arabic decimal system. In the 9th century, both al-Khwarizmi and the philosopher al-Kindi wrote books on the subject. Their work

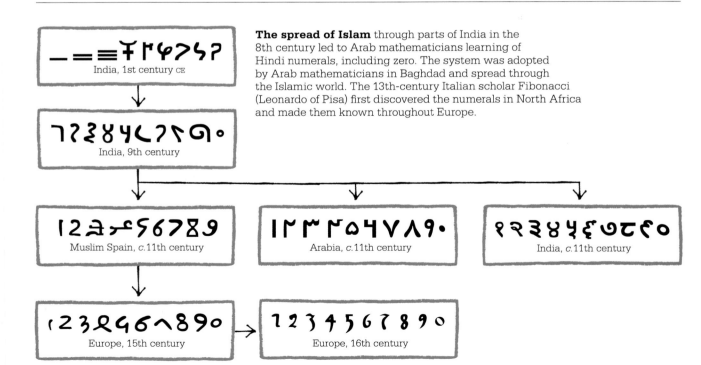

India, 1st century CE

India, 9th century

Muslim Spain, *c.*11th century

Arabia, *c.*11th century

India, *c.*11th century

Europe, 15th century

Europe, 16th century

The spread of Islam through parts of India in the 8th century led to Arab mathematicians learning of Hindi numerals, including zero. The system was adopted by Arab mathematicians in Baghdad and spread through the Islamic world. The 13th-century Italian scholar Fibonacci (Leonardo of Pisa) first discovered the numerals in North Africa and made them known throughout Europe.

Islamic mathematicians gather in the library of a mosque in this illustration from a manuscript by the 12th-century poet and scholar al-Hariri of Basra.

was later translated into Latin and published in the West, thus introducing Europeans to the decimal system, which was known in the Middle Ages only as Arabic numerals. However, decimal numbers were regarded for a long time as symbols of the heathen Muslim enemy. Instead, Europe persisted with Roman numerals, in which numbers are represented in letters. This continued to work well for most purposes in daily life, all numbers up to 1,000 being represented by combinations of just seven letters (I, V, X, L, C, D, M; representing 1, 5, 10, 50, 100, 500 and 1,000). However, it was incredibly cumbersome when applied to mathematics. For example, the basic multiplication 42 x 58 = 2436 becomes XLII x LVIII = MMCDXXXVI. It was only the interest in mathematics during the Italian Renaissance that finally saw Europe adopt Hindi-Arabic numerals, which came into widespread use by the late 15th or early 16th century.

The decimal point
The Arabs can also take the credit for introducing the decimal point, which allowed mathematicians to express fractions of whole numbers. This small but crucial symbol first appears in *The Book of Chapters on Hindu Arithmetic* (*Kitab al-Fusul fi al-Hisab al-Hindi*) by Abu al-Hassan al-Uqlidisi (*c.* 920–80), possibly written around 952 in

Whoever thinks algebra is a trick in obtaining unknowns has thought it in vain.
Omar Khayyam

Damascus. The name Uqlidisi refers to Euclid, and may mean that al-Uqlidisi earned his living by making and selling copies of Euclid's famous work *Elements*. In his book, al-Uqlidisi uses a slanted dash over the number that is the decimal; this would later evolve into the decimal point as we know it today.

Influence in the West
The discoveries and rules set down by medieval Islamic scholars are still the foundation of much of mathematics today, particularly algebra. When al-Khwarizmi's *Compendium on Calculating* was translated into Latin 300 years after his death, his style was so clear and authoritative that his book became the standard mathematical text in Europe for centuries to come. Its Latin title, *Liber Algorismi*, made its author's Latinized name (Algorismi) a household word synonymous with arithmetic itself. It also gave us the English word "algorithm," which stands as a tribute to the greatest of Muslim mathematicians. ∎

HAVE THEY NEVER OBSERVED THE SKY ABOVE THEM...?

THE QURAN, 50:6

IN CONTEXT

THEME
The uses of astronomy

WHEN AND WHERE
10th–13th centuries CE, across the Islamic world

BEFORE
2nd century CE The Greek polymath Ptolemy writes the *Almagest*, an astronomical treatise on the motion of the stars and planets.

476–550 The Indian mathematician Aryabhata produces the *Aryabhatiya*, a highly influential Sanskrit astronomical treatise.

AFTER
1543 Nicolaus Copernicus proposes a heliocentric model of the Solar System. His work is defended by Galileo Galilei (1564–1642).

1576 The first notable European observatory is established by Tycho Brahe, three centuries after Maragha.

Islam is one of the few religions in history in which scientific procedures are necessary for religious ritual. The observation of celestial bodies plays an essential part in the organization of the lunar calendar and religious festivals, and in the regulation of the five daily prayers, the timings of which are astronomically defined. The sun also plays another role in the rituals of Islam by helping to determine the *qibla*, or direction of prayer.

Locating Mecca

Five times a day Muslims around the world face Mecca to pray. Determining the compass direction of Mecca is therefore of the utmost importance. In the 10th century, Islamic astronomers discovered that there are two days in the year when at a precisely determined time the sun passes directly above Mecca. On those days, anyone in the same (northern) hemisphere as Mecca could easily determine the *qibla* by noting the position of the sun at the correct time of day and determining its compass direction. Two different days could be used to determine the correct direction of the *qibla* for worshippers in the southern hemisphere.

Baghdad was a major center of astronomy under the Abbasid caliphs from the 8th century onward. Working from the *Almagest*, a Greek astronomical treatise on the motions of the stars and planetary paths, written by Claudius Ptolemy in the 2nd century CE, House of Wisdom scholars double-checked its measurements. The Arab mathematician al-Khwarizmi (*c.* 780–*c.* 850) compiled the first known tables of daily prayer times, his calculations assisted by direct astronomical observations.

If the distance from the Kaaba is small, its direction may be determined by a diligent seeker, but when the distance is great, only the astronomers can determine that direction.
Al-Biruni

See also: The Five Pillars of Islam: *salat* 42–43 ▪ The Islamic calendar 116–17 ▪ The House of Wisdom 150–51 ▪ Arabic numbers and *al-jabr* 158–61

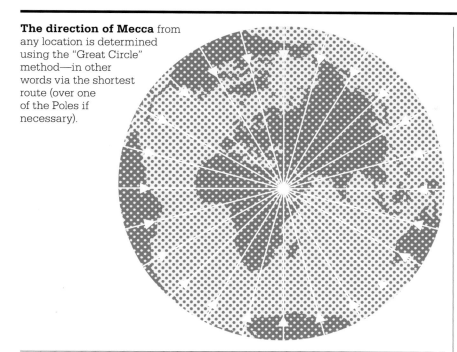

The direction of Mecca from any location is determined using the "Great Circle" method—in other words via the shortest route (over one of the Poles if necessary).

> Anyone who does not know that he does not know is stuck forever in double ignorance.
> **Nasr al-Din al-Tusi**

A succession of renowned Muslim astronomers built on al-Khwarizmi's work; among the greatest of these were the Syrian al-Battani (*c.* 858–929) and the Egyptian Ibn Yunus (*c.* 950–1009). One of al-Battani's best-known achievements was the determination of the solar year as 365 days, 5 hours, 46 minutes, and 24 seconds, which is only 2 minutes and 22 seconds off.

Earth at the center

Drawing from Ptolemy's *Almagest*, the early Islamic astronomers adopted his view that Earth was at the center of the solar system, and that the other planets rotated around it. Only occasionally was this questioned—the 10th-century astronomer al-Biruni did consider a heliocentric system that had the sun at its center, but he could not prove it and so settled for retaining an open mind on the subject.

The Maragha Revolution

By the 13th century, Islamic astronomy was at its zenith. In 1259, Mongol warlord Hulagu Khan built an observatory at Maragha in northwestern Iran. Here, Persian astronomer Nasr al-Din al-Tusi (1201–74) and his successors made use of a giant quadrant, which measured the planets' elevations as they crossed the meridian. With this apparatus the astronomers could produce increasingly accurate planetary tables (in Arabic, *zijes*).

The observatory attracted scholars from as far afield as China. They collectively contributed to what was known as the Maragha Revolution, which overhauled Ptolemy's work on astronomy and replaced the Greek's hypotheses

The direction of Mecca, or *qibla*, is commonly indicated in public buildings in the Muslim world.

with new solar and lunar theories. For example, in order to explain the varying speeds of some planets as they moved across the cosmos, Ptolemy had suggested that planets rotated around poles that did not coincide with their centers, which is impossible. Muslim astronomers invented new models that produced the same effects without violating the laws of physics.

Some of the ideas developed by Islamic astronomers inspired Polish astronomer Nicolaus Copernicus, who overturned the Ptolemaic universe in 1543 when he proposed that the planets revolved around the sun rather than around Earth. ▪

PEOPLE NEED STORIES MORE THAN BREAD ITSELF

THE THOUSAND AND ONE NIGHTS

IN CONTEXT

THEME
The chain of oral tradition

WHERE AND WHEN
9th–10th centuries, Baghdad

BEFORE
224–651 CE The collecting of entertaining stories becomes fashionable in pre-Islamic Sasanian Persia. *Hazar Afsaneh* (*A Thousand Stories*), for example, was translated into Arabic some time in the 8th or 9th centuries.

8th century The Homeric epics are translated into Arabic at the Abbasid court.

AFTER
1704–17 Antoine Galland's French translation introduces *The Nights* to a non-Arabic-speaking audience.

2019 Walt Disney Pictures produces a live-action musical film based on the tales of Aladdin from *The Nights*.

The Quran existed in oral form well before its parts were collected together and written down in the 7th century. Followers of the Prophet learned and faithfully repeated the words that had been revealed to him. Verses such as, "We have made the Quran easy to remember" (54:17) suggest the Muslim holy book was intended to be recited. Today, pious Muslims continue to memorize the Quran and recite its verses aloud. They quote it as a way of expressing their views.

The Quran emerged at a time and place in which writing was scarcely used. Pre-Islamic Arab society prided itself on orations of lengthy pieces of poetry. In fact, the tradition remains; in the Arabian Gulf, for example, *Million's Poet*—a reality television show in which contestants recite self-penned verses to compete for cash prizes—has become one of the most successful Arab television shows ever produced.

The *hakawati*, or professional teller of stories, largely vanished in the 19th century. Just a few individuals, such as this performer at a coffeehouse in Damascus, keep the tradition alive.

Tellers of tales

In a society that attached great importance to the ancient tradition of storytelling, tales of the Prophet Muhammad communicated the message of Islam most effectively. Individuals known as *qussa* specialized in telling religious stories in the mosques.

Outside of the mosque, the most popular tales were the epics of Islamic heroes. The romance of Abu Zeid, for example, was devoted to Arab victories over the Berbers in North Africa, and the stories of al-Zahir Beibars were loosely based on the exploits of a Mamluk sultan who ruled Egypt in the 13th century. While these story cycles

See also: *Al-Jahiliyyah*, the Time of Ignorance 20–21 ▪ Sayings and actions of the Prophet 118–23 ▪ The Umayyad and Abbasid caliphates 136–39 ▪ Orientalism 218

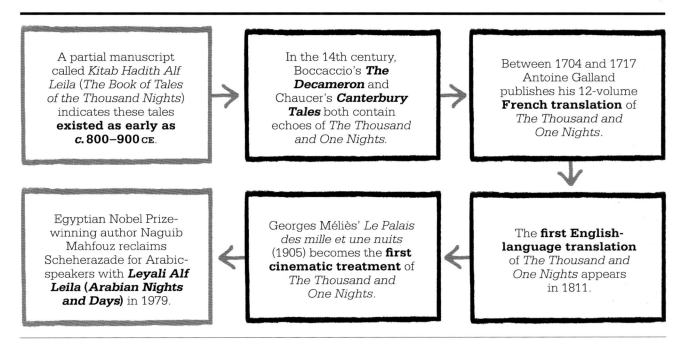

A partial manuscript called *Kitab Hadith Alf Leila* (*The Book of Tales of the Thousand Nights*) indicates these tales **existed as early as** *c.* **800–900** CE.

In the 14th century, Boccaccio's **The Decameron** and Chaucer's **Canterbury Tales** both contain echoes of *The Thousand and One Nights*.

Between 1704 and 1717 Antoine Galland publishes his 12-volume **French translation** of *The Thousand and One Nights*.

Egyptian Nobel Prize-winning author Naguib Mahfouz reclaims Scheherazade for Arabic-speakers with **Leyali Alf Leila (Arabian Nights and Days)** in 1979.

Georges Méliès' *Le Palais des mille et une nuits* (1905) becomes the **first cinematic treatment** of *The Thousand and One Nights*.

The **first English-language translation** of *The Thousand and One Nights* appears in 1811.

were occasionally written down, they existed primarily in the performances of professional storytellers known as *hakawati*. *Hakawati* were a common feature of life in Muslim cities as far back as Umayyad Damascus and Abbasid Baghdad. They told their stories wherever eager listeners gathered. They were still common as recently as the 19th century.

Tales of *The Nights*

Among all the tales told by the *hakawati*, those that have come to be best known outside the Muslim world are the stories that make up *Alf Leila wa Leila* or, as it is translated into English, *The Thousand and One Nights*, or *Arabian Nights*. This is a cycle of stories told to a sultan who is in the habit of taking to bed a new wife every night, only to have her killed in the morning. When the sultan selects the wily

Scheherazade, she spends the night telling him a beguiling story, which she promises to continue the next night, and in this way postpones the executioner's sword.

Arabic-language manuscripts of some of these stories exist dating back to the 9th century, but it is likely Scheherazade predates Islam. *The Nights* has no known author and no fixed table of contents. Like

He recites walking to and fro in the middle of the coffee room.
Alexander Russell
The Natural History of Aleppo (1794)

the suras in the Quran, some tales are one short paragraph, others are hundreds of pages long. The stories have no definite birthplace and have their roots in the folklore of the Middle East, India, and throughout the Muslim world—although the cultures of medieval Baghdad and Cairo are always present.

In spite of numerous allusions to the Prophet and echoes of the Quran, the stories are too full of magic and sorcery, bawdiness, and amorality to be found respectable. These are tales for the coffeehouse, not the family home or mosque.

The Nights became known outside the Arab-speaking world through a translation by the French Orientalist Antoine Galland, printed in 1704–17. This was the first printed version of *The Nights*, in any language. Since then the tales have been retranslated, retold, and adapted in the Western world, in books, music, ballet, and film. ▪

THE BRILLIANT ORNAMENT OF THE WORLD

THE SUFFERINGS OF PELAGIUS BY HROTSVITHA OF GANDERSHEIM (10TH CENTURY)

IN CONTEXT

THEME
The example of Islamic Spain

WHEN AND WHERE
912–61, Spain

BEFORE
From 5th century Spain is under the control of the Visigoths, Germanic tribes who invade the region as Roman power declines.

641 Muslim armies take over Egypt, then Libya. Tunisia falls in 647, Algeria in 680, and Morocco the following year.

711 Tarek ibn Ziyad leads a Muslim Arab and Berber army across the Straits to invade southern Spain.

AFTER
1492 The last Muslim ruler of Spain, Sultan Muhammad XII, surrenders Granada to Ferdinand of Aragon and Isabella of Castile.

If the Baghdad of the early Abbasid caliphs heralded a golden age of Islamic science and culture, its peak occurred roughly a century later, not in the Middle East but in Spain.

In 711, Umayyad general Tarek ibn Ziyad had crossed from North Africa into Spain (known as Iberia to the Romans) and thus extended Islamic rule into Europe. The Muslim presence in Spain, in territories they called al-Andalus, lasted almost 800 years. In its prime—from the early 10th to early 11th century—what the West dubbed Moorish Spain was the setting for a celebrated chapter of Islamic civilization, in which Muslims, Christians, and Jews coexisted to the benefit of all.

When ex-British prime minister Tony Blair wrote in 2007, "The standard-bearers of tolerance in the early Middle Ages were far more likely to be found in Muslim lands than in Christian ones," it was to al-Andalus that he was referring.

A new capital at Cordoba

Initially, al-Andalus was a distant province of the Islamic empire ruled from Damascus. But in the 750s the

The Ishmaelite citizens call it al-Andalus, and the kingdom is called Cordoba.
Hasdai ibn Shaprut
Jewish vizier to Abd al-Rahman III

Abbasids overthrew the Umayyads and eradicated their ruling class. A prince, Abdul Rahman, escaped the slaughter and fled westward to the farthest extents of Muslim reach—al-Andalus. There he won control of the Muslim soldiers and settlers in the recently conquered territory and founded an Umayyad state, politically autonomous from the caliph in Baghdad, with the city of Cordoba as its capital.

For the next century and a half, Abdul Rahman and his descendants ruled as emirs of Cordoba with nominal control over the rest of al-Andalus. But

The conquest of Spain

The Strait of Gibraltar, the stretch of sea that separates the tip of southwestern Europe from North Africa, is named after the Rock of Gibraltar (*pictured*), which derives its name from the Arabic *Jebel Tarek*, or Tarek's Mountain.

Tarek ibn Ziyad was the Umayyad general who led an invading Islamic army across the strait in 711. Accounts disagree, but it is likely that Tarek was a former Berber slave. The Berbers were the pre-Arab inhabitants of much of North Africa, who converted to Islam in the 7th century and now made up the

bulk of Tarek's army. Of the various historical accounts of the campaign, at least one has Tarek delivering a speech upon reaching Spain, saying, "We have not come here to return. Either we shall conquer and establish ourselves here or we will perish," and setting fire to his own fleet of ships to prevent his army from retreating.

The Muslims met the Visigoth army, led by their king, Roderic, at the Battle of Guadalete in 711—the Muslims emerged victorious and Roderic lost his life.

See also: Tolerating the beliefs of others 80–81 ▪ The Umayyad and Abbasid caliphates 136–39 ▪ Islamic art and architecture 194–201 ▪ Paradise on Earth 202–03

his grandson Abdul Rahman III, who became emir in 912, not only enforced his power throughout al-Andalus but extended it into western North Africa as well. In 929, he proclaimed himself caliph of the entire Islamic world, competing for influence with the Abbasid caliph in Baghdad.

The glory of al-Andalus

Under the rule of Abdul Rahman III, his son al-Hakam II (r. 961–76), and the regent al-Mansur ibn Abi Amir (r. 981–1002), al-Andalus became a beacon of learning. The city of Cordoba came to be known as one of the leading cultural and economic centers in the Islamic world.

A German nun, Hrotsvitha of Gandersheim (c. 935–73), visiting the region in the 10th century, wrote: "The brilliant ornament of the world shone in the west, a noble city known for the military prowess that its Hispanic colonizers had brought, Cordoba was its name." In addition to paved and well-lit streets, aqueducts to supply its

In 711, Muslim armies pour across the Mediterranean onto the Iberian Peninsula to **extend the rule of Islam into Europe**.

An Umayyad noble, **Abdul Rahman escapes the Abbasids**, flees to Cordoba, and establishes a rival state—al-Andalus.

Civil war topples Cordoba, and al-Andalus splits into warring factions.

The rule of **Abdul Rahman III** ushers in a golden age for al-Andalus.

Muslim Berbers from Morocco take over Islamic Spain but again succumb to **internal conflict**.

Christian armies retake Spain and Muslims are told to convert or be expelled.

citizens with fresh water, and hundreds of bathhouses and mosques, the city had a reputed 70 libraries. The royal palace had its own library, which was said to have held about 400,000 books—this at a time when the largest library in Europe had probably no more than 400. In the words of American historian Firas Alkhateeb, Cordoba was a "city that served as a bridge between undeveloped, generally illiterate Europe and the great cultured cities of the Muslim world".

Medinat al-Zahra was the fortified palace-city built by Abdul Rahman III as the capital of his caliphate. It was sacked in 1009. Its remains are located on the outskirts of modern Cordoba.

Flight and forceps

Science and scholarship relied initially on the Arabic books that arrived from Baghdad, but, over time, this western outpost of Islam made its own significant contributions to the world's intellectual and technological development. Abbas ibn Firnas (810–87) is regarded by some as the world's first aviator. He built a rudimentary hang-glider and launched himself from the side of a mountain. Some accounts maintain he remained airborne for several minutes before he came crashing to the ground. Abu al-Qasim al-Zahrawi (c. 936–c. 1013) was a physician to Caliph al-Hakam and invented more than 100 surgical » instruments, including the forceps used in childbirth. He supposedly developed inhalant anaesthetic sponges soaked in cannabis and opium, and perfected the procedure of tracheotomies. His 30-volume *Method of Medicine* (*Kitab al-Tasrif*) was translated into Latin to serve as a primary source for European knowledge of medicine.

Cordoba was also the place of birth of Ibn Rushd (1126–98), known in the West as Averroes, a highly influential philosopher who produced commentaries on the work of the Greek philosopher Aristotle. He is considered by many to be the father of secular thought in Europe and one of the most important philosophers of all time. It was also in al-Andalus that Moses ben Maimon (1135–1204), better known as Maimonides, wrote his definitive text on Jewish law, which remains central to the subject more than eight centuries later.

Jews and Christians

That major works of Jewish culture emerged from Islamic Spain is an indication of the pluralism and religious tolerance that came to

Europe lay in mud, Cordoba's streets were paved.
Victor Robinson
The Story of Medicine (1932)

characterize al-Andalus. When Abdul Rahman III became emir of Cordoba in 912, the Jews' civic and political status improved markedly. The Muslims were considerably more accepting of Judaism than the Christian Visigoths had been. Jews were now allowed to practice their religion and live according to the laws and scriptures of their community. They benefited from sharing in much of Muslim social and economic life.

The same rights were extended to Christians. There were, however, restrictions placed on both Jews and Christians: they were subject to special taxes (*jizya*) and dress codes, and could not make public displays of their religious rituals. They could flourish but remained second-class citizens.

Within a few generations, there was a vigorous rate of conversion from Christianity to Islam. This was encouraged by Muslims with a range of civil advantages for converts, notably exemption from paying *jizya*. Intermarriage further helped to create a society of mixed ethnicity and intermingled faiths. A variety of words came into use to denote the varied permutations of society: there were terms for a Christian living under Arab rule (*mozarab*); a Muslim living under Christian rule (*mudejar*); a Christian convert to Islam (*muladi*); a Jewish convert to Christianity (*converso*); a Jew who converted but remained a secret Jew (*marrano*); and, later, a Muslim who converted to Christianity (*morisco*).

The fall of al-Andalus

The downfall of the Islamic era in Spain was eventually brought about not by Christian–Muslim warfare but through a series of brutal wars of succession for the Cordoban caliphate, beginning in 1009. These ended in 1013, when an invading Muslim Berber army from Morocco sacked Cordoba, massacring its citizens and burning the palace complex and its library to the ground.

The new rulers of al-Andalus were the Almoravids, followed by the Almohads, two dynasties that emerged from the Atlas Mountain

The wealth and learning of al-Andalus were expressed in its architecture. The Great Mosque of Cordoba, begun in 784, has a prayer hall of unsurpassed magnificence.

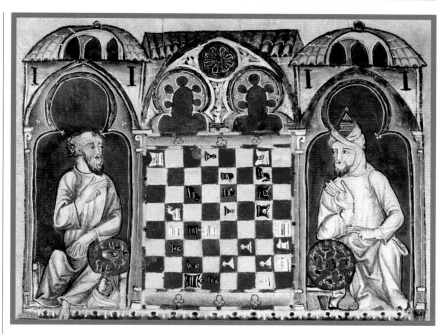

These Moors taught Spain and Italy for five centuries.
Voltaire
A Philosophical Dictionary

region of southern Morocco. Under them, the Islamic presence in Spain continued for almost another 280 years but the spirit of coexistence was diminished. Al-Andalus had disintegrated into a number of small principalities called *taifas*, ruled by politically weak emirs who competed among themselves. In time, Muslim control of Spain was also eroded by reconquest from the Christian kingdoms to the north. The last Muslim territory, the

Ferdinand II of Aragon was the king who led campaigns to reconquer Spain for the Christians. His tomb in Seville has inscriptions in Arabic, Hebrew, Latin, and Castilian.

Emirate of Granada, fell in 1492. The Christian monarchs—Isabella of Castile and Ferdinand II of Aragon—immediately ordered the expulsion of all Jews from Spain. Later, Muslims were also compelled to convert or be expelled.

The legacy of al-Andalus

The recapture of Spain gave Christian Europe access to the wealth of knowledge produced in the Islamic world. Several cities, notably Toledo, became centers of translation of Arabic texts into Latin. One of the first translations commissioned was a Castilian version of the series of animal fables known as *Kalila wa Dimna*, a book meant to instruct rulers and civil servants in making wise choices. In later centuries, when the first universities opened in the major European cities, a great part of their libraries consisted of Latin translations of Arabic texts from Cordoba.

Al-Andalus maintains a firm grip on the modern Muslim imagination. It remains a popular

A Christian and an Arab play chess in an illustration from a work made for Alfonso X (r. 1252–84) of Castile and León. Known as Alfonso the Wise, the king fostered a cosmopolitan court.

subject for literature, including verse, and movies, and is frequently invoked as an ideal for Islamic, if not global, society. ∎

For every [Christian] who can write a letter in Latin, there are a thousand who can express themselves in Arabic with elegance, and write better poems in this language than the Arabs themselves.
Alvaro of Cordoba
Christian scholar (c. 800–61)

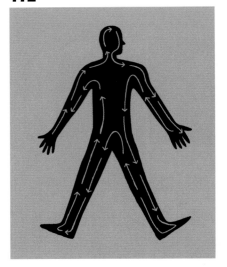

THE KNOWLEDGE OF ANYTHING IS NOT COMPLETE UNLESS IT IS KNOWN BY ITS CAUSES

IBN SINA (AVICENNA)

IN CONTEXT

THEME
Ibn Sina and the *Canon of Medicine*

WHEN AND WHERE
***c.* 1012, Bukhara**

BEFORE
9th century In Persia, al-Razi writes medical works, later translated into Latin.

***c.* 1000** In Cordoba, al-Zahrawi's encyclopedia of medicine includes the first illustrated guide to surgery.

AFTER
12th century Persian Ibn Rushd (Averroes) writes a medical encyclopedia, later known as the *Colliget* in Latin.

13th century Ibn al-Nafis from Damascus is the first to outline pulmonary circulation of the blood.

15th century Works by Ottoman physician Serefeddin Sabuncuoglu show advanced Muslim surgical procedures.

Medicine is "a science from which one learns the conditions of the human body with regard to health and the absence of health, the aim being to protect health when it exists and restore it when absent". If this sentence seems to be stating the obvious, it was much less so when it was first penned, sometime around 1012. It forms part of the opening statement of the *Qanun fi al-Tib*, or *Canon of Medicine*, written by Persian physician and philosopher Ibn Sina (980–1037).

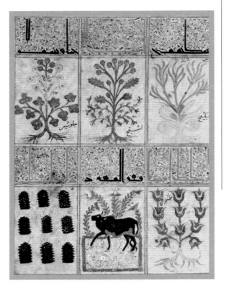

In his five-volume work, Ibn Sina sought to collate and organize all known medical knowledge, building on a well-developed legacy of Arab medicine. It was during the Islamic golden age that medicine first began to be treated as a true science, with an emphasis on empirical evidence and repeatable procedures.

Pioneering physicians
Early Islamic medicine drew on the ancient Greek theory of humors, which divides human fluids into four basic types: blood, phlegm, yellow bile, and black bile. The balance between them determines an individual's health. This theory was discredited by Muhammad ibn Zakariya al-Razi (854–925), a Persian pharmacologist and practicing clinician in a Baghdad hospital in the late 9th century. Hospitals had become widespread across the Islamic world under the Abbasid caliphs. Al-Razi introduced many progressive practices, including

Medical treatises by Muslim scholars included compendiums of plants and animals necessary for making a "theriac," an antidote composed from multiple ingredients.

See also: The House of Wisdom 150–51 ▪ The beginnings of Islamic philosophy 156–57 ▪ The example of Islamic Spain 166–71

establishing a psychiatric ward in his hospital at a time when in other parts of the world the mentally ill were regarded as possessed by demons. He ran clinical trials employing a control group, treating one set of patients with bloodletting but not the other, in order to compare the results.

In Islamic Spain, Abu al-Qasim al-Zahrawi (936–1013) compiled the *Kitab al-Tasrif* (*The Method of Medicine*), a 30-volume encyclopedia that documented accounts of his and his colleagues' experiences in treating the sick and injured, as well as the surgical

An ignorant doctor is the aide-de-camp of death.
Ibn Sina

Medicine in the Islamic world was far more advanced than the West during the Middle Ages. Muslim physicians wrote extensively on anatomy, ailments, cures, and clinical practice.

procedures and instruments used. Many of these instruments were invented by al-Zahrawi and his colleagues; he also pioneered the use of catgut for stitching up patients after an operation. The physician Abu al-Qasim Ammar ibn Ali al-Mawsili (996–1020) developed a hollow syringe to remove cataracts via suction.

Canon of Medicine

The studies and practices of these and other pioneers gave Ibn Sina a lot to draw on for his *Canon of Medicine*. It was a synthesis of all that had gone before, covering basic medical and physiological principles, and anatomy, as well as a compendium of drugs and their general properties. For diseases, one book covered the diagnosis and treatment of diseases specific to one part of the body, while another covered conditions not specific to one bodily part, such as poisonous

Ibn Sina (Avicenna)

Abu Ali al-Hussein ibn Abdullah ibn Sina was born in 980, near Bukhara, in what is now Uzbekistan. Bukhara at this time was part of the Persian Samanid Empire, and one of the intellectual centers of the Islamic world. The young Ibn Sina enjoyed a privileged upbringing. As a boy, he had memorized the entire Quran and a great deal of Persian poetry. After studying logic, philosophy, and natural sciences, he became interested in medicine and was a working doctor by the age of 18.

While his most famous work is on medicine, Ibn Sina is said to have written more than 450 works, of which roughly one third concerned philosophy, which has led to Ibn Sina being called "the most influential philosopher of the pre-modern era." He also wrote on alchemy, astronomy, geography, math, and physics, and penned poetry. He died in 1037 in Hamadan, Iran, where he is buried.

bites and obesity. The *Canon* also contained Ibn Sina's own work, such as his explanation of contagious diseases, and the suggestion that physical activity and exercise are important factors in preventing various chronic diseases.

When the work was later translated into Latin by Gerard of Cremona in the 12th century (and Ibn Sina became known in the West as Avicenna), it remained the predominant text for the teaching of medicine in Europe for the next six centuries. ▪

EVERYTHING IN THE UNIVERSE IS WITHIN YOU

JALAL AL-DIN MUHAMMAD RUMI (13TH CENTURY)

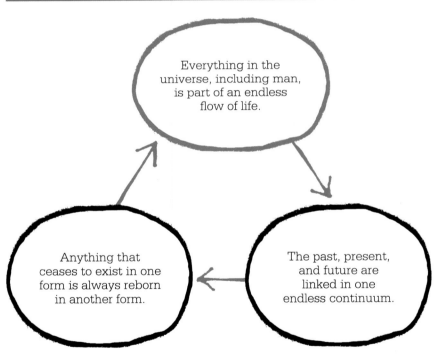

Everything in the universe, including man, is part of an endless flow of life.

The past, present, and future are linked in one endless continuum.

Anything that ceases to exist in one form is always reborn in another form.

Jalal al-Din Muhammad Rumi was born in 1207, in Balkh, Afghanistan, which was then a center of Persian culture. He was a devout Muslim, an Islamic scholar, an expert in Islamic law, a theologian, and a Sufi. He developed a version of Sufism that sought to explain the relationship of man with the divine. One of the greatest poets in the Persian language, he is also said to be the best-selling poet in the United States today.

Rumi was raised in the orthodox tradition of Islam. The family moved frequently, staying in Baghdad for a while,, before settling

See also: The emergence of Shia Islam 108–115 ▪ Sufism and the mystic tradition 140–45 ▪ The secularization of Turkey 228–31 ▪ The creation of Pakistan 242–47

in Anatolia in Turkey. Like his father, Rumi became an Islamic jurist and teacher, until in 1244 a meeting with a wandering dervish by the name of Shams al-Din Tabrizi is said to have completely changed his life. Rumi transformed himself into an ascetic devoted wholly to a life of Sufism.

The eternal flow of life

Rumi became a teacher in a Sufi order. In contrast to general Islamic practice, he placed emphasis on *dhikr*—ritual prayer or chanting—rather than rational analysis of the Quran for divine guidance, and became known for his ecstatic revelations. He believed it was his task to communicate the visions he experienced, and so he wrote them down in the form of poetry.

Central to Rumi's philosophy was the idea that the universe and everything in it is an endless flow of life, in which God is an eternal presence. Man, he believed, was a link between the past and future in a continual process of life, death, and rebirth—not as a cycle, or

I died as a mineral and became a plant, I died as a plant and rose to animal, I died as animal and I was Man.
Rumi

reincarnation, but in a progression from one form to another. Death is inevitable, but as something ceases to exist in one form, it is reborn in another. Because of this, Rumi taught, we should have no fear of death, nor should we grieve a loss. In order to ensure our growth from one form to another, however, we should strive for spiritual growth and an understanding of the divine-human relationship. Rumi believed that understanding comes from emotion, not from reason.

Among other works, toward the end of his life Rumi also wrote the *Masnavi*, a six-book epic poem, which frequently alludes to Quranic verses that offer moral lessons.

Rumi's legacy

The mystical elements of Rumi's ideas were inspirational within Sufism, and influenced mainstream Islam, too. They were also pivotal in converting much of Turkey from Orthodox Christianity to Islam. After his death in 1273, Rumi's followers founded the Mevlevi order of Sufism, which is famous for its whirling dervishes, who perform a distinctive form of *dhikr* unique to the sect.

Despite the ban imposed on the Mevlevi order by Kemal Atatürk's secular republic of Turkey in 1925, Rumi's work experienced renewed popularity in the 20th century, east and west. One of his greatest admirers was poet, philosopher, and politican Muhammad Iqbal, advisor to Muhammad Ali Jinnah, who campaigned for an Islamic state of Pakistan in the 1930s. ▪

Rumi in the West

The ideas and imagery used by Rumi in his poetry have transcended time and cultures. Their popularity is such that Madonna has recorded an English translation of one of his poems and the British band Coldplay incorporated a recitation of another poem on one of their albums. What is notable, however, is how many modern renderings of Rumi remove the Islamic and Quranic references from his verse. The most popular translators of the Persian poet's work, who include Coleman Barks and Deepak Chopra, prefer to present

Rumi as a mystical New Age poet or a writer of love poems. Love is an overwhelming part of Rumi's work, but for the poet himself this was a higher love, for God. Rumi's spirituality was undeniably of the religious kind, something that he makes explicit in the *Masnavi* when he writes: *I am the servant of the Quran as long as I have life. I am the dust on the path of [Muhammad], the chosen one. If anyone quotes anything except this from my sayings, I am quit of him and outraged by these words.*

THE EARTH IS ROUND LIKE A SPHERE

THE BOOK OF ROGER BY AL-IDRISI

IN CONTEXT

THEME
Mapping the Islamic world

WHEN AND WHERE
12th century, Sicily

BEFORE
c. **150** CE In his *Geography*, the Greek polymath Claudius Ptolemy compiles geographical coordinates that provide a basis for drawing maps.

7th century Spanish scholar Isidore of Seville provides a description of the world that inspires centuries of European maps that are largely symbolic rather than practical.

AFTER
1507 Following voyages by Christopher Columbus and others to the "New World," German cartographer Martin Waldseemüller's truly global world map is the first to use the name "America."

1569 Gerardus Mercator of Flanders (Belgium) develops a cylindrical projection that is still widely used for navigation charts and global maps.

Modern maps put north at the top, with the North Pole and Arctic on the roof of the world. But there is no actual "up" or "down" on Earth—maps simply represent how those who make them see the world. In the 15th and 16th centuries, when the empires of Spain and Portugal began to explore the world, the pioneering mapmakers were Europeans. They placed their own lands at the centre and top of the map, which resulted in north

See also: The House of Wisdom 150–51 ▪ Arabic numerals and *al-jabr* 158–61 ▪ The example of Islamic Spain 166–71 ▪ Spreading Islam through trade 182–85

Which way up?

In **ancient Egypt**, pictograms have **east at the top** because this is the direction from which the sun rises.

Early Islamic maps favored **south at the top** because for most Muslims that was the direction of Mecca.

In **early China**, the emperor lived in the north of the country, so **north was at the top of the map**.

Medieval **Christian maps** put **east at the top** because the Bible places the Garden of Eden in the east.

being "up." Before the European Age of Discovery (15th–17th centuries), the most advanced cartographers were Muslims, and for them the south was at the top.

Early Islamic maps
The earliest Muslim maps were produced in Abbasid Baghdad. The Caliph al-Mamun (r. 813–33) ordered the production of a new map of the world to update those the Arabs inherited from the Greeks. Led by al-Khwarizmi, 70 geographers and other scholars recalculated the coordinates of major cities and other landmarks, and added important Islamic cities such as Mecca and Baghdad. They corrected the Greeks' notion of the Atlantic and Indian oceans as landlocked seas, and adjusted what had previously been a gross overestimate for the length of the Mediterranean. Al-Mamun's map

no longer exists, but we know about it because scholars described some of its attributes in a compilation of geographical information called *Surat al-Ard* (*Picture of the Earth*), which was completed in 833.

The most influential of all Muslim maps appeared three centuries later. This was the work of Abu Abdullah Muhammad

al-Idrisi, more simply known as al-Idrisi. Born around 1100 in the town of Sabta (modern-day Ceuta), on the northern tip of what is now Morocco, he received his education in Cordoba, Spain, a major center of learning at the time. Al-Idrisi traveled widely as a young man, finally settling in Sicily, which was under the rule of the Christian Norman king Roger II. »

Islamic mapmakers were helped by the detailed accounts of journeys given by pilgrims making the Hajj to Mecca, as painted here by French artist Léon Belly in 1861.

Situated at the heart of the eastern Mediterranean, the Kingdom of Sicily traded with all the lands bordering this sea. Roger wanted more accurate maps, and turned to al-Idrisi for help. Although a Norman and a Christian, the king was well aware that Christian Europe's approach to mapmaking at this time was still highly symbolic. Its maps showed a circular earth composed of three continents equal in size—Asia, Africa, and Europe—separated by narrow bands of water. Jerusalem was at the center, while monsters occupied the unexplored regions.

Mapping routes

Muslims made better maps, and there were two reasons for this: economics and faith. While medieval Europe was fragmented and parochial, the Muslim world was unified by religion, culture, and a flourishing long-distance commerce. Muslim merchants and officials used so-called "road books" on their journeys that described routes and cities along the way. Such knowledge was also relevant to the Muslim populace in general, many of whom at some point in

For Muslims, pilgrimage rituals are something of the sublime.
Ibn Jubayr

their lives would make the Hajj to Mecca in Arabia. This pilgrimage could involve months of traveling by land and sea—the Islamic empire of the 12th century spread from the Atlantic coasts of Africa and Spain across to India.

The world atlas that the Sicilian king commissioned in 1138 took about 15 years to prepare. Al-Idrisi began by evaluating all available geographical knowledge, from the ancient Greeks and centuries of Islamic learning—and from contemporary sources, too. The Moroccan's assistants also asked the crews of ships in Sicily's ports about the places they had visited.

The Book of Roger

Once the research was complete, the task of mapmaking began. The resulting atlas was completed and presented to the king in 1154, just a few weeks before he died, probably of a heart attack. It was called *Nuzhat al-Mushtaq fi Ikhtiraq al-Afaq* (*For the Delight of One Who Wishes to Traverse the Regions of the World*), or more simply, *al-Kitab al-Rujari* (*The Book of Roger*).

The work contains 70 sectional maps, but its most famous element is a circular world map—presented to Roger engraved on a vast silver disc, and also included in the book.

Al-Idrisi's circular map reflected knowledge that he, like other cartographers in medieval Europe, had inherited from the Greeks. "The earth is round like a sphere, and the waters adhere to it and are maintained on it through natural equilibrium which suffers no variation," he explained in the accompanying notes to the atlas. The world, he added, remained "stable in space like the yolk in an egg". Al-Idrisi's great map, however, added an unprecedented level of cartographic detail and a very Islamic orientation.

Roger II of Sicily presided over a multicultural court mixing Eastern and Western Christians, Muslims, and Jews. This Greek-Norman-Islamic state was both powerful and prosperous.

The Hajj and beyond

Numerous accounts written by early pilgrims making the Hajj survive. One of the most famous is by Ibn Jubayr, who was born in Valencia, Spain, and served as secretary in the palace of the governor of Granada. He set off for Mecca in February 1183 and was gone for two years. During this time, he kept a meticulous account of his journey. He traveled by sea to Alexandria in Egypt and then up the Nile before cutting across the desert to the Red Sea. There he boarded a boat for Jeddah in Arabia and arrived at Mecca in August.

For his return journey, Ibn Jubayr joined a pilgrim caravan to Medina, then headed north to Baghdad, then to Damascus, and to the Mediterranean coast. He was shipwrecked off Sicily, which was ruled by the Arabic-speaking King William II, the grandson of Roger II. Ibn Jubayr finally arrived back in Spain in April 1185. The written accounts of his journeys inspired a new genre of writing, the *rihla*, or travelogue.

The Earth is essentially round but at no point is the roundness perfect.
Al-Idrisi

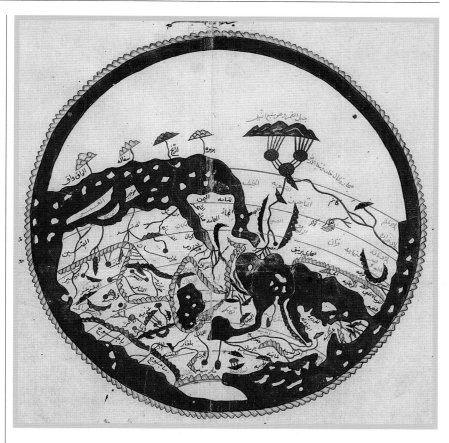

The world of al-Idrisi

Al-Idrisi's map shows a contiguous landmass surrounded by oceans. Europe up to the Arctic Circle, Asia, and North Africa are all clearly identifiable, as are numerous major rivers and lakes. The map includes the Canary Islands in the west and China in the east. The eastern Mediterranean and Arabia, the heartlands of the Islamic world, are at the center of the map. These areas, along with Asia, are depicted in some detail.

Overarching all the other continents is Africa. It includes the sources of the Nile, which were not explored by Europeans until the 19th century, but were evidently known to 12th-century Muslim travelers. Below the equator is empty, its southern temperate zone thought to be rendered unreachable by an impassable area of deadly heat. Northern Europe, which was generally an area of little interest to the Muslims, is squashed at the bottom of the map.

Seismic change

To a modern viewer, the most striking feature of al-Idrisi's map is that it is upside down, placing Africa at the top and Europe at the bottom. Islamic maps placed the south at the top because Mecca lay south of most Muslim lands but its importance demanded it be at the top of the map. In the same way, Christian maps from the medieval era put east at the top, because this is where the Bible locates the Garden of Eden, and they placed the holy city of Jerusalem at the center. The top of the world was to the east in ancient Egypt too, because this was the direction of sunrise.

Compared with the simplicity of the maps produced in Europe at this time, al-Idrisi's world map is remarkable. It was enormously influential, and for nearly three centuries afterward geographers continued to copy his work with only minor alterations.

The texts that accompanied the maps in Roger's book constitute the most elaborate description of

Of the 10 surviving manuscript copies of the *The Book of Roger*, or *Tabula Rogeriana* in Latin, this is the earliest. It is preserved in the Bibliothèque nationale de France.

the world produced in the Middle Ages. They describe the habitable world, proceeding from west to east and from south to north through 10 sections. Each section presents a general description of the region and an account of the principal cities, along with the distances between them.

Al-Idrisi went on to compose another geographical work for William I, Roger's successor. This work is said to have been even more extensive than his earlier effort, but only a few extracts have survived. ∎

MAY GOD GRANT VICTORY TO ISLAM
NUR AL-DIN (12TH CENTURY)

For Muslims, Jerusalem is the holy city of all of the prophets of Islam who came before Muhammad. As such, it was the first *qibla*, the place to which prayers are directed. The Prophet Muhammad is reported to have said, "Do not prepare yourself for a journey except to three mosques: Masjid al-Haram [Mecca], the Mosque of Aqsa [Jerusalem] and my mosque [Medina]." Thus, Jerusalem is confirmed as one of the three holiest cities for Muslims. Just six years after the death of the Prophet, in 638, Jerusalem was conquered by the Muslim armies of the caliph Umar ibn al-Khattab.

The First Crusade
On July 15, 1099, some 15,000 Christian soldiers surged into Jerusalem following a month-long siege. The victorious "crusaders"

Christian forces attempt to **capture Muslim territory** all around the Mediterranean.

Pope Urban II calls on **Christian soldiers** to launch a **holy war** to capture Jerusalem.

Crusading armies **capture Jerusalem** and establish **four Christian states** in Muslim lands.

Salah al-Din retakes Jerusalem for Islam and drives the Crusaders out of the Holy Land.

Western Christian **appropriation of Muslim lands** resumes with **colonization by European nations**.

See also: The early life of Muhammad 22–27 ▪ Islam in Europe 210–15 ▪ The rise of political Islam 238–41

slaughtered Muslim defenders and Jews alike in a bloody act that marked the beginning of 200 years of intermittent Muslim–Christian warfare in Muslim lands.

The campaign originated in a speech given by Pope Urban II in 1095 in Clermont, France. In it, he announced that: "A race absolutely alien to God has invaded the land of the Christians." The pope was referring to the Seljuk Turks, whose recent defeat of the Byzantines at Manzikert threatened to push the frontiers of Christianity back to the gates of Constantinople, but his goal was to capture Jerusalem, site of the tomb of Jesus Christ. Christian warriors rallied to the cause, eager to gain both salvation and plunder by joining a so-called "holy war" in God's name.

Enemies and friends

The Crusaders also captured the cities of Edessa, Antioch, and Tripoli, which, along with Jerusalem, became Christian city-states. Seljuk ruler Nur al-Din's counteroffensive from Damascus paved the way for

The 1099 siege of Jerusalem saw the First Crusaders capture the Holy City from Egypt's Fatimid Caliphate. It would be almost 200 years before the Muslims recaptured it.

Salah al-Din (Saladin), Sultan of Egypt and Syria, who retook Jerusalem in 1187. Yet the Christians maintained a presence in Muslim lands until they were ejected from their final stronghold of Acre in 1291.

The Muslims considered the Europeans, or *afranj* (from Franks, medieval rulers of most of Western Europe), barbarians. A Muslim noble from northern Syria, Usama ibn Munqidh (1095–1188), wrote about the *afranj* in his *Kitab al-Itibar* (*The Book of Learning by Example*). He railed against the invaders with expressions such as *qabbahum Allah* ("May God make them ugly") and labeled them *shayatin* ("devils"). To him, they were intellectually inferior, largely illiterate, and like beasts, with no virtues except courage. He was also appalled by the Europeans' worship of God as a young child (Jesus).

Yet despite cursing the *afranj*, ibn Munqidh made friends among them. One Crusader offered to take his son back to Europe, to teach him chivalry—a thought that filled the Muslim with horror.

Muslim warlords sometimes aligned themselves both politically and militarily with Crusaders against other Muslims in struggles for regional power. Trade continued between Muslims and Christians, as did mixed marriages. The Crusades also brought Muslim learning into Europe, as some of the *afranj* took home Islamic knowledge of science, mathematics, medicine, and philosophy. ▪

The ongoing crusade

Some Muslim historians do not regard the Crusades as beginning with Pope Urban II's 1095 speech and ending with the 1291 fall of Acre. They see the events that Western historians call the Crusades as one chapter in a continuing pattern of Western aggression against the Muslim world—including earlier Christian conquests of Islamic Spain and the Norman seizure of Sicily in the 11th century.

In the eyes of many Muslim historians, the Western threat did not end until the mid-15th century, when the Ottomans conquered Constantinople. There is also a view that later European colonial conquests of Muslim lands—starting with the French invasion of Egypt in 1798 and occupation of Algeria in 1830—were all part of a continuing crusading mindset. In the 1960s, the Egyptian Islamic theorist Sayyid Qutb claimed that "the Crusader spirit runs in the blood of all Westerners."

We never felt secure on account of the Franks, whose territory was adjacent to ours.
Usama ibn Munqidh

GOD OPENED THE HEART OF THE KING TO ISLAM

THE TRAVELS, IBN BATTUTA (14TH CENTURY)

IN CONTEXT

THEME
Spreading Islam through trade

WHEN AND WHERE
14th century, across the Islamic world

BEFORE
7th century According to Islamic tradition, Muslims reach as far as Ethiopia in the lifetime of Muhammad.

AFTER
1453 Following the Ottoman conquest of Constantinople, the city on the Bosphorus becomes the great trading hub of the Islamic world.

17th century The Ottomans dominate trade in Southeast Asia; by the time Europeans arrive in the 17th century, the region up to New Guinea is overwhelmingly Muslim.

The initial expansion of Islam was by conquest. During the 7th century, the followers of Muhammad spread quickly north and west through the territories of the Byzantine Empire. By the 9th century, the Islamic domain extended into Persia and Central Asia. Meanwhile, the message of the Prophet was traveling much greater distances across the world, carried not by armies and swords but by merchant ships and camel caravans.

Islam in Africa

Africa did not have to wait long to be exposed to Islam. While Muhammad was still alive, a group

See also: Mapping the Islamic world 176–79 ▪ The caliphate of the Ottoman Empire 186–89 ▪ Islam in Europe 210–15 ▪ Islam in Africa 278–79

From **Southeast Asia**, Muslim traders brought back **spices**, including cinnamon, pepper, cloves, and nutmeg. They exported all manner of goods, as well as their religion of Islam.

Muslim caravans traversed the **Silk Road** through Central Asia to **China** to bring back fine silks and other textiles, and technologies such as paper.

Major **Muslim trading cities** in Arabia and the eastern Mediterranean included Mecca, Medina, Baghdad, Damascus, and Cairo.

Europeans imported **mainly luxury goods** from the Islamic world, notably cotton, silk, perfumes, and exotic fruits and spices. They sent back lumber, metals, and wool.

In **East Africa**, the Muslims sent caravans of salt south, and in return received **gold and slaves**.

Ibn Battuta

At the age of 21, Ibn Battuta (1304–68/9) set out from his home city of Tangier on the Hajj, with the intention of studying Islamic law along the way. He spent most of the next 29 years on his travels, during which time he covered some 75,000 miles (120,700 km), visiting the equivalent of 44 modern-day countries. In that time, he served as an Islamic judge in India; met the Christian emperor in the city of Constantinople; was robbed, kidnapped, and shipwrecked; got married and divorced as many as 10 times; and fathered numerous children.

As a result of Islamic expansion, first by conquest and later by trade, the majority of countries he visited were under Muslim rule and belonged to the *dar al-Islam*, or World of Islam. Even those that were not Islamic had small Muslim communities. "I set out alone," he later wrote, "having neither fellow-traveler in whose companionship I might find cheer, nor caravan whose party I might join." But the fact is, the great wanderer would seldom have been far from his religious fellows on his travels.

of his followers fled persecution in Mecca to settle in what is now Ethiopia. Later, merchants from Arabia began to settle in cities along the East African coast—excavations in Kenya have revealed mosques that date as far back as the 10th century.

From the coasts of North Africa, Islam extended south into West Africa. Trade routes crossed the Sahara Desert, linking the Arabs of the north with the Africans who lived along the Niger river. Gold and slaves went north; salt and Islam came south. The Muslim religion gradually influenced the local culture—so much so, that by the 12th century, Mali had become the first Muslim kingdom of West Africa. When its king, Mansa Musa, made a pilgrimage to Mecca in »

The king of Mali, Mansa Musa, appears in the *Catalan Atlas* (1375) wearing a golden crown and holding a golden disc as an indication of the vast wealth of his African empire.

1324, he and his entourage of 8,000 courtiers reputedly spent so freely and gave out so much in alms along the way that the value of gold in Egypt and Arabia depreciated for the next 12 years. Returning to Mali, Mansa Musa took back with him some of the finest artisans, scientists, and Islamic scholars, and created a new hub of research and learning in Timbuktu, where he built mosques and madrasas.

The renowned Muslim traveler Ibn Battuta visited both East and West Africa in the 14th century. He remarked on the religious zeal of the people, who saw Islam not as a religion imposed on them but as a native African religion.

By sea to Asia

In 1343, Ibn Battuta visited the Maldive Islands in the Indian Ocean, where, by contrast, the formerly Buddhist population only recently had been converted to Islam. This happened, according to the traveler's account, as the result of the work of a North African missionary. "He stayed amongst them," writes Ibn Battuta, "and God opened the heart of the king to Islam and he accepted it before the end of the month."

Islam provided a glue that bound together trading routes from East Africa to Arabia, India, and beyond. Muslim traders carried their religion as well as goods to the ports along the Indian Ocean coast and onward to Southeast Asia— soon followed by missionaries, often Sufis. The first Muslim state in Southeast Asia was in northern

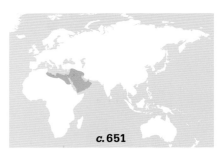

c. 651

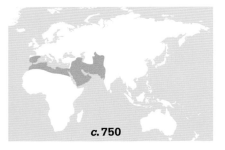

c. 750

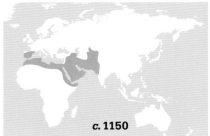

c. 1150

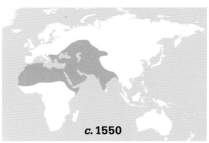

c. 1550

From the Arabian Peninsula the followers of Islam first spread their religion by conquest around the eastern Mediterranean and into Persia. Later, traders carried the religion south into Africa, and east into the islands of the Indian Ocean and Southeast Asia.

Sumatra (Aceh). When Italian merchant, explorer, and writer Marco Polo traveled through Asia in the 13th century, he noted the Sumatrans' adherence to the "Law of Mahommet." Islam soon spread eastward throughout the Malay Archipelago, one island at a time, and from there to Indonesia, the Philippines, and beyond.

Silk and spice routes

The Caliph Uthman ibn Affan sent an ambassador to the Tang Dynasty of China as early as 650. Islamic tradition has it that the emperor who received the envoy ordered a mosque built in honor of Muhammad, although there is no historical evidence for this. What is certain is that in the following centuries, trade between the Muslim dynasties in Damascus and Baghdad and the Chinese flourished along the mercantile Central Asian superhighway that was the Silk Road. But other than in the most westerly regions of the country, where the Silk Road terminated, Islam failed to take root in China. The Chinese were unsusceptible to the new religion. While Muslims did settle in

> If Paradise be on this earth, Damascus it is, and none but she.
> **Ibn Battuta**

Chinese cities, particularly ports on the southeastern seaboard, they remained in isolated communities.

Venice and the Mamluks

Europe also remained resistant to Islam while enjoying strong trading links with the Muslim world. The Muslims controlled the eastern Mediterranean, which was the nexus from which ancient trading networks stretching west to Europe and east into Asia met. The Muslims were the middlemen, organizing the transit and exchange of precious commodities. In Europe, the main destination for

luxury imports from the East was Italy. The city-states of Venice, Florence, and Genoa, which controlled maritime trade in the Mediterranean, formed close ties to Egypt, Syria, and other areas along the eastern Mediterranean shore from the 13th century onward.

Venice, in particular, became Christian Europe's most important interface with the Muslim lands of the Near East. Italian merchants did business predominantly with the citizens of Mamluk Egypt and Syria. Islamic arts and crafts flourished under this dynasty, and a dazzling array of goods—textiles, carpets, inlaid metalwork, precious stones, glass, porcelain, as well as paper—traveled in both directions. The Mamluks had a direct artistic influence on the fashions and architecture of Venice, whose artisans adapted and imitated the Muslims' tastes and techniques. Evidence of this remains in the polychromatic stonework and Arabesques that beautify much Venetian architecture until today.

While Europe held firm against the spread of Islam as a religion, it was happy to benefit from other bounties of the Islamic world. ∎

> They have converted the natives to the Law of Mahommet.
> **Marco Polo**

The Venetians became rich from trade with the Islamic world and were inspired by its cities, like Damascus here, to Orientalize their own buildings.

PUT ON THE HOLY MANTLE AND PRAY TO GOD

HOCA SALEDDIN EFENDI (1596)

IN CONTEXT

THEME
The caliphate of the Ottoman Empire

WHERE AND WHEN
1517–1923

BEFORE
1258 The Mongols sack Baghdad and execute the Abbasid caliph, bringing the caliphate era to an end.

1299 Osman I founds the Ottoman dynasty.

1453 Mehmet II captures Constantinople, establishing the Ottomans as the greatest power in the Muslim world.

AFTER
1952 In Jerusalem, Islamist party Hizb ut-Tahrir argues for the revival of the caliphate to unify all Muslims.

2014 So-called Islamic State (ISIS) proclaims itself as a new caliphate.

When Baghdad was finally taken by the Mongols in 1258, it marked the end of the Abbasid Caliphate. There was a shadow Abbasid Caliphate continuing in Cairo, Egypt, but these caliphs held no power and were token spiritual symbols serving the ruling Mamluk sultans only. After the Ottoman sultan Selim the Grim's conquest of Egypt in 1517, the shadow caliphate ended, and the sultan in Constantinople became caliph. In defeating the Mamluks, the Ottomans added not only Egypt to their empire, but also Syria and Arabia, including the holy cities of Mecca and Medina. From being an empire on the fringes of

See also: A successor to the Prophet Muhammad 102–03 ▪ The rightly guided caliphs 104–07 ▪ The Umayyad and Abbasid caliphates 136–39 ▪ Islam in Europe 210–15 ▪ The secularization of Turkey 228–31

On the death of the Prophet Muhammad in 632, a successor, or **caliph**, is nominated to succeed him as **leader of the *umma*, or Muslim community**.

The position of **caliph exists under Egypt's Mamluk sultans** as a purely ceremonial position with **no authority**.

The Ottoman sultan also takes the title of caliph and presents himself as **spiritual and political leader of the Islamic world**.

The **Ottomans defeat the Mamluks** and add Egypt, Syria, and Arabia to their empire.

the Islamic world, centered on Turkish Anatolia, the Ottomans now commanded most of the traditional lands of Islam. They could rightly claim to be heirs to the caliphate, and under them the title of caliph regained its old authority.

The rise of the Ottomans

The Ottoman dynasty was named for its founder, Osman I (r. 1299–1324), who led his Turkic tribesmen out of what is now known as Central Asia, to conquer much of the region now called Turkey. His successors extended this empire to Greece in 1345, and Serbia in 1389. Mehmet II (who ruled twice, from 1444–46 and again from 1451–81) conquered Constantinople in 1453, something that had first been attempted by the Umayyad caliphs seven centuries earlier, ending the millennium-old Byzantine Empire.

This map of Istanbul, capital of the Ottoman Empire, appears in a miniature by soldier-cartographer Matrakçi Nasuh from his 1537 account of Süleyman's campaign in Iran and Iraq.

Mehmet, whose achievements earned him the epithet "Mehmet the Conqueror," made Constantinople his capital and renamed it Istanbul. Signaling Muslim supremacy, Mehmet had the city's Haghia Sophia, one of the greatest cathedrals in Christendom, turned

into a mosque. Next to it he built a large madrasa (Islamic seminary) and a cluster of other Islamic institutions. In 1463, the new Fatih (or Conqueror's) Mosque, a huge monument to victory, was built on the site of the crumbling Church of the Apostles. Mehmet »

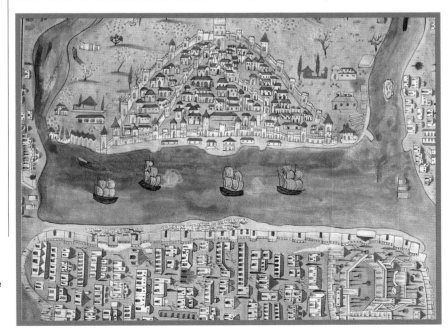

also began construction of the Topkapi Palace, a complex of public and private courtyards, gardens, halls, pavilions, barracks, harems, and imperial quarters on a promontory overlooking the city and Bosphorus Strait below. To promote the revival of the city, the sultan encouraged the elite to invest and build, and forcibly resettled people in his new capital, which became a vital trading port between East and West.

Mehmet spent most of his 30-year reign on campaigning, consolidating, and expanding Ottoman domains, unifying Anatolia (now central Turkey) and conquering southeast Europe as far west as Bosnia.

Governing the empire

To control their vast territory, the Ottomans evolved a strong system of government that combined local administration with central control. The sultan, whose brothers were customarily murdered at his accession to avoid rival claims, was supreme ruler, but a council of advisors—and later his deputy, the

Süleyman I (1494–1566) reigned for more than 45 years. The 10th ruler of the House of Osman, he was known locally as *Kanuni* ("the Lawgiver"), due to his important legal reforms.

grand vizier—ruled on the sultan's behalf. They appointed regional military governors (*beys*), with local councils to keep the *beys* in check.

The Ottoman army was also crucial to the empire's success. It was technologically advanced—employing cannon from the siege of Constantinople onward—and tactically sophisticated. Its high-

speed cavalry units could turn what looked like a retreat into a devastatingly effective flanking attack, surrounding the enemy in a crescent formation that would take them by surprise.

The Janissaries

At the heart of the army were the Janissaries, a unit of infantry that began as the imperial guard and expanded to become the most feared elite force of the period. Initially, the unit was made up of men who, as children, had been abducted from Christian families in the Balkans. Under the *devsirme* system, which was also known as the "blood tax," boys ages from eight to 18 were taken by the Ottoman military, converted to Islam (despite the Quran's prohibition on forced conversion), and sent to live with Turkish families, where they learned the Turkish language and customs. They were then given rigorous military training, and any who showed particular talent were selected for specialized roles ranging from archers to engineers.

Worship of God is the highest throne, the happiest of all estates.
Süleyman I

Istanbul's Süleymaniye Mosque was commissioned by Süleyman I. Inaugurated in 1557, its soaring dimensions and fine decoration testify to the might of the Ottoman Empire.

We Turks are
faithful Muslims.
Mehmet II

To ensure their loyalty to the sultan alone, Janissaries were not permitted to marry until they retired from duty, but they received special benefits and privileges. Although they constituted only a small proportion of the Ottoman army, they had a leading role and played a key part in many victories, including at Constantinople and in Egypt.

Ottoman heyday

The empire reached its economic, military, and cultural peak under the sultan Süleyman I (r. 1520–66). Known as Süleyman the Magnificent, he forged an alliance with the French against the Hapsburg rulers of the Holy Roman Empire, and signed a treaty with the Safavids of Persia that divided Armenia and Georgia between the two powers. He conquered much of Hungary and even laid siege to Vienna in 1529, although he did not succeed in taking it.

The Ottomans took their Islamic faith to their conquered territories, building mosques everywhere— and with the mosques came Islamic scholarship and education.

In the past, several Muslim states had made the claim to be caliphates—including the Fatimids of Egypt (909–1171), the Umayyads of Cordoba (929–1031), and the Almohads in Morocco (1121–1269)—

but, unlike the Ottomans, none fitted the criteria of ruling the majority of Muslims and having control of the holy cities of Mecca and Medina.

Leaders of Muslims

From the time of the capture of Egypt in 1517 until World War I in 1914–18, it was the Ottomans who protected the great annual Hajj caravans setting out from Damascus and Cairo against bandits, and who provided the *kiswa* each year, the ornate cloth that covered the Kaaba. This "sponsorship" of the Hajj would have done much to encourage all Muslims to regard the Ottomans as leaders of the Islamic world.

Some questioned the legitimacy of a Turkish caliphate on the grounds that only a member of the Prophet's Quraysh tribe could be caliph. In the mid-16th century, the Ottoman grand vizier Lutfi Pasha responded in a pamphlet that argued that the only qualifications for the office were power and competence, and that inheritance or kinship had nothing to do with it.

The legitimacy of the Ottoman caliphs was underscored by the possession of relics said to have belonged to the Prophet. These included a roughly woven mantle, the *Burda*. Sultan Mehmet III (r. 1596–1603) took this talismanic item on campaign in Hungary. At one point, when it looked as if his army was losing a battle, a courtier named Saadeddin told the sultan, "Put on the Holy Mantle and pray to God." The sultan did so and the battle was turned around.

The last of the caliphs

In the 18th century, with the Ottoman Empire increasingly threatened by the military might of

Ottoman artisans excelled in ceramics, carpet-weaving, and textiles, notably silk, such as this cloth, woven with gold and silver threads, and rich in motifs such as flowers and arabesques.

the European powers, the sultans embraced the idea of the caliphate to prop up their authority. When Abdul Hamid II took the throne in 1876, he was obliged by reformists to agree to a parliamentary system of government. As compensation for his loss of temporal power, a new constitution reasserted the sultan's role as caliph and leader of all Muslims.

This was not to last. With defeat in World War I, the Ottoman Empire came to an end and was replaced by Mustafa Kemal Atatürk's new Republic of Turkey in 1923. The role of caliph and caliphate was abolished the following year. ∎

THE FIRST THING GOD CREATED WAS THE PEN

PROPHET MUHAMMAD

IN CONTEXT

THEME
The divine art of Islamic calligraphy

WHEN AND WHERE
10th century, Baghdad

BEFORE
***c.* 150 BCE** The Nabataeans, whose capital is Petra (in modern-day Jordan), develop an alphabet. Used for writing the Aramaic language, it has 22 letters, all representing consonants, and is written from right to left.

3rd to 5th centuries CE
Nabataean Aramaic script develops into a recognizably Arabic form.

7th century After the fall of the Sasanian Empire, the Persians adopt Arabic script.

AFTER
1514 The first book printed in Arabic is a translation of the Christian devotional *Book of Hours* and is printed in Italy.

alligraphy is an enormously prestigious art in Islamic culture. The Quran is the word of God, which was delivered to Muhammad and recited by early Muslims. Following the death of Muhammad, it was written down. The first printed Quran was made in the 16th century, so for 900 years all Qurans were handwritten.

Copying the Quran's text was considered an act of devotion. As calligraphy was equated with glorifying the language of the Quran, it was seen as beautifying the unseen face of God. Not all Arabic calligraphy was religious in content, but the Arabic language was the language God chose for His revelation, and so Arabic is inextricably linked with Islam.

Scribes sought to make the word of God appear authoritative yet beautiful. To this end, they developed a stylized, rectilinear script that became known as *kufic*. It was in the city of Kufa in Iraq, an early center of Islamic culture, that the new script emerged, late in the 7th century.

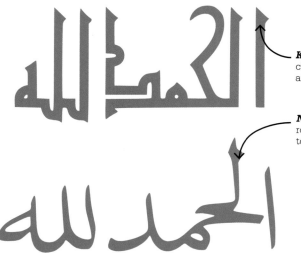

Kufic script is characterized by angular foms

Naskh is more rounded, and easier to write and read

Alhamdulillah
("Thank God") written in two different scripts illustrates the stylistic diversity of Arabic calligraphy.

See also: Depicting the Prophet 58–59 ▪ Compiling the Quran 64–69 ▪ The composition of the Quran 70–75 ▪ Islamic art and architecture 194–201

> If someone, whether he can read or not, sees good writing, he likes to enjoy the sight of it.
> **Qadi Ahmed**
> *"Calligraphers and Painters," 1606*

The style spawned many variants but all are recognizably *kufic* from their sharp angles and severely vertical and horizontal lines. For about 300 years, *kufic* was considered the only suitable script in which to write the Quran. It was used, for example, on the first surviving monument of Islamic architecture, the Dome of the Rock in Jerusalem (completed in 691–92), and on the earliest Islamic coins, minted during the reigns of the Rashidun caliphs (632–61).

The Six Styles

A civil servant at the Abbasid court in Baghdad, Ibn Muqla (886–940) is often cited as the inventor of *naskh*, a rounded script, easy to write and highly legible, which replaced the angular *kufic* as the standard of Islamic calligraphy. It was said of him, "He is a prophet in the field of handwriting. It was poured upon his hand, even as it was revealed to the bees to make their honey-cell hexagonal."

Ibn Muqlah is also credited with creating five more scripts, which, together with *naskh*, are known as the Six Styles (*aqlam al-sitta*) of classical Islamic calligraphy.

A profusion of calligraphy

Given Islam's general prohibition of figurative representation, calligraphers have traditionally been the most highly regarded artists in Islamic culture. Techniques were passed on from master to student, often within the same family. To become a master calligrapher, a student had to train for years by copying models to perfect his skills.

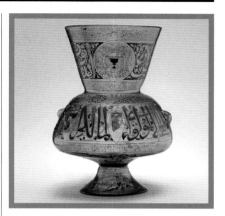

Islamic calligraphy, as on this mosque lamp, reflects the idea that God speaks to man through the Arabic language, whether spoken or written.

The calligrapher's pen, the *qalam*, was made of dried reed or bamboo, and dipped in ink. The introduction of paper from China in the 9th century allowed Muslim scribes to create many more books than their counterparts in Europe, who were still using expensive parchment.

Calligraphy appeared on sacred and secular objects in almost every medium—stone, stucco, ceramics, glass, jewelry, embroidery, carpets, woodcarving, and metalwork. It can provide valuable information about the object it decorates, especially in architecture, where in addition to Quranic verses, the lettering spells out the names of patrons and dates.

The practice of calligraphy in the Islamic world continues. New generations of artists continually reinvent the tradition, exchanging age-old media such as pen and paper for new techniques such as graffiti and digital graphics. Muslims today remain very much aware that the Arabic letters— the letters of the Quran—are precious heirlooms. ▪

Arabic script

Arabic is the second most widely used writing system in the world, based on the number of countries using it. The script is written from right to left. It has 28 letters, but many of them are differentiated by dots, so there are in fact only 18 letter forms for the 28 sounds. There are only letters for three vowels, and most vowel sounds are indicated by a system of diacritical marks.

Arabic letters have no capital forms, but their form changes depending on their position in the word (at the beginning, middle, or end, or placed on their own). In Latin-based scripts (such as French and English), letters are connected in handwriting or calligraphy, and unconnected when they are printed, but in Arabic it depends on the letters. All letters can connect to the preceding letter, but some letters do not connect to the letter that follows. A poetic tradition says these are "angelic letters," because they are attached to their origin (God) but detached from what follows (the world).

THE SHADOW OF GOD ON EARTH
SHAH ISMAIL (16TH CENTURY)

I n 1500, the 13-year-old Ismail became head of the Safaviyya Sufi order in Azerbaijan, and set out to avenge his father, who had been killed by the Turkic tribes that ruled most of Iran.

The following year, Ismail's followers captured Tabriz and took power in Iran. Ismail made Tabriz his capital and proclaimed himself shah (king), founding the Safavid dynasty that would rule until 1722. He also declared Twelver Shiism as the official religion of his new empire, thus changing the course of Islamic history.

The hidden Mahdi

Twelver Shiism was a major branch of Shia Islam that had never held wide-ranging political power. Its adherents held that no rule could be legitimate in the absence of the twelfth, "Hidden Imam," the Mahdi, who is concealed but will one day return to bring justice and peace to the world.

Before Ismail, most Shia had been Arabs and most Muslims in non-Arab Iran were Sunni. Ismail claimed descent from Ali, the First Imam, and presented himself as the hidden Mahdi of the Twelvers and the so-called "Shadow of God on

My name is Shah Ismail.
I am God's mystery.
Shah Ismail

Earth." He also wrote poetry that heralded his credentials: *My mother is Fatima, my father Ali; I am one of the twelve imams. I took back my father's blood from Yazid.* (Yazid was the Sunni Umayyad caliph who killed Ali's son Hussein at the Battle of Kerbala in 680.)

Ismail set about eliminating Sunnism in Iran. Sunni leaders were either executed or deported. In their place, religious scholars were invited from Arab centers of Twelver scholarship to set up Shia schools in Iran. Ismail's war against Sunnism extended beyond Iran. In 1510, he defeated the Sunni Uzbeks in Khorasan, a region covering what is now northeastern Iran and parts of Central Asia and Afghanistan.

See also: The rightly guided caliphs 104–07 ▪ The emergence of Shia Islam 108–15 ▪ Sufism and the mystic tradition 140–45 ▪ The Iranian revolution 248–51 ▪ Sunni and Shia in the modern Middle East 270–71

Shah Abbas's Isfahan was graced with public squares and gardens, and a profusion of beautiful, turquoise-tiled mosques and palaces.

He also campaigned against the Ottomans but was defeated by Sultan Selim I at the Battle of Chaldiran in 1514 and died in 1524. By the late 16th century, however, almost all Iranians were Shia, as they are to this day.

Philosophy and suppression

Under Ismail's great-grandson, Shah Abbas I (r. 1588–1629), the Safavid Empire reached its zenith. Abbas achieved decisive victories over the Ottomans and entered into diplomatic accords with European powers to keep Constantinople in check. His armies extended Safavid rule west into Iraq, south to the Indus, and north into the Caucasus.

Abbas also moved the Safavid capital to the city of Isfahan, where culture and intellectual activity flourished. Although he maintained the dominance of the Shia *ulema*—the "learned ones," a powerful class

who had an iron grip on theology and canon law—Islamic philosophy flourished under his rule, producing several great thinkers who made up what is now referred to as the School of Isfahan.

After Abbas, there was a shift away from the philosophical to a more literal reading of Shiism. A leading figure in this realignment was Muhammad Baqir Majlisi (1627–99). An influential cleric, Majlisi

outlawed Sufis as heretics, and suppressed the teaching of Islamic philosophy. Instead, he promoted the strict observance of mourning rituals in honor of Imam Hussein at Kerbala, and regular visits to the shrines of the Imams and their relatives in the shrine cities of Najaf and Kerbala in Iraq, and Mashhad and Qom in Iran. These remain notable features of the Iranian Islamic tradition today. ▪

Shia shrines

During the Safavid era, the Ottomans controlled Mecca and Medina, and so Shah Abbas promoted Mashhad in Iran as an alternative pilgrimage. The Shrine of Imam Reza at Mashhad (shown left) contains the tomb of Ali ibn Musa al-Reza (also known as Ali al-Rida), the eighth Twelver Shia Imam, and a direct descendant of the Prophet Muhammad. He died in 818 in a village near Mashhad. Thought to have been poisoned, al-Reza is revered as a martyr. Since he is the only Shia Imam buried in Iran, his tomb is extremely important to Shia

Iranians. On one occasion Shah Abbas I walked on foot from Isfahan to Mashhad in 28 days to show his devotion. He suggested this was equivalent to completing the Hajj.

Other sites holy to Shia Muslims include the Imam Ali Mosque in Najaf in Iraq, burial place of the first Shia Imam; the Imam Hussein Shrine in Kerbala, Iraq, burial place of the third Shia Imam; and the Sayyida Zeinab Mosque in Damascus, burial place of Zeinab, daughter of Ali and Fatima and thus the granddaughter of Muhammad.

GOD IS BEAUTIFUL

BEAUTIFUL

AND HE LOVES BEAUTY

THE PROPHET MUHAMMAD

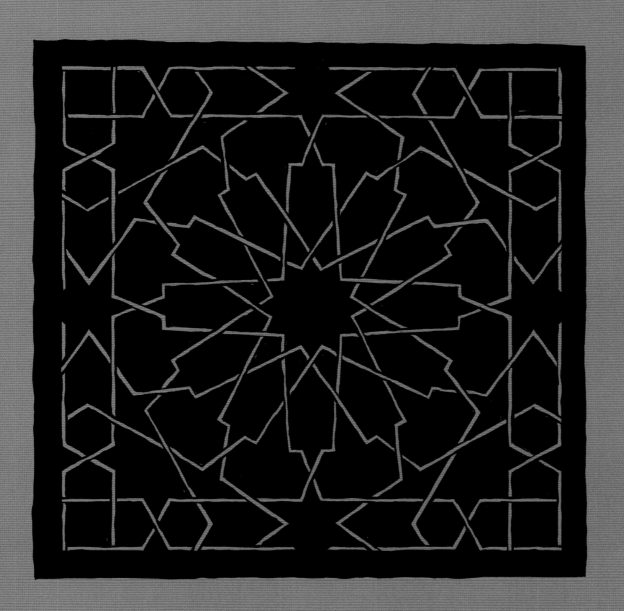

IN CONTEXT

THEME
Islamic art and architecture

WHEN AND WHERE
From 692, Islamic world

BEFORE
1st century CE The Romans extend their rule into the Near East, building temples at sites such as Jerash, in what is now Jordan, and Palmyra, in Syria.

4th century Successors to the Romans and recent converts to Christianity, the Byzantines start building churches in places of significance to the Christian story, in Jerusalem and throughout the Near East and in Egypt.

AFTER
2016 Architects Glenn Murcutt and Hakan Elevli design a strikingly modernist mosque at the Australian Islamic Center in Melbourne.

During its golden age, Islam was spread across regions as geographically distant and culturally diverse as the Iberian Peninsula, the deserts of North Africa and Arabia, and the steppes of Central Asia. Even so, it is still possible to talk about a common art and architecture of Islam. Art historians point to an extraordinary consistency of shared styles and motifs found across all of these regions—styles and motifs that were quite distinct from anything in Western artistic traditions.

The most significant of these characteristics is the general absence of people or animals (with a few notable exceptions). This trait distinguishes it not only from the Christian aesthetic, where the human being is arguably the artist's major subject, but also from the art of earlier times—of ancient Egypt, Mesopotamia, Greece, and Rome. In contrast, Islamic art favors pattern, both natural and

Exquisite blue, white, and gold tiling adorns the facade of the Dome of the Rock in Jerusalem. This was added in the 16th century by Süleyman I, replacing the original exterior mosaics.

> The principle which dominates over Islamic art and the philosophy of beauty which governs it, comes directly from the Quran and *hadith*.
> **Sayyid Hussein Nasr**
> *Islamic philosopher (b.1933)*

flowing (or "arabesque") and geometric. In the Western tradition pattern is applied sparingly; in Islam it is ubiquitous, covering every surface.

Another hallmark of the Islamic style is calligraphy, both religious and non-religious. Considered the highest of art forms, it appears on buildings and on many other decorative objects. This is in marked contrast with the West, where calligraphy is largely confined to manuscripts.

See also: Depicting the Prophet 58–59 ▪ An Islamic place of worship 98–101 ▪ The Umayyad and Abbasid caliphates 136–39 ▪ The divine art of Islamic calligraphy 190–91

Islamic decorative styles

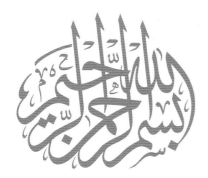

Calligraphy gives visible form to the revealed word of the Quran, and is therefore considered the most noble of the arts. It is widely used in the decoration of buildings.

Geometric patterns convey a certain quality of "oneness." They subsume the creativity of the artisan to a greater overall purpose.

Arabesque designs—repeating, interlacing patterns with foliate or floral motifs—are ubiquitous in Islam. They are a reflection of the presence of God in the natural world.

No early artist, architect, or artisan is likely to have thought of their work as "Islamic." They worked within local, regional, and national traditions. The idea of a universal Islamic style is an invention of 19th-century Western scholars. However, it is evident that Islam did foster a distinctive artistic language. Iranian philosopher Sayyid Hussein Nasr makes the claim that all Islamic art is a physical expression of "the inner reality that is Islam."

Borrowed beginnings

The art and architecture of early Islam was marked by the influence of other, pre-Islamic artistic traditions. This included Byzantine mosaic work: the two oldest surviving Islamic monuments, the Dome of the Rock in Jerusalem (completed in 692) and the Great Mosque of Damascus (715), both feature dazzling mosaics, crafted by artisans who were probably converts to Islam but who were also steeped in Byzantine tradition. Other influences were ancient Greek and Roman buildings, from which Muslim builders took—often quite literally—elements such as columns and capitals.

The Umayyads (661–750), the builders of the Dome of the Rock and the Great Mosque, also constructed many small palaces in the desert. The remains of one of these, Mshatta, 18 miles (30 km) south of Amman in Jordan, show clear Coptic (Egyptian Christian) and Sasanian (Persian) motifs in the form of carved figures and animals. But one section has no figures, and is carved only with floral designs. Historians speculate that this may have been the wall surrounding the palace's mosque, where artisans were instructed not to include any idolatrous representations.

Motifs and meaning

The Mshatta ruins represent an early example of the foliate scrollwork sometimes known as arabesque, which became one of the hallmarks of Islamic art. »

Kasr Mshatta was commissioned by Umayyad caliph al-Walid II (r. 743–44). It was abandoned before it was fully completed, but the palace's decoration is of great interest to historians.

The dome on the mosque of the Mamluk sultan Qaitbay in Cairo is a high point of stone carving, combining a vine-and-leaf motif with a repeating geometric star-shaped pattern.

It was probably inspired by the acanthus and vine decoration popular in classical Greece and Rome, but over time Islamic artisans developed the style to become increasingly elaborate.

In addition to foliate or floral motifs, artists worked with a repertoire of geometric shapes, such as stars, lozenges, and polygons, which they used in complex arrangements, so that they often appear almost like optical puzzles. These designs were applied to every surface of buildings, from domes and doorways to walls, ceilings, and floors, and to everyday objects.

Academics debate whether or not geometric motifs in Islamic art have meaning. One prevalent theory holds that the patterns symbolize the transcendent and infinite Oneness of God. Muslim craftsmen generally avoid obvious focal points, so that attention is not centered on any one area of a design; instead, it must be viewed as a whole. The laboriously created repetition of patterns directs the attention away from the individual in favor of a more holistic notion of beauty. The all-over patterning also draws the eye away from the form of a structure, which is earthly and only temporary.

Dynastic legacies

The Abbasids, who supplanted the Umayyads in 750, created two great capitals—in Baghdad and, later, Samarra—but little has survived of either from that time, making it difficult to assess their contributions to art and architecture. We can, however, trace the developments under the Fatimids (909–1171), who challenged the rule of the Abbasids and established a rival caliphate in North Africa.

A Shia Muslim dynasty claiming descent from the Prophet's daughter Fatima, the Fatimids governed first from Tunisia, then from their new capital, Cairo. In their buildings, they popularized the use of the "keel arch"—which comes to a point at its apex, like the upturned

The living image

Representing people and animals in art was generally frowned upon in Islam, but not all cultures recognized this prohibition. Fatimid ceramics, for example, frequently featured images of living beings. In Persia, Islamic dynasties often looked back to the pre-Islamic art of the Achaemenid (c. 550–330 BCE) and Sasanian (224–651 CE) Empires, which both depicted humans. Painting jewellike miniatures for wealthy patrons and illuminating manuscripts was a particular speciality of the Safavids (1501–1736). These stylized compositions often included calligraphy and geometric patterns, in scenes showing episodes from court life or from the great Persian poetic epics—such as the *Shahnameh* ("Book of Kings"), the mythical story of the Persian people written by Ferdowsi in the late 10th century. Miniatures also became part of the artistic heritage of the Turkish Ottomans and the Indian Mughals.

He who has not seen Cairo has not seen the world. She is the Mother of the World.
The Tale of the Jewish Physician
One Thousand and One Nights

hull of a boat—and introduced the "squinch," a structure that enables a dome to fit on top of a square room. Both of these would become signature features of Islamic architecture. The Fatimids also fashioned prized objects of intricately carved wood, ivory, and rock crystal, and their potters produced distinctive lusterware (ceramics with a metallic glaze).

Cairo became a city of even greater cultural riches under the Mamluks, former slave-soldiers who seized power in Egypt in 1250 and established their own sultanate controlling much of the Middle East. They used their acquired wealth to govern with great pageantry and ceremony, and embarked upon lavish building projects, making Cairo the economic, intellectual, and artistic center of the Arab Islamic world for the next two-and-a-half centuries.

The mosques, mausoleums, and *madrasas* (religious colleges) of the Mamluk era characteristically have exterior walls featuring striped stonework, intricately carved domes and minarets, and sumptuous interiors lined with polychromatic inlaid marble. Mamluk decorative artwork, enriched by influences from across the Islamic world, was highly sought after in the Mediterranean region and across Europe. Its treasures included enameled and gilded glass, and inlaid metalwork and woodwork.

In the second half of the 15th century, the arts flourished under the patronage of the Mamluk sultan al-Ashraf Qaitbay (r.1468–96), who, among other projects, extensively restored the shrines of Mecca and Medina. One of his earliest projects was his own funerary complex in Cairo, one of the most admired structures in Islamic architecture.

Techniques and color

The Berber dynasties of the Almoravids (c. 1040–1147) and the Almohads (1147–1248) ruled from Morocco over territories that included Muslim Spain, and developed a distinctive, but still wholly Islamic, aesthetic.

Artisans in this region took the art of carving plaster to a pinnacle of complexity and beauty, to the extent that their work almost resembles lace. They enhanced basic architectural forms by pinching the arch to look like a horseshoe, or adding scallops into the sides of arches. The intricate detail in brick and plaster was mirrored by extensive use of »

Patterned tiling in Marrakech, Morocco, decorates the base of the walls and columns. It is characteristic of the style that developed in Morocco and al-Andalus, or Muslim Spain.

patterned tiles: not only for floors but also on walls, or as decoration on minarets. One of the greatest examples of this is the fortress of the Alhambra, built at Granada in Spain from 1230–1492, during the twilight era of al-Andalus.

The tradition of architectural tiling, used to dazzling effect under the Berber dynasties of Morocco and Muslim Spain, was shared by the Mongol peoples of Central Asia,

Sheikh Lutfullah Mosque in Isfahan, Iran, is a UNESCO World Heritage Site and one of Islam's most exquisite architectural creations, built in 1619 for Shah Abbas and the women of his court.

and in Persia and Iraq, where the tradition predated the arrival of Islam. The Ilkhanid dynasty (1256–1335) only became Muslim in the late 13th century, which may explain why its artisans, who labored in the ceramic workshops of the capital Tabriz, produced distinctive star-shaped tiles that typically featured un-Islamic images of birds and animals.

The buildings of Central Asia's Timurid dynasty (1370–1507) have domes enameled in brilliant turquoise, meant to reflect the sky. They are so vivid because of a technique called underglazing, in which the painted surface is

covered with a transparent glaze and then fired. This was learned from the neighboring Chinese, from whom the Timurids also obtained their knowledge of blue pigments. The vivid Timurid palate, which included cobalts, yellows, rusts, and golds, was used to create almost psychedelic walls of pattern.

Such beauty might seem in stark contrast to the founder of the dynasty, Timur (known in the West as Tamerlane), who had a reputation for brutality. Rampaging through Persia and Iraq, he slaughtered fellow Muslims and created towers of their decapitated heads, but regularly spared artists and craftworkers, transporting them back to his glorious capital at Samarkand. When the Timurid Empire collapsed, its artistic legacy lived on in Persia, and in parts of Turkey and India.

Jewel in the crown

If any city matches Samarkand for brilliance, it is Isfahan, in what is now Iran. Rebuilt by the Safavid Shah Abbas I in the early 17th century, one historian has called the city "perhaps the most splendid and impressive gallery of Islamic architecture in the world"—a Persian pun on the city's name boasts that "Isfahan is half the world" (*Esfehan nesfe jahan*). Its

One of the greatest and finest cities, and most perfect of them in beauty.
Ibn Battuta
describing Samarkand in 1330

> If one had but a single glance to give the world, one should gaze on Istanbul.
> **Alphonse de Lamartine**
> *French writer (1790–1869)*

centerpiece is the great Maydan-e Naqsh-e Jahan ("Image of the World Square"), which is flanked by mosques, palaces, and pavilions.

Among these is the Sheikh Lutfullah Mosque, named for the shah's father-in-law, a venerated preacher. It is unusual in having no courtyard or minaret (it was a private mosque for the exclusive use of the royal court, so had no need for either), but its tiling is some of the most beautiful anywhere in the world.

Where the Sheikh Lutfullah Mosque is intimate and royal, the other mosque Shah Abbas had built on the square is immense and public. The Masjid-e Shah (Royal Mosque) was conceived by Abbas to be "without equal in Iran and quite possibly in the entire world." Its ambition is expressed in its foundation inscription, which reads "A second Kaaba has been built."

The great Sinan

The great artistic works of Islam tend to be credited to their patrons, the emperors, shahs, and sultans, while the names of their actual creators are generally passed over

The Süleymaniye Mosque, Istanbul is one of the most famous works of the architect Sinan, and was commissioned by Sultan Süleyman I in the 1550s.

in history. The one great exception to this is Mimar Sinan (*c.* 1488–1588), whose title "Mimar" is Turkish for "architect."

Sinan was appointed chief architect to the Ottoman court by Süleyman I in 1539, and over a 50-year career he designed and oversaw the construction of more than 370 works, from aqueducts, baths, and fountains to palaces, tombs, schools, hospitals, kitchens, granaries, caravanserai, and (most famously) a number of imperial mosques. These feature huge central domes that are surrounded by cascades of smaller domes and pencil-sharp minarets. Despite their size, they are buildings of superb lightness, externally and within.

Sinan's distinctive architecture left its imprint not only on the Ottoman capital at Istanbul, where his creations continue to dominate the modern city's skyline, but also over a vast empire stretching from the Danube to the Tigris rivers. ■

Keeping the arts alive

Completed in 1993, the Mosque of Hassan II in Casablanca, Morocco, could fit Rome's St. Peter's basilica in its prayer hall. It is an extraordinary building, set on a platform of reclaimed land jutting into the Atlantic Ocean. Glass panels in the floor allow visitors to see the waves below—a reference to verse seven of the 11th *sura* of the Quran: "Throned above the waters, He created the heavens and earth in six days." The mosque has one of the world's tallest minarets (689 ft, 210 m), which is topped with a laser whose beam, it is said, can be seen 30 miles (48 km) away.

However, it is not just the size of the mosque that impresses but the beauty of the craftsmanship. The mosque is the product of more than 10,000 artisans, employed to carve stone and wood, and to make mosaics. It served as a school for a new generation of craftsmen and women, keeping the arts of Islam alive.

THE RIGHTEOUS SHALL BE LODGED... AMID GARDENS
THE QURAN, 44:51

IN CONTEXT

THEME
Paradise on Earth

WHEN AND WHERE
13th–17th centuries, Spain, Persia, India

BEFORE
6th century BCE In ancient Persia, Cyrus the Great (559–30 BCE) creates a "royal garden" in his imperial capital at Pasargadae, with palaces, monuments, and fountains set in a tree-lined park.

c. 290 BCE The Babylonian priest Berossus writes of the Hanging Gardens of Babylon, which he attributes to King Nebuchadnezzar II (r. 605–562 BCE). Greek writers later list the gardens as one of the Seven Wonders of the Ancient World.

AFTER
2005 The Aga Khan funds an extensive new public park in Cairo, designed along Islamic lines with water features, lush planting, and lots of shade.

The idea of paradise as a garden far predates Islam. For example, a "Garden of the Gods" appears in the Sumerian epic *Gilgamesh*, which dates back to about 1800 BCE. Sumer was one of the ancient civilizations founded in Mesopotamia, whose name means "between two rivers" in Greek, reflecting the fact that it spanned the Tigris and Euphrates rivers. If paradise was a garden to the inhabitants of Sumer's fertile wetlands, how much more alluring must the concept have been to a people from the deserts of Arabia.

It is no wonder that the Quran includes more than one hundred references to the garden, mostly framed as a haven that awaits true believers in the afterlife: "Such is the Paradise the righteous have been promised: it is watered by running brooks: eternal is its fruit, and eternal is its shade" (13:35); "Trees will spread their shade around them, and fruits will hang in clusters over them" (76:14).

In the Quran, water is a symbol of God's mercy – He sends rain from the sky to water crops for the purpose of sustaining humans and animals (10:24, 16:65). Similarly, in God's mercy He caused "palm groves and vineyards to spring up" (23:18), yielding valuable fruit. Water, fruit, and the blessed shade provided by abundant foliage are the three key elements of the Islamic garden, offering both spiritual and physical sustenance.

It is no coincidence that the color most associated with Islam is the green of Paradise. It is reputed to have been Muhammad's favorite color and it specifically appears in a number of the Quran's descriptions of Paradise, such as "They shall recline on green cushions and fine carpets" (55:76) and "They shall be arrayed in garments of fine green silk and rich brocade" (76:21).

Brooks will run at their feet in the Gardens of Delight.
10:10

See also: The Quranic concept of Heaven 92 ▪ The example of Islamic Spain 166–71 ▪ The Safavid Empire 192–93 ▪ Islamic art and architecture 194–201 ▪ The Mughal Empire 204–05

Earthly paradise

Regardless of when or where they were created, or their size, almost all Islamic gardens share many of the same elements. The central axis or main feature is almost always water: either a pool or basin, or flowing channels. Planted areas are arranged around the water, either in symmetrical fashion or in geometric patterns. In Persia, a popular design was the so-called *chahar bagh*, or "four gardens," a quadrilateral layout based on *sura* 55 in the Quran, which includes a description of two pairs of gardens.

Unlike the great gardens of Europe, which could be vast, open spaces of greenery, in the Islamic world gardens are typically more private places. Historically, they were often attached to a palace or other noble residence, and were almost always walled to create a space suitable for contemplation. Planting was carefully ordered for maximum pleasure, incorporating tall trees with shade-giving leaves alongside smaller, fruit-bearing species. Flowerbeds were likely to be filled with fragrant shrubs such as jasmine and roses.

In certain regions, even the more modest houses of the *medina* (walled city) would have a small inner courtyard with a central fountain and a few fruit trees—a paradise garden in miniature. In Morocco, many of these courtyard houses, known as *riads*, have now been converted into guesthouses.

In Granada in Spain, the Moorish Nasrid dynasty (1230–1492) created the Alhambra, a citadel from which a series of terraced courtyards filled with pools, fountains, and greenery cascades down the hillside.

The formal garden was also prized in Persia, partciularly during the cultured era of the Safavids (1501–1722), who cultivated green spaces in the cities of Isfahan, Kashan, and Shiraz. But arguably the pinnacle of Islamic garden design was reached in Mughal India (1526–1857), where the construction of gardens was a beloved imperial pastime. To the standard elements of the Islamic garden they added water-lifting

The Alhambra Gardens combine color, shade, aromatic plants, and splashing water features to give pleasure to the senses.

devices for irrigation and to feed the water-channels, as well as canals, pavilions, and hillocks. The Shalimar Bagh in Lahore, built in 1619, had 450 fountains, some of which could shoot water 12 feet (3.6 m) into the air. ▪

MOST WORSHIPPERS OF GOD ARE INTENT ON THE ADVANCEMENT OF THEIR OWN DESTINY
EMPEROR AKBAR

IN CONTEXT

THEME
The Mughal Empire

WHEN AND WHERE
16th century, India

BEFORE
***c.* 1700 BCE** Hinduism arises in the valley of the Indus River.

8th century CE Islam arrives in India in the form of invading armies from Central Asia. It becomes a major religion under the Delhi Sultanate.

AFTER
18th century Hindu Marathas rout the Mughal armies and establish a rival empire on the subcontinent.

1857–58 The Indian Rebellion against British rule is quashed. The last of the Mughal dynasty, Delhi Sultan Bahadur Shah, dies in exile in 1862.

1947 India is partitioned along religious lines, leading to the creation of the new Muslim state of Pakistan.

The Mughal Emperor Akbar I fuses elements from the multiple faiths of his people to create a **new religion called *Din-i Ilahi*.**

From Sufism, the yearning for God as a key feature of spirituality.

+

From Christianity, the idea of celibacy as a virtue.

+

+

From Jainism, a condemnation of the killing of animals.

+

From Zoroastrianism, making fire and the sun objects of divine worship.

In the late 16th century, the third Mughal emperor, Akbar I, attempted to introduce a radical new interpretation of Islam into India. Called *Din-i Ilahi* ("Religion of God"), it combined Sufi Islam with elements of Christianity, Hinduism, Jainism, and Zoroastrianism. It was intended to provide a common set of beliefs to bind the Indian empire together, but its lasting effect was to trigger a strong orthodox reaction in the Islamic community in India.

Islam in India

The first Muslims had arrived in India in the 8th century, during repeated invasions of northern India by Muslim armies from Central Asia.

See also: The origins of Ahmadiyya 220–21 ▪ The creation of Pakistan 242–47 ▪ The demographics of Islam today 260–61 ▪ The rising tide of Islamophobia 286–87

By the late 12th century, one of these warlords—Muhammad of Ghur—had gained a lasting foothold, leading to the formation of the Delhi Sultanate, an Islamic empire based in Delhi that ruled over large parts of the Indian subcontinent for more than 300 years.

In 1526, another conqueror from Central Asia, Babur (r. 1526–30), who claimed direct descent from Genghis Khan, defeated the Sultan of Delhi at the Battle of Panipat. The empire he founded was known as the Mughal Empire in reference to Babur's Mongol heritage, and it lasted until 1857. Although the Mughals were Muslims, they ruled a country with a large Hindu majority. The new rulers did not attempt to impose Islam on their subjects and instead encouraged a mixing of cultures. The language of Urdu, for example, developed in the Mughal era as a fusion of Persian, Arabic, and Hindi.

Din-i Ilahi

The combining of cultures reached its peak during the reign of Akbar I (r. 1556–1605), Babur's grandson. He was a patron of the arts and an intellectual. He founded an academy, the *Ibadat Khana* ("House of Worship") in 1575, where representatives of all major faiths could meet to discuss issues of theology. From these debates, Akbar concluded that no single religion captured the whole truth and that they should be combined. From this emerged *Din-i Ilahi*.

Followers were encouraged to find purity through an Islamic God—who was acknowledged through prayers and incantations of *Allahu akbar* (God is great)—but they also worshiped light (in the

form of sun and fire) as the Zoroastrians did. The new religion encouraged celibacy, as did Catholicism, and forbade the slaughter of animals, in line with Jainism, but there were no sacred scriptures and no priestly hierarchy. At the center of the religion was Akbar himself, as a new prophet.

Din-i Ilahi was the emperor's solution to the problem of how a Muslim ruler could govern a majority Hindu state. However, the religion never spread beyond a tight circle of Akbar's own close associates. Most Muslim clerics declared it heretical.

After Akbar

Following the death of Akbar, his heirs steered a path back to more traditional ways. His son Jahangir (r. 1605–27) reinstated Islam as the state religion, while maintaining a policy of religious plurality. Under his successor, Shah Jahan (r. 1628–58), this plurality found its finest

> Take heart, my friends!
> There is a God!
> There is a God!
> **Emperor Aurangzeb**

Emperor Aurangzeb is frequently blamed for the downfall of the Mughal Empire. His religious intolerance, including demolishing temples, isolated several of his key Hindu allies.

expression in the Taj Mahal at Agra. The apex of Mughal art, this ivory-white marble mausoleum for the Shah's favorite wife, Mumtaz Mahal, is a gleaming fusion of the Hindu and Islamic, created with the talents of craftsmen from all over the Islamic empire.

Jahan's son Aurangzeb (r. 1658–1707) was the sixth and last great Mughal emperor. He came to the throne after imprisoning his father and having his older brother killed, and ruled for nearly 50 years. His reign was characterized by military might—his conquests expanded the Mughal Empire to its greatest size—and by his piety.

A devout and uncompromising Muslim, Aurangzeb ended the policy of religious tolerance fostered by earlier emperors. He no longer let the Hindu community live under their own laws and customs, demolished many temples, and imposed Sharia law over the empire. Aurangzeb disapproved of his father's Taj Mahal, believing it to be counter to the teachings of Muhammad. ▪

REFORM
REVIVAL
1527–1979

AND

Süleyman I leads an Ottoman army in a first attempt to capture the city of Vienna, capital of the powerful Hapsburg Empire.

Tribal head **Muhammad bin Saud** joins forces with religious leader **Muhammad Abdul Wahhab** to create the first Saudi state.

Sultan Mahmud II introduces the **Westernizing Tanzimat reforms** in the Ottoman Empire.

The British use the **Indian Revolt of 1857** as the pretext to exile the last Mughal Emperor, Bahadur Shah II.

1529 **1744** **1808** **1858**

1683 **1798** **1830** **1871**

Ottoman Grand Vizier Kara Mustafa Pasha lays **siege to Vienna**, and is soundly defeated by a coalition of European forces

French forces under **Napoleon Bonaparte invade Ottoman Egypt** in order to disrupt Britain's communications with its territories in India.

The **French invade and seize Algeria**, a province of the Ottoman Empire since 1529.

Persian activist **Jamal al-Din al-Afghani** inspires a circle of reformers who aim to revitalize Islam.

I n 1521, the Ottoman army of Süleyman I overran Belgrade, a major stronghold in the Christian Kingdom of Hungary, and eight years later they laid siege to Vienna, capital of the Hapsburg Empire. The city held and the Ottomans eventually withdrew, unconcerned by this setback. In 1571, the Ottoman Empire suffered its first major military defeat at the Battle of Lepanto, a clash at sea, during which the Venetians sank almost the entire imperial fleet. The Ottomans simply built a bigger, more modern fleet, and consolidated their power in the Mediterranean.

In 1683, an Ottoman army was at the gates of Vienna again, and once more it was repelled. This time, it did not make an orderly retreat but was routed by an alliance of European powers.

For the first time, the Ottomans were forced to surrender control of significant European territories. This marked the point at which the frontiers of Islam stopped expanding and went into retreat.

Colonizing Muslim lands
Europe had entered a period of dynamism, invention, and creativity, fueled by the Italian Renaissance of the 14th to 17th centuries. This cultural and economic rebirth was substantially inspired by the transfer of knowledge from Muslim lands and by the wealth acquired through trade with Muslim countries on the Mediterranean.

In 1499, Portuguese explorer Vasco da Gama found a sea route around Africa to India that gave Europeans direct access to the coveted spices of Southeast Asia,

which previously they could only obtain through Muslim merchants. Rising powers such as the Spanish, Portuguese, British, and Dutch explored and colonized much of the world. As the great empires of Islam—the Ottomans, Safavids, and Mughals—slowly unraveled, the European powers vied for the spoils. The Portuguese, British, and French all secured toeholds in India, where the British eventually brought the Mughal era to a close in 1857. France invaded Ottoman Egypt and Syria in 1798–1801, then Algeria in 1830.

Colonialism was not limited to European imperialists. In the 19th century, the Chinese and Russians absorbed the Muslim provinces of Central Asia. The Chinese province of Xinjiang was created from Silk Road oases that had been controlled for centuries by Muslims.

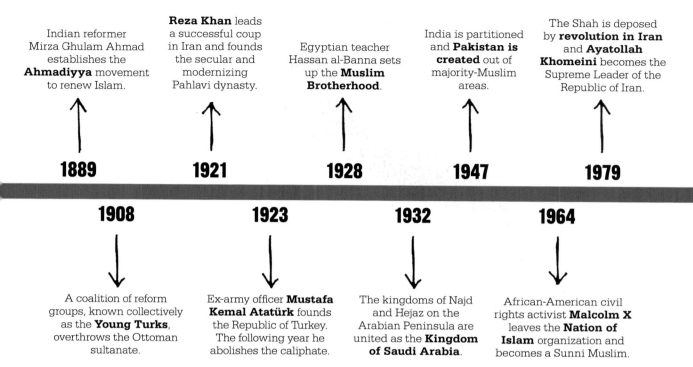

Indian reformer Mirza Ghulam Ahmad establishes the **Ahmadiyya** movement to renew Islam.

1889

A coalition of reform groups, known collectively as the **Young Turks**, overthrows the Ottoman sultanate.

1908

Reza Khan leads a successful coup in Iran and founds the secular and modernizing Pahlavi dynasty.

1921

Ex-army officer **Mustafa Kemal Atatürk** founds the Republic of Turkey. The following year he abolishes the caliphate.

1923

Egyptian teacher Hassan al-Banna sets up the **Muslim Brotherhood**.

1928

The kingdoms of Najd and Hejaz on the Arabian Peninsula are united as the **Kingdom of Saudi Arabia**.

1932

India is partitioned and **Pakistan is created** out of majority-Muslim areas.

1947

African-American civil rights activist **Malcolm X** leaves the **Nation of Islam** organization and becomes a Sunni Muslim.

1964

The Shah is deposed by **revolution in Iran** and **Ayatollah Khomeini** becomes the Supreme Leader of the Republic of Iran.

1979

Reawakening

By the mid-19th century, much of the Islamic world was controlled by colonial powers. There was no ideological clash—this was not a case of Christianity triumphing over Islam, as Islam was of little interest to the colonizers. However, for many Muslims who felt let down by national leaders who collaborated with the colonial powers, Islam now became a rallying cause.

From the mid-19th century, Islamic movements headed by charismatic ideologues emerged across the Islamic world. All shared the aim of awakening Muslims and shaking off colonial control, but their approaches varied. Some believed that Muslims had to emulate the West by modernizing and educating in order to compete on level terms. This was the view of Indian reformist thinkers Sayyid Ahmad Khan (1817–98) and Muhammad Iqbal (1877–1938)—who would be instrumental in the creation of Pakistan—and of Mustafa Kemal Atatürk (1881–1938), future founder of the Turkish Republic.

Some felt that Muslims needed to absorb lessons from the West, but at the same time renew their faith in Islam. This was the view taken by, among others, Persian writer Jamal al-Din al-Afghani (1838–97), founding father of Islamic Modernism, and Hassan al-Banna (1906–49), founder of Egypt's reformist Muslim Brotherhood.

Others advocated the complete rejection of everything Western in favor of a return to the pure, original form of Islam. Proponents of this approach included Egyptian intellectual Sayyid Qutb (1906–66).

To be Islamic or not?

The rise of political Islam was accompanied by a growing nationalism across the Muslim world. Following World War I, the Western powers had sliced up the former Ottoman Empire, bringing about the creation of the Arab nations of the modern Middle East. Many of these new nations began calling for their independence, which the majority achieved during the first half of the 20th century.

The question that then arose was the extent to which Islam would play a part in these modern nations. Reponses varied—from newly independent Turkey, where President Kemal Atatürk expunged religion from the state in the 1920s and 30s, to Iran, where the revolution of 1979 recast the country as a solely Islamic state. ∎

BETTER TURKISH THAN POPISH

DUTCH PROTESTANTS (1574)

IN CONTEXT

THEME
Islam in Europe

WHEN AND WHERE
16th–19th centuries, Europe

BEFORE
711 An Arab and Berber army led by Tarek ibn Ziyad crosses from North Africa to begin a Muslim conquest of Spain.

1299 Osman I founds the Ottoman dynasty, which will conquer Turkey, followed by Greece and Serbia.

1453 Mehmet II, also known as Mehmet the Conqueror, captures Constantinople, initiating centuries of glory for the Ottoman Empire.

AFTER
1920 Following Ottoman defeat in World War I, the Treaty of Sèvres partitions the Ottoman Empire, leading to the creation of Turkey and the modern Arab world.

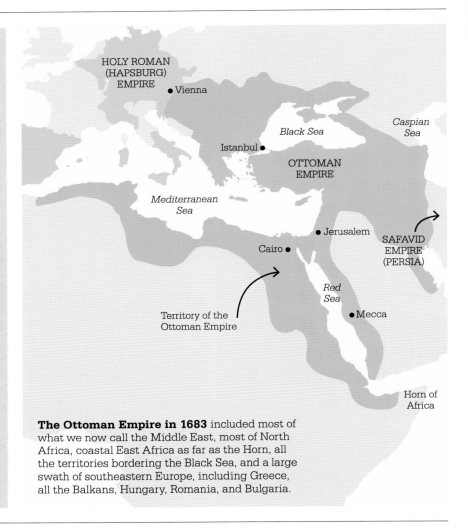

The Ottoman Empire in 1683 included most of what we now call the Middle East, most of North Africa, coastal East Africa as far as the Horn, all the territories bordering the Black Sea, and a large swath of southeastern Europe, including Greece, all the Balkans, Hungary, Romania, and Bulgaria.

I n 1683, as in 1529, an Ottoman army laid siege to Vienna, the capital of the Christian Holy Roman, or Hapsburg, Empire. This second attempt was a pivotal moment in the history of both Islam and Europe. Had Vienna fallen, then the Ottomans could have pushed deeper into Europe to seize control of major trade routes, changing the course of history on the continent. Instead, the Christian armies of Europe under the command of King John III Sobieski of Poland defeated the Ottoman army and sent it into retreat.

The 1683 Siege of Vienna is often portrayed as a defining clash of civilizations—of Islam versus the Christian West—but that is misleading. The truth is more nuanced: for example, while the citizens of Vienna were in dread of the Muslim foe camped outside their city, fellow Christians in France were openly relishing the idea of an Ottoman victory. And John Sobieski might not have won the battle were it not for the help of his country's Muslim Tatars. Also known as the Lipka Tatars, these were the descendants of refugees

from Timur who had found asylum in Eastern Europe in 1397. Skilled horsemen, they had fought for their new country ever since.

The enemy of my enemy
Just as there were political schisms in the Muslim world—the neighboring empires of the Ottoman Turks and Safavid Persians were frequently at war—enmity and rivalries also divided Europe. In 1517, a German monk named Martin Luther had initiated a reformation of the Christian Catholic Church, causing a schism in which his

See also: Spreading Islam through trade 182–85 ▪ The caliphate of the Ottoman Empire 186–89 ▪ The Safavid Empire 192–93 ▪ The secularization of Turkey 228–31

followers became known as Protestants. Europe became split between a predominantly Catholic south and a largely Protestant north. Islam—thanks to the Ottoman Empire's occupation of the Balkans, Greece, and the Kingdom of Hungary—constituted a third power in Europe. This made Muslim–Christian relations a complex political dance based on the ancient principle that "the enemy of my enemy is my friend."

The Ottomans were happy to use Christian schisms to political advantage, as illustrated by a letter from Sultan Murad III (r. 1574–95) to Protestant Lutherans in Catholic Spain, his arch rival: "You have banished the idols and portraits and bells from churches, and declared your faith by stating that God Almighty is one and Holy

I think it nothing offensive to God to set one of his enemies against the other, the [Ottoman] Infidel against the [Spanish] Idolaters.
William Harborne
English ambassador to Constantinople, 1583–88

Jesus is His Prophet ... but the faithless one they call Papa [the Pope] does not recognize his Creator as One, ascribing divinity to Holy Jesus ... thus casting doubt upon the oneness of God."

In 1600, in a similarly political vein, the court of Queen Elizabeth I of England hosted Muhammad al-Annuri, ambassador of the Saadian Sultan of Morocco. He was in London to negotiate a commercial and military alliance between the Protestant queen and the sultan against their common enemy, Catholic Spain.

There were many such examples of Christian–Muslim alliances against other Christians, or other Muslims. In 1598, English brothers Robert and Anthony Sherley looked to make a pact with the Safavids of Persia in a potential war against the Ottomans. France wanted the Ottomans as an ally against the Hapsburgs; Sweden wanted Ottoman help against the Russians; Hungary's Protestant princes were willing to become Ottoman vassals if they could defeat the Catholic Hapsburgs.

Protestant Christians observed that they received better treatment from the Ottomans than from the Catholics. Refugees from Catholic persecution often found shelter in the Ottoman Empire, including the Jews of Spain and Huguenots from France. Dutch Protestants under Spanish rule had a saying, "Better Turkish than Popish" (*Liever Turks dan paaps*), meaning it was better to be Muslim than Catholic.

Blueprint for pluralism

With territories stretching from North Africa to the border of Iran, and north to the fringes of Russia and Poland, the Ottoman Empire was home to large minorities of Jews and Christians. The Ottomans were not above turning churches into mosques and forcing Christians to convert, but they also presided »

Sultan Mehmet II by Italian Gentile Bellini, whose work launched European artistic interest in the Orient. He spent two years in Constantinople in 1479–81.

Painting of Moroccan ambassador Muhammad al-Annuri, whose stay at English Queen Elizabeth I's court may have inspired Shakespeare's Othello.

A Persian mission

In 1598, the English merchants and adventurers Sir Anthony and Sir Robert Sherley traveled to Isfahan in an attempt to befriend the Shah of Persia. They wanted to form an alliance that might break the monopoly the Spanish and Ottomans had on the lucrative trade with the Far East. By their own account, the Englishmen became close companions of Shah Abbas. They proposed to him a Persian–Christian pact that would defeat "the Turk" and give the Shah control over Central Asia. The Shah gave Anthony Sherley the authority to negotiate on his behalf with other European powers to form such a pact. Meanwhile, Abbas declared his lands open to all Christian people and their religion.

The Sherleys' schemes came to nothing, mainly because much of Europe, England included, already enjoyed a fairly profitable relationship with the Ottomans.

over an era of pluralism. Each faith community was allowed to organize itself into a separate *millet* or "nation," based on religion rather than ethnicity or nationality: all Jews in the empire, for example, belonged automatically to the Jewish *millet*. Each *millet* had its own education system and judiciary. Giving each of the faith communities more autonomy over its own affairs fostered greater social harmony between them. The system was far from perfect, but has often been described as a blueprint for religious pluralism.

Settlers and converts

Census data around the time of the 1683 Siege of Vienna suggests that only 20 percent of the population of the Ottoman territories in Europe was Muslim, formed of one third Muslim settlers and two thirds converts to Islam. The main incentive for conversion was probably economic and social, since Muslims enjoyed more rights and privileges than Christian subjects. But the spread of Islam was never the goal of Ottoman expansion—instead it was land, manpower, and plundered wealth. Young men from

… a certain Bean of Arabia whereof they make a Drink named Coffee … which is nowadays in very great request
Philippe Sylvestre Dufour
17th-century French merchant

captured territories were inducted into the Ottoman army to replenish and swell its ranks, and its soldiers fought not for Islam but for bonuses and promotions.

The lure of the East

At the height of their power, in the 16th and 17th centuries, the Ottomans exploited the religious struggles of European powers for their own political gain, and engaged in trade with their neighbors, but otherwise they were indifferent to the European Christians. This was in contrast to Europe's curiosity about "the Turk."

Europe developed a fascination with the Ottoman world that became known as "Turquerie," or "Turkomania," and peaked between 1650 and 1750. It became the fashion to imitate aspects of Ottoman culture, setting new operas and ballets in the Orient, borrowing motifs from its decorative arts and architecture,

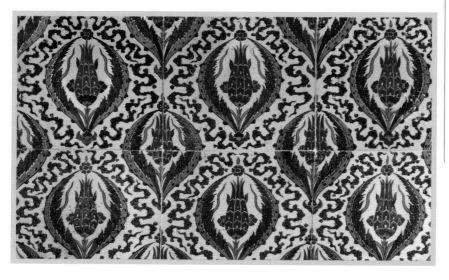

The tulip is native to Central Asia, the original homeland of the Ottoman Turks. It became a favored motif in Ottoman art, used in fabrics and on tiles, as here in tiles from the Rüstem Pasha Mosque (1563), in Istanbul.

> How helpful the experience of the Arabs could be if Europe wanted to carry its civilizing influence deep into Asia and Africa.
> **Michael Jan de Goeje**
> *Dutch Orientalist (1836–1909)*

Mostar in Bosnia and Herzegovina, Central Europe, thrived as an Ottoman frontier town in the 15th–16th centuries. The Old Bridge was designed by a student of the imperial architect Sinan.

donning Turkish dress for portraits and balls, and drinking coffee. Coffee originated in Arabia, and spread through the Ottoman Empire during the 16th century. The first coffeehouse in Europe is thought to have opened in Venice around 1630, followed soon after by coffeehouses in Paris and London. This blossomed into a Europe-wide coffeehouse culture by the 18th century.

Meanwhile, the Dutch had been struck by "tulipomania." A Dutch botanist imported the tulip from Istanbul to Holland in the late 16th century, where it was successfully cultivated. The flowers rapidly became a coveted luxury item and at one point, in the mid-1630s, bulbs were traded for staggering prices on the financial markets.

Europe also began to take an interest in "Oriental" languages, including Arabic. This was driven in part by commerce—a knowledge of Arabic was useful in the Asian and Indian Ocean spice trade. This

trade was dominated by the Dutch East India Company, and one of the earliest centers of Oriental studies was at Leiden, in Holland, from 1613 onward. A chair of Arabic was also established at the University of Oxford in 1636; its first professor was Edward Pococke, who had been working as a chaplain to the English merchant community in Aleppo.

Christian Europe's academics remained hostile towards Islam, with the attitude that it needed to be studied, but mostly with the purpose of proving it wrong.

The croissant, according to a popular story, was first baked in Vienna to celebrate the defeat of the Ottomans in 1683. Its shape is said to be inspired by the crescent on the Ottoman flag.

Shifting balance

Militarily, the Ottoman Empire never recovered from its defeat at the walls of Vienna in 1683. From then on, any battle fought by the Ottomans—mostly against the Hapsburg Empire and tsarist Russia—resulted in a loss of territory. The Ottoman–Hapsburg Treaty of Karlowitz in 1699 saw the Ottomans cede control of much of Central Europe and established the Hapsburg monarchy as the dominant power in the region.

Additional wars over the next 200 years saw Christian armies expel millions of Europe's Muslims, demolishing mosques as they advanced, pushing the Ottomans out of the Balkans and almost to the borders of what is now Greece, a position ratified in the 1878 Treaty of Berlin. Islam retained only a small presence in Europe, in what are now Albania, Kosovo, and Bosnia and Herzegovina.

In time, interest in the West began to take seed in Islamic lands. Muslim scholars attended universities in Europe and returned home with new ideas. These would reshape Islam as much as, if not more than, military encounters. ∎

UNIFIERS OF ISLAMIC PRACTICE

MUHAMMAD IBN ABD AL-WAHHAB

God reveals the Quran to Muhammad with its central message of the Oneness of God.

Generations of Islamic **scholars interpret the Quran**, and the words and actions of Muhammad, in order to arrive at an Islamic way of life, or *sunna*.

Wahhabism takes the **Quran and *hadith* at face value**, rejects interpretations, and regards Shias and Sufis as deviants.

Born in 1703 in the central Arabian region of Najd, Muhammad ibn Abd al-Wahhab came from a family of religious scholars. As a young man, he traveled to Medina and to Basra, in what is now Iraq, to study under scholars who followed the rigid Hanbali school of Islamic law. He emerged as a preacher with an absolutist ideology who condemned many aspects of contemporary Islamic teaching and practice, putting him at odds with other local religious authorities.

Initially, al-Wahhab was dismissed as a heretic and expelled from several towns. Eventually he did manage to attract supporters from two tribes, who accepted him as their religious leader. But he also attracted powerful enemies, and was once again forced to move on.

Moving to the town of al-Diriyah, near Riyadh, al-Wahhab gained new followers and a powerful patron in a local ruler named Muhammad bin Saud. Al-Wahhab and his disciples were given free rein by bin Saud to convert the locals to their cause, and in 1744 the two men swore an oath of mutual loyalty, forging the first Saudi (and Wahhabi) state.

The Wahhabis

The followers of al-Wahhab—known as Wahhabis and their doctrine as Wahhabism—opposed mainstream

See also: God's guidance through Sharia 128–33 ▪ The rise of Islamic Modernism 222–23 ▪ The birth of Saudi Arabia 232–37 ▪ The modern Sharia state 266–69 ▪ The new extremists 272–77 ▪ Salafism 304

Islam, and advocated strict adherence to Sharia and literal understandings of ambiguous Quranic verses, untainted by the contextual interpretations of past Islamic scholars.

Wahhabism claimed to more accurately represent the principle of *tawhid*, or proclamation of the oneness of God, than other strands within Sunni Islam. Followers called themselves *Muwahhidun*, which means "Unitarians" or "Unifiers of Islamic practice," and al-Wahhab himself was described as *mujaddid*, a renewer of Islam's basic message and components. His followers quoted a *hadith* that claims the Prophet once said, "God will raise for the *umma* every 100 years the one who will revive its religion for it."

Wahhabi militancy

The Wahhabis sent letters to religious scholars and political leaders in Muslim countries as far afield as Morocco, asking them to convert to the Wahhabi doctrine. If letter-writing failed, Wahhabis were encouraged to wage a *jihad* against non-Wahhabi Muslims, declaring them apostates who had abandoned Islam.

In 1812, a Saudi-Wahhabi army sacked Shia cities in Iraq. Shia drew the ire of Wahhabis in particular for their veneration of the shrines of the Imams, former religious leaders they revered as saints. In response, Ottoman sultan Mahmud II, whose empire embraced both Iraq and the Arabian Peninsula, sent his Egyptian viceroy Muhammad Ali to destroy the first Saudi-Wahhabi state. Its ruler Abdullah bin Saud was beheaded in Istanbul in 1818.

The revival of Wahhabism

Al-Wahhab died in 1792. He had six sons, and his descendants, known as the *Ahl ash-sheikh*, have historically dominated the religious institutions of the Saudi Arabian state. Outside the Arabian Peninsula, Wahhabism remained a fringe, heretical movement until the rise of the so-called Islamic Modernism movements and collapse of the Ottoman Empire in

Qatari Muslims outside Doha's national mosque, which is named after al-Wahhab. Qatar is the only country other than Saudi Arabia whose people are predominantly Wahhabi.

the early 20th century. At this time, al-Wahhab's ideas of a back-to-basics Islam were adopted by a number of reformers, notably the Lebanese intellectual Rashid Rida, who campaigned to rehabilitate some of the ideas of Wahhabism.

From the 1970s onward, now flush with oil money, the Saudi state began actively funding the spread of Wahhabism—building, for example, large numbers of Islamic schools, universities, and mosques around the world—to project its values far beyond the Arabian Peninsula.

Controversy over al-Wahhab's legacy persists. Critics allege that his strict interpretation of Islam directly inspired a generation of terrorists, including al-Qaeda leader Osama bin Laden (1957–2011). Supporters argue, however, that during his own lifetime al-Wahhab favored debate over violence, and not everyone agrees with drawing an ideological link to Bin Laden, pointing out that his largely political motivation was enmity with the West, particularly America. ▪

A forerunner of Wahhabism

Long before al-Wahhab began promoting his uncompromising reading of Islam, similar views were expressed by the 13th-century theologian Ibn Taymiyya (1263–1328). Born in Syria, he grew up studying under the Hanbali school of jurisprudence. He later courted controversy, denouncing Sufi leaders for their veneration of saints and, on at least one occasion, calling for the death of a Christian whom he accused of insulting the Prophet. He made himself unpopular with more orthodox religious scholars, on whose orders he was jailed on a number of occasions.

Ibn Taymiyya also infamously preached an extreme view of jihad. He declared a *fatwa* against the Mongols, who had begun converting to Islam in the 13th century, but whom he accused of not following God's law. His sanctioning of violence against fellow Muslims directly inspired extremist groups in the 20th century in acts of violence against their own governments.

A PROBLEMATIC EUROPEAN ATTITUDE TOWARD ISLAM
EDWARD SAID (1978)

IN CONTEXT

THEME
Orientalism

WHEN AND WHERE
18th–19th centuries, Europe

BEFORE
1479 Noted Italian artist Gentile Bellini arrives in Istanbul for a two-year stay, launching European artistic interest in the Orient.

1798 Napoleon Bonaparte invades Egypt, bringing with him scientists, archaeologists, and artists whose record of the country and its people inspires a new wave of interest.

AFTER
1978 Edward Said publishes *Orientalism*, challenging Western intellectuals on their ideas of the "Arab mind."

1998 Christie's auction house holds the first Orientalist sale; its primary buyers come from the Middle East.

I n the eyes of the European powers, the Ottoman Empire was both a fearsome military power and a valued trading ally. But from the 18th century, as the Turks suffered a series of territorial losses and the nation states of Europe grew economically stronger, the "Orient" (in this sense, primarily the Middle East and North Africa) was increasingly viewed as backward, uncivilized, and un-Christian.

Western religious authorities and others attacked Islam and the Quran. French political thinker Alexis de Tocqueville (1805–59), for example, pronounced that "by and large there have been few religions in the world as deadly to men as that of Muhammed." Such ideas were reinforced by so-called "Orientalist" experts and in art, which portrayed the Muslim world as licentious (women of the harem were a favorite subject for painters), brutal (swords and slaves were also popular), and fanatical.

This reductive view gave license to European powers to colonize Muslim countries, which were presented as badly in need of Christian intervention. In the post-colonial era, Palestinian-American academic Edward Said (1935–2003) articulated the Muslim perspective in his influential study *Orientalism*, which was published in 1978. In it Said wrote, "To say simply that Orientalism was a rationalization of colonial rule is to ignore the extent to which colonial rule was justified in advance by Orientalism, rather than after the fact." ■

Orientalist paintings played on Western fantasies of the exotic East and were typically dramatic and colorful, as in this work by French artist Jean-Léon Gérôme (1824–1904).

See also: The caliphate of the Ottoman Empire 186–89 ▪ Islam in Europe 210–15 ▪ The rising tide of Islamophobia 286–87

PURIFICATION BY THE SWORD
MUHAMMAD AHMED "THE MAHDI"

IN CONTEXT

THEME
The Mahdi of Sudan

WHEN AND WHERE
1881–85, Sudan

BEFORE
9th century The 12th Imam becomes hidden from human view (in "occultation"), destined to reappear to rescue his people at some future time.

***c.*1844** Sayyid Ali Muhammad Shirazi (1819–50) becomes the Bab ("Gate"), a Mahdi-like figure who launches Babism in Persia. The authorities execute him and thousands of his followers. He is subsequently venerated as one of the central figures of the Bahai faith.

AFTER
1882 In the Punjab, northern India, Mirza Ghulam Ahmad, founder of the Ahmadiyya movement, declares himself to be a minor prophet of Islam and the Mahdi.

While there is no reference to the Mahdi—meaning "the Guided One"—in the Quran, only in the *hadith*, Shia Muslims live in anticipation of this Messianic figure who will appear at the end of times, with Jesus, to bring peace to Earth. Over the years, several individuals have claimed to be the Mahdi.

In 1881, the religious leader of a Sufi order in Sudan, Muhammad Ahmed bin Abdallah (1844–85), who claimed descent from Fatima, the Prophet Muhammad's daughter,

This world is a carcass and those who desire it are dogs.
The Mahdi
Letter to the British, 1884

was proclaimed as the Mahdi by his disciples. At this time, there was widespread resentment among the Sudanese at the heavy taxation imposed by Egypt, which had conquered Sudan in the 1820s. The Mahdi regarded the Egyptians as hypocrites and apostates who had turned their back on Islam.

In 1881, the Mahdi sent a personal message to the governor-general of Sudan informing him that he, the Mahdi, was acting by the divine inspiration of the Prophet Muhammad—and that anyone who did not accept the Mahdi's divinely appointed mission would be "purified by the sword."

The Mahdist revolt amassed countrywide support and the rebels, armed with only swords and spears, scored victories over first Egyptian and then British forces, capturing the city of Khartoum in 1885. The Mahdi died of typhus later that year, and the revolt ended in 1898, but his name remained a potent symbol. A direct descendant, Sadiq al-Mahdi, was prime minister of Sudan twice, in 1966–67 and 1986–89. ∎

See also: The emergence of Shia Islam 108–15 ▪ The caliphate of the Ottoman Empire 186–89 ▪ The origins of Ahmadiyya 220–21

I HAVE BEEN COMMISSIONED AND I AM THE FIRST OF THE BELIEVERS

MIRZA GHULAM AHMAD

IN CONTEXT

THEME
The origins of Ahmadiyya

WHEN AND WHERE
Late 19th century, India

BEFORE
632 The Prophet Muhammad, the final prophet of Islam, dies in Medina.

1857 The Indian Rebellion is quashed, but launches the independence movement, which includes some militant elements.

AFTER
1908 Leadership of the Ahmadiyya movement passes to Hakim Noor-ul-Din, a companion of Ghulam Ahmad.

1984 The headquarters of Ahmadiyya moves to the UK.

1983 The annual Ahmadiyya conference in Pakistan attracts almost 250,000 participants; in 1984, restrictions placed on the group force its leader into exile.

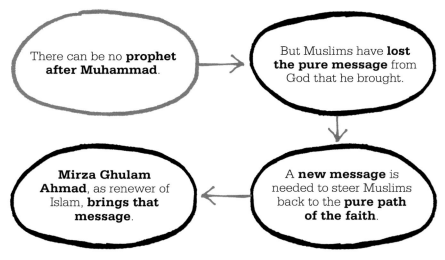

There can be no **prophet after Muhammad**.

But Muslims have **lost the pure message** from God that he brought.

A **new message** is needed to steer Muslims back to the **pure path of the faith**.

Mirza Ghulam Ahmad, as renewer of Islam, **brings that message**.

The Ahmadiyya movement emerged toward the end of the 19th century in the northwestern territories of British-ruled India. Its founder was Mirza Ghulam Ahmad who, in 1882, declared himself to be a divinely appointed reformer of Islam. The movement's name refers not to its founder but to "Ahmad," an alternative name for the Prophet Muhammad in some *hadith*.

Ghulam Ahmad's claim was that he had come to revive Islam and return it to the purity of its foundations. He did not claim to be a new prophet—in Muslim thinking, the Prophet Muhammad is the final prophet of Islam, and anyone else attempting to use the status of prophet should therefore be denounced. Ghulam Ahmad insisted that he was not bringing a new revelation, but a new interpretation, with the aim of guiding the Muslim community back to its roots. He saw himself as someone who could restore Islam to its original, pure state. He amassed followers in Punjab and Sindh and launched the movement with a ceremony of allegiance in 1889.

See also: The early life of Muhammad 22–27 ▪ The quest to make God's word supreme 134–35 ▪ The Mahdi of Sudan 219 ▪ The creation of Pakistan 242–47

Unorthodox teachings

In an atmosphere of growing anti-imperialist feeling in British-occupied India, Ghulam Ahmad controversially advocated only the spiritual form of jihad and the peaceful spread of Islam rather than any form of military confrontation.

Other teachings were more incendiary. Ahmad stated that Isa (Jesus) did not die on the cross, nor was he—as Muslims traditionally believe—saved from death on the cross by being raised up to heaven by God. Instead, Ahmad said, Isa fainted, recovered, and went to Afghanistan and Kashmir to search for the lost tribes of Israel, where he died of old age.

Ahmad declared himself not just to be a reformer of Islam, but a second coming of Muhammad and Isa. He was both the Mahdi (Guided One) and the Messiah who, in some *hadith,* was foretold by Muhammad to appear in the end times.

These claims went too far for many Muslims, and Ahmad was branded a heretic who challenged Muhammad's position as the Final Prophet, and the revelations given to him. When Ahmad died in 1908, his followers split into the Qadiani Ahmadiyyas, who accepted his claims and continued his teachings, and the Lahori Ahmadiyyas, who saw him as a renewer of the Islamic faith, but not as a minor prophet.

In 1973, Pakistani law ruled that Qadiani Ahmadiyyas were non-Muslims; from 1984, any Qadianis who claimed to be Muslims, used Islamic terminology, or referred to their faith as Islam could be punished. Persecuted, the Qadiani Ahmadiyyas moved their base from Pakistan to the UK, and now make up around 1 percent of the world's Muslims—although, universally, all other Muslims do not regard them as such. ▪

The Ahmadiyya movement has an evangelical mission and encourages the building of mosques around the world. This example in Berlin, Germany, was built in 1925.

Mirza Ghulam Ahmad

The son of a physician, Mirza Ghulam Ahmad was born in 1835 in Qadian, a village near Lahore, Punjab, which is now in Pakistan but was then part of northwest India. He studied Arabic and Persian, and some medicine with his father. Although he briefly took a job as a government clerk, he returned to Qadian and increasingly focused on religious study and public debates in defense of Islam.

In 1882, Ahmad declared that he had a divine mission. Seven years later, about 40 of his followers pledged allegiance to him, and in 1889 he published a set of rules to guide all who joined his movement. He traveled widely across northern India and to Delhi, spreading his message and debating with Islamic leaders. He wrote several books, including *Arguments of the Ahmadiyya* (1880–84), *Victory of Islam* (1891), and *The Star of Guidance* (1898).

When Ahmad died in 1908, leadership of the Ahmadiyya passed to Hakim Noor-ul-Din, who later passed it to Ahmad's eldest son. The movement is now thought to have 10–20 million followers worldwide.

THE CENTER OF ATTENTION IS NO LONGER ISLAM AS A RELIGION
JAMAL AL-DIN AL-AFGHANI

Only when **Islam** is seen as **relevant in the modern world** can it be regarded as a religion for all ages…

⬇

… so **Islam** must be **reconciled with Western values** such as democracy, civil rights, equality, and progress.

⬇

At the same time, Muslims must **resist Western colonial exploitation** and the imposition of Western secular values …

⬇

… and Muslims must also insist on the **importance of religious faith** in public life.

In the late 19th century, a movement arose to defend and modernize Islam in line with Western institutions and society. This movement, known as Islamic Modernism, had a number of leading lights, including Sayyid Ahmad Khan (1817–98) and his Aligarh movement in India, which pushed to establish a modern system of education for the Muslim population of British India.

The two most influential modernists, however, whose impact was felt around the Islamic world, were Jamal al-Din al-Afghani (1838–97) and his student and collaborator Muhammad Abdu (1849–1905). Al-Afghani argued that Islam should be seen first and foremost as a civilization rather than a religion, and he urged Muslims to engage with the modern world, not retreat from it.

Rise of a modernist
Al-Afghani claimed Afghan Sunni descent, hence his name, but many believe he was in fact of Persian Shia origin, from a village in western Iran. What is clear is that he had an eclectic education in Iran and the Shia shrine cities of Iraq, which ultimately led to him

See also: God's guidance through Sharia 128–33 ▪ Islam in Europe 210–15 ▪ Wahhabism, or an Islamic reformation 216–17 ▪ The rise of political Islam 238–41 ▪ The creation of Pakistan 242–47

Al-Azhar University in Cairo is the leading center of Sunni Islamic thought. As Egypt's Grand Mufti, Muhammad Abdu looked to reform its teachings, impacting all of Sunni Islam.

merging Sufi, Shia, and rationalist ideas into the framework of his thought. He was a modernist both in his use of media, specifically newspapers, to mobilize society against the colonial powers and in his approach to Islam—insisting that Islamic theology and the legal tradition (Sharia) needed streamlining to meet the challenge of the West. He came to these views through work and study in India, Afghanistan, Istanbul, and also Cairo, where he met a student of Islamic mysticism Muhammad Abdu in 1868.

Born into the Egyptian elite in the Nile Delta, north of Cairo, Abdu was immediately impressed by al-Afghani's ideas. Together they created the journal *al-Urwa al-Wuthqa* (a Quranic term meaning "the firmest bond"), of which they produced 18 issues in Paris in 1884. Circulated in the aftermath of France's 1882 occupation of

I went to the West and saw Islam, but no Muslims; I got back to the East and saw Muslims, but not Islam.
Muhammad Abdu

Tunisia, Britain's 1882 occupation of Egypt, and Ottoman bankruptcy to European creditors, the journal was revolutionary in creating a sense of Islamic unity founded on opposition to European colonization of Muslim lands.

A rationalist approach

Al-Afghani and Abdu's rationalist approach to the Quran and Islamic law earned them hostility among the Islamic authorities in Cairo and Istanbul but gained them a respectful hearing among Western officials and scholars. In 1883, when French scholar Ernest Renan claimed publicly that Muslims rejected education and science, al-Afghani's insistence that Islam could be a motor for rationalism and scientific progress was widely discussed.

As Grand Mufti of Egypt (chief Islamic jurist) from 1899, Abdu went on to become a close confidant of Lord Cromer, Britain's agent and consul-general in Egypt. Following al-Afghani's death, Abdu

worked with a Lebanese religious scholar, Rashid Rida, who had come to Egypt in 1897. They established the journal *al-Manar*, which promoted reformist ideas. Rida encouraged Muslims to interpret the primary sources of Islam themselves, as he did. His ideas were considered controversial by many—not the least of which was his support for Darwin's theory of evolution, which is something some Muslims still do not accept.

Abdu also continued to push for reform. He argued that Muslims could not rely on the interpretations of texts provided by medieval scholars—they needed to use reason to keep up with changing times. He reinterpreted Sharia to loosen strict requirements such as avoiding usurious interest in financial transactions and eating only halal meat. He was also an advocate for the education of women. His Muslim opponents called him an infidel, but his legacy was a trend of liberal thought in 20th-century Islam. ▪

AMERICA NEEDS TO UNDERSTAND ISLAM

MALCOLM X (1964)

IN CONTEXT

THEME
Early Muslims in America

WHEN AND WHERE
Early 20th century, US

BEFORE
12th century Mali becomes the first Muslim kingdom of West Africa, after centuries of trade with Morocco's Arabs.

1503 The transatlantic slave trade begins, transporting more than 10 million Africans to the Americas by 1867.

AFTER
1984 American rapper William Michael Griffin converts to Islam. As Rakim, he becomes one of the the most influential hip-hop artists of all time, and references Islam in his lyrics.

2006 Keith Ellison, the first Muslim elected to Congress, takes his oath of office using Thomas Jefferson's Quran.

On May 29, 1921, the *Detroit Free Press* newspaper carried a story with the headline "Sheik Helps Build Moslem Mosque." The "sheik" in question was Hassan Karoub, a Syrian immigrant to the United States, who presided over the opening of what would be the first specifically designed mosque in America.

The Karoubs had come from Damascus, Syria, to Detroit in about 1912, to find work in the automobile industry, like many other Muslim immigrants. They were part of a local Muslim community that was estimated to be about 16,000 strong at this time.

See also: Spreading Islam through trade 182–85 ▪ The origins of Ahmadiyya 220–21 ▪ The demographics of Islam today 260–61 ▪ Muslims in the West 282–85

From **1503** onward, large numbers of Muslims arrive as **slaves captured in West Africa**.

In the **late 19th century**, a wave of Muslim immigrants arrives from the **Middle East and South Asia**. This is halted by the 1924 Immigration Act.

An estimated **3.45 million Muslims** live in the United States today. This represents just over **1 percent** of the total **US population**.

Large-scale Muslim immigration resumes following the **Immigration and Naturalization Act of 1965**.

In the **1920s and 30s**, various Black Muslim movements emerge, including the **Nation of Islam**.

Most of these would have been recent immigrants, although Islam in America already had a long history, with roots that predate the nation's founding in 1776.

Islam in chains

The first Muslims to arrive in America were brought as slaves. They came as early as 1503, when the Spanish took the first African captives across the Atlantic Ocean to the Caribbean and the New World. Researchers debate the exact number of Muslim slaves transported to the Americas, but estimate that about one-third of all African slaves came from largely Muslim parts of West Africa—mostly from what are now Senegal, Gambia, Guinea, Mali, and Nigeria. Put to work on plantations, most Muslim slaves, forced by their owners to convert to Christianity, abandoned their

religion. However, despite this coercion, some enslaved Muslims did hold onto their religious practices. Among them was Ayuba Suleiman Diallo, an educated man from a family of Muslim clerics in Senegal. Captured in 1730, he was sent to work on a tobacco plantation in Maryland. He ran away and eventually arrived in London in 1733, where he wrote his memoirs.

Omar ibn Said was taken from Senegal in 1807 and transported to America. He, too, was a learned »

Ayuba Suleiman Diallo, painted by William Hoare of Bath in 1733, the year Diallo escaped slavery in America and made his way to England.

Malcolm X was a dynamic, influential, and polarizing figure who initially fought for black nationalism under the banner of the Nation of Islam.

Post slavery

Islam as brought to America by African slaves did not survive. Under pressure to convert to Christianity, they could not pass their religion on to their children. However, by the late 19th century, the millions of economic immigrants coming to America included tens of thousands from Muslim-majority countries in the Middle East and South Asia. They formed communities, built mosques, and integrated Islam into the fabric of American life.

man and before his capture he had been an Islamic scholar. Omar spent the rest of his life enslaved in North Carolina and died in 1864, the year before the abolition of slavery in America. He left a short memoir and other writings in Arabic, which reveal that while he appeared to have converted to Christianity, he continued to write verses of the Quran in Arabic in his Bible.

Firsthand accounts by Muslim slaves such as Ayuba Suleiman Diallo and Omar ibn Said are rare, but they show that, by the time of its founding in 1776, the United States already had a significant Muslim population. Lists of soldiers serving under George Washington during the American War of Independence in 1775–83 include Muslim names such as Bampett Muhammad and Yusuf Ben Ali.

Thomas Jefferson, chief author of the Declaration of Independence in 1776 and third president of the United States (1801–09), had his own copy of the Quran, the 1734 translation into English by George Sale. Why Jefferson had the Quran is unknown, but it possibly hints at an awareness of a religious diversity in the newly forged nation that many have now forgotten.

The legacy of the early Muslim slaves made itself felt early in the 20th century, however, with the movement to promote the idea of Islam as a lost part of African-American heritage. In 1914, Jamaican immigrant Marcus Garvey founded the United Negro Improvement Association (UNIA), in New York City's Harlem. The UNIA championed black separatism and advocated a return to Africa to end white colonialism and unite the continent under black rule.

The United States of America ... has in itself no character of enmity against the laws, religion, or tranquility of Muslims.
John Adams
2nd US President (1735–1826)

From Spain to California

There is a theory that Islam was present in the Americas even before the first Muslim slaves were landed in the 16th century: Moors expelled from Spain in the 14th century may also have crossed the Atlantic. And when Christopher Columbus sailed from Spain in 1492 and discovered the "New World," he is said to have brought Muslims with him as part of his crew.

A more lasting legacy might exist in the name of one of the territories the Spanish found and then claimed in 1542—California. Some think they took the name from *The Deeds of Esplandián*, a romance novel popular with the conquistadors. It features a rich island called California, which is ruled by black Amazons and their queen Calafia. The book was published in 1510 in Seville, a city that had until recently been part of al-Andalus and under the rule of a Muslim caliph: from "caliph" comes the female Calafia and so perhaps California.

> [Islam] is the one religion that erases from its society the race problem.
> **Malcolm X**

Although a Christian, Garvey sometimes mentioned Islam in his speeches, while the UNIA's house newspaper, *Negro World*, ran many stories about Muslims in the 1920s, playing a role in spreading the connection between Islam and black nationalism.

The Moorish Science Temple of America, founded in Chicago by Timothy Drew—or Noble Drew Ali —in 1913, proposed a more explicit connection, claiming that African Americans were of Moorish ancestry, from the Moroccan Empire, and were therefore Islamic.

More influential was the Nation of Islam, established in Detroit in 1930 by Wallace D. Fard, or Wali Fard Muhammad. Thanks to its charismatic leaders, notably Elijah Muhammad, who led from 1934 to 1975, the Nation helped lay the groundwork for the emergence of Islam as an influential part of the Black Power and broader civil rights movements of the 1950s and 1960s.

The Nation's teachings drew on elements from the Bible and the Quran to argue that Africans were

A mosque rises out of the northwest Ohio countryside. It belongs to a Muslim community with roots in the area going back to the 1930s.

Earth's original people and that Americans of African descent should be given a state of their own, separate from the white race.

While in prison in 1946–52, Malcolm Little converted to Islam and joined the Nation, changing his name to Malcolm X—as a protest at the loss of identity when white slave owners imposed new surnames on their slaves. Upon release, he became one of the Nation's most high-profile members, but he grew disillusioned, left the organization, and embraced mainstream Sunni Islam, making the Hajj in 1964. Then a stern critic of the Nation's separatist beliefs, he was assassinated by three of its members in 1965.

While each campaigned for the betterment of African Americans, the unorthodox religious beliefs and practices of these groups lie outside mainstream Islam; most Muslims do not view followers of the Nation and similar movements to be Muslims.

Islamic unity in the US

The mosque that Muhammad Karoub founded in Detroit in 1921 closed in 1927. However, a mosque built in Chicago in 1922 still stands; the Sadiq Mosque is named for

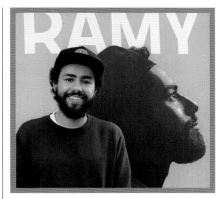

Ramy Youssef, the American-Egyptian comedian whose 2019 hit TV show *Ramy* is all about the experience of being an American Muslim.

Muhammad Sadiq, who was sent to America in 1920 as a missionary of the Ahmadiyya movement. Looking to build bridges between African-American and other US Muslims, he made thousands of converts.

The Ahmadis are the oldest continuous Muslim community (although other Muslims do not accept them as Muslims) in the US, with 10,000 to 20,000 followers, out of the estimated 3.45 million Muslims in America today. As 44th US president Barak Obama said in 2015, Islam is "woven into our country's fabric." ∎

PROVIDED IT DOES NOT INTERFERE WITH SANE REASON

MUSTAFA KEMAL ATATÜRK

IN CONTEXT

THEME
**The secularization
of Turkey**

WHEN AND WHERE
1923, Turkey

BEFORE
1299 CE Osman I founds the
Ottoman dynasty, which will
conquer Turkey, then Greece
and Serbia.

1453 Mehmet II, also known
as Mehmet the Conqueror,
captures Constantinople, thus
ending the Byzantine Empire
and initiating centuries of
glory for the Ottoman Empire.

AFTER
2001 Politicians form the
Turkish AKP party, which
looks to the conservative
tradition of Turkey's Ottoman
past and seeks to restore the
country's Islamic identity.

By the 19th century, the
Ottoman Empire, whose
sultans had been ruling
much of the Islamic world for more
than 500 years, was in decline—
a situation underlined by a series
of failed military campaigns.
The court attempted to reverse
the trend through a policy of
Westernization. In the mid-19th
century, officials launched large-
scale reforms in administration,
law, the military, and education.
Ultimately, this desire to reinvent
itself would lead Islam's most
powerful empire to largely abandon
the Muslim faith at state level and
transform itself into an almost
entirely secular society.

See also: The caliphate of the Ottoman Empire 186–89 ▪ Islam in Europe 210–15 ▪ The demographics of Islam today 260–61 ▪ Islam and democracy 264–65

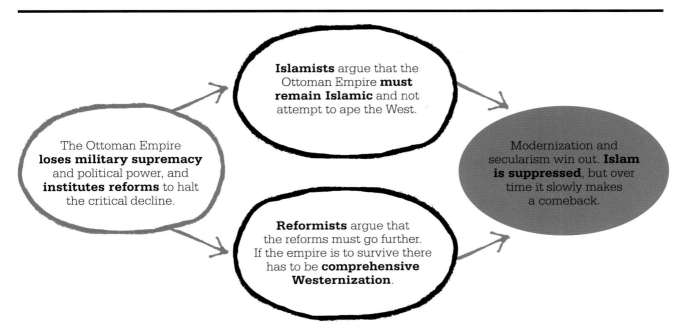

The Ottoman Empire **loses military supremacy** and political power, and **institutes reforms** to halt the critical decline.

Islamists argue that the Ottoman Empire **must remain Islamic** and not attempt to ape the West.

Reformists argue that the reforms must go further. If the empire is to survive there has to be **comprehensive Westernization**.

Modernization and secularism win out. **Islam is suppressed**, but over time it slowly makes a comeback.

Roots of secularization

Several factors led to the collapse of the sultanate, but the seeds of its dismantling lay in the Tanzimat program instituted in 1839. This had the aim of reforming the political structure of the state along Western lines—creating new cadres of bureaucrats, technical experts, and military elites conversant in European methods and languages. Reformists also legislated to reduce the power of the religious establishment by restricting the remit of Sharia law. Unfortunately, the financial cost of the reforms meant that the state had bankrupted itself to Western creditors by the 1870s. Meanwhile, territorial losses continued as the Ottomans lost the Balkans and the Caucasus to the Russians.

The response of Sultan Abdul Hamid II, who ruled from 1876 to 1909, was a policy of reasserting Islamic power—which included reinforcing his status as caliph— and a regime of repression that began with shutting down a brief experiment in government by parliament in 1878. But reform had already progressed too far to allow this reversion to authoritarian rule. Small clandestine groups, later known as "Young Turks," kept up the pressure for change. Most were weeded out and crushed, but one, the Committee of Union & Progress (CUP), succeeded in seizing control of the Ottoman army in Macedonia. By 1908, the CUP was powerful enough to send a telegram to the »

Keeping Islam alive in Turkey

Said Nursi (1877–1960) was an Islamic theologian and scholar. He founded the Nur Movement, which advocated reinterpreting Islam according to the needs of a modern society. Originally a member of the Young Turks, he later fell out of favor, and was accused of taking part in anti-government revolts. While in prison he wrote a work of Quranic commentary that ran to more than 6,000 pages. Parts of this were distributed to his disciples all over Turkey in what he called a "jihad of the word," which he characterized as the struggle to revive Muslim ethics in a world that had become highly secularized.

Following Nursi's death, one of those who continued his work was fellow scholar and preacher Fethullah Gülen. Rivalry between the millions-strong Gülen movement and the ruling AKP party erupted in 2013, and in 2016 the AKP blamed Gülenists for an attempted coup in Turkey.

aging sultan demanding the restoration of parliament. Faced with a rebellious revolutionary army marching on Constantinople, Abdul Hamid agreed to their demands. Elections to the new parliament saw the CUP win all but one seat.

Collapse of empire

The Ottoman Empire entered World War I in 1914 by attacking Russia, which declared war in response, as did Russia's allies France and Britain. When the war ended in defeat and occupation, the disgraced CUP government fell from power. The British and French planned to divide the empire into European-backed spheres of influence. Renegade army units began banding together under the leadership of Mustafa Kemal, a young Turkish general who had successfully repelled the Allied invasion of the Dardanelles in 1915–16. In 1919, Kemal led a revolt from the interior, formally declaring independence and creating a new

If I see my nation's belief secured, I will not even care about burning in Hell.
Said Nursi

government in the city of Ankara. "Henceforth," he declared, "Istanbul does not control Anatolia, but Anatolia Istanbul."

For two years, rival authorities in Istanbul and Ankara were at a stalemate, but by October 1922, Mustafa Kemal's forces prevailed. The sultanate was abolished and the last sultan fled Istanbul for Italy. The Turkish Republic was proclaimed in October 1923 with Mustafa Kemal "Atatürk" ("father of the Turks") as its president and Ankara as its capital. The caliphate was abolished the following year.

De-Islamification

Several years of dismantling Islamic institutions followed, including shutting down the Sharia courts, banning the Sufi orders, and excising Islam from the constitution. This was part of a general policy of reducing the presence of Islam in Turkey; other measures extended to banning the headscarf in state institutions, forcing men to wear Western-style fedora hats instead of the fez, the exclusive use of the

Le dernier calife

L'Assemblée d'Angora poursuit l'œuvre d'évolution de la Turquie. Après avoir proclamé la République et exilé le sultan, elle vient de rompre le dernier lien avec le passé. Abdul Medjid, qui, en qualité de calife, représentait la tradition religieuse à la tête des Ottomans, a reçu notification de sa déchéance et est parti pour l'étranger avec les princes et princesses de sa famille.

The National Assembly notifies the sultan of the end of the caliphate in 1924, following the proclamation of the Turkish republic the previous year, on the cover of a French newspaper.

> There may be a great many countries in the world, but there is only one civilization, and if a nation is to achieve progress, she must be a part of this civilization.
> **Mustafa Kemal Atatürk**

Mustafa Kemal Atatürk is celebrated at his mausoleum in Ankara on Republic Day, but there are many critics of the aggressive secularism that removed Islam from Turkish public life.

Gregorian rather than the Islamic calendar, and the obligatory adoption of Turkish rather than Islamic–Arabic surnames.

The most radical measures were the language reforms, which saw Arabic script replaced with Latin script in 1928, alongside a purging of Arabic and Persian words to be replaced by, in many cases, made-up words. Other reforms were attempted that never gained much traction, even during the lifetime of Atatürk, such as the introduction of pews and wearing shoes in mosques.

The combined effect of these policies was to cut off Turkey from both its Middle Eastern neighbors and its Ottoman past. The goal of the new regime was to create a new European Turk who could take his or her place as a member of the "advanced group of nations."

Atatürk's own attitude towards Islam appears ambiguous. He is quoted as saying, "Religion is an important institution. A nation without religion cannot survive," but he also declared, "I have no religion, and at times I wish all religions at the bottom of the sea. He is a weak ruler who needs religion to uphold his government," although to this he adds, "Every man can follow his own conscience, provided it does not interfere with sane reason."

Following Atatürk

The fervor of the new radicalism began to wane after World War II. Multiparty elections were instituted by Atatürk's successor, Ismet Inönü, from 1950. Over subsequent decades, a series of parties came to power that drew their support from the conservative Anatolian hinterland, which had never fully subscribed to the secular revolution. Despite a series of military coups to remove these governments, political Islam grew in strength, supported by Sufi networks and the work of religious scholar Said Nursi.

Political Islam eventually overcame its secular adversaries through electoral victories from the 1980s onward. From 2002, the Justice and Development Party (AKP) governments formed under the leadership of Recep Tayyip Erdogan are the culmination of this. Appealing to a coalition of religious conservatives and secular forces attracted by its language of civil rights and promises of EU membership, the AKP proved to be surprisingly durable. Under the AKP, Sufism also made a comeback.

The legacy of Atatürk remains, however, and in recent years one of the fiercest areas of contention in public discourse has been between secular and religious interpretations of Ottoman imperial and Turkish republican history. ■

> A political party cannot have a religion. Only individuals can.
> **Recep Tayyip Erdogan**

OUR CONSTITUTION IS THE QURAN

KING FAISAL (1967)

IN CONTEXT

THEME
The birth of Saudi Arabia

WHEN AND WHERE
1932, Arabian Peninsula

BEFORE
967 During the Abbasid era, the position of Sharif of Mecca is created for the steward of the holy cities of Mecca and Medina and surrounding Hejaz region. The term *sharif* is Arabic for "noble," and describes the descendants of the Prophet's grandson Hassan.

1919 Sharif Hussein of Mecca refuses to ratify the Treaty of Versailles at the end of World War I, forfeiting British support for his claims to rule Arabia.

AFTER
1946 Abdullah, son of Sharif Hussein, becomes the first king of the newly independent Hashemite Kingdom of Jordan.

I'm telling you,
you can't compare Saudi
Arabia to other countries.
Al-Walid bin Talal
*Member of the Saudi royal family
(b.1955)*

n the 7th century, armies swept out of Arabia to conquer vast territories in the name of Islam. Within a short time, new dynasties emerged in Damascus, Baghdad, and later in Cairo and Istanbul, relegating the birthplace of Islam to a political backwater. From the 10th century onward, the holy cities of Mecca and Medina were under the control of a local Arab ruler known as the Sharif of Mecca, a position that mostly owed allegiance to other powers— notably the Abbasids, Mamluks, and, from the 16th century, the Ottomans. The rest of Arabia reverted to tribal rule, as it was before the coming of the Prophet.

The 20th century, however, saw a remarkable turnaround—through a combination of conquest, shrewd diplomacy, and luck, the Arabian Peninsula regained control of the destiny of Islam once again.

Useful alliances

The first state in Arabia, called the Emirate of Diriyah, was the result of an alliance between a local ruler, Muhammad bin Saud (1710–65), and the preacher of a puritanical form

Elephant Rock in northern Saudi Arabia is a rare rocky landmark in a country that consists almost entirely of desert—and vast oil reserves, mainly in the Eastern Province.

of Islam, Muhammad ibn Abd al-Wahhab (1703–92). The two men formed a partnership in 1744, cemented by marriage between their children, and established the House of Saud. Wahhab's religious ideologies gave the House of Saud a legitimacy and potency other tribes lacked. Those same ideologies also brought down the first Saudi state in 1818, after the Wahhabis' jihad-inspired territorial expansions had provoked the Ottoman Empire to intervene and execute their leaders.

The Sauds established a second Saudi–Wahhabi state six years later. Known as the Emirate of Najd, it pragmatically limited itself to its home territory of the Najd region, in central Arabia. Even so, the Sauds' rule was contested by a rival tribe, the Rashidi, and in 1891 the Sauds were decisively defeated and went into exile in Kuwait, where they sought the protection of the ruling al-Sabah family.

See also: Wahhabism, or an Islamic reformation 216–17 ▪ The modern Sharia state 266–69 ▪ Sunni and Shia in the modern Middle East 270–71 ▪ The new extremists 272–77

In 1902, Abd al-Aziz (1875–1953), also known as Ibn Saud, son of the expelled Saudi ruler, managed to retake the family's hometown of Riyadh in a surprise nighttime attack. Using Riyadh as his base, Ibn Saud followed this up with attacks on small villages in southern Najd, forcing the Rashidi fighters to retreat.

In seeking to form a new state, Ibn Saud was careful to avoid past mistakes. At the outbreak of World War I, he courted favor with the British, who were eager to control the seas around Arabia; they encouraged the Sauds to capture the Arabian Peninsula from Ottoman control. Backed by British funding and weapons, Ibn Saud captured Mecca and Medina.

With the collapse of the Ottoman Empire at the end of World War I, the Rashidis lost their backers and by 1927, the Sauds had taken control of most of Arabia. In 1932, Ibn Saud formally united his realm into the Kingdom of Saudi Arabia, with himself as king. He reimposed the Wahhabi brand of Islam over the entire population, and appointed two of his sons as viceroys of the country's most important regions, Najd and Hejaz. He also brought in Muslim Arabs from Iraq, Syria, and Egypt to help administer a territory that was almost two-thirds as big as India, although only sparsely populated.

The infant kingdom was still extremely poor. Its main source of revenue came from fees paid by Hajj pilgrims, but even this income was unreliable. As a consequence of the worldwide Great Depression of the 1930s, the number of pilgrims dropped to a fifth of what it had been only a few years before.

Saudi Arabia is the heart of the Muslim world.
Abul Ala Mawdudi
Pakistani political leader (1903–79)

Oil and America

The kingdom's fortunes—and the politics of the Middle East—were transformed when drillers struck oil in 1938 at Dhahran, in the country's Eastern Province. The cash-strapped Ibn Saud granted American oil companies concessions to explore and drill further. This discovery would turn out to be the first of many, eventually revealing Saudi Arabia to be the largest source of crude oil ("black gold") in the world.

So significant were the finds that in 1945, as World War II entered its final year and the Cold War loomed, US President Franklin D. Roosevelt met Ibn Saud to secure assurances of unrestricted access to Saudi Arabia's oil. The two men reputedly got along so well that Roosevelt presented the king with one of his wheelchairs, while the king's gifts to the president included a diamond-encrusted dagger.

The meeting laid the foundations for a close relationship between Saudi Arabia and the United States that continues to this day and has profoundly influenced the history of the modern Middle East. In the years that followed, the American presence in Saudi Arabia grew, with the establishment of a US airbase in Dhahran and a plan to sponsor young Saudis to go to college in America, as a way of ensuring that the Saudi nation remained pro-American.

Problems of succession

On his death in 1953, Ibn Saud was succeeded by his second son, Prince Saud, who became King Saud. His reign was marked by conflict with his brother Faisal—given that their father had had 45 sons, 36 of whom survived to adulthood, sibling rivalry was almost inevitable, and highly dangerous. Faisal took advantage of the king's absence abroad because of illness to seize power in 1964. Worried that he himself might in turn fall to a coup, Faisal engaged in brutal internal suppression. »

Ibn Saud, King of Saudi Arabia, met US President Roosevelt on a warship on the Suez Canal in 1945. The meeting sealed an enduring special relationship between the countries.

When Faisal's brother Prince Talal and other liberal Saudi princes demanded political reform and a written constitution, which he feared might constrain his actions, the king responded, "our constitution is the Quran".

There followed a number of attempts to overthrow Faisal's government, most of which were foiled by a sophisticated Saudi internal security apparatus trained and equipped by the United States. So it was a shock to the West when, in 1973, Faisal withdrew oil from world markets in protest over Western support for Israel in that year's Arab–Israeli War.

The action earned the King great prestige among his fellow Arab nations. The oil embargo quadrupled the price of oil internationally and flooded Saudi Arabia with money, creating an economic boom in the Arabian Gulf region. Faisal was unable to enjoy the benefits of the windfall, however, —he was assassinated in 1975.

Large retractable umbrellas shelter pilgrims from the sun at the Prophet's Mosque in Medina. Saudi Arabia has invested heavily in developing the holy sites to accommodate more pilgrims.

A pipeline once carried oil from eastern Saudi Arabia all the way, via Jordan and Syria, to a Mediterranean port in Lebanon. It ceased operation in 1990 because of regional disputes.

Oil-fueled politics

Saudi Arabia's oil embargo of 1973 deeply shocked the West. So, too, had President Gamal Abdel Nasser of Egypt, when he took power in 1956 and nationalized the Suez Canal, a vital artery for international shipping and oil supplies. Nasser's vision of secular Pan-Arabism had made him a hero not just to Arabs but throughout the developing world.

Hoping to curb Nasser's growing influence, the Saudi monarchy opened its arms to his opponents— notably Egypt's Islamist group, the Muslim Brotherhood—giving them the money and arms they needed in the fight against Nasser. Meanwhile, many Egyptians—as well as Syrians, Iraqis, and other Arabs—poured into Saudi Arabia, where they received not just housing and work in the civil service, oil fields, and universities, but also first-hand exposure to the doctrine of Wahhabism.

From 1975 onward, under Faisal's successors, Saudi Arabia began to truly make its weight felt in the wider world through lavish spending. Many of its foreign policy goals aligned with those of the United States: Palestinian leader Yasser Arafat received money to keep things peaceful in Israel; the Somalis received money to expel the Soviets from their country; Zaire was given funds to fight pro-Soviet rebels in Angola.

The old alliance whereby the Saudi state backed its Wahhabi clerics still held, ensuring that they were well funded and able to impose their strict interpretation of Islam on the country and its holy sites. However, following Iran's overthrow of its monarchy in February 1979 and a failed Saudi insurrection by Wahhabi dissidents later that year, the state resolved to keep the clergy away from domestic

The Saudi Arabian capital Riyadh is the third-largest city in the Arab world. Dating from the pre-Islamic era, it has become a modern metropolis with a population of over 6 million people.

politics and instead occupy them with promoting Saudi–Wahhabi interests abroad. Over the next decade, Saudi Arabia allied with the United States in funding tens of thousands of *mujahideen* fighters from around the Muslim world to combat the Soviet Union's incursion into Afghanistan.

Moderate reforms

In 1990, following Iraq's invasion of Kuwait and fearing an attack on Saudi Arabia, the kingdom joined the military coalition against Iraqi leader Saddam Hussein. However, when King Fahd (r. 1982–2005) invited coalition forces to station themselves in Saudi Arabia, factions within the kingdom denounced Saudi dependence on the United States. In the wake of the Gulf War, Saudi Arabia suffered a wave of terrorist bombings thought to have been carried out by al-Qaeda and other Islamic extremists as part of a campaign against Westerners and Westernization.

In 1992, partly in response to civic unrest, King Fahd decreed the Basic Law of Saudi Arabia, a charter divided into nine chapters. It reassured citizens that the constitution of Saudi Arabia is "the Holy Quran, and the *sunna*" of the Prophet Muhammad. While the Basic Law contains many of the characteristics of a constitution, it does not override Islamic laws.

Saudi Arabia also realized that the export of Wahhabism was seen as a problem by its American allies. This led to a new era of domestic reform driven by Crown Prince and later King Abdullah (r. 2005–15), who instituted a restructuring of the judicial system and curbs on the religious establishment. The reforms have continued under his successor, King Salman.

Saudi Arabia has approximately 20 percent of the planet's known oil reserves, and Saudi Aramco, which extracts this oil, is believed to be the world's most profitable company. In addition, the annual revenue from pilgrims making the Hajj and Umra is expected to exceed $150 billion by 2022. Such wealth ensures that Saudi Arabia will continue to exert a strong influence on the practice of Islam for some time to come. ■

Far-reaching media

Saudi Arabia commands a powerful position in Pan-Arab media, influencing how it presents the news, politics, entertainment, and religious affairs. This media tends to support Saudi Arabia's agenda in foreign policy, and attacks those who do not conform to a Wahhabi line on Islam— notable targets are Iran, and Shia Islam in general. Since the late 1990s, Saudi's MBC, Orbit, and ART have been some of the most heavily watched TV channels in the Arab world. The rise of Saudi media marks the eclipse of Egypt as a political, economic, and media force in the region.

In 2003, the Saudis also set up Al Arabiya as a news channel to challenge Qatar's Al Jazeera. In coordination with the United Arab Emirates (UAE), where Al Arabiya is based, Saudi media is at the forefront of a new struggle for dominance between Saudi Arabia and the UAE on one side, and Turkey and Iran on the other.

We have developed a case of oil addiction in Saudi Arabia.
Muhammad bin Salman
Crown Prince of Saudi Arabia

ISLAM IS THE SOLUTION

THE MUSLIM BROTHERHOOD

he Muslim Brotherhood
(*Jamaat al-Ikhwan*) was
formed in 1928, in the Suez
Canal city of Ismailia in Egypt, by
schoolteacher Hassan al-Banna
(1906–49). He was influenced by
the likes of Jamal al-Din al-Afghani,
Muhammad Abdu, and Rashid Rida
of the Muslim modernist movement,
and their project to recast Islam to
meet the challenge of the West.
Today, the Brotherhood—as it is
commonly abbreviated—is the
world's oldest political Islamist
group. It has always campaigned
for a system of rule based on
Islamic law—its slogan is "Islam
is the solution." The Brotherhood
has married the idea of political

See also: *Al-Jahiliyya*, the Time of Ignorance 20–21 ▪ The rise of Islamic Modernism 222–23 ▪ The secularization of Turkey 228–31 ▪ The new extremists 272–77

All Muslims **not living according to Sharia** are living in **jahiliyya**, or a state of ignorance brought about by the influence of the West.

↓

A vanguard of **true Muslims** must pursue **jihad** to bring enlightenment to the greater Muslim nation.

↓

The goal is to bring about the **absolute sovereignty of God**, or *hakimiyyat Allah*, and the liberation of service by humans to other humans.

activism with social responsibility, offering aid to often-marginalized elements of society. However, in the past, members and affiliates of the party have resorted to extremist violence, and in recent times the organization has found itself demonized and persecuted by the Egyptian state.

Militant beginnings

In founding the Brotherhood, the charismatic al-Banna was influenced by a number of factors, including the belief that Britain had pressured the Turks into abolishing the Islamic caliphate in 1924, and the continued presence of British troops of occupation in supposedly independent Egypt. Al-Banna's

organization, which quickly spread throughout Egypt, was built around a structure of *usra* ("families" of four or five initiates led by a *naqib*, or "captain") and held together by a strict culture of obedience. By 1936 it was able to organize mass protests against British rule in

Palestine. After World War II the Brotherhood sent paramilitary units to take part in the 1948 war in Palestine. Alarmed by the group's size and reach, and fearing it would carry out a coup, the British-backed government of Egypt outlawed the organization in December 1948. In retaliation, a member of the Brotherhood assassinated Egyptian Prime Minister Mahmoud al-Nokrashi. In February 1949, unknown assailants shot and killed al-Banna.

Sayyid Qutb

The Brotherhood now entered its most influential period, dominated by its greatest intellectual, Sayyid Qutb (1906–66). Qutb was a civil servant and well-known liberal writer of literary criticism who underwent a transformation to Islamic ideologue in the late 1940s. After two years of study in the United States, Qutb returned to Egypt in 1950 and became a vociferous critic of not just America but of the secular culture of the West in general. Qutb openly »

The headquarters of the Muslim Brotherhood in Cairo burns in 1954, set on fire by angry crowds in retaliation against the attempted assassination of prime minister Gamal Abdel Nasser.

> The civilization of the West, which was brilliant by virtue of its scientific perfection for a long time, is now bankrupt and in decline.
> **Hassan al-Banna**

supported the Brotherhood, although he did not formally join it until 1953. When army officers led by Gamal Abdel Nasser seized power in a military coup in 1952, overthrowing the British-backed monarchy, Qutb and the Muslim Brotherhood cooperated enthusiastically with the coup leaders. The relationship soured when Qutb turned down then-prime minister Nasser's offer of the post of minister of education, and the Brotherhood as a whole was unwilling to place its huge

organization at the service of the new military regime. After an assassination attempt against him in 1954, Nasser cracked down on the Brotherhood, and Qutb was one of many who were arrested.

Vanguard of believers

While in prison, Qutb wrote a book called *Signs on the Road* (*Maalim fi'l-Tariq*), which was published in 1964 and became an international manifesto for an Islamic revolution. The book is based around the twin concepts of *jahiliya* (ignorance) and *hakimiyya* (sovereignty); Qutb believes that the modern world, including the parts inhabited by Muslims, is no better than the pre-Islamic "Age of Ignorance." He argues that a vanguard of true believers is needed to bring about a truly Islamic society for all mankind, one in which clerics and rulers ensure that parliament only passes laws that accord with Sharia. Qutb was scathing about contemporary non-Islamic, nationalist ideologies including Nasser's ideas about Pan-Arabism, and suggested the vanguard would need to be prepared to defend itself from the forces of the state.

> A society cannot be Islamic if it expels the religious Laws of Islam, so nothing of Islam is left except rites and ceremonials.
> **Sayyid Qutb**

Qutb implied that only the vanguard were true Muslims—all other Muslims living in states, whether Arab or non-Arab, in which Sharia law was not applied (for example, Egypt) were by default non-Muslim. In Qutb's view, Muslim governments and societies were corrupted by the West to the point that they had abandoned Islam. Only a return to Islam could free people to become true Muslims living under the sovereignty of God. This was a revolutionary plan to save humankind. Two years after

Inspiration from Europe

In two books, *Islam and the Problem of Civilization* (1962) and *The Future Belongs to This Religion* (1964), Sayyid Qutb cited heavily from French biologist-turned-eugenicist Alexis Carrel's 1935 critique of industrial civilization. Carrel's idea of a new elite of the mentally and physically superior who should withdraw from society in preparation for its renewal clearly foreshadows Qutb's notion of the Muslim vanguard. Critics point out that although Qutb did not translate anything from Carrel's passages arguing for sterilization and

euthanasia of society's "defectives," he presented no challenge to them either.

Qutb's work is also compared with that of West Indian anti-colonial theorist Frantz Fanon (1925–61) and his study of Algeria's war of independence. Both authors dealt with the perpetuation of colonial attitudes by successor regimes. Fanon sounds very much like Qutb when he writes: "So comrades, let us not pay tribute to Europe by creating states, institutions and societies that draw their inspiration from it."

Supporters of Muhammad Mursi, the Muslim Brotherhood candidate who became Egyptian president, march in 2013. The former fringe Islamic party briefly headed the country.

presidential elections held in 2012, its candidate Muhammad Mursi won the vote. But Mursi's secretive style of leadership and restrictive policies soon led to a fall from grace, allowing the military to mount a coup.

After Mursi was ousted, the state imposed a brutal crackdown. Hundreds of Brotherhood members were killed on the streets and thousands more imprisoned. Its leadership went into exile. The group had proved incapable of managing Egypt's democratic transition. It was still driven by the Qutbist model of the vanguard, while party thinking on social and political questions, such as the rights of women and the freedoms of secularism, was too far out of step with that of the more moderate Egyptian public.

Disturbing legacy

Although the mainstream Muslim Brotherhood no longer identifies with the teachings of its former figurehead Sayyid Qutb, he remains enormously influential. His call for Muslims to replace the sovereignty of man with that of God continues to inspire some extremist thinking—although it should be noted that Qutb never sanctioned violence, and once wrote that the killing of innocents finds no justification in the Quran. Apart from Middle East specialists, few in the West have heard of Sayyid Qutb, yet he is widely studied across the Muslim world, where his legacy continues to be a source of division decades after his death in 1966. ∎

Signs on the Road was published, Qutb was hanged for treason, becoming a martyr for the cause of radical Islam.

The Brotherhood today

Following the initial era of al-Banna and the radical era of Qutb, a third act in the history of the Brotherhood saw the group return to active participation in civil society.

After President Anwar Sadat took office in 1970, he released large numbers of prisoners and allowed the Brotherhood to operate again. A new generation of members entered into politics. The group made great strides, becoming the strongest opposition group not only in Egypt but across the region through affiliate parties such as Ennahda in Tunisia and Milli Görüs (National Vision) in Turkey.

This period came to an end during the Arab uprisings of spring 2011. After Egyptian president Hosni Mubarak was forced out by mass public protests in February of that year, the Brotherhood emerged as the dominant political player. In

Only in the Islamic way of life do all men become free from the servitude of some men to others.
Sayyid Qutb

LAND OF THE PURE

REHMAT ALI (1933)

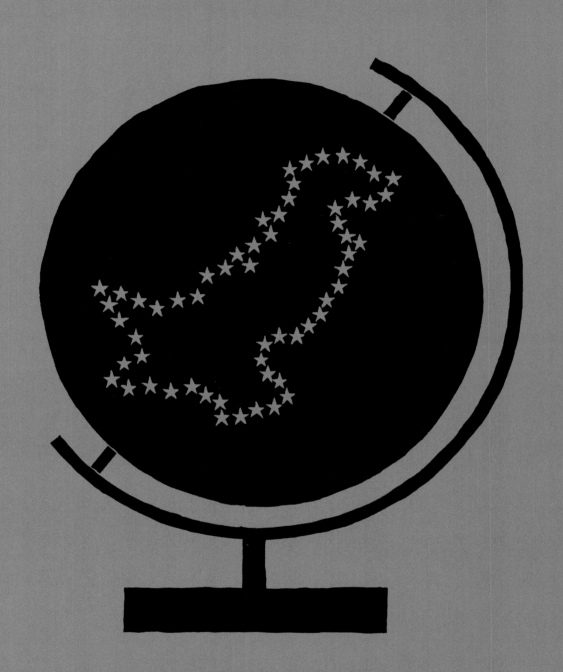

IN CONTEXT

THEME
The creation of Pakistan

WHEN AND WHERE
1947, India

BEFORE
8th century Islam arrives in India, brought by invading armies from Central Asia; it becomes a major religion under the Delhi Sultanate.

1526 Babur defeats the Sultan of Delhi at the Battle of Panipat and founds the Mughal Empire.

AFTER
1977 General Zia-ul-Haq takes control of Pakistan in a coup; he commits to establishing an Islamic state and enforcing Sharia to restore the country's Islamic identity.

1988 Following Zia-ul-Haq's death, Benazir Bhutto becomes Pakistan's first female prime minister, as well as the first female head of government in a Muslim-majority country.

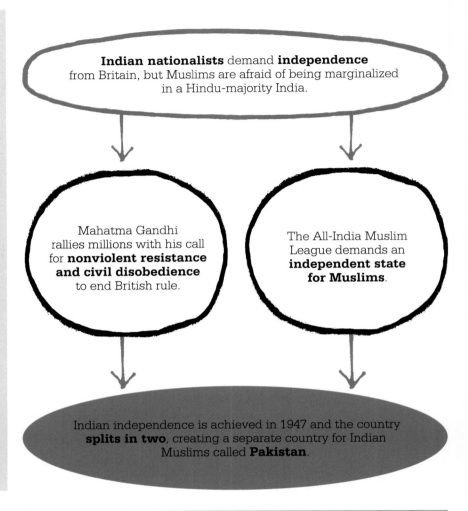

Indian nationalists demand **independence** from Britain, but Muslims are afraid of being marginalized in a Hindu-majority India.

Mahatma Gandhi rallies millions with his call for **nonviolent resistance and civil disobedience** to end British rule.

The All-India Muslim League demands an **independent state for Muslims**.

Indian independence is achieved in 1947 and the country **splits in two**, creating a separate country for Indian Muslims called **Pakistan**.

P akistan is often said to be the only country to have been created in the name of Islam. It was formed in 1947, when India was partitioned along religious lines into two separate nations: the predominantly Hindu India and Muslim Pakistan. As a result, about 97 percent of Pakistanis are Muslims, and the country has the second-largest number of Muslims in the world (only Indonesia has more). The name of the country was invented in 1933 by Rehmat Ali, a Muslim Indian student in Britain, who came up with the acronym

"Pakstan" to describe a future Muslim state that would include the Punjab, the North-West Frontier Province (also known as the Afghan Province), Kashmir, Sind, and Baluchistan. The letter "i" was added to ease pronunciation. *Pak* also means "pure" in Urdu—so Pakistan was to be the wholly Islamic "Land of the Pure."

The British threat
At its height under Akbar the Great in the late 16th century, the Mughal Empire ruled almost all of South Asia: an area including what are

now Afghanistan, Bangladesh, Nepal, India, Pakistan, and Sri Lanka. The Mughals had built on the legacy of previous Muslim sultanates that had governed most of north India since the late 12th century. After the Mughal Empire began to disintegrate in the early 18th century, Muslim successor dynasties continued to control much of India, although Hindus made up most of the population.

The main threat to Muslim dominion came not from Hindus, however, but from the British. The British East India Company opened

See also: The Mughal Empire 204–05 ▪ The origins of Ahmadiyya 220–21 ▪ The secularization of Turkey 228–31 ▪ The demographics of Islam today 260–61 ▪ The rising tide of Islamophobia 286–87

The aim of Islam
is to bring about
a universal revolution.
Abul Ala Mawdudi

a first trading post in 1619, but in the 18th century its interests turned from trade to territory. In 1757, it took control of Bengal, followed by Bihar, and gradually increased its territories until it commanded most of the Indian subcontinent.

There were also other challenges to Muslim rule. In northern India, Sayyid Ahmad Barelvi (1786–1831)

preached Islamic revival and led a jihad against growing Sikh power in the Punjab. He was killed, along with many of his followers, at a battle at Balakot in 1831. Some scholars believe he anticipated the idea of modern Islamists, in waging jihad to try to create an Islamic state. A more critical moment in the struggle for power came with the rebellion of 1857 against the British. Although many Hindus took part, the British saw the Muslims as the principal force behind the uprising, and they bore the brunt of British wrath in the aftermath. From this time on, Hindus were favored by British officials over their Muslim counterparts.

Two-nation theory

Mughal aristocrat Sayyid Ahmad Khan (1817–98) argued that Muslims needed to cooperate more with the British and learn the ways of the modern West to develop their

Don't compare your nation
with the nations of the West.
Distinctive is the nation of
the Prophet of Islam.
Muhammad Iqbal

education and compete with the Hindus. He warned that "India is inhabited by two different nations," who would inevitably vie with each other for power if the British left.

In 1885, less than three decades after the uprising of 1857, the Indian National Congress was formed in order to give political representation to Indians in British-ruled India. Membership in the Congress was open to all, but Hindus significantly outnumbered Muslims—reflecting the fact that only a quarter of the population of India was Muslim. In response, in 1906 Muslims founded the All-India Muslim League, which sought to counter the growing influence of the Hindus.

The Muslim League originally grew from an intellectual group at the Aligarh Muslim University, founded by Sayyid Ahmad Khan. Poet Muhammad Iqbal was »

The partition of India in 1947 led to one of the biggest displacements of people in peacetime, as both Muslims and Hindus fled to their respective sides of the new border.

elected president of the League in 1930, and in his presidential address at Allahabad, Iqbal put forward the demand for a separate Muslim state in India, made up of the Punjab, North-West Frontier Province, Sind, and Baluchistan. In his words, "Self-government within the British Empire, or without the British Empire, the formation of a consolidated North-west Indian Muslim state appears to me to be the final destiny of the Muslims, at least of North-west India."

The so-called "two-nation theory" gained popularity among Muslims but was rejected by the Indian National Congress. In 1935, the British agreed to grant self-government to India in the form of a parliamentary democracy. Congress made an informal promise to the Muslim League that the two parties would form coalition governments in provinces with substantial Muslim populations, but after elections they reneged on this promise. In the Lahore Resolution (also known as the Pakistan Resolution) of 1940, the League's then-leader, Muhammad Ali Jinnah, laid out the formal demand for an independent Muslim state.

Birth of the new state
In 1942, after two decades of leading India's mass movement of nonviolent protest, Mahatma Gandhi made his "Quit India" speech, urging Hindus and Muslims to unite in ending British rule. Muslim–Hindu violence increased, however, and in 1947, crippled by debt after World War II, Britain agreed with Congress and the Muslim League on the partition

Pakistan's flag, waved here at a cricket match, is the Crescent and Star. The green represents the country's Muslim majority; the white, its minorities; the star is light, the crescent is progress.

of India. The area that was then being referred to as Pakistan was to consist of two halves: in the east, the Muslim-majority area of Bengal, and in the west the Muslim-majority

Jamaat-e Islami

In 1867, a group of Indian scholars founded a madrasa that was hostile to British colonial rule. The school was called the Darul Uloom Deoband and its followers became known as Deobandis. The movement spread across South Asia, and in 1941, it was the ideas spread by the Deobandis that inspired Islamic philosopher, jurist, journalist, and imam Abul Ala Mawdudi (1903–79) to found the Jamaat-e Islami (Party of Islam) in India. Mawdudi sought to revive Islam in response to what he saw as the threat of Western secular imperialism.

The Jamaat initially opposed the idea of the creation of Pakistan, preferring to struggle for a more perfect Muslim society within India. After Partition, the party split into separate groups in India and Pakistan; the Pakistan group led the movement to transform the country into an Islamic state. After General Muhammad Zia-ul-Haq seized power in Pakistan in a military coup in 1977, the Jamaat supported him in introducing "Sharization" to Pakistan. Since Zia's death in 1988, the Jamaat's influence has dwindled.

area of Punjab and adjoining territories. The two were separated by almost 1,000 miles (1,600 km) of Indian territory. Jinnah was made governor-general, and his lieutenant in the League, Liaquat Ali Khan, was named prime minister.

Pakistani identity

Partition caused one of the largest movements of people ever seen. Muslims moved north out of India into Pakistan, and Hindus left what was now Pakistan for Indian territories. Some 12 million people became refugees, and between half a million and a million people were killed in religious violence.

Despite the creation of a new Muslim homeland, more Muslims stayed on in India than those who left, while about two million Hindus remained in Pakistan. The crisis over who controlled the region of

Take Islam out of Pakistan and make it a secular state; it would collapse.
Muhammad Zia-ul-Haq
President of Pakistan 1978–88

Kashmir led to war between the two nations. In 1971, Pakistan itself split into two countries, with the creation of an independent Bangladesh in the east.

Both Jinnah and his prime minister were dead within four years of the creation of Pakistan,

and the influence of the Muslim League dwindled. Since then, government of the country has swung between civilian democracy and military dictatorship.

While Islam is the state religion, Pakistan is not an Islamic state; its rule of law is not set by Sharia. Political parties hold opposing views about whether Pakistan was intended as a secular homeland for Indian Muslims (which was the view of Jinnah) or as an Islamic state. Many ask what the point is of creating a Muslim state if it is not Islamic, but Islamist parties have never been able to garner significant support in elections. ∎

Faisal Mosque in Pakistan's capital, Islamabad, is one of the largest mosques in the world. Built with funding from the Saudi King Faisal in 1976, its design echoes the shape of a Bedouin tent.

ISLAM IS POLITICS OR IT IS NOTHING

AYATOLLAH KHOMEINI

IN CONTEXT

THEME
The Iranian Revolution

WHEN AND WHERE
1979, Iran

BEFORE
1501 The 15-year-old Ismail proclaims himself shah and becomes the first of the Safavid dynasty. He replaces Sunnism with Shiism as the Persian state religion.

1789 The Qajar clan, which had been prominent under the Safavids, takes control of Iran.

AFTER
1980 Iraq invades Iran, worried that the 1979 Iranian Revolution could cause Iraq's Shia majority to rebel against the country's Sunni regime. The war ends in 1988, at a cost of an estimated 500,000 lives.

I n 1979, Iran underwent a popular revolution whose seismic impact on the country and beyond has been compared with the French Revolution in 1789 and the Russian Revolution in 1917. Rule by a constitutional monarchy was replaced with rule by theocracy, as the people of Iran installed a religious leader as the highest authority in the land.

The revolution within Iran was supposed to be only the beginning of a larger Islamic revolution that would extend throughout the *umma*, or global Muslim community. More than 40 years later, that wider Islamic revolution has yet to materialize, but Iranian-backed

See also: The emergence of Shia Islam 108–15 ▪ The Safavid Empire 192–93 ▪ The secularization of Turkey 228–31 ▪ Sunni and Shia in the modern Middle East 270–71

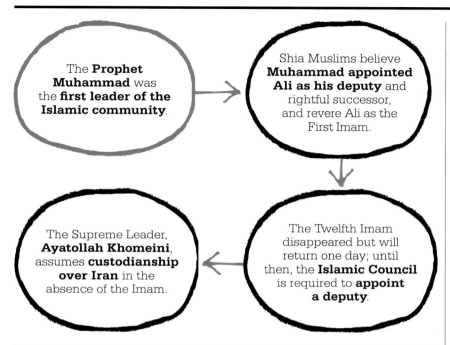

The **Prophet Muhammad** was the **first leader of the Islamic community**.

Shia Muslims believe **Muhammad appointed Ali as his deputy** and rightful successor, and revere Ali as the First Imam.

The Twelfth Imam disappeared but will return one day; until then, the **Islamic Council** is required to **appoint a deputy**.

The Supreme Leader, **Ayatollah Khomeini**, assumes **custodianship over Iran** in the absence of the Imam.

Only God, the Exalted, is the light; everything else is darkness.
Ayatollah Khomeini

Shia groups continue to influence events in the Middle East in a significant way.

The Shah
The revolution ended the unpopular rule of the Pahlavi shahs (kings), which had begun when Reza Khan, a military commander, seized power in 1921 and became shah in 1925. The Qajar dynasty he deposed had been propped up by loans from Britain and Russia in return for crippling economic concessions— including the exploitation of Iran's oil fields, which had first been discovered in 1908.

An admirer of Mustafa Kemal Atatürk's reforms in Turkey, Reza Shah wanted Iran and Iranians to look modern. He sidelined the *ulema* (religious council) and banned the *hijab*. When the *ulema* protested in 1935 at the ongoing secularization, dozens were machine-gunned in the precincts of the Imam Reza Shrine in Mashhad. In 1941, Reza Shah was forced to abdicate and was succeeded by his Swiss-educated son, Muhammad Reza Pahlavi.

The new shah continued his father's policies, and after World War II he drew Iran close to the United States, a country that his government viewed as a suitably modern and anti-colonial partner. Iran became filled with American products, from cars to Coca-Cola, as well as American expatriates, particularly oil workers and military personnel.

Iran became an important Middle Eastern ally of the US as the Cold War set in, due to its long border with its neighbor, the Soviet Union. After the popular prime minister Muhammad Mosaddegh nationalized the oil industry in 1951, a US-led coup two years later allowed the Shah to reassert his grip on power.

In 1971, the Shah threw a lavish party at the ancient site of Persepolis to celebrate 2,500 years of Iranian monarchy. He invited global heads of state to an event that was said to have cost in excess of $100 million. Meanwhile, average working-class Iranians were mired »

Muhammad Reza Pahlavi (center) visits the United States in 1962, at the height of the Cold War, and is received by President John F. Kennedy.

in poverty and, although the middle classes did enjoy some of the benefits of the country's oil wealth, the Shah's autocratic and repressive regime stifled free speech and ignored human rights. Many disaffected groups found common cause in an opposition movement that had coalesced around the black-garbed figure of an exiled religious leader, Ayatollah Khomeini.

The Ayatollah

Ruhollah Khomeini was born in 1902 in Khomein, a small town between Tehran and Isfahan. He came from a family of *sayyids*, or descendants from the Prophet; the family traced its lineage back to the Shias' Seventh Imam and thus to the First Imam: Ali, Muhammad's rightful successor, according to the Shia. Khomeini studied religious law in Qom, and become a *mujtahid* at the precocious age of 34.

In 1963, Khomeini spoke out against a new raft of reforms proposed by the Shah, which he considered to be an attack on Islam. He condemned the Shah for spreading moral corruption in Iran, and accused him of submission to

Islam is the religion of militant individuals who are committed to truth and justice.
Ayatollah Khomeini

America, and to Israel, whom the Iranian regime supplied with oil. In 1964, Khomeini denounced a new law that extended diplomatic immunity to US military personnel in Iran, saying, "They have reduced the Iranian people to a level lower than that of an American dog." He was forced into exile—first in Turkey, then Iraq, and finally Paris.

A theory of Islamic rule

Khomeini remained an important figure during his exile, with many supporters in Iran displaying his picture and following his speeches, which were smuggled into the

country on cassette tapes. Khomeini used this time to develop his ideas on Islamic rule. In his book *Hukumat-e Islami: Velayat-e Faqih* ("Islamic Government: Regency of the Jurist"), published in 1970, Khomeini argued that the actions of the Prophet constituted proof of the legitimacy of an Islamic government—Muhammad himself had established a government and engaged in the implementation of laws and administration of society.

According to Twelver Shia Islam, Muhammad had been followed by his rightful successor, Ali and the rest of the Imams. In the absence of the "Hidden Imam" (the Twelfth), the responsibility to rule passed to those selected by the *ulema*. Khomeini demanded the removal of the Shah and his administration, and the establishment of an *ulema*-appointed government instead.

Khomeini represented only one camp in the opposition to the Shah. Another figure who commanded a large following was the Western-educated intellectual Ali Shariati, who was inspired by Marxism and Western anti-colonial scholars, and incorporated their ideas into the concepts of Shia Islam. However,

---

Mujtahid and ayatollahs

After the collapse of the Safavid Empire in the 18th century, many of the Shia *ulema* (religious authorities) emigrated from Iran. From these emerged two distinct schools of legal thought. The first school, the Akhbaris, took the theological position that everything a Muslim needed to know was in the Quran and the *hadith*. The other school, the Usulis, argued that *ijtihad* (independent legal ruling) was necessary to reinterpret religious law afresh for each generation.

Ultimately, the Usulis prevailed in Iran, coming to prominence in the 19th century under the Qajar dynasty. While most Akhbaris believe no one can give new religious rules until the return of the Mahdi, in the Usuli system, there is a special class of religious scholar called *mujtahid*, who are qualified to interpret and pronounce an opinion on matters of law. The title of ayatollah (which means "sign of God") is bestowed on the highest level of *mujtahid*.

In January 1979, fervent crowds in Tehran proclaimed allegiance to Ayatollah Khomeini. Within weeks, the Shah left Iran and Khomeini returned.

> The *sunna* and path of the Prophet constitute a proof of the necessity for establishing government.
> **Ayatollah Khomeini**

After 14 years in exile, Ayatollah Khomeini returned to Tehran on February 1, 1979—a day still celebrated each year as a public holiday in Iran.

as a result of his political activity he was imprisoned and then exiled, and died in the UK in 1977.

The following year, an attack on Khomeini in government-backed newspapers in Iran led to protestors in the shrine city of Qom calling for the Ayatollah's return. A number of students were killed by security forces. The demonstrations spread to other cities and were met with more violence. Factory workers went on strike in sympathy with the demonstrators, and the government declared martial law, sending tanks out into the streets. On the holiday of Ashura, which that year fell on December 11, more than a million people demonstrated in Tehran. Soldiers began to desert. In January 1979, the Shah relinquished power and left the country. On February 1, Khomeini flew back to Iran.

Revolutionary government

Four days after his return, Khomeini addressed his followers in Tehran and announced the formation of a new government. "This is not an ordinary government. It is a government based on the Sharia," he said. "Opposing this government means opposing the Sharia of Islam … Revolt against God's government is a revolt against God. Revolt

against God is blasphemy." Khomeini appointed a new prime minister, even though the previous incumbent was still in office. Rival supporters battled in the streets, but the fighting was short-lived; on February 11, the Supreme Military Council ordered all military personnel back to their bases, ceding control to Khomeini. Two months later, a referendum was held on whether Iran should become an Islamic Republic: 98 percent of the voters were in favor.

The new administration was a hybrid. Its head of state, known as the Supreme Leader, was a religious figure, placing the Islamic faith at the center of the state, and Ayatollah Khomeini filled this role for the rest of his life. Ostensibly, the Supreme Leader's authority is supplemented by a democratic structure, with an Iranian president serving as the head of government,

elected by the Iranian people for a maximum eight-year term. However, the theocracy holds ultimate power, since presidential candidates have to be approved by a panel of clerics before they can run for election.

The Iranian Revolution was not necessarily about religion, but Islam was the single most important force in uniting the people against a shah who was characterized as despotic and under the sway of the Western governments. Despite being in exile from Iran during the period that led to the toppling of the Shah, Khomeini was the leading architect of the Islamic Republic, and it was he who provided its composite model of governance. ∎

ISLAM TODAY

General Muhammad Zia-ul-Haq leads a **military coup in Pakistan**. He becomes president and adopts Sharia law.

1977

A **popular revolution in Iran** replaces the regime of the Shah with an Islamic state led by Ayatollah Khomeini.

1979

The **Soviet Union invades Afghanistan** in support of the ruling but unpopular communist government.

1979

Led by Saddam Hussein, Iraq invades the newly declared Islamic state of Iran, beginning the eight-year **Iran–Iraq War**.

1980

Islamic extremists **assassinate Egyptian president Anwar Sadat** after he makes peace with Israel.

1981

Iraq invades Kuwait. After the United Nations condemns the invasion, a US-led coalition force liberates Kuwait.

1990

On 9/11, al-Qaeda launches coordinated **terrorist attacks against the US**, killing almost 3,000 victims.

2001

The United States leads an **invasion of Iraq** with the aim of toppling the regime of Saddam Hussein.

2003

The Islam of today is very much shaped by events that took place as the 1970s ended and the 1980s began. In 1977, a coup in Pakistan saw Muhammad Zia-ul-Haq take charge of the country and introduce *Nizam-e-Mustafa* or the "rule of the Prophet"—Sharia law. Two years later, the Soviet Union invaded Afghanistan, and Pakistan allied with Saudi Arabia, Iran, and the United States, among others, in funding and arming the Afghan resistance. Also in 1979, the secular regime of the Shah in Iran was overthrown by a popular revolution that brought Ayatollah Khomeini to power and transformed the country into an Islamic state. In 1981, another reliable ally of the West, the Egyptian president Anwar Sadat, was assassinated by Islamists. In a little over four years, large parts of the Muslim world had been swept by a wave of Islamic conservatism and anti-Westernism.

Seeds of conflict

The Iranian Revolution swept hardline Shia clergy into power, triggering alarm in other countries with sizeable Shia populations of their own. One such country, Sunni-ruled Iraq, invaded Iran, setting off a bloody eight-year war.

Iraq had barely made peace with Iran when it launched another invasion, this time of Kuwait in 1990. With international oil supplies in jeopardy, not just in Kuwait but also in neighboring Saudi Arabia, the United States led a rescue coalition. This first Gulf War culminated in Operation Desert Storm, which lasted about six weeks in early 1991 and resulted in the liberation of Kuwait. However, the presence of US forces in the Middle East, particularly in Saudi Arabia, home to the holy cities of Mecca and Medina, caused resentment among some Muslims, some of whom had only recently returned from Afghanistan, where they had been successful in driving out the Russians. It was from among the ranks of these Islamic fighters that militant Islamist groups such as the Taliban and al-Qaeda emerged.

Perceptions of Islam

Al-Qaeda's goal was to strike at the West in retaliation for its perceived oppression of Muslims. On September 11, 2001, al-Qaeda agents launched terror attacks on America with massive loss of life.

Starting in Tunisia, anti-government protests and uprisings, known as the **Arab Spring**, spread across North Africa and the Middle East.

A 17-year-old Pakistani activist for female education, **Malala Yousafzai**, becomes the youngest winner of the Nobel Peace Prize.

In Indonesia, **Islam Nusantara** is launched as an alternative interpretation of an Islam from a non-Arabic perspective.

Rashida Tlaib and Ilhan Omar become the **first Muslim women to sit in the US Congress**.

2011   **2014**   **2015**   **2019**

2013   **2014**   **2018**   **2019**

The Somali-based terrorist organization **al-Shabab** attacks the Westgate shopping mall in Nairobi, Kenya, killing 67 people.

Militant group **Islamic State** captures large areas of Iraq and Syria and declares a new caliphate.

Saudi Arabia lifts its ban on women driving cars and issues its first licenses to female drivers.

Brunei implements new Sharia laws in which adultery and sex between men are punishable by stoning to death.

The US responded by attacking al-Qaeda bases in Afghanistan and invading Iraq, ultimately deposing its ruler Saddam Hussein.

The 9/11 attacks led many in the West to view every expression of Islam as a threat. This was a cause of particular anguish for the millions of Muslims living as minorities in the West, who became subjected to mistrust and an increasing tide of Islamophobia.

The West's perception of the Muslim world underwent another profound change in 2011 with the Arab Spring uprisings against regimes across North Africa and the Middle East. The fact that many of the revolutionary movements were led by young people, that women were as present at the protests as men, and that the protestors' demands were for free, democratic elections led the watching world to believe that a new era was dawning in the region. This has yet to materialize, but the image of young Muslims—of both sexes—battling for their civil and human rights has helped to promote a more nuanced view of the Muslim world.

Opposing forms

Even though less than one fifth of the global Muslim population lives in the Middle East, the region retains an outsized influence on the rest of the Islamic world. Indonesia, which has the world's largest Muslim population, has developed its own Southeast Asian take on Islam, but thanks to huge oil wealth, it is Saudi Arabia and the Arab Gulf states that have the most prominent say in the form in which Islam is observed around the world. This takes the form of a strict, back-to-basics approach, known as Wahhabism (in its strict Saudi form) or Salafism.

In the Middle East, Saudi Arabia's hegemony within Islam is challenged by Iran. Since Saddam Hussein's demise, Iranian influence has expanded into Iraq – which has a Shia majority – and across Syria into Lebanon. Recent conflict in Iraq and Syria—including the war against the Islamic State—has created millions of Muslim refugees. Some of these have been absorbed by neighbouring countries, but many have fled to Europe. As a result of this forced migration, allied with high Muslim birth rates, the numbers of Muslims in Europe, and worldwide, are predicted to increase rapidly in the coming decades, quite possibly altering the story of Islam once more. ∎

WE BELONG TO GOD, AND TO HIM WE SHALL RETURN

THE QURAN, 2:156

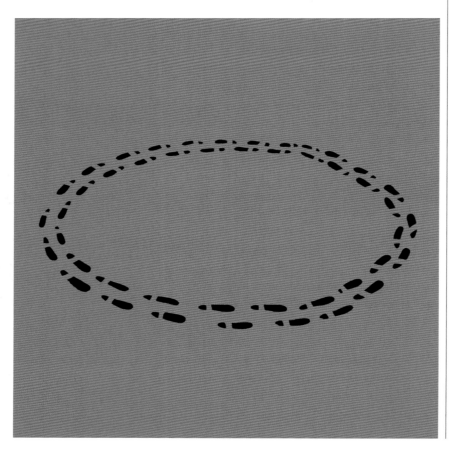

IN CONTEXT

THEME
Rites of passage

WHEN AND WHERE
Today, worldwide

BEFORE
595 The future prophet Muhammad marries Khadija, who is 15 years his senior. He remains monogamous, but after she dies, he marries another 10 times.

8th century Legal scholar al-Shafii decrees that it is desirable for a man to confine himself to a single wife, although it is permissible for him to marry more than one.

2007 Egypt's al-Azhar University, an Islamic institution that rules on social conduct, conducted a study of ways to inhibit the spread of *urfi*, or unofficial, marriages, which, it stated, had "reached alarming proportions."

All Muslims, whether practicing or not, still embrace the rituals of their faith at important moments in their lives, notably birth, marriage, and death.

On the birth of a Muslim child it is traditional in some cultures for the *Shahada* to be whispered into its right ear—"There is no god but God, and Muhammad is the messenger of God." The central message of Islam is the first thing the child ever hears. Tradition also states that the baby's first taste should be something sweet, so parents may chew a piece of date and rub the juice on the baby's gums, or alternatively use honey.

See also: The Five Pillars of Islam: *Shahada* 36–41 ▪ The Quranic concept of Heaven 92 ▪ Sayings and actions of the Prophet 118–23 ▪ God's guidance through Sharia 128–33

An Indonesian grandfather cuts a baby's hair as part of the *aqiqa* ceremony. Many Muslims believe that by performing *aqiqa* they will keep their children safe from harm.

Preparing for life

Babies are usually named on the first or seventh day after birth, based on a tradition recorded in a *hadith*. Names are usually derived from those of the prophets, their wives, or the Companions, with Muhammad being the most common choice for boys. Some sources claim that Muhammad is the world's most popular boys' name, and not just in Muslim-majority countries: the UK's Office for National Statistics revealed that Muhammad, and its 14 different registered spellings, was the most popular boys' name for babies born in Britain in 2017.

There are a number of events that take place on or after the seventh day, including shaving the baby's head. The hair removed is weighed and the equivalent weight in silver (or its monetary value) is given to charity. It is also traditional to observe *aqiqa*, which is the sacrifice of a goat or sheep to express thanks to God for the child. For a boy, two animals are sacrificed, for a girl, it is one; the meat is given to relatives and neighbors, and also to the poor. These days there are special *aqiqa* charities that will carry out the sacrifice on behalf of the family and then distribute the meat to the poor.

Muslim boys are circumcised, which ideally takes place at the age of one week, but can take place any time before puberty. In Malaysia, for example, the procedure serves as a rite marking the boy's passage into adulthood. Circumcision is something that predates Islam, and is thought to date back to the time of the prophet Ibrahim (Abraham). There is no mention of circumcision in the Quran, but it is addressed in the *hadith*. For example the *Sahih al-Bukhari* and *Sahih Muslim* quote the Prophet as including circumcision in a list of things that are *fitra*—a term that describes the state of purity all humans are born into—along with trimming the mustache and clipping one's nails.

In rural areas, the operation might be performed by a barber, but it is more commonly done at a clinic or hospital. Being a custom rather than a part of Islamic doctrine, circumcision is not obligatory for converts to Islam.

Female circumcision, or female genital mutilation (FGM), is not a part of Islamic religious observance and is widely banned as a violation of human rights. Where it is practiced—including in rural Egypt, Sudan, and Muslim and non-Muslim communities in East Africa, as well as some immigrant communities in the West—it is a cultural tradition, rather than anything authorized by the Quran.

Getting married

Dating between young Muslim men and women in the majority of Muslim countries is not common, and premarital sex is an absolute taboo. Instead, families play a large role in bringing young couples together. It is commonly accepted that parents are in the best position to find a good life partner for their »

Lord, give us joy in our wives and children, and make us examples to those who fear You.
25:74

***Sura* 35** "The Creator," verse 11, succinctly outlines the cycle of life: we are born, we reproduce, we die. It also reveals that how long everyone lives or dies is preordained.

Birth
"God created you from dust, then from a little germ…"

Marriage
"Into two sexes He divided you…"

Pregnancy
"No female conceives or gives birth without His knowledge…"

Death
"No one grows old or has his life cut short but in accordance with what a Book decrees."

children. The parents have to agree the terms of the dowry (in Arabic, *mahr*), paid by the groom to the bride, before the marriage.

Marriage is a civil contract in Islam, not a religious rite. At the heart of it is the *nikah*, the legal contract between a man and a woman that says that they marry of their own free will. This is signed in the presence of two Muslim witnesses. Unlike Christian weddings, which traditionally take place in a church, the *nikah* is more likely to occur in a clerical office than a mosque. There is no requirement for an imam or any other religious official to be present. Whatever wedding ceremony happens after the *nikah* is shaped by the cultural traditions of the couple rather than Islam.

Marital variants

At the time of the Prophet, it was common for men to have more than one wife, as long as they could support them and honor them equally, and the Quran condones this. While most Islamic authorities maintain that it is legal for a man to take up to four wives (but not for a woman to have multiple husbands), polygamy is illegal in some Muslim countries, including Turkey and Tunisia, and is in decline in many others—in Egypt, for example, the number of polygamous marriages is below 3 percent.

Some Muslims also recognize a form of unofficial short-term marriage known as an *urfi* marriage. The high cost of marriage forces many young couples to wait years before they officially marry—an *urfi* marriage allows them to be together without being officially registered. *Urfi* marriages are conducted by a Muslim cleric in the presence of two witnesses. The couple can register

An Indian Muslim bride signs a marriage certificate in the presence of religious leaders during the *ijaazat* ("permission") ceremony.

the marriage later and have a full wedding when finances allow. In the Shia tradition, *mutah* marriages are permitted where a man and woman marry privately, for a short to medium-term period, and no witnesses are required.

These temporary marriages are highly contentious and are often kept secret from family members. They are also dangerous for the women involved because the arrangement gives them no legal protections, such as the right to alimony or child support.

Getting divorced

In Islam a man can divorce his wife by pronouncing the *talaq*, by which he announces that he repudiates her. However, in Islam marriage is both a sacramental and a contractual institution, and divorce is presented only as a last option, after a couple has pursued all possible remedies to rebuild the relationship. Prophet Muhammad is reported to have said, "Of all the lawful things, divorce is the most hated by God."

The more common and proper procedure is that if a couple agree to divorce by mutual consent, they petition a *qadi* (someone learned in Sharia) to annul the marriage in front of two witnesses. If one partner wishes to divorce but the other does not, he or she can still petition the *qadi* and, if there are reasonable grounds, the divorce will be granted. A marriage can also be annulled if the couple have been living apart for at least two years and one partner has no intention of returning to the other.

When the divorce is initiated by the husband, the wife has full rights to keep the dowry that was paid to her. If the wife initiates a divorce, she may forgo the right to keep the dowry since she is the one

A Shia family tends the grave of a relative in one of the world's biggest cemeteries, in Najaf in Iraq. Visits are traditionally made during the *Eid al-Fitr* celebrations at the end of Ramadan.

seeking to break the marriage contract, unless she can prove just cause before the *qadi*.

The end of life

Islam sees death as a transitional stage between life in this world and the afterlife. Death is divinely willed and when it arrives it should be readily accepted. The deceased should be buried as soon as possible after death, preferably on the same day (cremation is not allowed). Adult members of the

deceased's family wash the body to remove impurities—men are washed by men, women by women. They then wrap the body in a modest white shroud. Mourners say a funeral prayer for the deceased at the mosque, after which the body is carried to the cemetery. It is laid in a grave, with the body facing Mecca, while the mourners recite the *Shahada*, the same attestation of faith that was whispered into the baby's ear at birth. Many of those present throw three handfuls of earth into the grave while reciting from *sura* 20 in the Quran: "From the earth We have created you, and to the earth We will restore you; and from it We will bring you back to life" (20:55).

Specific funerary rituals differ by country, but usually the family and relatives give money or food to the poor in the name of the deceased in expiation for any sins they may have committed. ∎

LGBT+ and Islam

The Quran tells the story of the people of Lot—which is also in the Bible—who were destroyed by God due to their "obscene" behavior, which included homosexuality: "Will you fornicate with the males of humans and eschew the wives whom God has created for you?" (26:165–66). In light of this, early Muslim scholars declared a prohibition on homosexuality.

Some Muslims today view homosexuality as a lifestyle choice and believe that a person who feels homosexual urges should strive to change or abstain. There are some Muslim countries in which same-sex intercourse is legal, including Jordan, Lebanon, Turkey, and most of Indonesia, but in the majority of Muslim countries, committing homosexual acts is against the law. The specific punishment varies by country, ranging from jail sentences and lashings, to the death penalty in states such as Brunei, Saudi Arabia, Sudan, and Yemen.

THE SEVEN HOUSES OF ISLAM

ED HUSAIN (2018)

IN CONTEXT

THEME
The demographics of Islam today

WHEN AND WHERE
Today, worldwide

BEFORE
7th century Conquests take Islam into Africa and Europe, and to the borders of India.

651 The third caliph, Uthman, sends an embassy to China.

922 Volga Bulgaria becomes the first Muslim state in what is now European Russia.

12th century The Muslim Kilwa Sultanate, based in East Africa, spreads as far south as Mozambique.

1492 The first Muslim arrives in the Americas as part of Christopher Colombus's crew.

AFTER
2050 Data published in 2017 predicts there will be 2.76 billion Muslims by 2050—29.7% of the world's population.

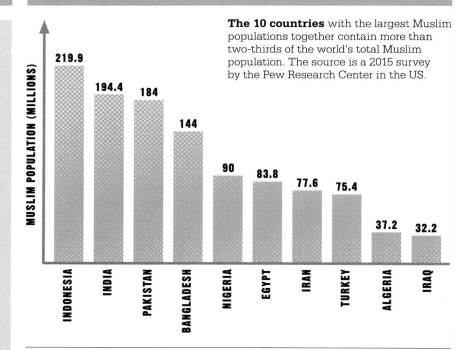

The 10 countries with the largest Muslim populations together contain more than two-thirds of the world's total Muslim population. The source is a 2015 survey by the Pew Research Center in the US.

MUSLIM POPULATION (MILLIONS)

INDONESIA	219.9
INDIA	194.4
PAKISTAN	184
BANGLADESH	144
NIGERIA	90
EGYPT	83.8
IRAN	77.6
TURKEY	75.4
ALGERIA	37.2
IRAQ	32.2

According to a 2015 survey by the Pew Research Center, there are roughly 1.8 billion Muslims in the world. The global population in 2019 is 7.7 billion, which means that almost one in four people in the world today is a Muslim. Of those, only 317 million, or less than 18 percent, live in the Middle East and North Africa (MENA). More Muslims live in India and Pakistan than the whole of the MENA region. The five countries with the highest Muslim populations are Indonesia (219.9m), India (194.4m), Pakistan (184m), Bangladesh (144m), and Nigeria (90m). The sixth country on the list, Egypt, is the Middle Eastern country with the largest Muslim population, with approximately 83.8 million.

See also: Spreading Islam though trade 182–85 ▪ Islam in Europe 210–15 ▪ Early Muslims in America 224–27 ▪ The creation of Pakistan 242–47 ▪ Islam in Africa 278–79 ▪ Islam in Indonesia 280–81 ▪ Muslims in the West 282–85

The houses of Islam

Students of the Islamic world divide it into several cultural and geographic spheres. Author Ed Husain lists seven of these. The first is the Arabic-speaking world of the Middle East, North Africa, and northern East Africa (Djibouti, and Eritrea). The region that gave birth to Islam is home to less than one fifth of its followers, but it has the world's highest concentration of Muslims.

The Persian-speaking countries of Iran, Afghanistan, and Tajikistan form the second region. Iran has the world's largest Shia population.

Sub-Saharan Africa forms a third region: non-Arabic-speaking Muslim countries including Gambia, Ghana, Kenya, Mali, Niger, Nigeria, Senegal, Sierra Leone, and Somalia, account for about 250 million Muslims. In countries such as Niger and Somalia, Muslims make up 99 percent of the population, though almost one in three Muslims in Sub-Saharan Africa lives in Nigeria.

The fourth region is the Indian subcontinent of India, Pakistan, Bangladesh, Burma, Nepal, and Sri Lanka. India has the world's second-largest Muslim population, despite Muslims making up less than 15 percent of the populace. By 2050, India could have the world's largest Muslim population, while remaining a Hindu-majority nation.

The fifth region is Turkic, and includes Turkey and people with a Turkic heritage: Azerbaijanis,

Men pray at a workplace in Lagos, Nigeria, where roughly 50 percent of the country is Muslim (concentrated in the north) and 50 percent is Christian (mostly in the south).

The ultimate vision is to instate in the Muslim world the notion of multiculturalism.
Feisal Abdul Rauf
American Sufi imam

Chechens, Kazakhs, Kyrgyz, Turkmen, Uzbeks, and Chinese Uighurs. China has about 22 million Muslims, mostly concentrated in Xinjiang, the only Muslim-majority province, where the population was roughly 53 percent Muslim in 2019.

The sixth region is Southeast Asia, which includes Indonesia, Malaysia, Brunei, and minorities in Thailand and the Philippines.

Indonesia has the world's largest Muslim population: about 13 percent of all Muslims in the world live there.

Spreading Islam

The seventh house is the "West." Europe has experienced a recent surge of migrants fleeing conflicts in Africa and the Middle East, so numbers are unreliable, but it is thought to be home to about 44 million Muslims. Russia has the largest population, with more than 16 million Muslims. France is home to 5.7 million Muslims (8.8 percent of the country's population) and Germany 5 million (6.1 percent). European countries with the highest concentration of Muslims are Kosovo (90%), Albania (80%), Bosnia-Herzegovina (40%), and the Republic of Macedonia (33%).

Of the approximately 4.6 million Muslims in North America, roughly 3.45 million live in the US and just over 1 million in Canada. Less than 1 percent of the US population is Muslim, a figure that is projected to double by 2050. ▪

AN ARAB HAS NO SUPERIORITY OVER A NON-ARAB
PROPHET MUHAMMAD

IN CONTEXT

THEME
The Arabization of global Islam

WHEN AND WHERE
Today, worldwide

BEFORE
8th century The Shuubiyya movement sees a controversial promotion of non-Arab, notably Persian, culture at the Abbasid court in Baghdad.

1962 Saudi Arabia founds the Muslim World League, in order to propagate a Saudi version of Islam worldwide.

2019 A Sri Lankan news report says that Quranic *madrasas* and Arabic colleges funded largely by Saudi Arabia "have mushroomed in their thousands around Sri Lanka" over the past decade.

AFTER
***c.* 2040** Gulf oil (and with it, perhaps, Gulf influence) is predicted to peak mid-century.

Islam was born in Arabia—the Prophet Muhammad was an Arab and the Quran was revealed to him in Arabic. Muslims all over the world turn to face Mecca, in Arabia, to pray; and every Muslim hopes to make the Hajj to Mecca at some point in their life. It is common for non-Arab Muslims to learn Arabic in order to be able to read the Quran and understand the words they are saying when they pray.

Despite the fact that less than 20 percent of the world's Muslim population is Arab, Arabic and

If there are some of you who wish to practice Arab culture, and do not wish to follow our Malay customs, that is up to you. I also welcome you to live in Saudi Arabia.
Sultan Iskandar of Johor

Arab culture and ideology exert an influence out of proportion to that figure, and it is an influence that is on the increase—a modern phenomenon known as Arabization.

This was not always the case. Muslims in Turkey, India, and Southeast Asia were once culturally distinct, but since the latter part of the 20th century, the "Gulf Arabic" culture of the Arabian Peninsula has been adopted as a marker of Muslim identity. The most visible example is the traditional Arabian white *thobe* for men and the black *abaya* for women, which have become everyday Muslim attire in many countries. The *niqab* (face veil) was rarely seen outside the Arab world until recently, but it is now common from Somalia in East Africa to Brunei in Southeast Asia.

Ramzan or Ramadan?
Arabic phrases are increasingly finding their way into national languages in place of local equivalents. For example, a Malay newspaper reports the growing use of the Arabic term *hijab* (headscarf) over the Malay *tudung*, and *shukran* (thank you) over the traditional Malay phrase *terima kasih*. The Persian *Ramzan*, which has always

See also: The secularization of Turkey 228–31 ▪ The birth of Saudi Arabia 232–37 ▪ The demographics of Islam today 260–61 ▪ Islam in Indonesia 280–81

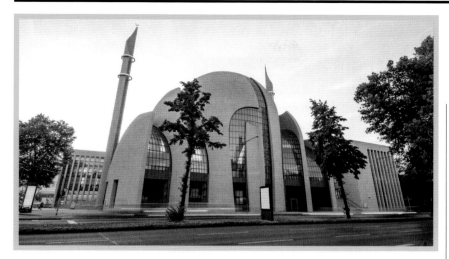

The Cologne Mosque, inaugurated in 2015, was funded by a branch of the Turkish government's religious affairs authority, as a way of enhancing Turkey's status in the Islamic world.

been the pronunciation widely used on the Indian subcontinent for the month of fasting, has now largely been replaced with the Arabic *Ramadan*. Similarly, Arabic names are now favored for children. In Malaysia in 2016, the Sultan of Johor urged Malays not to discard their traditional phrases and culture in favor of copying Arab ways.

Since the 1970s, when they became rich on oil, the Gulf States —Qatar and Saudi Arabia, in particular—have been increasing their influence over global Muslim communities. They tap into the deep-rooted religious connection that the world's 1.8 billion Muslims hold for the Arabian Peninsula as the cradle of Islam and home to its holiest sites. This has involved recruiting and training imams to send out to teach Islam according to Gulf and Saudi custom and law, and funding mosques in cities and villages across the world. There is also a drive to centralize global Muslim community decision-making, such as declaring when Ramadan has started and when Eid should be celebrated.

The Arab media strengthens these bonds. The Gulf States successfully export literature, television, and online content that emphasizes an Arabian world view. The prime example is the Qatari state-funded Al Jazeera news broadcaster.

Pushback

Countermovements have been pushing back against Arabization, with a desire to reclaim and promote their own particular Muslim cultures as equally valid expressions of Islamic faith. In 2015, the Indonesian Islamic movement Nahdatul Ulama started promoting "Islam Nusantara" as a form of Islam that takes into account local Indonesian customs. In the US, black Muslim Americans have run social media campaigns to promote their identity, using the hashtag #BlackoutEid. Turkey has been exporting television as a way of asserting a Turkish version of Islamic heritage; dubbed versions of its soap operas—often depicting historical events from Muslim history, such as the life of Süleyman the Magnificent—have been popular throughout the Arab world. It is a way of reminding Muslims that until the 20th century, under the Ottoman Empire Turkey was the preeminent power in the Islamic world. ∎

Muslim is not a race

Unlike being Jewish or Sikh, being Muslim is not considered a race or ethnicity. Confusion between what is religion and what is race sometimes leads to the idea that Arab and Muslim are interchangeable, which is not the case. Islam is blind to race and embraces all tribes and cultures.

In his Farewell Sermon, in 632, the Prophet Muhammad is reported to have said, "All mankind is from Adam and Eve, an Arab has no superiority over a non-Arab nor has a non-Arab any superiority over an Arab; also a white has no superiority over a black nor has a black any superiority over white except by piety and good action." The Quran states that the best people are those who are pious, irrespective of race. It presents the existence of different tribes and nations as positive for humanity. Islam is taught as embracing all cultures as long as their traditions do not conflict with Islamic religious practice.

DEMOCRACY AND ISLAM ARE NOT INCOMPATIBLE
BENAZIR BHUTTO (2007)

IN CONTEXT

THEME
Islam and democracy

WHEN AND WHERE
Today, worldwide

BEFORE
632 A successor to the Prophet Muhammad as leader of the Muslims is chosen by a *shura*, or a council of wise men.

1945 In Turkey, a multiparty political system replaces the autocratic regime established by founder of the modern state, Mustafa Kemal Atatürk.

1947 Following Partition, the newly independent nations of both India, with its large Muslim minority, and Pakistan, with its Muslim majority, become democracies.

2011 Pro-democracy uprisings erupt throughout the Arabic-speaking world, beginning in Tunisia and spreading to Morocco, Libya, Egypt, Syria, and Bahrain.

Millions of the world's 1.8 billion Muslims live in democracies, or countries with open elections. The country with the world's greatest number of Muslims, Indonesia, is also the world's third-largest democracy by population. The country that is projected to have the biggest Muslim population in the world by 2050 is India, which is the world's largest democracy. Mali, Senegal, Tunisia, Turkey, Pakistan, Bangladesh, and Malaysia are all Muslim-majority countries that have democratic political systems, of varying degrees of success. All of these facts would suggest that there is no inherent contradiction between Islam and democracy.

The Quran contains a number of ideas that might be read as supporting democratic ideals: one is the *shura*, or communal decision-making; another is *ijma*, or the principle of consensus. *Sura* 42:38, for example, recommends that believers "conduct their affairs by mutual counsel."

However, Muslims who follow a stricter interpretation of the Quran could argue that a strict implementation of Sharia law, for example, takes governance out of the hands of humans and regards God as the sole giver of laws. More extreme religious scholars believe that even participating in everyday politics—joining a political party or voting, for example—is *haram*, or religiously forbidden. Wahhabi clerics in Saudi Arabia, the Taliban in Afghanistan and Pakistan, and some followers of the Salafist movement adopt this position.

Islamists support the vote

Not all Islamist organizations oppose democracy. There have been occasions in recent history

You have Christian democracy in Europe. Why can't we have Muslim democrats in the Muslim world?
Anwar Ibrahim
Malaysian reformist leader

See also: God's guidance through Sharia 128–33 ▪ The rise of political Islam 238–41 ▪ The demographics of Islam today 260–61 ▪ Salafism 304

> The development of both political Islam and democracy now appear to go hand in hand, albeit not at the same pace.
> **Olivier Roy**
> *Professor at the European University Institute in Florence*

when democracy has appeared as the most realistic path to political legitimacy for Islamist parties. In Algeria, for example, the popular Islamic Salvation Front was poised to defeat the ruling National Liberation Front in democratic elections held in 1991. To prevent this from happening, those in power cancelled the elections. Instead, the military took control, and more than 100,000 people were killed in a decade-long civil war.

More recently, after the 2011 Arab Spring uprisings brought down the unpopular government of President Hosni Mubarak in Egypt, elections the following year saw the Muslim Brotherhood candidate Muhammad Mursi voted in as the country's president. Once in power, the Brotherhood did not share the democratic culture of the protestors who had put them there; the

Tunisians cast their votes at a polling station during parliamentary elections in 2019. Tunisia has built a political system that includes Islamists and their former adversaries.

military removed Mursi from office in a coup in 2013 and restored authoritarian rule.

A national uprising in Muslim-majority Tunisia also resulted in the ousting of a long-standing, authoritarian president in 2011, paving the way for democratic elections. The experiment was more successful than in Egypt. The formerly banned Islamic party Ennahdha, only legalized in 2011, became the party with the most seats in the Tunisian Constituent Assembly. Since then, Tunisians have participated in several more peaceful elections and have approved a new constitution that is one of the most progressive in the Arab world.

Who is against the vote?

To date, Tunisia is the Arabic-speaking world's sole successful experiment in democracy. The rest of the region is typically associated with leaders who are not prepared to give citizens a say in who rules them, and who curtail personal freedoms to keep it that way. Why this should be is a matter of debate among political scientists. Some point the finger at the West's long-standing willingness to support the region's despots and dictators, particularly during the Cold War, when both the United States and the Soviet Union backed politically repressive regimes in order to secure regional allegiances. Today, the West continues to support leaders with poor democratic credentials in order to safeguard crucial supplies of oil and gas from the Middle East.

The unpredictability of open elections, with the risk that they may, for example, put Islamist parties in power, means that democracy in the Middle East has frequently not been seen as in the best interests of Western powers. ▪

SHOULD YOU DISAGREE ABOUT ANYTHING REFER IT TO GOD

THE QURAN, 4:59

IN CONTEXT

THEME
The modern Sharia state

WHEN AND WHERE
Today, Saudi Arabia

BEFORE
8th century Scholars eager to standardize Islamic jurisprudence emerge in many Muslim communities, and independently codify Sharia, or Islamic law.

19th century In the face of European colonialism, Muslims increasingly associate Sharia with self-determination.

1928 The Muslim Brotherhood decrees that only by restoring Islamic law to its central place in the lives of Egyptians can Egypt expect national renewal.

1932 Tribal leader Ibn Saud takes control of the Arabian Peninsula and allows religious scholars to enforce Islamic law.

Since the mid-20th century, some Muslim countries have sought to revive the pre-modern Sharia state—in other words, implement an entirely Islamic legal system, and corresponding code of behavior, derived from the Quran and *sunna*. Those who promote this path see it as living a life directed not by the rulings of man, but by the eternal, concrete rulings of God. Adherents of Sharia believe they are following the word of God when he revealed, "Should you disagree about anything refer it to God and the Messenger" (4:59).

How Sharia should be applied in today's world is a subject of dispute between "conservative"

See also: God's guidance through Sharia 128–33 ▪ Wahhabism, or an Islamic reformation 216–17 ▪ The birth of Saudi Arabia 232–37 ▪ The creation of Pakistan 242–47 ▪ The new extremists 272–77 ▪ Salafism 304

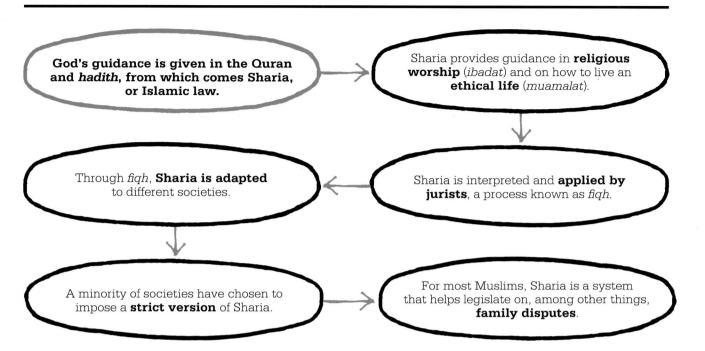

God's guidance is given in the Quran and *hadith*, from which comes Sharia, or Islamic law.

Sharia provides guidance in **religious worship** (*ibadat*) and on how to live an **ethical life** (*muamalat*).

Through *fiqh*, **Sharia is adapted** to different societies.

Sharia is interpreted and **applied by jurists**, a process known as *fiqh*.

A minority of societies have chosen to impose a **strict version** of Sharia.

For most Muslims, Sharia is a system that helps legislate on, among other things, **family disputes**.

and "moderate" Muslims. Full implementation extends into all areas of public life. Some aspects are widely accepted, such as halal foods and Islamic banking (non-interest banking). Other aspects are more contentious: *hudud* ("boundaries"), for example, which are the punishments specified in the Quran and *hadith*, meted out for sins ranging from adultery and homosexuality to robbery and murder. Under a strict Sharia regime, Muslims are obliged to modify their everyday behavior, including how they dress and with whom they spend their time.

Sharia states
The vast majority of the roughly 50 Muslim-majority countries in the world have replaced Sharia law with criminal and civil law systems based on European models. They retain Sharia only with regard to family law. Just a handful of nations employ full Sharia law—Afghanistan, Brunei, Qatar, and Saudi Arabia. Indonesia, Nigeria, and Sudan apply Sharia in certain regions. Iran's legal code is based on Sharia integrated with civil law.

Tomorrow, Thursday, May 1, 2014, will see the enforcement of Sharia law.
Sultan Hassanal Bolkiah of Brunei

The most prominent example of a Sharia state is Saudi Arabia. The clerics have a position in Saudi Arabia that is unique among Islamic countries. In addition to the Islamic affairs ministry, clerics have traditionally controlled the justice and education ministries. »

Hassanal Bolkiah became sultan of the small, oil-rich, Muslim-majority island of Brunei in 1967. In 2019, he decreed Sharia law for his country.

They also control a religious police force, formally known as the Committee for the Promotion of Virtue and the Prevention of Vice, and commonly referred to as the *mutaween*. Saudi judges follow the notably strict Hanbali school of Islamic law, supplemented by regulations issued by royal decree that cover more modern issues, such as intellectual property rights.

Criminal law

Although Sharia covers a vast range of human behavior, it is the area of criminal law (a small component) that sparks the most controversy. The Quran can be highly specific on crime and punishment: "As for the man or woman who is guilty of theft, cut off their hands to punish them" (5:37). And, "The adulteress and adulterer you shall give each a hundred lashes" (24:2). In other places it is more vague: "If two men among you commit a lewd act, punish them both" (4:16) and "He that kills a believer by design shall burn in Hell forever" (4:93). In such cases, in which the Quran does not stipulate a punishment, judges look to the *hadith* for guidance.

Avoid condemning the Muslim to *hudud* whenever you can, and when you can find a way out (of *hudud*) for the Muslim, then do so.
Prophet Muhammad

Serious criminal offenses that are covered by Sharia include not only internationally recognized crimes such as murder, rape, theft, treason, and drug smuggling, but also apostasy (renouncing religious beliefs), adultery, blasphemy, and witchcraft. The Saudi version of Sharia theoretically allows the death penalty for all of these crimes. Execution is usually carried out in public by beheading with a sword. Homosexual acts or acts promoting homosexuality are punishable by lashings, prison, or even death.

Supporters of Sharia argue that courts require incontrovertible proof before any punishment can be carried out. For example, in the case of adultery, the Quran says that there must be four reliable witnesses to the act. Anyone who accuses someone of adultery without those witnesses is liable to be punished themselves with 80 lashes for slander. However, critics maintain that these strictures are not always met.

Women in Sharia

The status of women in Sharia is another area of intense debate. Segregation of the sexes, which clerics justify under the Sharia notion of *dar al-fasad* ("shielding from corruption"), has traditionally meant bans on the mixing of men and women. This has had the unfortunate effect of keeping many women out of employment. Women's alleged "lack of capacity" (*adam al-kifaah*) has required the presence of a male guardian (a father, brother, husband, or other family member), whose permission must be granted for travel, medical procedures, or to open a bank account. Women's dress is

Sharia in non-Muslim countries

Sharia tribunals exist in non-Muslim countries to serve the needs of Muslim communities. Often attached to a mosque, they are not courts of law, and their rulings do not have legal force and cannot overrule regular courts. Such bodies are typically consulted on family issues; for example, a couple seeking divorce might go to a Sharia tribunal for help reaching agreements about children and finances. A couple might get married at a Sharia tribunal, although this would not mean they were married in the eyes of the state.

Some in the West have sought to make Sharia a political issue. In the United States, for example, a number of US states have banned Sharia tribunals. Yet virtually every religious group in the US, including the Jewish community, uses its own arbitration committees in family disputes. In this respect Sharia tribunals are nothing out of the ordinary.

Until 2018, Saudi women were banned from driving—since a woman was not allowed to travel without a man, it was argued, they did not need to drive.

Sharia police stop passing motorists to check on Sharia-compliant dress in Aceh, the sole Indonesian province that observes Sharia law.

governed by a strict interpretation of Islamic law that requires extreme modesty, usually only satisfied by a long cloak, or *abaya*, and a head scarf. The face does not necessarily need to be covered with a *niqab* (face veil)—some scholars say it does, but most see it as a cultural rather than religious practice.

The situation is changing, albeit slowly. In 2017, Saudi Arabia's King Salman decreed that women no longer need permission from their male guardian for some activities, including attending college, taking a job, and undergoing surgery. Saudi Arabian women may now drive and they can have a passport and travel abroad without a guardian's consent. However, Saudi women are still legally classified as minors for their entire lives.

Sharia around the world

The other modern state that has come close to the Saudi model of Sharia is Afghanistan under the Taliban. A group of Sunni Muslim Pashtuns established an Islamic state there from 1996 to 2001, with cleric-judges and a morality police that patrolled the streets to enforce Islamic rules on behavior. The Taliban went much further than Saudi Arabia in forbidding education and employment for woemn, and by carrying out the *hudud* punishment of stoning for adultery—something from which even Saudi Arabia has refrained. Saudi Arabia was one of only three countries in the world to extend diplomatic recognition to the Taliban, along with Pakistan and the United Arab Emirates. There are major points of difference between the ideologies of the Taliban and the Saudia Arabian clerics, but both believe that the Sharia state has no need for any political parties or forms of legislative elections.

Elsewhere, Sharia has often been introduced as a means for modern rulers to burnish their Islamic credentials for political reasons. Sharia was written into the 1968 and 1973 constitutions of Sudan, and remains the country's guiding principle. Critics claim it has been used as a tool to persecute Christian women, who face being whipped in public for wearing "immoral" dress, such as a pair of trousers.

In 1979, as part of his Islamization of Pakistan, military ruler Muhammad Zia-ul-Haq introduced the Hudood Ordinances. These regulations added new criminal offenses to the penal code, including adultery and fornication (sex outside marriage), with new punishments, including whipping, amputation, and stoning to death.

In 2014, the Sultan of Brunei introduced a new legal code that extended the scope of Sharia courts from civil laws to criminal law. In 2019, he extended this to include *hudud* punishments. The decision triggered an outcry from countries and rights groups around the world.

A wider sense of Sharia

While non-Muslims are prone to associating Sharia only with the severe *hudud* punishments, for many Muslims this represents only a small part of a broader system of justice, one that is intimately linked to their Islamic identity. Almost all Muslim countries employ Sharia to some extent, usually relating to family laws concerning marriage, divorce, and succession. By far the majority of modern Muslim countries see Sharia as a system that can and does coexist within other kinds of legal systems, and extreme implementations of Sharia are as much anathema to the majority of Muslims as they are to non-Muslims. ■

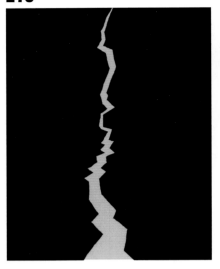

MORE POLITICAL THAN RELIGIOUS
THE GUARDIAN NEWSPAPER (2015)

IN CONTEXT

THEME
Sunni and Shia in the modern Middle East

WHEN AND WHERE
Today, the Middle East

BEFORE
1501–1722 Rule by Iran's Safavid dynasty ends the mutual tolerance between Sunni and Shia as the Shia Safavids wage war with their Sunni Ottoman neighbors.

1935–36 Iraqi Shia stage uprisings against the minority Sunni government.

1979 The Iranian Revolution replaces the Shah (King) with a Shia Islamic Republic.

2005 Following the toppling of Saddam Hussein in 2003, Iraqi Shia celebrate the end of Sunni dominance in the country.

2019 Iranian-backed militias intervene in Iraq to suppress mass protests against state corruption and unemployment.

Shia account for roughly 15 percent of all Muslims worldwide. However, they have a greater presence in the Middle East than elsewhere. Recent estimates are that of all Muslims in the Middle East, 191 million are Sunni and 121 million are Shia, which means Shias make up just over 38 percent.

The greatest concentration of Shia Muslims today is in Iran, where Shiism became the official state religion during the reign of the Safavids (1501–1722), and where 87 percent of the population identifies as Shia. Iraq, too, has a sizeable Shia majority, as does the small island kingdom of Bahrain. Other notable Shia populations are in Lebanon, Yemen, and Saudi Arabia, and away from the Middle East, in India and Pakistan.

Although the Shia Safavids spent two centuries skirmishing with the Sunni Ottoman Empire

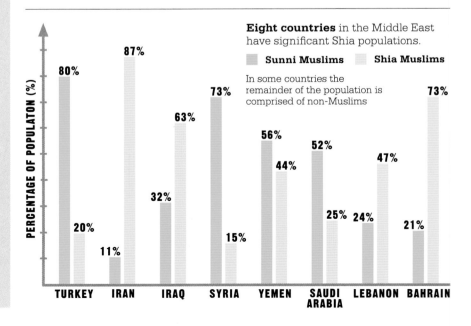

Eight countries in the Middle East have significant Shia populations.

■ **Sunni Muslims**   ■ **Shia Muslims**

In some countries the remainder of the population is comprised of non-Muslims

See also: The emergence of Shia Islam 108–15 ▪ The Safavid Empire 192–93 ▪ The birth of Saudi Arabia 232–37 ▪ The Iranian Revolution 248–51

along their borders, Sunnis and Shiites have peaceably coexisted for most of their history.

The specter of sectarianism

Iran's Islamic revolution of 1979 changed everything—Shias had overthrown the monarchy, and Shia Islam was now regarded as a more militant force. Saddam Hussein, the Sunni ruler of predominantly Shia Iraq, was so alarmed by the threat of this revolution influencing his own population that he invaded Iran in 1980. In what was portrayed as an Arab war against "Persians," Iraq was bankrolled by the Sunni Gulf States. The Iran–Iraq War was fought to an inconclusive standstill in 1988, but when American-led coalition forces overthrew Saddam in 2003, the subsequent parliamentary elections brought in a majority Shia government.

Iranian influence has since extended to backing the Lebanese Shia militia movement Hezbollah, which is now the strongest party in Lebanon. Iran also backs the Houthis, Shia militants in Yemen who

ousted the country's internationally recognized government in 2015, and the regime in Syria, where the Assad family's repression of Syria's majority Sunni population in favor of its own Shia Alawite clan sparked protests in 2011. The ensuing civil war has became a flashpoint for regional rivalries and global superpowers.

Nationalism

Despite appearances, Islamic sectarianism is not the sole or even the main cause of divisions in the Middle East. For the majority of

A Shia sheikh leads Friday prayer in the Kingdom of Bahrain, where the Sunni al-Khalifa dynasty rules over a Shia majority population.

Muslims, their national identity matters more than which tradition of Islam they follow.

Iraqi Shias, for example, made up the bulk of the Iraqi army that fought Iran during the Iran–Iraq War. When Iraq's Saddam Hussein invaded Kuwait in 1990, one Sunni country was invading another; numerous Sunni Arab countries then signed up to the coalition to liberate Kuwait. The Houthis in Yemen are Zaydi Shia but they deposed and later assassinated President Ali Abdullah Saleh, who was also a Zaydi.

The wars of today's Middle East have their roots in nationalism as well as theology. Many of these conflicts are proxy wars between Iran and Saudi Arabia, two major powers in the region pursuing strategic rivalries for control of the Muslim world, particularly in places where governance has collapsed. ▪

Let people stop boasting about their ancestors. One is only a pious believer or a miserable sinner.
Prophet Muhammad

Alawites

The Alawites are a group within Shiism, reputed to have been founded in the 9th century by Ibn Nusayr—they were formerly known as Nusayris. Like all Shiites, they revere Ali, the First Imam, but they have also added elements of other faiths into their own, including Christianity, and have a Holy Trinity of the Prophet Muhammad, Ali, and Salman al-Farsi, a Companion of the Prophet. They are relatively liberal—they drink alcohol and women do not cover their hair.

The Alawites are mainly found in Syria, where they make up between 10 and 15 percent of the population. The Assad family, which assumed power in 1971, is of Alawite heritage. Presidents Hafez al-Assad and his son Bashar al-Assad strengthened loyalty to their regime by appointing many Alawites to senior positions in the government and security services. Historically, some Sunni clerics have denounced Alawites as heretics, making the Alawites fearful of ever ceding power to the Sunnis.

NO NEGOTIATIONS, NO CONFERENCES, AND NO DIALOGUES

ABDULLAH AZZAM (1980s)

IN CONTEXT

THEME
The new extremists

WHEN AND WHERE
Today, worldwide

BEFORE
Late 8th century Early Islamic jurists discuss jihad as a collective defensive struggle against injustice by infidels and apostates.

1898 In Egypt, Islamic reformer Rashid Rida launches *al-Manar*, a journal in which he chastises Muslim societies for facilitating colonialism, and calls for a return to the "true Islam," purged of Western influences.

1964 Egyptian Islamic reformer Sayyid Qutb publishes his landmark book *Signs on the Road*, which urges Muslims to create an Islamic society based solely on the precepts of the Quran.

In the late 19th to mid-20th centuries, when Islamic thinkers such as Jamal al-Din al-Afghani and Sayyid Qutb sought to right the wrongs that they believed Muslims faced due to Western imperialism, they sought to apply Islam to social and political life in order to create a utopian Islamic society. In the late 20th century, the idea of reconciling Islam and Western-style modernism turned into rejection, as the new Islamic extremists scorned the West and everything it stood for. This uncompromising approach was summed up in a phrase employed by Palestinian Islamic scholar Abdullah Azzam (1941–89): "Jihad and the rifle alone: no negotiations, no conferences, and no dialogues."

The 21st century has seen a high incidence of what some Western commentators refer to as "jihadism" (war against unbelievers), perpetrated by Islamist groups. The term "Islamist" is debated, but is generally taken to mean a supporter of militancy in the name of a strict interpretation of Islam, pitting Muslims against non-Muslims—or sometimes, in the case of extremists known as *takfiri*, against

> Jihad must not be abandoned until Allah alone is worshipped. Jihad is the way of everlasting glory.
> **Abdullah Azzam**

all other non-Islamist Muslims, whom they consider to be apostates. Islamic extremist groups see themselves as soldiers in a struggle for God's sovereignty on Earth.

These groups follow the teachings of Abdullah Azzam, who preached that all Muslims, regardless of nationality, are obliged to fight against any enemy who invades a Muslim land. By 1980, the land Azzam specifically had in mind was Afghanistan.

Generation Afghanistan
In December 1979, the Soviet Union had invaded Afghanistan in order to support the country's communist (and therefore atheist, un-Islamic) government. Volunteers from all over the Muslim world heeded Azzam's call and streamed into Afghanistan to take up arms against the Soviets. Known as *mujahideen*, these Afghan and Muslim resistance fighters were supported by an unlikely grouping that included Iran, Pakistan, Saudi Arabia, and the United States.

For nine years the Soviet army battled Muslim *mujahidin* forces in Afghanistan before conceding defeat in February 1989 and abandoning the country.

See also: The quest to make God's word supreme 134–35 ▪ The crusades through Muslim eyes 180–81 ▪ The rise of Islamic Modernism 222–23 ▪ The birth of Saudi Arabia 232–37 ▪ The rise of political Islam 238–41 ▪ Islam in Africa 278–79

Among the *mujahideen* was Ayman al-Zawahiri, a doctor from Cairo. An ardent follower of radical Islamic thinker Sayyid Qutb, al-Zawahiri was a member of an Egyptian group called al-Jihad. Their spiritual leader was the blind sheikh Omar Abdel Rahman, who would later be given a life sentence for conspiring to bomb New York City's World Trade Center in 1993.

In 1981, al-Jihad killed Egypt's President Anwar Sadat, who had angered the Islamists by signing a peace deal with Israel. Following his assassination, many Islamists were rounded up and jailed, including al-Zawahiri. He was released in 1986 and moved to Pakistan to treat wounded *mujahideen*. There he met and befriended a rich young Saudi Arabian named Osama bin Laden.

As a student at King Abdulaziz University in Jeddah, Bin Laden had attended lectures given by Muhammad Qutb, younger brother of Sayyid. Both brothers had spent time in prison in Egypt, but while Sayyid was hanged, Muhammad

Al-Qaeda can best be understood as an engine that runs on the despair of the Muslim world.
Lawrence Wright
Author of **The Looming Tower: Al-Qaeda and the Road to 9/11**

was released and moved to Saudi Arabia, where he became a professor of Islamic studies and promoted his brother's work. Bin Laden, inspired by what he learned, headed to Pakistan in 1981, where he found another mentor in Abdullah Azzam.

The road to 9/11

Al-Zawahiri viewed Afghanistan as a training ground for revolution in his own country against what was termed the "near enemy"—in this case, the Egyptian government. Bin Laden's focus was the "far enemy"—which meant the West.

When the Soviets withdrew from Afghanistan in 1989, al-Zawahiri continued to lead al-Jihad in a campaign of bombings and attacks on Egyptian political figures. Meanwhile, Bin Laden, Abdullah Azzam, and others formed a new group, which they called al-Qaeda ("the Base"). Its objective was to purge Islam of Western influence, destroy Israel, and establish a new caliphate across the Muslim world.

In August 1990, US troops arrived in Saudi Arabia at the request of its ruler, King Fahd, ahead of Operation "Desert Storm," which expelled Iraqi forces from Kuwait by February 1991.

In 1990, the invasion of Kuwait by Iraqi leader Saddam Hussein put Saudi Arabia's oil fields at risk. Bin Laden offered the use of the *mujahideen* to defend the oil fields, but the kingdom's rulers opted to join an American-led coalition and allow it to deploy troops on Saudi territory. Bin Laden denounced the coalition and what he saw as the profaning of sacred soil. Banished from Saudi Arabia, he fled first to Sudan in 1991, then to Afghanistan in 1996.

In 1996, Bin Laden issued a "Declaration of War against the Americans Occupying the Land of the Two Holy Places." It called on all Muslims to liberate Saudi Arabia from the Americans, who had retained a presence there after driving the Iraqis out of Kuwait. **»**

This *fatwa* was followed by another statement in 1998—this time issued under the name of the World Islamic Front, a new umbrella organization that brought together Bin Laden's al-Qaeda, al-Zawahiri's al-Jihad, and three other groups. It ruled that "to kill the Americans and their allies—civilians and military—[is] an individual duty for every Muslim who can do it."

In August that year, suicide bombings by al-Qaeda destroyed US embassies in Nairobi, Kenya, and Dar es Salaam, Tanzania, killing 224. In 2000, al-Qaeda militants bombed the US naval ship USS *Cole* in a suicide attack off the coast of Yemen, killing 17 US servicemen. On September 11, 2001, members of al-Qaeda flew two commercial airliners into the twin towers of the World Trade Center in New York City, and a third into the Pentagon in Washington DC, while a fourth plane that was intended to target either the White House or the Capitol was crashed in a field in Pennsylvania. In total, al-Qaeda's 9/11 attacks killed 2,996 people, including 2,507 civilians, 343 firefighters, 72 law enforcement officers, and 55 military personnel.

Combatting al-Qaeda

Almost all Muslim leaders—political and religious—condemned the 9/11 attacks, including the leaders of Egypt, Iran, Libya, Syria, and the Palestinian Authority.

In 2002, as Muslims and non-Muslims around the world struggled to understand what could have inspired such a shocking attack, Bin Laden posted a "Letter to America"

So-called Islamic State fighters display the group's black banner, which is emblazoned with the second phrase of the *Shahada*: "Muhammad is the messenger of God."

in which he gave his justifications for al-Qaeda's campaign. These included America's support of the State of Israel since its creation in 1948, allowing Israel's occupation of Palestine and incursions into Lebanon; its actions in Somalia; its inaction over Muslim oppression in Chechnya and Kashmir; its "looting" of Arab oil; and its sanctions in Iraq.

The US response to 9/11 was to declare a "War on Terror" and go after al-Qaeda in its home territory of Afghanistan. Although nearly 80 percent of al-Qaeda in Afghanistan were then eliminated, the group's wider network of affiliated cells continued to plan and execute attacks. On July 7, 2005, four British suicide bombers killed 56 people on London's Underground train network and on a London bus, and hundreds more civilians were killed in further attacks in Bali, Istanbul, Algiers, Madrid, Paris, and elsewhere.

In 2011, US president Barack Obama announced that Bin Laden had been killed in a covert operation in Abbottabad in Pakistan. While the influence of al-Qaeda has since waned, some of its affiliates remain active—notably the Somali-based al-Shabab ("The Youth"), which killed almost 700 people with its truck bombs in Mogadishu, Somalia, in 2011 and 2017, and carried out further attacks in Nairobi, Kenya, in 2013 and 2019.

The Taliban

After the Soviets withdrew from Afghanistan in 1989, defeated by the *mujahideen*—a victory celebrated by both Islamists and the West—the victors turned on each other. Civil war broke out, and factions were backed by external forces, including Iran and Saudi Arabia. One group that emerged in 1994 was made up of Pashtun (an ethnic group split across Pakistan and Afghanistan) and Pakistani Deobandi students. Known as the Taliban (from the Arabic *talib*, or "student"), it aimed to establish a pure Islamic society.

From 1996 until its overthrow in 2001, the Taliban ruled roughly three-quarters of the country, and enforced a brutal interpretation of Sharia—from the rejection of humanitarian aid to widespread massacres and the destruction of the 1,500-year-old Buddhas of Bamiyan statues in 2001. Only

> There will come a people from the east, young men with shaved heads and foolish ideas, who recite the Quran without it penetrating beyond their throats. Wherever you find them, fight them.
> **Prophet Muhammad**

Pakistan, Saudi Arabia, and the United Arab Emirates formally recognized the Taliban government. In 2001, in the aftermath of 9/11, the Taliban rejected a US ultimatum to turn over Bin Laden and expel the al-Qaeda forces they sheltered. In response, the US and its allies invaded Afghanistan and deposed the Taliban government.

Since then, however, the group has steadily reasserted its presence in Afghanistan; by 2019, the Taliban controlled 15 percent of the country and was active in 70 percent.

Islamic State

The so-called Islamic State—also known as ISIS (Islamic State in Iraq and Syria), ISIL (Islamic State of Iraq and the Levant), or Daesh (an Arabic acronym)—grew out of the remnants of al-Qaeda in Iraq. It took advantage of instability in Iraq and in Syria (where civil war had broken out in 2011) to seize territory, capturing the Iraqi cities of Mosul and Tikrit in 2014.

That same year, ISIS leader Abu Bakr al-Baghdadi announced the formation of a caliphate. Where al-Jihad and the Taliban had sought only to control a single country, Islamic State (IS), as it was now called, laid claim to the leadership of the whole of the Muslim world. "Soon," al-Baghdadi declared, "by God's permission, a day will come when the Muslim will walk everywhere as master."

A US-led coalition began airstrikes against the Islamic State in Iraq in 2014, while combined Iraqi, Kurdish, and Syrian forces fought the Islamic State on the ground. Cells of Islamic State operatives bombed a Russian plane in Egypt in 2015, and carried out a series of deadly attacks in Paris, but by 2018, the campaign against the Islamic State could focus on its few remaining strongholds in eastern Syria.

In December of that year, US president Donald Trump declared that ISIS was defeated. In late 2019, the US announced the death of al-Baghdadi, killed in a raid by US special forces.

Misguided beliefs

According to a report by the Global Extremist Monitor, Islamist extremism was responsible for the deaths of 84,000 people (including 22,000 civilians) across 66 countries in 2017 alone. The majority of extremism's victims are Muslims, and Muslim activists such as Malala Yousafzai (see right) protest against its injustices.

Abdullah Azzam's "Jihad and the rifle alone" is a message that still finds too many willing recruits. At its height, the Islamic State controlled a vast area of territory from western Iraq to central Syria, containing an estimated 8 to 12 million people. However, although it called itself a caliphate, it never controlled the holy sites of Mecca and Medina, and has only succeeded in unifying Arab and other Muslim countries against it. ∎

Resisting the Taliban

On October 9, 2012, two men stopped a school bus in the northern Swat district of Pakistan, and asked, "Who is Malala?" When she identified herself, they shot 15-year-old Malala Yousafzai in the head.

The daughter of a teacher, Malala had been raised to be politically aware. Inspired by figures such as reformist Muhammad Ali Jinnah and former prime minister Benazir Bhutto, from the age of 12 she had spoken out in public and online about basic rights of education for girls and how these rights were threatened by the Taliban. Their attempt on her life was in retaliation for her activism.

Malala was left in a critical condition but was transferred to a hospital in the UK, where she recovered. She became an even more prominent activist for the right to education for girls, and in 2014 she was the corecipient of the Nobel Peace Prize, becoming the youngest-ever Nobel laureate. In 2017, she began studying at the University of Oxford, and she continues to campaign for the 130 million girls around the world who are not in school.

PEOPLE REALLY LIVE ISLAM HERE
YOUSSOU N'DOUR, SENEGALESE SINGER (2004)

IN CONTEXT

THEME
Islam in Africa

WHEN AND WHERE
Today, Africa

BEFORE
***c.* 614** Prophet Muhammad advises a group of followers facing persecution by the Meccans to seek refuge across the Red Sea in Aksum.

14th century Musa I is emperor of the West African Mali Empire. He is thought to be the richest man in history, thanks to vast reserves of precious salt and gold.

2013 Al-Qaeda insurgents fleeing Timbuktu in Mali set fire to a library containing thousands of priceless historic Islamic manuscripts.

2018 Italian police arrest a Somali planning to plant a bomb in St. Peter's Basilica in Rome on Christmas Day.

I t has been estimated that 48 percent of the population of Africa is Muslim, while 50 percent is Christian. In addition to the Arabic-speaking countries of North Africa, Islam has a large presence in the Horn of Africa, the Sahel region south of the Sahara, and much of West Africa. With about 550 million Muslims across the continent, Africa is home to almost one third of the world's Muslims.

An African religion

Islam has been present for so long in much of the continent that many Africans consider it an African religion. Islamic tradition says that the first Companions of Muhammad to flee persecution in Mecca settled in the Christian kingdom of Aksum, present-day Ethiopia and Eritrea. They are said to have returned to Arabia when Muhammad founded a Muslim community in Medina, but excavations at a 7th-century cemetery in northern Ethiopia reveal traces of a Muslim community that survived the exiles' departure.

Muslims make up approximately 34 percent of the population in Ethiopia, which is otherwise largely Christian, but in Nigeria, the continent's most populous nation,

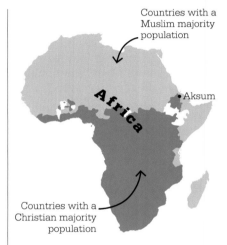

Countries with a Muslim majority population

Aksum

Africa

Countries with a Christian majority population

From its beginnings in Aksum, Islam has become Africa's dominant religion in the north, while the south is predominantly Christian.

the figure rises to roughly 50 percent, with more than 100 million Muslims. In Sierra Leone, Muslims account for 77 percent of the population, while in Guinea it is 85 percent, the Gambia 90 percent, Senegal 94 percent, Mali 95 percent, and Niger 98 percent.

Despite the dominance of Islam in these countries across northern Africa, many Africans who consider themselves Muslims (or, for that

See also: *Hijra*, the flight from Mecca 28–31 ▪ Sufism and the mystic tradition 140–45 ▪ Spreadng Islam through trade 182–85 ▪ The demographics of Islam today 260–61 ▪ The new extremists 272–77

Senegalese Sufi Muslims in front of the Great Mosque of the Mourides in Dakar, before its 2019 inauguration. It is the largest mosque in West Africa.

matter, Christians) also continue to believe in witchcraft, traditional religious healers, and animism—the idea that objects, places, and creatures all possess a spiritual essence.

One example of Africanized Islam is found in Senegal, where almost all Muslims are Sufis, belonging to mystical orders linked to holy men or *marabouts*. The most famous of these is Cheikh Ahmadou Bamba (1853–1927), founder of the Mouride brotherhood. His followers attribute miraculous powers to him, but he himself preached a simple message of devotion to God and hard work: his motto was "Pray to God but plow your fields." Bamba's image can be seen all over Senegal today, on wall murals and stickers on taxi dashboards. In his hometown of Touba, his tomb—inside one of the largest mosques in West Africa—is a major site of pilgrimage.

Extremist scourge

While there are almost as many Muslims in Africa as there are Christians, broadly speaking, the north of the continent is heavily Muslim and the south is mostly Christian. The two religious groups have coexisted largely peacefully, but in the 21st century the region in which the two meet—a 4,000-mile (6,400-km) band across the middle of Africa, from Senegal in the west to Somalia in the east—has turned into a zone of bloodshed, not because of Muslim–Christian sectarian violence, but because of Islamist extremism and terrorism.

In recent decades, poor governance and state corruption have created a space for radical religious groups to offer an alternative solution to a disaffected populace. These groups have stepped in where government has failed, raising money for schools and hospitals, while also spreading a radical version of Islam.

One of the most notorious groups is the Nigerian Islamist Boko Haram. Founded in 2002, it rejects the secular state, since it is created by man, not God, as well as

Islam demands peace and not the kind of egotism where you kill people with Kalashnikovs.
Cheikh Tidiane Samb
Senegalese Mouride

all Western, non-Islamic learning; the name Boko Haram means "Western education is a sin" in the local Hausa language. In 2014, the group sparked international outrage (and the hashtag #Saveourgirls) when it kidnapped 276 female students from a government school. In areas of the country affected by Boko Haram, almost no one gets schooling, health care, or other public services.

On the opposite side of Africa, Somalia's Islamist group al-Shabab ("the Youth") has repeatedly attacked the capital Mogadishu since 2006. Its aim is to create an Islamic state in Somalia, but it also operates in neighboring countries, notably Kenya, where it has staged at least 150 attacks: in 2013, al-Shabab attacked a shopping mall in Nairobi, killing 67; in 2015, the group killed 148 in an attack on a university in Garissa; and in 2019, it bombed a Nairobi hotel, killing at least 21. However, groups such as Boko Haram and al-Shabab, which both have links with al-Qaeda, are at odds with an otherwise moderate African Islam across the continent. ▪

ALL TOO MANY MUSLIMS FAIL TO GRASP ISLAM
ABDURRAHMAN WAHID (2005)

IN CONTEXT

THEME
Islam in Indonesia

WHEN AND WHERE
2015, Indonesia

BEFORE
1405–33 Chinese Muslim
admiral Zheng He leads a
series of voyages across the
Indian Ocean, linking Muslim
communities in southern
China with those throughout
Southeast Asia.

1613–46 Sultan Agung of
Mataram in Central Java leads
a "holy war" against Bali, the
only Hindu state in the midst
of the predominantly Muslim
islands of the Indian (now
Indonesian) Archipelago.

AFTER
2019 Indonesia's president
Joko Widodo is reelected with
a commitment to religious
pluralism, while hardline
Muslims back his opponent.

Indonesia has the world's largest Muslim population. While 99 percent of its 229 million Muslims are Sunni, they mostly practice a distinctively local form of Islam, called Islam Nusantara—*Nusantara* being a local term for the Indonesian archipelago, which is made up of more than 17,000 islands.

Islam first arrived in Southeast Asia with Muslim traders in the 13th century, and spread to islands and archipelagos across the region. By the end of the century, a Muslim sultan ruled Pasai on the north coast of Sumatra, one of the islands that form Indonesia. Over the next two centuries, major Muslim centers sprang up at Melaka (now Malacca, in Malaysia) and Aceh, in Sumatra.

With Mecca some 4,350 miles (7,000 km) away, this process of Islamization occurred without any intervention from the caliphates or dynasties, Arab or otherwise, who were extending Islamic interests across North Africa, Asia, and Europe. Rather than being imposed on Indonesia, Islam was gradually absorbed into local traditions, such as pilgrimages to the tombs of local saints, festivals celebrating their birthdays, and ceremonies to send the spirits of the deceased into the Afterlife. The retention of such traditions gave this regional Islam a distinctively mystical accent.

Imported ideas
The sense of isolation began to change in the 1870s, when the Dutch—whose Dutch East Indies colony included Indonesia—began to switch from sail to steamships

Islam Nusantara is challenged in many parts of the country by local laws that compel women and girls to wear the hijab in schools, government offices, and public spaces.

See also: God's guidance through Sharia 128–33 ▪ Spreading Islam through trade 182–85 ▪ Wahhabism, or an Islamic Reformation 216–17 ▪ The demographics of Islam today 260–61

| Observance of **Islam**, including following the Quran, the *sunna*, and the Five Pillars of Islam … | **+** | maintaining pre-Islamic **local traditions**, including pilgrimages to local saints' tombs and celebrating saints' birthdays … | **=** | Islam Nusantara, a **liberal and inclusive** form of Islam that can be adapted to any culture across the globe. |

---

for faster journey times. This enabled many more Southeast Asian Muslims to make their first pilgrimage to Mecca, and Indonesians soon became the largest contingent of pilgrims from any nation on the annual Hajj.

While on the Hajj, these pilgrims were exposed for the first time to the religious and intellectual ideas of Arabia—and specifically to Wahhabism. They took these ideas home, leading to calls for stricter forms of Islamic observance, including the introduction of Sharia.

In 1926, moderate Indonesian Muslims responded by coming together to found the Nahdlatul Ulama (NU), or the "Revival of the Ulama." The organization presented itself in opposition to Wahhabism, and argued for a more tolerant interpretation of Islam. During the Indonesian war of independence in 1945–49, the NU supported the struggle against Dutch colonial forces, calling it a holy war.

In the new republic, the NU became a political party, first as part of a coalition of Islamic groups, later as an independent party. In 1984, the NU withdrew from politics and returned to its original purpose as a socio-religious organization. That same year, Abdurrahman Wahid (popularly known as Gus Dor), grandson of NU founder Hasyim Asyari, became chairman of the NU. He would remain a promoter of liberal ideas and supporter of interfaith dialogue when he served as Indonesia's president in 1999–2001.

Islam Nusantara

In 2015, the NU coined the term *Islam Nusantara*, or Indonesian Islam, to refer to the type of localized Islam practiced by the majority of the country's Muslims. This followed the example set by Abdurrahman Wahid, who once said, "All too many Muslims fail to grasp Islam, which teaches one to be lenient toward others and to understand their value systems, knowing that these are tolerated by Islam as a religion."

The NU has since embarked on a project to promote its vision of an inclusive Islam to the rest of the world. It seeks to offer a counter-narrative to what the NU sees as the rigid ideology propagated by stricter elements of Islam in the Middle East. Its aim is not to insert Indonesian culture into the Arab world, but to promote an approach that accommodates local culture within Islam.

The NU sees this as a blueprint for developing, for example, a uniquely American, European, or Australian Islam—understandings of Islam that take account of where Muslims live. Opponents, including many within Indonesia itself, contend that Islam Nusantara seeks to legitimize practices at odds with the teachings of Islam; supporters maintain that it is an inclusive Islam, tolerant of local culture. ▪

Sharia in Aceh

Not all of Indonesia follows a liberal interpretation of Islam. As a result of concessions to help end an armed separatist conflict that had run for almost 30 years, ending in 2005, the semiautonomous province of Aceh on the northwest tip of Sumatra was granted special rights to set some of its own regulations. One of these was the implementation of Sharia as an adjunct to civil and criminal law, which was presented as a way to address social issues.

Sharia police now monitor public behavior and enforce the rules, including prohibitions on alcohol and gambling, the wearing of suitably modest clothing by women, and restrictions on the mixing of sexes. Penalties for offenses take the form of public canings. Some politicians in Aceh have called the tsunami that hit the region in December 2004 "a punishment from God" and have warned that a bigger disaster will come if the people of Aceh do not follow Sharia.

WHY DO I HAVE TO PROVE TO YOU THAT I'M A GOOD GUY?

ABE AJRAMI (2018)

IN CONTEXT

THEME
Muslims in the West

WHEN AND WHERE
Today, the West

BEFORE
1889 The Shah Jahan Mosque in Woking, near London, becomes the first custom-built mosque in Great Britain.

1957 Dwight D. Eisenhower becomes the first US president to visit an American mosque when he speaks at the Islamic Center of Washington DC.

2016 The US's Pew Research Center estimates the number of Muslims in Sweden at 810,000, or 8.1 percent of the population. In western Europe, only France (at 8.8 percent) has a higher percentage of Muslims.

In 2018, German chancellor Angela Merkel told the German parliament, "It is beyond question that our country was historically formed by Christianity and Judaism. But it's also the case that with 4.5 million Muslims living with us, their religion, Islam, has also become a part of Germany." She could also have been speaking for the rest of Europe, which, leaving out Russia and Turkey, is home to an estimated 25.8 million Muslims.

Muslims are found in significant numbers across western Europe, with large populations in France, Germany, and the United Kingdom, and smaller numbers in most other

See also: The caliphate of the Ottoman Empire 186–89 ▪ Islam in Europe 210–15 ▪ Early Muslims in America 224–27 ▪ The demographics of Islam today 260–61

A 2016 survey published by the Pew Research Center lists the total number of Muslims in Europe as 25.8 million, or 4.9 percent of the population. Countries with more than a million Muslims are labelled on this map.

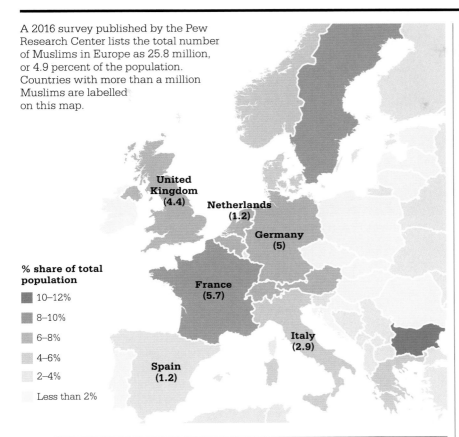

% share of total population

- 10–12%
- 8–10%
- 6–8%
- 4–6%
- 2–4%
- Less than 2%

United Kingdom (4.4)
Netherlands (1.2)
Germany (5)
France (5.7)
Italy (2.9)
Spain (1.2)

conflicts in the Middle East and Africa. The traditional preference for large families means that Muslims tend to have more children than non-Muslims. Statistics state that the average Muslim woman in Europe has 2.6 children, while the average non-Muslim woman has 1.6 children.

Guests turned citizens

In each European country, the makeup and relationship of the Muslim minority to the host country is different. Following World War II, Germany desperately needed labor and initiated a program of *gastarbeiters*, or guest laborers. These migrant workers, mostly from Turkey's rural Anatolian heartlands, were expected to leave when their work was done, but instead they brought their families. Germany eventually granted them and their German-born children citizenship, starting in 1990. Today, it is estimated that there are upward of 4 million people of full or partial Turkish origin living in Germany, making them the largest immigrant group in the country. More recently, »

countries, including Austria, Belgium, the Netherlands, Sweden, and Switzerland.

Historic presence

Muslims have governed parts of Europe for centuries, since Tarek ibn Ziyad conquered southern Spain in 711, and the Ottomans extended their domains into the Balkans in the 14th century. Islam is tightly woven throughout the continent's history and culture. Today, Muslims in Europe range from Bosniaks (Bosnian Muslims) who can trace their heritage back to the conquests of Süleyman the Magnificent (r. 1520–66), to descendants of Yemeni *lascars* (sailors) who settled

in northeast England in the 19th century, and the communities of migrants in Tromsø in the Arctic region of Norway who arrived in the 21st century.

Europe has seen a significant increase in its Muslim population since the reconstruction and decolonization that followed World War II. The 1950s and 1960s saw several European countries actively soliciting Muslim immigrants to fill labor shortfalls. Between the peak years of mid-2010 and mid-2016, migration again became significant as 3.8 million Muslims arrived in Europe, some as students, some seeking employment opportunities, but many others as refugees fleeing

People are of two types ... either your brother in Islam, or your brother in humanity.
Ali ibn Abi Talib
Son-in-law of Prophet Muhammad

between 2014 and 2016, when about 1 million migrants arrived in Europe, most of them Muslim, Germany took in half of them.

France has the largest Muslim population in Europe, with 5.7 million Muslims, primarily from its former colonies in North Africa. The country has pursued a policy of assimilation, where migrants have been viewed as permanent citizens and strategies have been employed to encourage integration into the state. Muslims have achieved success in all walks of life, from captaining the French football team to World Cup glory (Zinedine Zidane) to being appointed minister of justice (Rachida Dati). However, despite the presence of grand mosques in major cities such as Paris and Lyons, integration policies also mean that the display of Islamic religious symbols, including the veil, is banned in most institutions (the policy applies equally to the symbols of other religions).

Integration or not
Britain's 2 million Muslims come primarily from India, Pakistan, and Bangladesh, which once formed part of the British Empire. They

Soccer player Mohammed Salah is one of a growing number of global sports icons who provide positive Muslim role models in the West.

are largely concentrated in the industrial cities of the north and the Midlands, where in the 1950s and 1960s migrants were invited to settle and work in factories. Many of those factories are long since closed, but second and third generations of Muslims have integrated into British life, with Muslims represented in every sector of society from politics (a Muslim mayor of London, Sadiq

If he scores another few, then I'll be Muslim too.
Liverpool FC supporters
Soccer chant in honor of the club's Egyptian striker Mohammed Salah

Khan) to sports (one of Britain's greatest ever athletes is Sir Mohammed "Mo" Farah). British law protects diversity in faith and practice, which means Britain's Muslim communities tend to retain a strong sense of identity.

The different approaches of Germany, France, and Britain each bring their own problems. There has been a rise in support for right-wing politicians in Germany who oppose immigration. In France, Muslim youths complain that their religion causes many French to see them as second-class citizens. In Britain, Muslim communities are accused by some politicians and commentators of not doing enough to integrate.

In North America
Except in a few cities, such as Dearborn, Michigan (which is at the heart of an industrial area that drew many Muslim migrants in the early years of the 20th century), Muslims in the United States are thinly spread. In 2017, they totaled about 3.45 million, or just over 1 percent of the nation's total population.

The Muslim experience in North America tends to be quite different from that of Muslims in Europe.

Islam Down Under

Numbers released by the Australian Bureau of Statistics in 2017 revealed that Arabic was the third most spoken language in Australia behind English and Mandarin. The same census put the number of Australians who identified as Muslims as 604,200, or 2.6 percent of the total population.

Islam in Australia goes back to at least the 18th century, when Indonesian Muslims from Sulawesi visited the coast of northern Australia. Muslims—or Mohammedans—were listed in the musters (colony headcounts) of 1802, 1811, and 1822, and in the first census of 1828. The Muslim population was boosted in the second half of the 19th century by the arrival of Central Asians, who came as camel drivers to lead the camel trains that transported goods across the country's deserts and also built the country's first mosque in 1861. The Adelaide to Darwin railway is named "the Ghan" (short for Afghan) after them.

American Muslims gathered on Capitol Hill in Washington, DC on September 25, 2009 for Friday prayer, to "pray for understanding between America and its Muslim community."

Muslim migrants to Europe have traditionally come from poorer segments of society. The relatively close distance between Europe and North Africa and the Middle East means they retain close contact with their countries of birth and, when they succeed in Europe, they often seek to bring over their families. America's Muslims are generally more middle class. With fewer of them in relation to the total population, they are more integrated.

After 9/11, however, America's relationship with its Muslim community changed. This group—until then a largely "invisible" minority—became perceived as "the enemy within," accused of harboring disloyalty to their nation. Then-president George W. Bush voiced what many Americans were thinking when he asked in the days after the attack, "Why do they hate us?" In a 2017 survey, 42 percent of Muslim children ages 11 to 18 in America said they were bullied at school because of their faith. Another survey revealed that one in five Americans would deny Muslim citizens the right to vote. Abe Ajrami, a Palestinian American medical professional in Texas, spoke for many Muslim Americans when in 2018 he told a reporter from *National Geographic* magazine, "Why do I have to prove to you that I'm a good guy?"

Canada has a significantly higher percentage of Muslims than the US. The 2011 census recorded 1,053,945 people who identified as Muslims in Canada, or about 3.2 percent of the population. Based on patterns in previous censuses, experts predict that in 2019, Canada probably had about 3 million Muslims.

Closing the gap

Despite recent difficulties, Muslims in the US are thriving. Each Friday, for instance, Washington's Church of the Epiphany near the White House turns into a mosque. It is

A Muslim nurse assists a patient in a UK hospital. According to a 2015 report, of the UK's 4.4 million Muslims, 47 percent were UK born, and 33 percent were ages 15 and under.

reported that the congregation includes Homeland Security agents, State Department bureaucrats, and lawyers from the Department of Justice. The New York Police Department set up a Muslim Officers Society, the first in America, which has resulted in a significant increase in police recruitment among Muslims. There is a Muslim Barbie – modeled on Olympic medal-winning fencer Ibtihaj Muhammad. In 2017, the television channel Hulu invested in *Ramy*, a show about an American Muslim navigating his way through life in New Jersey. It premiered in 2019 and became a hit, finding an appreciative audience far beyond the Muslim community.

In many ways, the 20th-century wave of Muslim arrivals in the West has done remarkably well. Many came from humble backgrounds to carve out new lives in their adopted countries. In the 21st century, two or three generations later, their children and grandchildren have closed the gaps in education, salary, and lifestyles, with the only differentiator being religion. ■

DON'T PANIC, I'M ISLAMIC

LYNN GASPARD (2017)

IN CONTEXT

THEME
The rising tide of Islamophobia

WHEN AND WHERE
Today, worldwide

BEFORE
1993 In the first terror attack on US soil, extremists bomb the World Trade Center in New York City, killing six people.

1995 The Federal Building in Oklahoma City is bombed, killing 168 people. Media reports blame "Islamic extremists." In fact, the bomber is Timothy McVeigh, a white, Christian man.

2001 *Reel Bad Arabs*, a book by Jack Shaheen, looks at how Hollywood vilifies Arabs and Muslims on screen.

2019 A white supremacist gunman kills 51 people and injures 49 in shooting attacks at mosques in Christchurch, New Zealand.

The word Islamophobia entered the *Oxford English Dictionary* in 2006, where it is defined as: "Intense dislike or fear of Islam, especially as a political force; hostility or prejudice toward Muslims."

As the OED notes, the word has been around since at least 1923, when it was used in an article in *The Journal of Theological Studies*. Britain's Runnymede Trust, a think tank on race relations, brought the word to public attention in 1997, with a widely discussed report entitled *Islamophobia: A Challenge for Us All*.

Triggers

The 1997 report came as a result of growing anti-Muslim prejudice, not just in Britain but around the world. Among myriad contributory factors, experts point to two main triggers. The first was the Iranian Revolution of 1979, reports of which were dominated by images of Iranians burning American and British flags in the Western press, without necessarily explaining the roots of the uprising. The second came in 1989, when Iran's Supreme Leader Ayatollah Khomeini issued his *fatwa* (ruling) calling for the death

of Salman Rushdie, author of a novel, *The Satanic Verses* (1988), that many Muslims considered offensive toward Islam. The anger felt by Muslims the world over was matched by that of non-Muslims in the West in response to the *fatwa*.

In the 20 years between the first Runnymede report and its follow-up in 2017, anti-Muslim prejudice grew into a significant geopolitical force. Perceptions of Muslims have been harmed by events such as the 9/11 attacks in the United States, the 7/7 London bombings in the UK in 2005, the *Charlie Hebdo* and

Islamophobia has now crossed the threshold. ... For far too many people, Islamophobia is seen as a legitimate—even commendable—thing.
Baroness Warsi
First Muslim member of Cabinet in a UK government, 2010–14

See also: God's guidance through Sharia 128–33 ▪ The Iranian Revolution 248–51 ▪ The new extremists 272–77 ▪ Muslims in the West 282–85 ▪ A feminist Islam? 292–99

Muslim activist Mona Haydar offers free coffee and doughnuts in Cambridge, Massachusetts, in 2016, along with an invitation to "Ask A Muslim," as a way of countering Islamophobia.

November 2015 Paris attacks in France, and the surge of so-called "jihadis"—some 40,000, according to the UN in 2017—heading to Iraq and Syria to join (or marry) ISIS fighters. As a result, much of public discourse on Muslims and Islam has been framed in terms of terrorism.

Reponses

While the terrorist threat is very real, many misleading or outright incorrect stories in the media have served to stigmatize Muslim communities that are every bit as horrified by terrorist actions as their non-Muslim neighbors. Each attack fuels the proliferation of hostile far-right groups with an anti-Islam agenda. In the 21st century, these have extended across the US and many European countries and have included campaigns against immigration,

the building of mosques and minarets, and halal meat, along with calls for "burka bans."

Islamophobic comments made by a number of politicians in the West have resulted in spikes in anti-Muslim hate crime. More often than not, Muslim women have borne the brunt of this. In Britain, a prominent politician's comments made in 2018 equating *niqab*-wearing women to "bank robbers" was followed by a

reported surge in Islamophobic incidents. According to Tell MAMA, an organization that records hate crime in the UK, the week following the comment saw an almost four-fold increase (375 percent) in anti-Muslim incidents compared to the week before.

In the United States, the New America organization notes that anti-Muslim activities have increased markedly in recent times. It documents 763 separate incidents between 2012 and the end of 2018.

Us and them

Anti-Muslim hate crime attempts to promote the separation between "us" and "them," creating mutual suspicion, hostility, and fear. It fails to recognize that the Muslim community consists of many diverse and fluid national, racial, and ethnic communities, whose adherence to Islam ranges from devout to not at all. The book *Don't Panic, I'm Islamic* (edited by Lynn Gaspard) is a witty reply to an American travel ban in 2017 that largely targeted Muslims, and celebrates their diversity. ▪

Discrimination in Asia

About a quarter of Muslims in Asia live as minorities within their countries. Despite Asian economic growth, these Muslim minorities have experienced a persistent decline in their status, often accompanied by violence. In India, there has been a marginalization of Muslims since the election of the Hindu nationalist BJP party in 2014. Many nationalists express the idea that Muslims can never truly be Indians because, unlike Hindus, their

holy sites are not in India. In Sri Lanka, there were anti-Muslim riots in 2018 and 2019.

In 2016, state authorities in Myanmar began a crackdown on the country's Muslim Rohingya population. Employing killing, rape, and arson, the Burmese military has forced more than one million Rohingya to flee to neighboring countries. In China more than one million Muslim Uighurs are reported to have been detained and placed in so-called "reeducation camps."

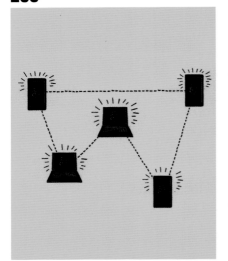

MY IDENTITY Z ISLAM & UMMA IS MY FAMILY
ROSE @CHOCOLATE9933 (TWITTER)

IN CONTEXT

THEME
Islam in the digital age

WHEN AND WHERE
Today, worldwide

BEFORE
2011 Young activists working through social media are instrumental in organizing the Arab Spring protests that sweep North Africa and the Middle East.

2012 Some friends in New York jokingly tag themselves "Muslim hipsters" and the "Mipsterz" quickly evolve into a global online community.

2015 Apple introduces Kaaba, mosque, and prayer beads emojis for Muslim users.

2019 A Malaysian start-up launches SalamWeb, a new browser that is compliant with Islamic values, vetting web pages as appropriate, neutral, or inappropriate.

Muslims have embraced the internet, smartphones, and related technologies just as the rest of the world has— and, in some ways, the results have been even more significant. The best example of this is the way in which social media was directly responsible for the spread of the uprisings throughout the Middle East in 2010 and 2011, known as the Arab Spring. In Egypt, it was a Facebook campaign in support of Khaled Saeed, a young man murdered by the police, that led to an initial protest march, which then rapidly escalated to mass protests in Tahrir Square and the downfall of then-president Hosni Mubarak.

Digital *umma*
The Arab Spring was not religious in nature—the protestors were against oppressive regimes—even if, in the case of Egypt and Tunisia, subsequent free elections saw Islamic parties voted into power. However, the internet has provided new ways for Muslims to explore their own Islamic identity. The notion of *umma*, or the global Muslim nation, is embedded in Islam. Prophet Muhammad reportedly said that anyone who wakes up in the morning and does not think of their Muslim brothers and sisters is not a Muslim. Formerly, *umma* would only be experienced on occasions of mass gathering, such as Friday prayers or the Hajj, but thanks to the internet, Muslims around the world share a strong sense of belonging to a global, digital *umma*.

Online resources allow Muslims to easily explore scripture and gain a deeper understanding of their faith. Forums allow discussion of religious issues of a sometimes difficult or personal nature, such as

Muslim youngsters are adopting technology to distance themselves from older, traditional practices while also challenging Western models.
Bart Barendregt
Associate professor, Leiden University

> Is it haram for girls to post their pics on the internet without *hijab*?
> **Question posted on Stack Exchange/Islam forum**

sexual health, relationships, and spiritual well being, without having to rely on local preachers.

#MosqueMeToo

The internet's impact is even greater for Muslim women, for whom traditional learning spaces such as mosques and *madrasas* have traditionally been off limits. This is the subject of American Muslim Hind Makki's Tumblr, called Side Entrance, which contrasts photographs of attractive prayer spaces reserved for men with the dismal spaces—often basements—set aside for women. The internet, at least, offers an alternative forum in the form of "virtual mosques" that offer online sermons and instruction, or *dawah* (Islamic information-sharing) programs on YouTube.

In 2011, in protest against Saudi Arabia's ban on women behind the wheel, Manal al-Sharif uploaded a

video to YouTube showing herself driving. The video went viral and earned al-Sharif a spell in detention, but in 2018 Saudi Arabia began issuing its first driving licenses to women.

In 2018, women used the hashtag #MosqueMeToo to share stories of sexual assault and abuse in places of worship.

Sheikh Google

The internet is also a prime source for religious rulings, or *fatwas*. However, this reliance on what is playfully referred to as "Sheikh Google" is open to abuses—for instance, "*fatwa* shopping," which is the term for taking a question to multiple online religious scholars until the questioner gets the answer they want.

Software developers have used technology to aid good Islamic practice in many other ways. Phone apps give prayer time notifications, indicate the direction of Mecca,

and deliver Quranic verses to read each day. There are apps to locate the nearest mosque or halal restaurant, and numerous Muslim networking and dating apps, with names like buzzArab and Muzmatch. In a uniquely Islamic slant on a global obsession, when millions of Muslims gather in Mecca each year to perform the Hajj, Twitter is deluged with self-portraits tagged #HajjSelfie.

Technology cuts both ways. Militant Islamist groups continue to use online forums to attract recruits to their causes and to post propaganda videos featuring horrific killings. Social media has also increased the reach of controversial clerics, such as Saudi Arabian Muhammad Al Arefe, who has advocated violence against non-Muslims. However, the internet's potential to encourage open discussion and spread understanding and knowledge of Islam is overwhelmingly positive. ▪

United Arab Emirates nationals Khalid Al Ameri and his wife Salama Mohamed are prominent Muslim social media influencers; they have 3.2 million followers on Facebook.

WHAT MUSLIMS CONSUME AFFECTS WHO THEY ARE

SHELINA JANMOHAMED, AUTHOR OF *GENERATION M: YOUNG MUSLIMS CHANGING THE WORLD* (2016)

IN CONTEXT

THEME
The global business of halal

WHEN AND WHERE
Today, worldwide

BEFORE
2004 Malaysia launches the Malaysian International Halal Showcase, with companies from 19 different countries.

2008 CrescentRating launches as the world's first online site to rate hotels according to their halal facilities.

2018 Three former students from Nottingham University (a Palestinian, Jordanian, and Russian) launch Halalivery, an on-demand halal food delivery service in the UK.

2019 Brazil, the world's top exporter of halal beef and meats, announces that its halal food exports are worth $5 billion annually.

Traditionally the term halal (permitted) has been applied to indicate a food that has been prepared in accordance with Sharia law, and is acceptable for Muslims to eat. However, increasingly the term is applied to products other than food, as the definition of halal widens to encompass anything that is *tayyab* ("wholesome"). For many, consuming halal products and engaging in halal activities is a daily part of being a good Muslim. "Going halal" also becomes a badge of identity for Muslims wanting to publicly assert their faith.

With some products, such as toothpaste, skin creams, and cosmetics, Muslims want to know that no alcohol or *haram* (forbidden) animal products have been used in their making. Manufacturers offer halal nail polishes that claim, unlike normal types, to let water through, so they do not need to be removed before ablutions for prayer. Other products that might normally be *haram* have also been changed to become halal compliant—for example, there is alcohol-free "halal beer" and "halal wine," and even halal "bacon" (made from beef). The halal travel industry caters to the desire for hotels serving halal food, gender-segregated pools, and no alcohol. Halal dating agencies match Muslims who want to get married; clients start by exchanging "halal" (virtuous) chat-up lines. Halal is big business: according to a 2019 forecast, the global halal market is expected to be worth $9.71 trillion by 2025. ∎

Halal tourism is a rapidly growing sector in the travel industry. Popular destinations include Muslim countries such as Turkey and the Maldives, pictured above.

See also: Muslim dietary laws 124–25 ▪ Islam and alcohol, gambling, and drugs 126 ▪ God's guidance through Sharia 128–33

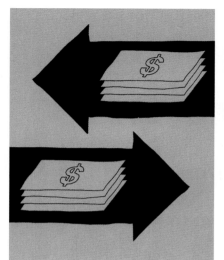

ETHICAL FINANCE CAN BE A FORCE FOR GOOD

CORDOBA CAPITAL, ISLAMIC FINANCE CONSULTING

IN CONTEXT

THEME
Islamic banking

WHEN AND WHERE
Today, worldwide

BEFORE
1940s–50s Islamic scholars condemn commercial banks and propose a banking system based on *mudaraba*, where shared profit on investment would replace interest.

1976 Following the First International Conference on Islamic Economics in Mecca, the first interest-free bank is established in Dubai in 1979.

2004 The Islamic Bank of Britain becomes the UK's first Islamic bank. In 2014, it was rebranded as Al Rayan Bank.

2016 CNBC reports on the "quiet financial revolution going on under the radar," which is the rise of Islamic financial institutions in the US.

The Quran forbids usury (*riba*), or the earning of interest, a key component of modern international banking. Sharia-compliant Islamic banking does not pay or charge interest. In an Islamic mortgage, for instance, a bank does not lend money to a person to buy a property; instead, the bank buys the property. The customer either buys it back from the bank at a higher price, paid in instalments (*murabaha*), or makes payments that are both a

You have to understand the basics of Sharia, what's allowed and not allowed in Islam.
Sheikh Hussein Hassan
Scholar on applying Sharia to finance

repayment of the purchase price and rent until he or she owns the property, an arrangement known as *ijara*. Islamic banks loan money to businesses in exchange for a share in profits. If the business defaults or does not earn a profit, the bank also does not benefit.

Islamic banks also promise customers that they will not invest in things that Islam forbids—so no alcohol, armaments, drugs, pork, gambling, tobacco, or pornography.

Both Muslims and non-Muslims can benefit from Islamic banking, which many customers value as a more transparent and fairer system of finance. In the UK, Al Rayan Bank estimates that more than one third of its customers are non-Muslim. Many conventional banks also offer Islamic banking services. The fact that investments can only be made in activities in keeping with the ethical values of Islam appeals not just to Muslims but to anyone who shares the ideals of fair trading, and prefers banks that invest in real assets rather than speculating in financial markets. ∎

See also: Islam and alcohol, gambling, and drugs 126 ▪ Money-lending in Islam 127 ▪ God's guidance through Sharia 128–33

ISLAM IS A RELIGION THAT EMPOWERS WOMEN

MARIAM KHAN (2019)

IN CONTEXT

THEME
A feminist Islam?

WHEN AND WHERE
Today, worldwide

BEFORE
c. **595** Wealthy Meccan trader Khadija bint Khuwaylid marries Muhammad, future prophet of Islam.

1236 Razia Sultana becomes empress of the Delhi Sultanate and the first sovereign female ruler in Islamic history.

1250 Shagaret al-Dur ("Tree of Pearls") becomes sultana of Egypt on her husband's death.

1918 Azerbaijan is the first Muslim-majority country to give women the vote—the same year as Austria, Germany, Poland, and Russia, and a year before the 19th Amendment would state that the right to vote of all citizens could not be denied by any US state on the basis of sex.

Feminism and Islam are often seen as incompatible, particularly by those outside the Muslim world. Western commentators and media typically present Islam as responsible for marginalizing women's role in society and acting as an obstacle to their careers. For many Muslim women, however, feminism and faith can and do happily coexist.

The very beginnings of Islam provide a feminist role model in the form of Khadija bint Khuwaylid, the first wife of Prophet Muhammad. A successful businesswoman in Mecca, she chose Muhammad as her husband—not the other way around—and provided him with the opportunity to become a successful merchant in his own right. After Muhammad began receiving the revelations that would form the Quran, Khadija became the first Muslim. She challenges the erroneous assumption that Muslim women's so-called subjugation stems from the Quran.

Challenging assumptions

It is not hard to see why feminism and Islam are so often viewed as being at odds with each other. For

Often, women are immediately identifiable as Muslims in a way men are not, by what they wear, notably the *hijab*, or headscarf.

example, in 2013 the Pew Research Center published the results of a survey conducted in Muslim-majority countries that asked whether a wife should always obey her husband—the majority of respondents answered she should. In Turkey, 65 percent were in favor of a husband's right to obedience, while in Malaysia the figure was 96 percent. On the question of how women should dress in public,

Huda Shaarawi

In 1919, Egyptian Huda Shaarawi led women onto the streets to demonstrate against the British occupation of her country. She was equally critical of the rules of the patriarchal world in which she was raised, which saw her married off at the age of 13 to a cousin 40 years her senior.

Shaarawi's activism began in 1908, when she helped create the first medical dispensary for underprivileged women and children. The act that she is most remembered for came in 1922 when, returning from a conference in Rome, she

removed her face veil in public at Cairo railway station. Those who had come to greet her were shocked. However, many women soon followed her lead.

Shaarawi and her followers made further important gains, including establishing 16 as the minimum age for marriage for women, and founding the first secondary school for young women and the Egyptian Feminist Union. After Shaarawi's death in 1947, President Nasser banned Egypt's women's movements—they would not reemerge until the 1980s.

See also: Women in the Quran 82–85 ▪ The new extremists 272–77 ▪ Islam in Africa 278–79 ▪ Muslims in the West 282–85 ▪ The *hijab* and *niqab* 300–03

another survey (this one carried out by the University of Michigan's Institute for Social Research in 2014) conducted in seven Muslim-majority countries found that most respondents, both male and female, preferred that a woman should completely cover her hair.

Patriarchal and conservative views may remain commonplace, but that is far from the whole story. Many middle-class Muslim women lead lives that ar not much different from their non-Muslim counterparts. They are often well educated, have jobs, run businesses, and enjoy busy social lives.

Education and opportunity

Muslim societies have frequently faced criticism from outside for failing to adequately educate women. The Taliban's attack on Pakistani women's education activist Malala Yousafzai and the Nigeria-based Boko Haram group's kidnapping of schoolgirls have contributed to this perception. However, data published by the Pew Research Center in 2018 suggests that it is not Islam that limits the education of Muslim women, but economics. The Center's analysis shows that a country's wealth is the most important factor in women's education. Women in the oil-rich states of Bahrain, Kuwait, and Qatar, for example, receive as many years of schooling as women in Germany and the United Kingdom (about 12 years)—which is only slightly less than the United States

Women in the Islamic world are increasingly becoming better educated. For example, in Saudi Arabia, fewer than 2 percent of women went to college in 1970; today, the figure is 57 percent.

at about 13 years. By contrast, women in economically poor Muslim-majority countries, such as Afghanistan, Mali, Niger, Sierra Leone, and Yemen receive on average less than two years of education (three years in the case of Nigeria).

What the Pew Research Center survey does not reflect is that even in those countries in which women benefit from education, far too few join the workforce. In Saudi Arabia, where there are more women in »

I'm a feminist and a Muslim.
Malala Yousafzai
Pakistani activist for female education

Egyptian women gathered on Tahrir Square in Cairo during the demonstrations of spring 2011. This was a gender-equal revolution that saw both sexes on the front lines.

college than men (52 percent women versus 48 percent men), only 27 percent of women go on to get a job. In one university in Cairo, while 80 percent of students studying architecture are women, anecdotal evidence suggests that women make up less than half of all practising architects. Despite any equality in education, the idea that offices are a male environment and that women belong at home still prevails in many parts of the Islamic world.

However, this may be changing. A report by the World Economic Forum in 2018 revealed that one in three start-ups in the Arab world is founded or led by women, which is a higher percentage than in Silicon Valley in California. Being relatively young, the technology industry is not afflicted by the inherited prejudices of older and traditionally male-dominated fields.

Women leading
The Arab Spring uprisings that began in 2010 shattered stereotypes as women, young and old, from Tunisia to Egypt to Bahrain stood on the frontlines to protest and play

A whole series of people opposed me simply on the grounds that I was a woman.
Benazir Bhutto
Former Pakistani prime minister, assassinated in 2007

their part in shaping their nation's revolutions. It was a reminder that without rights for women, no country can become a true democracy. Since then, eight countries in the Middle East and North Africa region have criminalized domestic violence. Six governments have repealed laws that allowed a rapist to escape prosecution by marrying his victim.

Progress on women's rights is most pronounced in Tunisia, where the Arab Spring pro-democracy uprisings started. The country's 2014 constitution affirms equal rights for male and female citizens and promises the state will strive to achieve parity in all elected assemblies. Following elections in 2018, it was reported that women make up 47 percent of the local council positions. Tunisia is also notable for overturning legislation banning Muslim women from marrying non-Muslim men—a taboo in most Muslim countries,

> My life's work has been informed by the belief that religion and culture must never be used to justify the subjugation of women.
> **Mona Eltahawy**
> *Author and journalist*

although men can marry non-Muslim women because it is assumed that children will take the father's religion.

Across the Middle East and North Africa, female representation in national parliaments rose to an average of about 17.5 percent in 2017, up from less than 5 percent 20 years previously – the global average is 23.4 percent. In fact, in 2019 women held 25 percent of all top ministerial posts in Egypt, one of the world's most populous Muslim countries, including high-profile portfolios such as health, investment, and tourism. The same year, the cabinet of the United Arab Emirates could boast nine women ministers out of 32, which is close to 30 percent.

Beyond the Arab world, Muslim-majority Pakistan elected a woman as head of state in Benazir Bhutto, who served as prime minister from 1988 to 1990 and again from 1993 to 1996. In Bangladesh, Khaleda Zia served as the prime minister from 1991 to 1996, and again from 2001 to 2006—the first woman in the country's history and second in a Muslim-majority country to head a democratic government. Another woman, Sheikh Hasina, served as Bangladesh's prime minister from 1996 to 2001, and took up the post again in 2009.

In contrast, the first 45 presidents of the United States have all been men. Women made up 23.2 percent of the US Congress in 2019, but the first two Muslim women ever to serve in Congress have faced hostility. Rashida Tlaib (born to working-class Palestinian

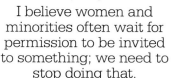

> I believe women and minorities often wait for permission to be invited to something; we need to stop doing that.
> **Ilhan Omar**
> *US Congresswoman*

parents in Detroit) serves as the representative for Michigan's 13th congressional district, while Somali-born Ilhan Omar represents Minnesota's 5th congressional district. Both took office in 2019. Omar, who wears a headscarf, has been the subject of inflammatory, anti-Muslim rhetoric at rallies, including one in South Carolina in 2019 where the crowd repeatedly chanted "send her back."

We are not oppressed

Women such as Ilhan Omar and Rashida Tlaib are frequently held up as rare examples of Muslim women breaking through barriers. The Western media often portrays such women as exceptions to the rule that Muslim women are oppressed by either their husbands or their religion—or both—and are lacking in aspiration or the capability for independent thought. In 2016, a British newspaper reported that former British prime minister David Cameron had »

Somali-born Ilhan Omar (shown here), along with her colleague Rashida Tlaib, became the first two Muslim women to assume office in the US House of Representatives, in 2019.

implied during a private meeting that the traditionally submissive nature of British Muslim women made their sons vulnerable to radicalization. In response, thousands of women took to Twitter using the hashtag #TraditionallySubmissive to list their achievements.

A similar incident occurred following a Democratic Party convention in the US in 2016 when Ghazala Khan, mother of a Muslim American soldier killed in Iraq, remained silent while her husband spoke. Republican presidential candidate Donald Trump said at the time, "If you look at his wife, she was standing there. She had nothing to say … maybe she wasn't allowed to have anything to say. You tell me."

While this view of Muslim women as passive, voiceless victims is prevalent in the West, women in the Muslim world are moving on with being doctors, journalists, university professors, soldiers, technology entrepreneurs, airline pilots, sporting stars, and government ministers.

> I am both … believer and feminist, enlightened and sometimes very traditional, East and West.
> **Seyran Ates**
> *Muslim feminist*

Equality at the mosque

Women are also carving out new roles within the practice of Islam—although, so far, this is only happening outside the Muslim-majority world. In Western Europe, a number of Muslim women have sought to reform male-dominated religious worship and education and reflect the needs of a new generation of believers. In the UK, the Inclusive Mosque Initiative, which was established in London in 2012 by two British Muslim

women, considers itself a "feminist" mosque. Its entire team—including imams—are also women.

A number of Muslim women have sought to not only reform male-dominated mosques across Western Europe, but to reflect the needs of the new generation of Muslims across the continent. Berlin is home to the Ibn Rushd–Goethe mosque, the first liberal mosque of its kind in Germany, cofounded in 2017 by Turkish-born lawyer, imam, and human rights campaigner Seyran Ates. In a move that elicited controversy, women and men pray together, while women can lead the prayer and preach. Ates has since received death threats and hate mail from conservative Muslims, and the main religious authority in Turkey has attacked the mosque for "depraving and ruining religion."

Scandinavia's first female-led mosque opened in Copenhagen, Denmark, in 2016. Named the Mariam Mosque (after the mother of Jesus), it was founded by two female imams, Sherin Khankan and Saliha Marie Fetteh. As Khankan, a mother herself, has said, "having female imams affects not only the structure in the mosque at a society level, but challenges the family structure"—children grow up in the faith seeing women as leaders. Friday prayers are exclusively attended by women.

Author and academic Dr. Amina Wadud is perhaps the most high-profile female imam in the US. Although America has yet to see its first mainstream female-run mosque, Dr. Wadud has led mixed

Sherin Khankan, of the Mariam Mosque in Copenhagen, has called for the reformation of Islam with a feminist agenda, a vision outlined in her book *Women Are the Future of Islam*.

Ibtihaj Muhammad was the first Muslim American woman to wear a *hijab* while competing for the US at the Olympics. She earned a bronze team medal in fencing at Rio 2016.

Friday prayers. Meanwhile, other women are establishing spaces that reflect previously taboo aspects of American Muslims' identities. For example, Chicago-based Mahdia Lynn runs Masjid al-Rabia, a women-centered LGBTQ and trans-inclusive mosque.

Reclaiming the narrative

Muslim women are often the most visible representatives of their religion, because of the simple fact that many of them wear the *hijab*. In this way, they often become the subject of any discussion about Islam, even as their own voices are rarely heard.

In 2019, feminist and writer Mariam Khan published *It's Not About the Burqa*, a collection of essays by Muslim women talking about their faith and their lives. "When was the last time you heard a Muslim woman speak for herself without a filter?" she asked in her introduction. Two years earlier in

the United States, Amani al-Khatahtbeh, who founded MuslimGirl.com in 2009, launched the first Muslim Women's Day. Like her website, it aimed to celebrate the voices of Muslim women around the world, and counter misrepresentation in the media. Al-Khatahtbeh is notably critical of the way that Muslim women are treated as if they are one single entity. "Muslim women come from

every single walk of life on the planet," she told allure.com. "You can't talk about them in any way that's different than Christian women, for example."

In 2016, during a panel discussion at the White House's first United State of Women Summit, al-Khatahtbeh was asked, "How do we empower the people we call the voiceless?" Her simple answer was, "Pass the mic." ∎

The most dangerous misconception about Muslim women is that we're one homogenous group.
Amani al-Khatahtbeh
Editor-in-chief of MuslimGirl.com

Scholars against the patriarchy

There is a modern tradition of "Islamic feminists" working on interpreting the main texts of Islam from a distinctly feminist perspective. The pioneer in the field was Moroccan sociologist Fatema Mernissi (1940–2015). She produced one of the first books in the field, called *Beyond the Veil*, published in 1975. This and her many subsequent works reexamine traditional Islamic jurisprudence, to offer alternative interpretations that are less male-oriented.

American professor of Islamic studies Dr. Amina Wadud courted controversy in her *Inside the Gender Jihad: Women's Reform in Islam* (2006). Citing the example of slavery, which she believes is condoned in the Quran, she argues that if something seems to be against the standards of modern society, it has to be discarded. So when the Quran says that if a wife is disobedient her husband can hit her, this, too, is no longer acceptable in the modern world.

BEAUTIFUL TO GOD RATHER THAN PEOPLE

YASMIN MOGAHED (2019)

The Quran prescribes a code of behavior and dress for both men and women. In *sura* 24, the prescription is to men first: "Enjoin believing men to turn their eyes away from temptation and to preserve their chastity. This will make their lives purer" (24:30). It is then followed by a prescription for women: "Enjoin believing women to turn their eyes away from temptation and to preserve their chastity; not to display their adornments (except such as are normally revealed); to draw their veils over their bosoms ..." (24:31).

The instruction is for men and women to be respectful in how they look at each other—often described

Styles of head covering

Hijab The generic name for many styles of headscarf. This is by far the most common type of head covering.

Niqab Covers the face and head with an opening for the eyes. It is most common in the Arab Gulf States.

Burka Covers the entire face and body, and there is a mesh screen over the eyes. Worn mainly in Afghanistan.

as the "*hijab* of the eyes"—but with the additional stipulation for women concerning what they wear. It is this directive "not to display their adornments" that has led to the modesty-preserving clothing that many Muslim women wear.

The *hijab*

Women who wear the *hijab* are sometimes referred to as *hijabis* or *muhajaba*. The word *hijab* is used to refer to the headscarf, as stipulated in *hadith,* but it also acts as a generic descriptor for modest dressing. In the Quran, *hijab* only means a curtain or partition (between men and women or deity and mortals); verses also mention the *khimar* ("cover," in 24:31) and *jilbab* ("cloak," in 33:59), but do not specify the head or hair.

Attitudes toward "modest dress" vary by region. In more moderate countries, such as Egypt, Turkey, and Tunisia, there is no official dress code for women, but dressing modestly, covering knees and shoulders, is expected, particularly in rural areas. Dress codes are also subject to shifting social attitudes and fashions at different times in history. In Turkey, for example, after Kemal Atatürk declared the country a secular state in 1923, headscarf-wearing went into rapid decline and all but

So even if you hate it, I still wrap my *hijab*. Wrap my *hijab*, wrap my *hijab* Wrap, wrap my *hijab*.
Mona Haydar
Lyrics to 2017 song "Hijabi (Wrap My Hijab)"

disappeared. Following a military coup in 1980, a total ban was enforced. However, since the rise to power of Islamic parties, notably the AKP (Justice and Development Party), in the 21st century, the headscarf is very much back.

Even when Muslim women do wear the *hijab*, it is is not a uniform look. West African women favor a brightly colored wrap like a turban, while in South Asia it is a loosely draped cloth that hangs down around the shoulders. Woman in the Gulf States sometimes wear the *khaleeji hijab* (*khaleej* is Arabic for Gulf). Nicknamed the "big bun," "beehive," or "camel hump," it has a rounded bulge at the back of the head to give the impression of a mane of hair that has been neatly coiled up into a bun.

Other countries—notably Iran, but also Saudi Arabia and other Sharia states—strictly police what women wear in public. In Iran, they have to put on either a *chador*, which is a long, black, shapeless garment covering the whole body, or (in less conservative circles) a headscarf, trousers, and a long-sleeved coat called a *manteau*. Women in Mecca and Medina are obliged to wear an *abaya* (a robe-like dress) whenever they go out, and a cloth wrapped around the hair called the *shayla*; this has been promoted as the most authentic Islamic expression of modest dress, short of the full *niqab*.

The *niqab*

The influence of Saudi Arabia and the more conservative Sharia states in the Gulf, such as Qatar, has also been responsible for the spread of the *niqab*, the full face covering. Globally, however, the number of »

For some Muslims in the West the *hijab* has almost become a symbol of defiance, a way to reassert an Islamic identity in the face of widespread Islamaphobia.

Personal choices

Women give a range of reasons for wearing the *hijab*. For some it is a personal act of obedience to God, and strengthens their worship and their relationship with God. For others, it is a form of modest dressing that aims to reclaim their bodies from objectification and commercialization. It can also be a way of reclaiming an identity that has been demonized, or a defiant expression of pride in their faith. Or it can just be a case of fitting in or following fashion.

Conversely, in some Muslim countries in which modest clothing is mandatory by law, women have conducted protests by removing their headscarves as an act of defiance—echoing the act of early Egyptian feminist Huda Shaarawi back in 1922. The act of deveiling becomes not about religion, but about politics and human rights.

Modest fashion

A recent development is the rise of "modest fashion"—clothing that is designed to appeal to women who consider themselves to be observant Muslims but who still like to dress stylishly. For a younger generation of Muslims especially, faith and modernity go hand in hand.

This has led to a grassroots fashion movement developed by Muslim women who feel that main street and online retailers are not responding to their fashion needs, and are building their own brands, often online. What began as a niche market is now a global phenomenon. The movement has been fueled by dedicated *hijabi* fashion bloggers,

women who wear the *niqab* is a fraction of the number who wear the *hijab*. For many women, the *hijab* is simply an everyday item that may or may not have religious significance for the wearer, while the *niqab* is associated, even among Muslim women, with extreme conservatism.

Because the *niqab* obscures all but the wearer's eyes, it has become highly politicized and has been banned in schools, the workplace, and public spaces in a number of countries, both non-Muslim and Muslim.

France and Belgium were the first countries to ban the *niqab* in public areas, in 2011. In 2019, the Netherlands became the 15th European country to ban face coverings. The Canadian province of Quebec imposed a ban in 2017. Tunisia and parts of West Africa and China have also restricted where women can wear the *niqab*.

Although wearing the *hijab* is framed as a personal choice, I think there's a lot of social pressure.
Shalini Gopalan
Marketing director, Indonesia

I wear the *niqab* as a personal act of worship, and I deeply believe that it brings me closer to God.
Sahar al-Faifi
British geneticist, activist, skydiver

A model showcases a look during a 2018 event in Milan organized by the Islamic Fashion & Design Council and dedicated to modest fashion, which is now a multibillion-dollar market.

> The *hijab* has become deeply politicized.
> **Azzah Sultan**
> *Malaysian artist*

who post about how to create modest fashion looks. Major international clothing, cosmetics, and fashion brands have caught on. In 2016, Nura Afia, an American beauty vlogger, became the first brand ambassador to wear a *hijab*, Dolce & Gabbana released a line of *hijabs* and *abayas* (robes), and Indonesian fashion designer Anniesa Hasibuan presented an all-*hijab* collection at New York Fashion Week. In 2018, Somali-American model Halima Aden became the first woman of color to appear on the cover of *Vogue* magazine wearing a *hijab*.

Modest clothing is also making a splash in sports. In 2016, Olympic athletes wearing the "burkini" (see below) made headlines, and fencer Ibtihaj Muhammad, America's first *hijab*-wearing Olympian, won bronze. Seeing a trend, Nike launched the first made-for-athletes *hijab* in 2017 and modest swimwear in 2020.

The meaning of *hijab*

Critics point out that reducing the *hijab* to a piece of fashion apparel dilutes its meaning as an act of observance. Yasmin Mogahed, a Muslim scholar in the United States, reinforces this view when she says that the *hijab* is "a personal choice to submit to God rather than the fashion of society. To be beautiful to God rather than people." What is clear is that the *hijab* means many different things to many people. ∎

The burkini

Part of the modest fashion trend, the "burkini" is an all-over body swimsuit and swimcap, and sometimes has an additional loose layer, such as short dress or skirt. The original burkini was created by Lebanese-born Australian fashion designer Aheda Zanetti in 2004, who coined the name as a cross between "burka" and "bikini." Zanetti had noticed the struggles that Muslim women face at the pool and in other sports. "I created the burkini to give women freedom, not to take it away," she says. "It's not something that symbolizes anything."

In 2016, however, the burkini was banned from a number of French towns and beaches. A newspaper picture that was reproduced globally showed a woman in a burkini surrounded by armed policemen forcing her to disrobe. The photo sparked outrage, and the ban was overturned by higher courts.

The burkini also made headlines at the 2016 Rio Olympics, when beach volleyball player Doaa Elghobashy of Egypt and sprinter Kariman Abuljadayel of Saudi Arabia wore similar attire.

THE BEST PEOPLE ARE THOSE LIVING IN MY GENERATION
PROPHET MUHAMMAD

Salafism is a back-to-basics movement within Islam that has its roots in Egypt in the 19th century, and which was itself inspired by the example of Saudi Wahhabism. Salafism experienced a surge in popularity in the late 20th century. It aims to reconnect Muslims with the original sources of Islam, specifically the first three generations of Islam, who are collectively known as the *salaf al-salihin*, or "pious predecessors." Followers of Salafism reject the authority of the medieval schools of law, since they appeared after the *salaf al-salihin*, and instead look only to the texts of the Quran and the *hadith*, which they read literally.

To many Muslims, the Salafist approach is uncompromising. Its adherents wear traditional dress (robes for men, rather than trousers, for example) and send their children to segregated Muslim schools. Non-Islamic holidays, such as national holidays, are not observed by Salafis, and nonreligious greetings such as "Good morning" are avoided.

Salafism is an ideology, not a single organization, and it includes many strands of thought. There are Salafis who are apolitical and focus on education and missionary work. However, there are also militant Salafis, who aim to overthrow "apostate" rulers of the Muslim world and replace them with "true" Muslims. Al-Qaeda and Islamic State are militant Salafists. The rise of such organizations reflects a struggle within Salafism itself, as much as it does a battle between Islam and the West. ∎

Its appeal is like that of Protestant reformation in Christianity.
Yasir Qadhi
American Muslim scholar

See also: God's guidance through Sharia 128–33 ∙ Wahhabism, or an Islamic reformation 216–17 ∙ The new extremists 272–77 ∙ Islam in Africa 278–79

ISLAM HAS BEEN A PROGRESSIVE FAITH SINCE THE BEGINNING
MECCA INSTITUTE (2019)

Progressive Islam is an umbrella term for a diverse array of individuals and groups, with no central authority but with a shared goal of reforming interpretations of the Quran to better accord with the values of the wider modern world, particularly with regard to issues such as human rights and female equality.

Progressives believe that early Muslim scholars did their best to interpret the Quran and *sunna* through consensus, analogy, and *ijtihad* (independent reasoning), which they used to formulate Sharia law. However, they argue, these early interpreters were fallible and mortal men, and the product of their time and culture.

Progressives argue that the spirit of Islam—a religion of justice and compassion—cannot be sustained by observing laws that were made in a time and place that condoned slavery and marrying off girls below the age of puberty. They back their arguments by pointing out that the Quran frequently urges Muslims to think independently.

It saddens our hearts to see how traditionally conservative Muslims today are frozen in time and place.
Akmal Ahmed Safwat
Democratic Muslims of Denmark

In addition to many academics engaged in this debate, bodies such as the US-based MECCA Institute and UK-based *Critical Muslim* magazine aim to promote dialogue to do with liberal thinking about Islam. Although conservative Muslims reject the Progressive view, liberalism is spreading in Islam—for instance, a 2017 poll in the United States showed that acceptance of gay marriage is now stronger among American Muslims than among white evangelical Christians. ∎

See also: Women in the Quran 82–85 ▪ God's guidance through Sharia 128–33 ▪ An Islamic feminism? 292–99

DIRECTO

RY

DIRECTORY

In addition to the individuals featured throughout the book, notably in the biography boxes in the articles, there are many other people who have played a key role in the history of Islam. These include the early leaders of the faith, caliphs, commanders, scholars, mystics, poets, and the later political leaders. Brief biographies of these figures who formed and developed the Muslim faith and Islamic civilization around the world are listed in chronological order below.

KHADIJA BINT KHUWAYLID
555–619

First wife of Muhammad, Khadija bint Khuwaylid came from a merchant family of the powerful Quraysh tribe, which ruled Mecca. She was a wealthy trader in her own right. She married Muhammad at the age of 40, after hiring him to take a caravan to Syria. Sunni sources suggest she had already been widowed twice before marrying Muhammad, although according to Shia tradition he was her first husband. Of their children, four, all daughters, survived to adulthood. After Muhammad's first revelation, in 610, Khadija became the first convert to Islam. She fully supported his preaching for the rest of her life.

MUHAMMAD
570–632

The Prophet Muhammad was born in Mecca, into the Banu Hashim clan of the Quraysh tribe. When he was 40 years old, he received a visitation from the angel Jibreel (the Arabic for Gabriel), which laid the foundations for the Quran. After two years of further revelations, he began to publicly preach and gain converts to his religion, which became known as Islam. Muhammad's monotheism challenged the paganism of the rulers of Mecca, and he and his followers faced persecution, leading them to migrate to the city of Medina in 622. War started between Mecca and the Muslims in 624, and Muhammad gained victory in 630. By 632, Muhammad had gained control of most of Arabia. That year he led the Farewell Pilgrimage to Mecca, and died shortly afterward in Medina.

ABU BAKR AL-SIDDIQ
573–634

See box on p103.

UMAR IBN AL-KHATTAB
584–644

Umar ibn al-Khattab, second Islamic caliph, converted to Islam in 615. Born in Mecca, he joined Muhammad in Medina in 622, and became one of the Prophet's most important counselors. His daughter Hafsa married Muhammad in 625. After Abu Bakr became caliph, Umar's influence grew, and he succeeded him as leader of the Muslim community in 634. Under Umar's leadership the caliphate became a global power, conquering territory from the Byzantine and Sasanian Persian empires, and thus extending its territory from North Africa to the Caucasus. Umar's life was brought to a sudden end at the age of 60, when he was fatally stabbed by a Persian slave.

UTHMAN IBN AFFAN
c. 576–656

A wealthy Meccan merchant from the powerful Umayyad clan, Uthman ibn Affan converted to Islam in 611. He would later marry two of Muhammad's daughters. After Umar died in 644, Uthman was on the committee of six nominated to choose his successor. Despite having little political or military experience, Uthman himself was selected as the third of the Rashidun ("Rightly Guided") caliphs. He oversaw the collation of an official version of the Quran and continued the campaigns of conquest. However, there was rising dissent against his regime, which erupted finally into revolt, and Uthman was murdered at his home in Medina by his opponents.

KHALID IBN AL-WALID
c. 585–642

Born into a clan of the Quraysh tribe that was initially hostile to Muhammad, Khalid ibn al-Walid fought in some of the early battles against the Prophet. However, in 629 Khalid migrated to Medina and converted to Islam, becoming an important military commander. After Muhammad's death, Khalid played a central role in defeating rebel Arab tribes. He then led campaigns against the Sasanians as well as the Byzantines during the conquest of Iraq and Syria, becoming known as the "Sword of God." Despite being undefeated in battle, he was dismissed from the army by Umar in 638, and died in Homs, Syria, four years later.

ALI IBN ABI TALIB
601–61

A cousin of Muhammad, Ali ibn Abi Talib was raised by him from early childhood. He was the first male to convert to Islam, at the age of just nine. He joined Muhammad in Medina, becoming his deputy and marrying his daughter Fatima. Ali distinguished himself during the wars with Mecca, earning a reputation as a courageous warrior. After the death of Muhammad, Ali was passed over for leadership of the Muslims twice, before he was selected as fourth caliph in 656. The caliphate descended into civil war as rebels, known as the Kharijites, sought to overthrow Ali. He was assassinated while at prayer in Kufa, Iraq. Shia Muslims revere Ali, and view him and his descendants as the rightful successors of Muhammad.

MUAWIYA IBN ABI SUFYAN
602–80

Muawiya ibn Abi Sufyan became a convert to Islam after Muhammad's conquest of Mecca. Muawiya led campaigns against the Byzantines and in 640 was made governor of Syria. After Muawiya's kinsman Uthman was murdered in 656, he rebelled against Ali, believing he had not done enough to catch the culprits. Following Ali's assassination, Muawiya succeeded him, founding the Umayyad caliphate and moving the capital to Damascus. As Muawiya I, he continued to extend the caliphate further into North Africa and Asia Minor. Before his death, Muawiya named his son, Yazid, as his successor, setting the precedent of hereditary rule.

FATIMA BINT MUHAMMAD
605–32

Fatima was the youngest daughter of Muhammad and his first wife Khadija. In 622, shortly after the migration to Mecca, she married Muhammad's cousin Ali. Theirs was a devoted union, and four of their children survived to adulthood: two sons, Hassan and Hussein, and two daughters. After Muhammad's death in 632, Fatima clashed with caliph Abu Bakr; like Ali, she was reluctant to recognize his authority. Abu Bakr's supporters gathered at Fatima's house in Medina to gain her support. Some sources, mostly Shia ones, suggest there was then a violent altercation, with Fatima suffering injuries and a miscarriage, which, they claim, contributed to her death from illness later that year.

AISHA BINT ABU BAKR
614–78

The daughter of Abu Bakr, Aisha married Muhammad at a young age, becoming, after Khadija, his next most favored wife. Following the death of Muhammad she concentrated on religious study, memorizing the Quran, as well as narrating *hadith* (2,210 are attributed to her). She joined the opposition to the third caliph, Uthman, but after he was killed, she criticized Ali, who had now become the fourth caliph, for not apprehending Uthman's murderers. Aisha raised an army against Ali and was defeated by him in 656 at the Battle of the Camel in Basra, in Iraq. Aisha was allowed to return to Medina, where she lived peacefully, focusing on religious and charitable endeavors until her death.

HASSAN IBN ALI
624–69

Hassan was the eldest son of Ali and Fatima, and the grandson of Prophet Muhammad. After his father was murdered in 661, Hassan succeeded him as caliph, but was challenged by Muawiya I, governor of Syria, who declared his decision not to recognize him. Both men prepared for conflict, but when it became clear to Hassan that his forces would be outnumbered, he entered into negotiations with Muawiya to prevent civil war. Under the terms of the resulting treaty, Hassan abdicated and retired to Medina, where he lived until his death in 669. According to some accounts, he was poisoned by one of his wives, who had conspired with Muawiya.

HUSSEIN IBN ALI
626–80

The second son of Ali and Fatima, Hussein (also spelled Husayn) joined his older brother Hassan in accepting Muawiya I as caliph in 661. Muawiya had agreed that he would not nominate the next caliph, but before he died in 680, he named his son Yazid I as his successor. Hussein refused to recognize the succession. He fled from Medina to Mecca before being invited by the people of Kufa, a city in Iraq where many opposed the Umayyads, to lead a rebellion against Yazid. Hussein set out for Kufa but was intercepted by Umayyad forces at Kerbala; despite being overpowered, he refused to surrender and was beheaded. He is mourned by all Muslims as a martyr.

ZEINAB BINT ALI
c. 627–c. 682

Zeinab (also spelled Zaynab) was the daughter of Ali ibn Abi Talib and Fatima, and the grand-daughter of Prophet Muhammad. She was sister to Hassan and Hussein ibn Ali. She married Abdullah ibn Jafar and had three sons and two daughters with him. When her brother, Hussein, fought against Yazid ibn Muawiya in 680 at Kerbala, Zeinab accompanied him. According to tradition she saved the life of her nephew, Ali ibn al-Hussein, by throwing herself over his body, and later secured the release by Yazid of herself and other prisoners taken at Kerbala. For this, she became known as the "Heroine of Karbala." Her shrine at Damascus remains an important place of pilgrimage, particularly for Shias.

ABD AL-MALIK IBN MARWAN
646–705

Abd al-Malik was the son and successor of Marwan I—the fourth Umayyad caliph, who reigned briefly from 684 to 685. As caliph, Abd al-Malik faced ongoing civil war, having to battle for the caliphate with the Mecca-based Abdullah ibn Zubeir. Abd al-Malik killed his rival in 692, reestablishing Umayyad control over the entire caliphate. He then resumed war with the Byzantine Empire, making advances into Anatolia and Armenia, and across North Africa. By the time of his death, Abd al-Malik had consolidated the government of the caliphate. He is also known for founding the Dome of the Rock in Jerusalem, one of the earliest surviving Islamic religious monuments.

YAZID IBN MUAWIYA
647–83

The son of Muawiya I, the first Umayyad caliph, Yazid I faced opposition when he succeeded his father in 680—initially from supporters of Hussein ibn Ali, who was executed by Umayyad forces in Kerbala. The murder of Hussein, in addition to rumors of Yazid's dissolute lifestyle, led to a rebellion against him in Arabia. In the fall of 683, Yazid's army defeated the rebels outside Medina, pillaging the city, before laying siege to Mecca, during which a fire damaged the Kaaba. The campaign ended prematurely when Yazid died in Syria that November, although conflict within the caliphate continued until 692.

ABU HANIFA
699–767

Abu Hanifa was a renowned legal scholar whose work formed the basis for the Hanafi school of Islamic law, which is still widely followed today. Born in the city of Kufa in Iraq, the son of a merchant, he initially studied theology before turning his attention to jurisprudence. Abu Hanifa rationally applied Islamic doctrine to legal questions, and by about 738 was one of the foremost scholars in Iraq. Although he was repeatedly offered official positions, he refused them in order to retain his independence. Late in his life, he moved to Mecca, where he was to die in prison—having been incarcerated by caliph al-Mansur, possibly as a result of refusing to serve him as a judge.

MALIK IBN ANAS
711–95

Born in Medina, Malik ibn Anas forged a reputation as a jurist, theologian, and philosopher, and attracted a wide following of disciples. He became the founder of one of the four schools of Sunni law, the Maliki, which became influential throughout much of North Africa, and with some of the prominent Sufi orders. He was an outspoken man; in 762 he offered support to a rebellion against caliph al-Mansur by declaring that forced oaths of loyalty were not binding. As a result he was flogged. He later made amends with the caliphate so that he could continue his work. Malik compiled the *Muwatta* ("Well-trodden path"), one of the oldest and most important Islamic legal works.

AL-MANSUR
714–75

Al-Mansur was a member of the Abbasid family, who were descended from Muhammad's uncle, and who, in 750, overthrew the Umayyad caliphate. Al-Mansur's brother al-Saffah became the first Abbasid caliph. He was succeeded by al-Mansur in 754. Al-Mansur consolidated Abbasid power by eliminating rival claimants and putting down the scattered revolts that broke out against him. In 762 he founded Baghdad as his capital, which would house the increasingly large bureaucracy that governed the caliphate. Al-Mansur died while on a pilgrimage to Mecca and was succeeded by his son al-Mahdi.

RABIA AL-ADAWIYYA
714–801

The origins of the most celebrated female Sufi saint are contested. Popular histories tell how Rabia al-Adawiyya was born into a poor family, orphaned, and sold into slavery. However, scholars believe it more likely she came from a well-off branch of the Quraysh tribe. She grew up in the thriving port city of Basra, in Iraq, where she practiced renunciation—turning away from this world to contemplate the next and living in seclusion. There are a number of anecdotes emphasizing her piety and asceticism. For example, it was said that once, after many days of fasting, a bird flew over and dropped food into her bowl. Many pieces of poetry and prose are also attributed to al-Adawiyya, which express her love of and devotion to God.

HARUN AL-RASHID
c. 766–809

Son of the Abbasid caliph al-Mahdi, Harun al-Rashid succeeded his older brother al-Hadi. As caliph, al-Rashid relied heavily on his mother, al-Khayzuran, a Bedouin former slave, until her death in 789; he then was advised mainly by his former tutor and vizier Yahya the Barmakid, whose family became highly influential until falling from grace in 803. Although he faced many local uprisings, al-Rashid's reign is often viewed as the zenith of the Abbasid caliphate and his Baghdad is memorialized in *The Thousand and One Nights*. He died in 809 in the Khorasan region of Central Asia, after falling ill while trying to put down a revolt.

AL-SHAFII
767–820

Muhammad ibn Idris al-Shafii was born in Gaza, but moved to Mecca as a child, growing up in a poor household. He studied in Medina with Malik ibn Anas, becoming known as a skilled jurist. At the age of 30 he was appointed by the Abbasids as governor in Yemen, but in 803 was involved in a revolt against the caliph and was briefly imprisoned. After he was freed, he devoted himself to legal scholarship until his death in Cairo. Thanks to his many followers, the Shafii school of Islamic law would become highly influential.

AL-KHWARIZMI
c. 780–c. 850

See box on p159.

AHMAD IBN HANBAL
780–855

Born in Baghdad, Ahmad ibn Hanbal began his religious and legal studies at a young age, traveling across Iraq, Syria, and Arabia to learn from leading scholars, as well as making five pilgrimages to Mecca. He eventually settled back in Baghdad, founding the Hanbali school of Islamic law, which emphasizes the importance of strictly following the Quran and *hadith*. Ibn Hanbal refused to change his beliefs to conform with doctrines approved by the caliph, and as a result was imprisoned, flogged, and briefly banished from the city. Despite this, he was a popular and highly respected figure, and his funeral was attended by 800,000 people.

AL-KINDI
c. 800–73

See box on p157.

AL-BUKHARI
810–70

Muhammad al-Bukhari came from Bukhara, in modern-day Uzbekistan. When he was 16 he went on pilgrimage to Mecca, and then began his search for accurate knowledge about the Prophet's life and sayings, journeying for many years across Arabia, Iraq, Syria, Egypt, and Central Asia. On his return home, he compiled his *Sahih al-Bukhari*, a compilation of 7,275 *hadith* he had deemed to be wholly reliable. Sunni Muslims regard this as one of the most important of all religious works.

AL-TABARI
839–923

As a child, Muhammad al-Tabari left his birthplace of Amol, in Iran, to study with scholars in Iraq, Syria, and Egypt. He later settled in Baghdad. Thanks to family wealth, he had no need to take up any official positions, and was able to pursue his many academic interests for the rest of his life. He wrote extensively, including a highly influential commentary on the Quran, the *Tafsir al-Tabari* (*Commentary of al-Tabari*), which in some editions runs to 30 volumes. His most famous and influential work was the *Tarikh al-Rusul* (*History of the Prophets and Kings*), which chronicled events (focusing mainly on the Near East) from Creation up to the year 915. This has been translated into many languages, including an English edition in 38 volumes.

ABDUL RAHMAN III
891–961

Grandson of the sole surviving member of the Umayyad dynasty, in 912 Abdul Rahman III inherited the mantle of Emir of Cordoba. He consolidated his authority over all of al-Andalus (Muslim Spain) and into North Africa. In 929, Abdul Rahman III declared himself caliph of Cordoba, challenging the rule of the Abbasid caliphate. Merciless with his opponents, he presided over the most prosperous era of Muslim Spain, when the economy, culture, and architecture of the city of Cordoba were greatly enriched. Following his death, Abdul Rahman III was succeeded by his son al-Hakam II.

IBN AL-HAYTHAM
965–1040

Known in the West as Alhazen, Ibn al-Haytham was a mathematician and astronomer. Born in Basra, he became a local official there. He then moved to Egypt, to work for the Fatimid caliph al-Hakim, claiming that he could regulate the Nile's flooding. Although unable to do this, Ibn al-Haytham remained in Egypt, pursuing his studies of science and nature in Cairo until his death in 1040. A prolific and wide-ranging writer, Ibn al-Haytham believed that theories had to be proved by experiments. His most famous treatise was the *Kitab al-Manazir* (*Book of Optics*), which was the first work to correctly model human vision.

AL-BIRUNI
973–*c.*1050

The Persian polymath Muhammad al-Biruni was one of the greatest scholars of his age, researching and writing on a phenomenal range of subjects and laying the groundwork for modern scientific method. Born in the Khwarazm region of Central Asia, he studied theology, law, medicine, and a wide array of sciences, and exchanged ideas with contemporary thinker Ibn Sina (Avicenna). He served under several royal patrons, and in 1017 was made court astrologer to Mahmud of Ghazni, joining him on his forays into India. Al-Biruni's extensive study of that country is one of his most significant works. Many of his treatises concerned astronomy and physics, and he explored experimental methods that are still relevant today.

IBN SINA (AVICENNA)
980–1037

See box on p173.

OMAR KHAYYAM
1048–1131

Born and raised in Nishapur, in north-eastern Iran, Omar Khayyam excelled in studies of astronomy, mathematics, and philosophy, and was welcomed at the court of Samarkand, in modern Uzbekistan, where he wrote his famous *Treatise on Demonstration of Problems of Algebra* (1070). Much of his life was spent under the patronage of various courts. Although a gifted polymath, Khayyam is best known as a poet, his verses invoking the mystical state of Sufi spirituality. His name achieved such fame that many works are probably inaccurately attributed to him. Despite this, his popular appeal can be credited with bringing a strain of ancient mysticism to a wide audience, even almost 1,000 years after his own time.

AL-GHAZALI
*c.*1058–1111

Abu Hamid al-Ghazali was born around 1058 near Tus in Iran. As a teenager he studied in the Persian city of Nishapur, which at this time was a major center of learning. In 1091 he took up a post as a tutor at a *madrasa* (theological college) in Baghdad. Four years later, he abandoned his prestigious post and embarked on several years of travel, including to Damascus and Jerusalem, in search of spiritual enlightenment. He eventually returned to Tus, where he spent a number of years in seclusion, dedicating himself to writing. By the time of his death he had authored some 70 works. Prominent among these are the *Ihya ulum al-din* (*The Revival of the Religious Sciences*), an influential work that brings together orthodox Sunni theology and Sufi mysticism, and *Tahafut al-Falasifa* (*The Incoherence of the Philosophers*), which argues for faith over philosophy, and which is considered a landmark work in the history of philosophy.

AL-IDRISI
1100–65

Muhammad al-Idrisi was one of the foremost geographers and cartographers of the medieval era. Born in Ceuta in North Africa, he studied in Cordoba, and traveled across North Africa, Asia Minor, and Europe. In 1136, he entered the service of Roger II of Sicily, a Christian Norman king. Working at his court in Palermo, al-Idrisi produced several important works, including the *Tabula Rogeriana*, an extensive description of the world with accompanying world maps. Completed in 1154, it took al-Idrisi 15 years to produce, and combined his own experiences with ancient and contemporary knowledge. Despite lacking parts of some of the continents, the map would be the most accurate in existence for many centuries.

IBN RUSHD (AVERROES)
1126–98

Ibn Rushd, known in the West as Averroes, was born in the Andalusian city of Cordoba. He rose to become chief judge of his home town, as well as serving as court physician to the Almohad caliph in Marrakech. In addition to his official career, Ibn Rushd was a polymath and prolific writer; he achieved his greatest influence as a philosopher, and he was highly regarded for his commentaries on Aristotle. He often had to defend his philosophy against criticism from orthodox religious figures, and in 1195 such attacks led to him being dismissed from his posts. He was restored to favor and recalled to the Almohad court three years before he died.

SALAH AL-DIN YUSUF
1137–93

The warrior-sultan known in the West as Saladin (whose Arabic name "Salah al-Din" means "Righteousness of the Faith") was a Kurd, born in Tikrit, in Iraq. He fought for the Turkish Zengid dynasty in their wars to gain influence in Egypt. By 1169 he was vizier to the Fatimid caliph in Egypt; two years later he overthrew the caliphate to establish his own Ayyubid dynasty. From 1174 to 1186, Salah al-Din battled other Muslim rulers to gain control of much of the Middle East, before defeating the Crusader states, and conquering Jerusalem and most of Palestine. From 1189 he spent three years fighting off the Third Crusade, Christendom's attempt to regain the territory; he died in Damascus one year later.

IBN JUBAYR
1145–1217

See box on p178.

IBN ARABI
1165–1240

The poet, mystic, and philosopher Ibn Arabi was born in Murcia, Spain, and raised and educated in Seville, where he worked for the Almohad governor. After adopting Sufism, he received a vision that he should travel east, and in 1200 he left Spain to journey across the Muslim world. He visited Arabia, Egypt, Anatolia, and Iraq, before settling in Damascus in 1223, where he stayed until his death. He became a famed scholar and was a prolific writer: the work that is often considered his most significant is *Fusus al-Hikam* (*The Bezels of Wisdom*), which summarizes his teachings and beliefs.

AL-TUSI
1201–74

A Persian intellectual of great talents, Nasr al-Din al-Tusi was most distinguished as an astronomer. Born in Tus, north-eastern Iran, he traveled widely as a young scholar, driven partly by the incursions of the Mongol Genghis Khan's armies. In 1256 he became scientific adviser to Mongol ruler Hulagu Khan, who had just destroyed the fortress of Alamut, where al-Tusi resided, and who agreed to fund the building of a grand observatory near Maragha, a city in Azerbaijan. Completed in 1262, the site hosted a scientific community that included Chinese astronomers. Here, al-Tusi and his peers made hitherto impossible calculations, transforming their field of study with new models and theories: a period that became known as the Maragha Revolution.

RUMI
1207–73

Jalal al-Din Muhammad Rumi was a Persian Sufi mystic and poet. He was born in Balkh, in modern-day Afghanistan. When he was about 11, he and his family left and migrated to Anatolia, eventually settling in the city of Konya. By 1244 Rumi had begun to practice Sufism. That year he met Shams al-Din Tabrizi, a wandering dervish, and the two developed a close friendship and spiritual bond. Shams disappeared about three years later, and it seems likely that he was murdered. Grief-stricken, Rumi began writing poems, eventually composing some 30,000 of them. After he died, in Konya in 1273, his followers founded the Mevlevi (or Mawlawi) order, known for performing a whirling dance as an act of religious devotion.

MUSA I
c. 1280–c. 1337

Musa I was the tenth *mansa* (king) of the West African Islamic Mali Empire. This was an empire that covered a vast swath of land mostly north of the Niger River, and which flourished from 1235 to 1670. At its peak, the empire grew rich from taxes on trade and the wealth accrued from three large gold mines that made Mali the largest producer of gold in the world. Musa I ruled for about 25 years, and he is believed to have been one of the richest people in history. He is famed for his pilgrimage to Mecca, made between 1324 and 1325, on which he was accompanied by a lavish retinue of some 60,000 men and women, and lots of gold.

IBN BATTUTA
1304–c. 1368/69

See box on p183.

IBN KHALDUN
1332–1406

Ibn Khaldun started his career as a calligrapher for the ruler of his native Tunis. This was the first of the many different leaders for whom Ibn Khaldun worked, across North Africa and Muslim Spain—moving frequently because court intrigues meant that he sometimes fell out of favor. In 1375 he began the *Muqaddimah* (*Introduction*), a general philosophy of history that touched on sociology and economics. This was the first book of *Kitab al-Ibar* (*Book of Lessons*), a world history that focused on Muslim North Africa. In his later years, Ibn Khaldun still held some political offices, but concentrated on teaching and writing; he died in Cairo, while in the service of the Mamluk sultans.

MEHMET II
1432–81

Known as "Mehmet the Conqueror," Mehmet II became Ottoman sultan at the age of 12, when his father, Murad, abdicated in 1444. However, civil disorder led to Murad II coming out of retirement to reclaim the throne in 1446, ruling until his death in 1451. Mehmet II then began his second reign. His first great achievement was to conquer Constantinople in 1453, which became his capital. Mehmet followed this triumph with a series of campaigns across Anatolia and eastern and southern Europe, adding huge swaths of territory to the Ottoman Empire.

SHAH ISMAIL
1487–1524

Shah Ismail, also known as Ismail I, founded the Safavid dynasty, which ruled Iran from 1501 to 1736. His father, Haydar, was the leader of the Safawiyya, a Sufi group that later became associated with Shia beliefs, and who was killed fighting Sunnis in 1488. Ismail remained in hiding until 1501, when he publicly succeeded his father, took the city of Tabriz, in northwestern Iran, and proclaimed himself shah. He then conquered the rest of Iran, as well as parts of modern-day Afghanistan, Azerbaijan, Iraq, and Turkey. Ismail declared Twelver Shiism the official religion of his empire, leading to conflict with his Sunni Ottoman neighbors.

MIMAR SINAN
c. 1488–1588

The most esteemed architect of the Ottoman Empire, Sinan was born into a Christian family, possibly of Greek or Armenian origin, in central Anatolia. The son of a stonemason, he converted to Islam when he was conscripted into the Janissary infantry units, rising to become a senior officer. His skill as a military engineer led to architectural work, and from 1539 he was employed as chief royal architect, overseeing public buildings including mosques, palaces, and bridges. His most famous design is the magnificent Süleymaniye Mosque in Istanbul; he is buried in a tomb nearby.

SÜLEYMAN I
1494–1566

Süleyman I became sultan of the Ottoman Empire upon the death of his father, Selim I, in 1520. He enjoyed military success, leading his armies personally and conquering Belgrade in 1521 and Rhodes in 1522. However, his westward expansion of Ottoman power was checked in 1529, with the failed Siege of Vienna. Later, Süleyman I defeated the Safavids, gaining territory in the Middle East and the Caucasus, while victories in the Mediterranean gave him control of most of North Africa. Domestically, he oversaw major legal reforms and sponsored public works across his empire, notably in Istanbul. He died in 1566 while campaigning in Hungary; he was succeeded by his son, Selim II.

AKBAR
1542–1605

The greatest of the Mughal emperors, "Akbar the Great" succeeded his father Humayun in 1556, at just 13 years old. For the first four years of his reign there was a regency, but in 1560 Akbar began governing for himself. He modernized his army, winning a series of victories that gave the Mughals dominance over the northern Indian subcontinent. To consolidate his huge empire, he instituted a centralized taxation and administrative system, while adopting tolerant and conciliatory policies to his non-Muslim subjects, particularly local Hindu rulers. Akbar died after a reign of nearly 50 years, with his son Jahangir ascending the throne in his place.

ABBAS I
1571–1629

Shah Abbas I came to the throne in 1588, at the age of 17. At that time the Safavid Empire was in disarray under his weak father, with significant territories claimed by the Ottomans and the Uzbeks. Abbas I made a peace treaty with the Ottomans, ceding large areas of land to them, then built up a new army with which he crushed the Uzbeks in 1598. He increased his lands further and made Isfahan his new capital, which became one of the most beautiful cities in the world. Credited with restoring his empire to glory, Abbas I was a skilled but ruthless leader, whose suspicion of betrayal led to the merciless treatment of many members of his own family. He died with no heir to succeed him.

AURANGZEB
1618–1707

The last of the great Mughal emperors, Aurangzeb (meaning "Ornament of the Throne") ruled for nearly 50 years and expanded his empire over almost the entire Indian subcontinent. He ascended the throne in 1658 having conspired against the brother whom his father, Shah Jahan, had named as his successor. Aurangzeb was a pious and orthodox man, disapproving of luxury, and put an end to his predecessors' tolerance of a multi-faith land. Sharia law was imposed and many Hindu temples destroyed. Ultimately, Aurangzeb's persistent spending on military campaigns damaged his economy, and following his tenure the empire went into decline.

MUHAMMAD IBN ABD AL-WAHHAB
1703–92

The theologian Muhammad ibn Abd al-Wahhab was born in the village of Uyaynah in Arabia, and finished his education in Medina. He became convinced that many Islamic practices of the time, such as venerating the tombs of saints, were heretical innovations. He preached a traditionalist message, and was expelled from several towns before settling in al-Diriyah, at the invitation of its ruler Muhammad bin Saud. The two men agreed to work together to make the House of Saud rulers of Arabia, with "Wahhabism" as their ideology. Wahhabism remains the dominant doctrine in Saudi Arabia, which continues to sponsor its global spread.

MUHAMMAD BIN SAUD
1710–65

Muhammad bin Saud started as the emir of al-Diriyah, a town in central Arabia. In 1744 he made a pact with the religious leader Muhammad ibn Abd al-Wahhab. They would unite the local tribes to create a state, free from the influence of the Ottoman Empire, ruled by Bin Saud and spiritually guided by Wahhab's version of Islam. The alliance was sealed with the marriage of Wahhab's daughter to Bin Saud's son. Diriyah thus formed the nucleus of the First Saudi State, which Bin Saud ruled until his death. His descendants extended the boundaries of the state, which was the forerunner of the Kingdom of Saudi Arabia, officially founded in 1932.

AHMAD IBN IDRIS
1760–1837

Ahmad ibn Idris was born in Fez, Morocco, and studied there before settling in Mecca in 1799, where he began to teach his version of Sufism. He warned his followers against rigid adherence to any particular religious school, and stressed that people should seek a personal relationship with God through gaining their own independent understanding of the Quran and other religious texts. In 1828 he moved to Yemen, where he stayed until his death. By then his set of teachings, known as the Idrissiya, had gained many students and followers, who disseminated it across the world.

MUHAMMAD IBN ALI AL-SANUSI
1787–1859

The founder of the Sanusi (also spelled Senussi) mystical order, Muhammad ibn Ali al-Sanusi came from northwestern Algeria and spent his early life studying and traveling across North Africa, during which time he became convinced that Islam needed to be revitalized and reformed. He settled in Arabia, where he established his own Sufi school of thought, the Sanusi, in 1837, remaining there until he was expelled by the Ottomans in 1841. Al-Sanusi relocated his order to Cyrenaica, in northeastern Libya, where he spread his message among local tribes. After he died, his son assumed leadership of the Sanusi order. His grandson Idris I later reigned as king of an independent Libya from 1951 until 1969.

SAYYID AHMAD KHAN
1817–98

Islamic reformist Sayyid Ahmad Khan was born in Delhi, when the Mughal emperor Akbar II was a figurehead under British rule. Khan worked for the East India Company, later becoming a judge. Following the Indian uprising of 1857, he published a damning critique of British policies, although he remained loyal to the British Empire. He had a powerful belief in modern education, and founded many schools, as well as the first Muslim university in Southern Asia. His writings included commentaries on both the Quran and the Bible.

MIRZA GHULAM AHMAD
1835–1908

See box on p221.

JAMAL AL-DIN AL-AFGHANI
1838–97

Born in Iran, Jamal al-Din al-Afghani was a political reformer who rose to prominence in 1866, when he emerged as counselor to the emir of Afghanistan. Following a regime change, al-Afghani left Afghanistan in 1868, and from then on led a peripatetic existence, living around the world including in Istanbul, Cairo, India, Paris, London, Russia, and Iran until his death from cancer in 1897. He spoke out against Western imperialism, believing that it could be combated by pan-Islamism as well as political reform, and improved technical and scientific education within the Muslim world.

MUHAMMAD AHMED
1844–85

Muhammad Ahmed bin Abdallah was a Sudanese leader who became known as "the Mahdi" and led a war against the British. As a young man he joined the Samaniyya Sufi sect and became a Quranic teacher. He gained a large following and in 1881, he was proclaimed as the Mahdi, the messianic redeemer of the Islamic faith, by his disciples. The colonial government in Khartoum sent a military expedition against him, which was defeated. Mahdi-led forces similarly defeated a British army sent from Egypt. He created a vast Islamic state extending from the Red Sea to Central Africa and founded a movement that remained influential in Sudan a century later.

MUHAMMAD ABDU
1849–1905

Born into an elite Egyptian family, as a student in Cairo Muhammad Abdu became a dedicated follower of Jamal al-Din al-Afghani. Inspired by al-Afghani, Abdu agitated for political reform in Egypt to ensure that it did not fall under Western imperialism—a view that led to him being exiled in 1882, after the British military occupation of Egypt began. He was permitted to return to Egypt in 1888, and held the role of a judge before being appointed Grand Mufti (chief Islamic jurist) of Egypt in 1899, remaining in the post for the rest of his life. As one of the leading figures in the country, he supported liberal, rationalist reforms in both government and religion. He also wrote several religious treatises.

RASHID RIDA
1865–1935

Born in modern-day Lebanon, near Tripoli (then part of the Ottoman Empire), Muhammad Rashid Rida was a founding figure in the Salafi movement, which sought, in the face of Western imperialism, to reform the Muslim world by returning to the spirit of early Islam. He declared that adherence to Sharia law was essential for all Muslims. However, he was also open to change and modernization, willing to embrace innovations in science and technology. Rida moved to Egypt in 1897, where he founded the influential reformist journal titled *Al-Manar (The Lighthouse)*, which he published and edited from 1898 until his death in 1935.

IBN SAUD
1875–1953

Abdulaziz ibn Abdul Rahman ibn Faisal ibn Turki ibn Abdullah ibn Muhammad Al Saud was born in Riyadh, Arabia, a small, mud-walled town in the middle of the desert. His family was driven into exile in Kuwait when he was ten, but in 1902 he returned to capture Riyadh at the head of a Bedouin war party mounted on camels. He went on to subdue the rest of Central Arabia, followed by Mecca, Medina, and Jeddah. In 1932 he unified his territories as the Kingdom of Saudi Arabia, with himself as monarch. Initially the kingdom subsisted on profits from the pilgrim trade to Mecca, then oil was discovered in the late 1930s. Oil exports began to bring in colossal wealth and by the time of his death in 1953, Ibn Saud was one of the world's richest men.

MUHAMMAD ALI JINNAH
1876–1948

Born in Karachi to a wealthy merchant family, Muhammad Ali Jinnah moved to London in 1892, where he qualified as a barrister before returning home in 1896. After ten years of practicing law in Bombay (now Mumbai), Jinnah became involved in the Indian independence movement, and in 1913 joined the All-India Muslim League. This organization aimed to secure the rights of Muslims, and Jinnah came to favor the creation of a separate state for them. His leadership was central to achieving this in 1947. When India gained independence from the British Empire, Pakistan was created from Muslim-majority areas. Jinnah was the new country's first governor-general, but died a year later.

MUHAMMAD IQBAL
1877–1938

After leaving his homeland in the Punjab in Northern India in 1905, Muhammad Iqbal qualified as a barrister in London and earned a doctorate in philosophy in Munich. He returned to Lahore in 1908 and practiced law, as well as gaining fame as a writer of poetry. Iqbal, who was knighted in 1922, was also prominent in the Indian independence movement, advocating the establishment of a separate nation state for provinces with a majority-Muslim population. He saw this as a way to guarantee their religious and political rights. His vision helped to inspire the creation of the nation of Pakistan in 1947, nine years after his death in 1938.

HUDA SHAARAWI
1879–1947

Huda Shaarawi was an Egyptian feminist and nationalist. Forced to marry her cousin at the age of 13, she was subsequently estranged from him, enabling her to pursue her education. She spearheaded a wave of reforms for women in Egypt, and was a key figure in the Revolution of 1919 against British rule. In 1922, she shocked society by publicly removing her face veil, inspiring others to do the same. The following year, Shaarawi founded the Egyptian Feminist Union and was elected its first president. The Union achieved legislation that included a minimum age for marriage, and access to university education for women.

MUSTAFA KEMAL ATATÜRK
1881–1938

The founder of modern Turkey was born in Thessaloniki, in present-day Greece. He entered the Ottoman Army after graduating from military college in 1905, and became involved with the reformist Young Turks movement, before fighting in the Balkan Wars and World War I. From 1919 to 1923, Kemal masterminded nationalist victory in the Turkish War of Independence, which led to the overthrow of the Ottoman sultanate and the declaration of the Republic of Turkey. Kemal was its first president, and initiated sweeping reforms that created a modernized and secular nation state. In 1934, the Turkish parliament honored him with the surname Atatürk, meaning "Father of the Turks."

ELIJAH MUHAMMAD
1897–1975

American Elijah Muhammad, born Elijah Robert Poole, left his home state of Georgia in 1923 to settle in Detroit. There he became involved in the Nation of Islam, a black nationalist group that aimed to promote unity and self-help in the African-American community. Adopting the surname Muhammad, by 1934 he had become leader of the organization and turned it into a nationwide movement, with its own mosques, businesses, and schools. Although Muhammad often clashed with others in the Nation, including Malcolm X, he retained the leadership until his death in 1975.

AYATOLLAH RUHOLLAH KHOMEINI
1902–89

Ruhollah Khomeini, known in the West as Ayatollah Khomeini, was an Iranian politician and cleric who, as a young man, rose to prominence as a scholar in the Shiite holy city of Qom. He became a vocal critic of Iran's ruler, Shah Muhammad Reza Pahlavi, particularly after the Shah launched a raft of modernizing reforms, known as the White Revolution, in 1963. Khomeini was imprisoned and banished; while exiled in Iraq and then France, he continued to oppose the Shah, and helped inspire the movement against him that culminated in his overthrow in 1979. That year Khomeini returned to his home country, and was named supreme leader of the Islamic Republic of Iran, remaining in office until his death in 1989.

ABUL ALA MAWDUDI
1903–79

Abul Ala Mawdudi was born into a middle-class Sunni family in Aurangabad, in northwestern India. A prodigious scholar and writer on a wide range of subjects, he argued that Western influences must be removed from Islam. In 1941 he founded the Jamaat-e-Islami, an organization that aimed to create an independent Islamic state in British India. After the founding of Pakistan in 1947, Mawdudi reestablished his group and became politically active. He was imprisoned several times, although by the time he died in 1979 the ruling regime of General Zia-ul-Haq had embraced many of Mawdudi's values.

HASSAN AL-BANNA
1906–49

In 1928, Egyptian schoolteacher Hassan al-Banna founded the Muslim Brotherhood. This was an organization that aimed to revive Islam through social reform, charitable works, and educational efforts. As it gathered members across Egypt, the Brotherhood became more political in outlook. It espoused pan-Islamism and opposed Western imperialism; it also became involved in the conflict in the Holy Land by sending volunteers to fight for the Palestinian Arabs there. Al-Banna's popularity and influence as both a religious and political leader made him a threat to the Egyptian government's authority, and in 1948 the Brotherhood was outlawed. Al-Banna was assassinated in Cairo the following year.

SAYYID QUTB
1906–66

Sayyid Qutb began his career working for Egypt's Ministry of Education. Initially a secularist, he shifted toward Islamist views, joining the Muslim Brotherhood in 1953. The group criticized the regime of President Nasser for its secularism, and, when a member of the Brotherhood attempted to assassinate Nasser in 1954, Qutb and many of his colleagues were imprisoned. While incarcerated, Qutb grew increasingly radical. In 1964, he published *Maalim fi'l-Tariq* (*Signs on the Road*), an influential work that called for Muslims to establish a society based on the Quran. A few months later he was found guilty of plotting to overthrow the government, and in 1966 he was executed.

MUHAMMAD ZIA-UL-HAQ
1924–88

Muhammad Zia-ul-Haq deposed the prime minister of Pakistan, Zulfikar Ali Bhutto, in a military coup in 1977. He declared martial law and became the country's sixth president in 1978. When the Soviets invaded Afghanistan in 1979, Zia worked closely with the Afghan *mujahidin* against the Soviets. He undertook a process of Islamization of Pakistan, replacing the largely secular law inherited from the British with curbed civil liberties and the introduction of new criminal offenses, including adultery and fornication, with new punishments including stoning, flogging, and amputation. He was killed in a mysterious plane crash in 1988.

MALCOLM X
1925–65

Born in Omaha, Nebraska, Malcolm Little became involved in crime during his youth, leading to jail. While in prison he joined the Nation of Islam and changed his name to Malcolm X. Following his release he became a national figure, criticizing the integrationist and nonviolent views of other civil rights leaders. Eventually, he grew disillusioned with the Nation of Islam and left the group in 1964. Having made the Hajj, Malcolm X converted to the Sunni tradition of Islam and changed his name to al-Hajj Malik al-Shabazz. His life ended tragically in 1965, when he was assassinated in New York by three members of the Nation of Islam.

EDWARD SAID
1935–2003

Born in Palestine to Christian parents, Edward Said was brought up between Jerusalem and Cairo, before being sent to the US to complete his education, including studies at Princeton and Harvard universities. He became a professor of literature at Columbia University, New York, a public intellectual, and a founder of the academic field of postcolonial studies. He became a high-profile spokesperson for the establishment of a Palestinian state. He is best known for his highly influential book *Orientalism* (1978), which is a critique of the ways in which the Western world has historically portrayed the Arab and Islamic worlds, presenting a distorted image that was intended to serve colonialist interests.

AGA KHAN IV
b. 1936

Aga Khan is the title held by the Imam, or spiritual leader, of the Ismaili Shia. The first to hold the title was Hassan Ali Shah, who was the 46th Imam of the Ismailis. The current, and fourth, Aga Khan is Prince Karim, who took up the role in 1957 at just 20 years old. He was born in Geneva, brought up in Nairobi, and educated at, among other places, Harvard. He has a British passport but resides at an estate near Chantilly in northern France. In addition to looking after the material as well as spiritual needs of his followers, Aga Khan IV heads the Aga Khan Development Network, which employs 80,000 people in 30 countries and is known for the nonprofit work it does in poor and war-torn parts of the globe, benefiting people of all faiths.

SHEIKH AHMED MUHAMMAD AL-TAYYEB
b. 1946

Born in Upper (southern) Egypt, Ahmed Muhammad al-Tayyeb was a student at Egypt's prestigious al-Azhar University in the 1960s and 1970s. Later he studied at the University of Paris before returning to his alma mater. He served as president of al-Azhar for seven years and since 2010 he has been the Grand Imam, or Sheikh, of al-Azhar—the 50th person to hold the role since it was established in the late 17th century. The world's second-oldest university, al-Azhar represents the center of Sunni Islamic jurisprudence and issues authoritative religious rulings. The Grand Imam is among the most prominent individuals in the Sunni tradition of Islam, considered by some Muslims to be the highest authority in Islamic jurisprudence worldwide. While serving as the grand Sheikh, al-Tayyeb has spoken against the Muslim Brotherhood and Islamic State (ISIS) for their exploitations of Islam as a political ideology, while also resisting calls by Egyptian president Abdel Fatah al-Sisi to revoke the verbal divorce law in Egypt.

BENAZIR BHUTTO
1953–2007

Benazir Bhutto served as prime minister of Pakistan from 1988 to 1990 and from 1993 to 1996. She was the first woman to head a democratic government in a Muslim-majority nation. She was born in Karachi to a political family: her father was prime minister until he was ousted in a military coup and executed. After his death, Oxford University-educated Bhutto led a movement for the restoration of democracy, for which she was imprisoned and then exiled to Britain. She returned to Pakistan in 1986 and was elected prime minister two years later. She lost her position but regained it in the 1993 elections. During her terms in office she worked to advance women's rights. While on the campaign trail in 2007, she was assassinated; al-Qaeda claimed responsibility. She has since become an icon for women's rights in the developing world.

MALALA YOUSAFZAI
b. 1997

See box on p277.

GLOSSARY

In this glossary, terms defined within another entry are identified with **bold** type.

Abaya A long, loose-fitting robe that is worn by women, originating on the Arabian Peninsula.

Abbasids A dynasty descended from Prophet Muhammad's uncle Abbas ibn Abd al-Muttalib that formed the third Islamic **caliphate** (750–1258).

Adaan The call to prayer.

Afranj The Arabic term for European Christians, or "Franks," during the Crusades.

Aga Khan The title of the hereditary spiritual leader of the **Ismaili** branch of **Shia** Islam.

Ahl al-beit "People of the House:" specifically, the Prophet himself, his daughter Fatima, cousin and son-in-law Ali ibn Abi Talib, and Ali and Fatima's sons Hassan and Hussein.

Ahl al-dhimma Non-Muslim "protected peoples." Christians, Jews, and others who were free to practice their own religion under Muslim rule, subject to the **jizya** tax.

Ahl al-kitab "People of the Book:" followers of the other religions based on divine revelations enshrined in holy books—mainly Jews and Christians, but also Zoroastrians and Sabaeans.

Ahmadiyya Followers of Mirza Ghulam Ahmad, who claimed to be God's "renewer" of Islam. Most traditional Muslims do not consider Ahmadiyya to be true Muslims.

Allah The Arabic name of the one God.

Allahu akbar "God is great:" the phrase that invokes the supremacy of God.

Almohads Berber tribesmen from southern Morocco who formed an Islamic empire in North Africa and Spain in the 12th century.

Almoravids Berber tribesmen from southern Morocco who formed an Islamic empire in North Africa and Spain in the 11th century.

Amir al-Muminin "Commander of the Faithful:" a title given to Ali by **Shia** Muslims but to Umar, the second **caliph**, by **Sunni** Muslims and adopted by many later leaders.

Al-Andalus The region of the Iberian peninsula occupied by Muslims from 711 CE to the late 15th century.

Ansar The "helpers:" the people of **Medina** who aided the Prophet and his followers after their flight (**Hijra**) from **Mecca**.

Apostasy The renunciation of a religion by former believers (who are branded apostates). In Islam, apostasy is a serious crime that can be punishable by death under **Sharia** law.

Aqiqa A ceremony, traditionally with animal sacrifice, for a newborn child, held seven days after birth.

Arabesque A style of decoration using curled lines that avoids depicting humans or animals.

Arabic numerals The Hindu-Arabic decimal system. Invented in India, it was developed by medieval mathematicians in Baghdad and reached Europe in the 15th century.

Arkan al-Iman See **Six Pillars of Faith**.

Arkan al-Islam See **Five Pillars of Islam**.

Ashura The 10th day of the month of Muharram that for **Shia** Muslims marks the martyrdom of the third **Imam**, Hussein, at **Kerbala**.

Aya A verse of the Quran.

Ayatollah A religious leader in the Shia tradition of Islam.

Bedouin An Arabic-speaking desert nomad.

Beit al-Hikma "House of Wisdom:" the Grand Library of Baghdad, established in the 9th century by the **Abbasid caliphate** as a repository of all the world's knowledge.

Bismillah The opening phrase of the Quran: "In the name of God, the Compassionate, the Merciful." Recited before every **sura** except one, and used as an invocation before any significant undertaking.

Black Stone The special stone, possibly a meteorite, embedded in the eastern corner of the **Kaaba**.

Boko Haram A militant Islamist group founded in Nigeria in 2002, whose original stated goal was to "purify Islam."

Buraq The winged mount that Muslims believe transported Muhammad to Jerusalem and to Heaven on his **Night Journey**.

Burka Modest dress for women of a robe and headcovering, with a mesh screen over the eyes. It is associated with the **Taliban**, and is worn mainly in Afghanistan and parts of Pakistan.

Burkini Modest swimwear consisting of an all-over body swimsuit and swimcap.

Caliph Spiritual and political leader of the Islamic community. From the Arabic word *khalifa*, meaning "successor" (of the Prophet).

Caliphate Islamic state under the leadership of a **caliph**, consisting of the Muslim community and all those under its dominion.

Chador Full-length outer garment or cloak draped over the head and held closed under the chin; worn by women in Iran, Iraq, and other predominantly **Shia** communities.

Chahar bagh Rectangular Persian garden layout divided into four by water channels and designed to reflect paradise on Earth.

Charter of Medina A constitution written for the residents of **Medina** following Prophet Muhammad's arrival with his followers in 622 CE.

Companions of the Prophet Those followers of Muhammad who saw or spent time with him during his lifetime. In Arabic, they are called the **Sahaba**.

Day of Judgment The event in which all Earth is destroyed, along with all living beings, followed by resurrection and the weighing up of every person's deeds to determine whether they go to Heaven or Hell.

Deobandi Revivalist Islamic movement founded in India in 1867.

Dervish Follower of **Sufism** who seeks to reach a trancelike state by dancing and whirling around.

Dhikr Ritual acts, usually prayer or repetition of a devotional phrase, central to **Sufi** worship.

Dhimmi "Protected person:" a term referring to non-Muslims living in a Muslim state who are given legal protections.

Dikka A platform in larger mosques on which a cleric stands to repeat the sermon and lead the prayers for those too far from the front to hear.

Din-i Ilahi "Divine Faith:" a new interpretation of Islam introduced in India by the **Mughal** emperor Akbar in the late 16th century, with elements of **Sufism**, Christianity, Zoroastrianism, and Jainism.

Djinn Supernatural creatures formed out of fire.

Dome of the Rock An Islamic place of worship built in the 7th century on Temple Mount in Jerusalem. It covers a rock from which the Prophet is said to have ascended to Heaven on the **Miraj**.

Eid al-Adha The "Feast of the Sacrifice," commemorating Ibrahim's devotion to God, when he intended to sacrifice his son and God provided a lamb to sacrifice instead. It follows the **Hajj** rituals for pilgrims in Mecca, but is celebrated by all Muslims.

Eid al-Fitr The "Feast of Breaking the Fast," marking the end of the fasting month of **Ramadan**.

Emir Prince, ruler, or commander.

Ennahdha The "Renaissance Party," a moderate Islamist political party founded in Tunisia in 1981.

Fanous Colorful lanterns used in the celebration of **Ramadan**.

Faqih An expert in **fiqh**, or Islamic jurisprudence.

Fatiha The "Opening:" the first **sura** of the **Quran**. It is frequently recited silently whenever believers feel the need to praise or thank God.

Fatimids Dynasty (909–1171) founded in North Africa whose rulers claimed descent from the Prophet's daughter Fatima. They were the first **Shia** dynasty. They established their capital al-Qahira (Cairo) in 969 CE.

Fatwa A decision or ruling on a matter of Islamic law given by an Islamic legal expert.

Fiqh The study of **Sharia**, or Islamic law.

Fitna "Unrest" or "civil strife." The First Fitna (656–61 CE) was the struggle between Ali and Muawiya for control of the Islamic **caliphate**, which led to the split between the **Sunni** and **Shia** branches of Islam.

Five Pillars of Islam The core practices of **Sunni** Islam, which should be observed by all Muslims. These are: **Shahada** (profession of faith); **salat** (offering prayer to God); **zakat** (almsgiving); **sawm** (fasting); and **Hajj** (the pilgrimage to **Mecca**).

Fivers See **Zaydis**.

Furu al-Din The ten practices of **Shia** Islam: **salat** (offering prayer to God); **zakat** (almsgiving); **sawm** (fasting); **Hajj** (the pilgrimage to **Mecca**); *khums* (a tax in addition to zakat); *jihad* (the struggle to do good); *amr bil-maaruf* (encouraging others to do good); *nahi anil-munkar* (forbidding what is evil); *tawalla* (expressing love for the Prophet); and *tabbara* (disassociation from those who insult God).

Hadith Account (or accounts) of the sayings and actions of Prophet Muhammad, as recorded by those who were close to him. Hadith are the second prime source for the practice of Islam after the **Quran**.

Hafiz A "guardian" of the **Quran**—in other words, somebody who has learned it by heart.

Hajj The pilgrimage to the sacred city of **Mecca**, which every Muslim who can should make at least once. It is performed during the last month of the **Hijra** calendar, Dhu al-Hijja. Hajj is one of the **Five Pillars of Islam**.

Hakawati A professional storyteller.

Halal Food, products, or behavior that is permitted, or lawful under Islamic law. It is often used with reference to meat slaughtered to prescribed Islamic methods.

Hanafi One of the four schools of Sunni Islamic law. Founded by Abu Hanifa (699–767), it emphasizes a process of systematic reasoning.

Hanbali One of the four Sunni schools of Islamic law. Based on the teaching of Ahmad ibn Hanbal (780–855), it is considered the most conservative on matters of doctrine.

Haram Food or behavior that is forbidden, or unlawful.

Hejaz The holy land of Islam: western Saudi Arabia, including the cities of **Mecca** and **Medina**.

Hijab A head covering worn by some Muslim women to conceal the hair.

Hijra The "flight" of the Prophet Muhammad and his followers in 622 CE from persecution in **Mecca** to safety in **Medina**.

Hijra calendar The lunar calendar used by Muslims. Its year zero is dated from the **Hijra** in 622 CE.

Houri A beautiful maiden who, according to the **Quran**, waits in Paradise for devout men.

House of Wisdom See **Beit al-Hikma**.

Hudud Fixed **Sharia** punishments for crimes as prescribed in the **Quran** and the **hadith**.

Ibadat The collective term for the different forms of worship in Islam.

Ibadat Khana "House of Worship:" an academy founded in India by the **Mughal** emperor Akbar in 1575, where representatives of major faiths met to discuss theology.

Ibadism An early strand of Islam formed by Muslims who opposed the rule of the third **caliph** Uthman. Ibadis diverge from mainstream Islam in minor aspects of theology. Ibadism is dominant in Oman and is also found in parts of North and East Africa.

Iftar The sundown meal that breaks the fast during **Ramadan**.

Ihsan The Muslim duty to obtain perfection in worship—to worship God as if the believer sees Him.

Ijma A legal concept meaning "consensus," or the agreement of the Muslim community or of a body of Muslim scholars on a particular point of law.

Ijtihad The concept of intellectual reasoning in the understanding and advancement of Islam.

Ilkhanid A Mongol dynasty (1256–1335) that emerged from the fragmentation of the greater **Mongol Empire** to rule most of Iran, Iraq, and Central Asia. Its rulers converted to Islam in 1295.

Ilm al-Rijal "Science of the learned men:" the study of the individuals who transmitted the **hadith**.

Imam 1) In **Shia** Islam, the leader of the community, and a rightful successor to the Prophet, starting with Ali ibn Abi Talib, the first Imam. 2) In **Sunni** Islam, an **imam** is a religious official who leads a congregation in prayer.

Infidel Unbeliever. Said by Muslims of Christians and vice versa.

Inshallah A popular Arabic phrase meaning "If God wills it."

ISIS See **Islamic State**.

Islam The religion established by Prophet Muhammad and practiced by Muslims. The word means "submission" in Arabic and refers to the act of submission that Muslims are expected to make to God.

Islamic State A militant group founded in 1999, previously known as ISIS (Islamic State of Iraq and al-Sham), or ISIL (Islamic State of Iraq and the Levant), or by its Arabic acronym Daesh.

Islamism A movement to reform government and society so they conform to a strict interpretation of Islamic law. Adherents of Islamism are Islamists.

Ismailism A branch of **Shia** Islam that considers Ismail, son of Jafar al-Sadiq, to have been the legitimate **Imam** after his father. The main branch of Ismailism today follows the leadership of the **Aga Khan**.

Isnad The chain of attribution that links a **hadith** back to the Prophet.

Isra The first part of the Prophet's Night Journey, in which he traveled on the winged steed **Buraq** to the "furthest mosque," identified with al-Aqsa Mosque in Jerusalem.

Jahannam Hell.

al-Jahiliya The "Time of Ignorance," before Islam and the revelation of the **Quran** to the Prophet. The word *jahiliya* can also refer to life in modern times that is incompatible with Islam.

Jamaat al-Ikhwan See **Muslim Brotherhood**.

Jamaat-e Islami Islamic religious party founded in 1941 in India by Mawlana Abul Ala Mawdudi and still active in Pakistan.

Janna Paradise.

Jebel al-Nur Location of the Hira cave, the spiritual retreat of Muhammad, where **Jibreel** first delivered the divine revelations that became the **Quran**.

Jerusalem One of the three most sacred sites of Islam, along with **Mecca** and **Medina**. Originally, Muslims faced Jerusalem in prayer, before the orientation of the **qibla** was changed to Mecca c. 624 CE.

Jibreel The angel who conveyed the message of the **Quran** to the Prophet, and who brought a ram for Ibrahim to sacrifice in place of his son. Jibreel is known as Gabriel in Judaism and Christianity.

Jihad The struggle for a particular cause, in the name of God. The "greater jihad" (*al-jihad al-akbar*) is the inner, spiritual struggle against the demands of the lower self. The "lesser jihad" (*al-jihad al-asghar*) refers to physical struggle.

Jizya A tax payable by **ahl al-dhimma** living under Muslim rule, in return for the freedom to practice their own religion.

Juma Friday prayers. See **Salat**.

Kaaba The most sacred site in Islam, a large stone cubelike structure within the Great Mosque at **Mecca**. It existed as a pre-Islamic, pagan shrine before becoming the focal point for Muslim prayer and pilgrimage following Muhammad's capture of Mecca in 630 CE.

Kafir Unbeliever.

Kalam The "science of debate" or a system of philosophical and theological argument.

Kerbala Site of a battle in 680 CE at which Hussein, grandson of the Prophet Muhammad, was killed, accentuating the split between the **Sunni** and **Shia** traditions of Islam.

Kharijites Originally supporters of Ali ibn Abi Talib, the "seceders" were dissenters who urged strict adherence to Islamic law.

Kiswa The silk cloth that covers the **Kaaba** in **Mecca**.

Koran See **Quran**.

Kufic A highly stylized, rectilinear Arabic script, often used in monumental inscriptions.

Leilat al-qadr The "Night of Power," the holiest night of the year, commemorating the first revelation of the **Quran** to the Prophet. It falls in the last 10 days of **Ramadan**.

Madrasa A school for Islamic religious education.

Mahdi A savior and restorer of true Islam who, according to some traditions, will appear before the **Day of Judgment** and rid the world of evil.

Makruh Food or behavior that is considered "detestable" but (unlike **haram**) not forbidden absolutely.

Maliki One of the four Sunni schools of law. Based on the teachings of Malik ibn Anas, it relies on the **Quran** and the **hadith** as primary souces.

Mamluks Freed slave-soldiers who founded a dynasty that ruled Egypt, Syria, and the **Hejaz** from 1250 to 1517.

Marwa One of two small hills of **Mecca**, now enclosed within the Great Mosque, which pilgrims walk between as part of the rituals of **Hajj**. The second hill is **Safa**.

Mashallah A phrase meaning "God wills it" used to express appreciation, resignation, or joy.

Mashhad Iranian city that is the site of the revered **Shia** shrine of Imam Reza. Mashhad means "Place of Martyrdom."

Masjid The Arabic word for **Mosque**.

al-Masjid al-Haram The Great Mosque of Mecca, which contains the **Kaaba**. It is the largest **mosque** in the world and the second-largest building in the world.

al-Masjid al-Nabawi The Mosque of the Prophet, in **Medina**, which contains Muhammad's tomb.

Matn "Backbone:" the main text of a **hadith**, the record of what the Prophet said or did. See also **Isnad**.

Mawlid al-Nabi The birthday of the Prophet, which is widely celebrated on the 12th day of the month of Rabi al-Awwal. Also spelled Moulid al-Nabi.

Mecca (Makkah) The desert town in Arabia where Muhammad was born and first spread the message of Islam. Location of the holy **Kaaba**, and one of the three most sacred sites in Islam, along with **Medina** and **Jerusalem**.

Medina (Medinah) Called Yathrib in pre-Islamic times, the city to which Muhammad and his early followers fled when they faced persecution in **Mecca** in 622 CE. It is the second holiest city in Islam after Mecca.

Mevlevi An order of **Sufis** founded in Konya (in modern-day Turkey) by followers of Jalal al-Din Muhammad Rumi. Their form of **dhikr**, a slowly spinning dance, led to their other name of "whirling dervishes."

Mihrab A niche in a **mosque** that indicates the **qibla**, the direction of the Kaaba in **Mecca** for prayer.

Millet A self-governing religious community of non-Muslims, during the **Ottoman Empire**.

Mina A site near **Mecca** associated with rituals of the **Hajj**, in particular the "Stoning of the Devil."

Minaret A tower typically attached to a **mosque** from which the **muezzin** traditionally makes the call to prayer.

Minbar An elevated pulpit found in a **mosque**, used by the imam to deliver the sermon.

Miraj The second part of Prophet Muhammad's Night Journey, when he ascended from Jerusalem to the heavens. See also **Isra**.

Mongol Empire Established by Genghis Khan in 1206, the empire stretched across Central Asia to the Persian Gulf and the Danube River. The Mongols razed Muslim cities but later converted to Islam.

Mosque From the Arabic *masjid*, meaning a "place of prostration."

It is a building for prayer but also a place where Muslims can come together as a community.

Mount Arafat A site near **Mecca**, associated with rituals of the **Hajj**.

Muezzin The person who calls Muslims to prayer.

Mughal Empire Created in India after the invasion of Babur from Central Asia in 1526. Its Muslim emperors ruled predominantly Hindu subjects.

Muhadithun Specialists in the study of **hadith**.

Muhajirun Those who followed the Prophet in his flight from **Mecca** to **Medina** (the **Hijra**).

Mujahidin From the Arabic "those who fight for jihad." Most closely linked with the Afghani and foreign forces who fought the Soviet Union in Afghanistan (1979–89).

Mujtahid Someone who is able to interpret and make independent rulings on Islamic law.

Murid A disciple in a **Sufi** order.

Muslim A follower of Islam: literally "One who submits" (to God).

Muslim Brotherhood Political **Islamist** group, founded in Egypt in 1928 by schoolteacher Hassan al-Banna.

Mutawin Islamic religious police.

Mutazilites "Those who separate themselves:" a Muslim group established in the 8th century whose followers believed in open questioning and rational enquiry.

Najaf Iraqi city containing the burial place of the First **Imam** Ali ibn Abi Talib, a sacred site in **Shia** Islam.

Najd A rocky plateau in central Saudi Arabia, scene of early Muslim victories over rebel tribes, and later the birthplace of **Wahhabism**.

Naskh A rounded, easily legible Arabic script, used in early copies of the **Quran** and other documents.

Night Journey See **Isra** and **Miraj**.

Niqab A face veil worn by some Muslim women that leaves only the eyes uncovered.

Niyya The concept of intending an act for the sake of God.

Orientalism A Western view of Arab and Muslim culture as exotic, backward, and uncivilized that flourished in the 19th and 20th centuries.

Ottoman Empire Founded in Turkey in the 13th century by Osman I, at its height the empire included all of modern Turkey, much of the Middle East and North Africa, and much of southeastern Europe. It was abolished in 1923 with the formation of the Turkish Republic.

Pan-Arabism The idea of a political and cultural alliance across Arab states that was popular from the 1950s to 1970s.

People of the Book See **ahl al-Kitab**.

Persian Empire An empire ruled by a series of dynasties from the Achaemenids, established by Cyrus the Great in 550 BCE, to the Qajars, whose reign came to an end in 1925. With the Arab conquest of Persia in 651 CE, Islam became its dominant religion. The modern name for Persia is Iran.

Qadar The concept of divine destiny in Islam—the recognition that God knows all that has happened and all that will happen.

al-Qaeda A militant organization that was formed in the late 1980s by participants in the war against the Soviets in Afghanistan. Its goal was specifically to target the West. Under the leadership of Osama bin Laden, it carried out attacks against the United States— including 9/11—and its allies.

Qajar A dynasty that ruled Persia (Iran) from 1796 to 1925.

Qawwali A **Sufi** musical tradition that aims to elicit a state of ecstasy in its listeners.

Qibla The direction of prayer for Muslims, originally **Jerusalem**, but later changed by the Prophet Muhammad to **Mecca**, following a divine revelation in 624.

Qital Literally "combat," a temporary form of **jihad** sometimes known as the "lesser jihad," which may take the form of armed struggle.

Qiyas A way of establishing rulings in Islamic jurisprudence by reasoning. It is applied in the absence of any guidance from the **Quran** or the **hadith**.

Quran The holy book and foundational scripture of Islam. It is God's message to humanity as revealed to Prophet Muhammad.

Quranists A minority of Muslims who believe that the **Quran** alone is sufficient for guidance, and dismiss all **hadith** as unreliable.

Quraysh A leading tribe of **Mecca**. Muhammad was born into the Banu Hashim branch of the tribe in 570 CE.

Qurra "Reciters:" those who memorized the Quran during the Prophet's lifetime, enabling it to be collated in written form.

Rakat A sequence of prescribed physical movements performed while offering prayers. Each daily prayer comprises a specified number of rakats. See also **salat**.

Ramadan The ninth month of the **Hijra** calendar, when Muslims fast during the hours of daylight.

Rashidun The four "rightly guided" **caliphs** in **Sunni** Islamic tradition, and the Prophet's first successors: Abu Bakr, Umar ibn al-Khattab, Uthman ibn Affan, and Ali ibn Abi Talib.

Rehal A foldable bookrest to support the **Quran** for reading.

Riad A traditional Moroccan house with a central courtyard garden.

Ridda Wars The "Wars of Apostasy," fought after the Prophet's death when a number of tribes in Arabia refused to acknowledge his successor, the **caliph** Abu Bakr.

Safa See **Marwa**.

Safavid Empire The ruling regime in **Persia** (Iran) between 1501 and 1722. The Safavid founder Ismail made **Twelver Shiism** the official form of Islam in Persia.

Sahaba See **Companions of the Prophet**.

Sahih al-Bukhari "The Authentic Collection:" a collection of around 7,275 **hadith** compiled in the 9th century by Muhammad al-Bukhari and considered by Sunnis the most reputable source on the words and actions of Prophet Muhammad.

Saint See **Wali**.

Salafism A reform/revivalist movement rooted in 18th-century **Wahhabism** that gained popularity in the 20th century. Its followers (Salafis) advocate a return to the traditions of the *salaf*, the first three generations of Muslims: the Prophet Muhammad and his Companions (the **Sahaba**); their successors (the **Tabiun**); and the successors of the successors (the **Tabi al-Tabeen**).

Salat Prayer: one of the **Five Pillars of Islam**. Formal worship of God takes place five times every day, at dawn (*fajr*), early afternoon (*dhuhr*), late afternoon (*asr*), dusk (*maghreb*), and evening (*isha*). The weekly congregational prayer, on Friday afternoon, is known as al-*juma* (the Arabic for Friday), meaning gathering together.

Sawm Fasting: one of the **Five Pillars of Islam**.

Seljuk Empire A Turkish empire lasting from 1037 to 1194. At its height it controlled a vast area, from western Anatolia (in modern-day Turkey) and Syria to the Hindu Kush in the east, and from Central Asia to the Horn of Africa in the south.

Sevener A branch of Shia Islam that believed that Ismail ibn Jafar was the seventh and last **Imam**, and that his son Muhammad ibn Ismail would return as the Imam al-Mahdi.

Shafii One of the four schools of **Sunni** Islamic law. Founded by Muhammad ibn Idris al-Shafii (767–820), it is the dominant school in East Africa, Indonesia, and parts of Arabia, and for the Kurds.

Shah Persian for "king." The last shah of Iran was exiled in 1979.

Shahada One of the **Five Pillars of Islam**. A profession of faith, it states that "there is no god but God and Muhammad is His messenger."

Sharia The code of conduct and law of Islam, which was evolved largely in the 9th century, based on the **Quran** and the **hadith**.

Sheikh A senior, respected figure. The title is often given to the head of a tribe or clan, the leader of a **Sufi** order, or a man of religious learning.

Shia The tradition of Islam that supported the Prophet's cousin and son-in-law Ali ibn Abi Talib and Ali's descendants as leaders of the Muslim community. Now the dominant form of Islam in Iran and in parts of Iraq and other countries.

Shirk Idolatry: the worship of anyone or anything besides God. Shirk is a crime under **Sharia** law.

Shura A consultation process or body. Early in Islamic history, the second caliph Umar set up a body of people (or *shura*) to elect his successor. Now it refers to a court of law or a parliament.

Silsila Literally "chain:" the lineage of spiritual teachers in a **Sufi** order.

Sira The body of literature devoted to the life of the Prophet Muhammad.

Six Pillars of Faith In Arabic, *arkan al-iman*—the Sunni belief in the Oneness of God (**Tawhid**) and in His angels, His scriptures (the Quran, the Gospels, the Torah, and the Psalms), His prophets (who received His scriptures and spread His message), the **Day of Judgment**, and divine destiny (**Qadar**).

Sufism From the Arabic, *tasawwuf*, meaning "to dress in wool," a branch of mystical Islam that emerged in the **Umayyad** period and which places an emphasis on attaining a spiritual closeness with God through rituals known as **dhikr**.

Suhur The predawn meal that is taken during the fasting month of **Ramadan**.

Sunna The Muslim way of life, in the form of its social and legal practices derived from the life of the Prophet Muhammad. Together with the **Quran** and the **hadith**, the Sunna forms the basis of **Sharia** or Islamic law.

Sunni The tradition of Islam that grew from the supporters of succession to the caliphate by election rather than by blood; now the dominant form of the religion in most parts of the Islamic world. The second most dominant is **Shia**.

Sura A chapter of the **Quran**.

Tabi al-Tabeen The generation that comes after the **Tabiun**.

Tabiun The "successors:" the generation of Muslims who came after the **Companions of the**

Prophet (Sahaba). A *Tabi* is one who received Muhammad's teachings secondhand.

Tafsir The field of scholarship that interprets and comments on the meanings of the **Quran**.

Takfir The act of one Muslim declaring another Muslim to be a nonbeliever (*kafir*) guilty of **apostasy**. It is usually associated with extremists, who use *takfir* to justify killing other Muslims who do not share their views.

Taliban A mostly student movement of Pakistani origin that succeeded in taking control of Afghanistan in the 1990s, following the withdrawal of Soviet forces.

Tanzimat A series of reforms instituted during the 19th century with the aim of modernizing the **Ottoman Empire**.

Tariqa A school, or order, of **Sufi** thought.

Tawaf Circumambulation of the **Kaaba**, performed by pilgrims during the **Hajj**.

Tawassul In **Shia** tradition, the appeal to **Imams** at their shrines to intercede with God.

Tawhid The concept of the Oneness of God, who is the sole deity.

Thobe An ankle-length robe with long sleeves (often white) worn by men in the Arabian Peninsula and parts of North Africa.

Timurid Empire The dynasty (1370–1507) founded by Timur (or Tamerlane), who was descended from Genghis Khan, founder of the

Mongol Empire. At its peak, the Timurids controlled most of Central Asia and Iran, as well as parts of India, Pakistan, Syria, and Turkey. India's **Mughal Empire** was an offshoot of the Timurid.

Twelver The branch of **Shia** Islam that believes in a line of 12 **Imams** and that the Twelfth Imam did not die but went into a hidden existence and will return as the Imam al-Mahdi.

Ulema "Those with knowledge:" the *ulema* are Islamic scholars, traditionally educated in **madrasas**. The *ulema* also produce religious officials, judges, and teachers.

Umayyad Empire The first Islamic **caliphate** after the era of the **Rashidun**. The Umayyads (661–750) made the position of caliph hereditary and ruled from Damascus. See also **al-Andalus**.

Umma The Islamic community.

Umra The "lesser pilgrimage" to **Mecca**, which can be made at any time of the year. See also **Hajj**.

Usul al-Din The five "Principles of Religion" of **Shiism**: belief in the Oneness of God (**Tawhid**), His justice (*Adl*), His messengers and prophets, the **Imam** successorship, and the **Day of Judgment**.

Usury The practice of charging interest (*riba*) on loans, which is specifically forbidden in the **Quran** and consequently in **Sharia** law.

Yathrib The former name of the city of **Medina**.

Yom al-Din See **Day of Judgment**.

Wahhabism Sunni Islamic movement started by Muhammad ibn Abd al-Wahhab in 18th-century Arabia. It was taken up by the Saudi family and is practiced in Saudi Arabia and Qatar.

Wali In Islam, a "friend of God" (*wali*, plural *awliya*), chosen by God and endowed with special, even miraculous, powers. Tombs of the saints are centers of pilgrimage.

Whirling dervishes See **Mevlevi**.

Wudu Ritual ablutions made prior to prayer.

Wufud Delegations sent by tribes to the Prophet in **Medina**, to express their loyalty.

Yazidi Kurdish minority mainly found in northern Iraq, northern Syria, and southeastern Turkey. Their faith includes elements of Iranian religions, Judaism, and Nestorian Christianity, and they venerate **Umayyad** caliph Yazid I. Long persecuted as **apostates**, most recently by the **Islamic State**.

Zakat One of the **Five Pillars of Islam**: the charitable giving of a portion of wealth to the needy.

Zakat al-Fitr A charitable obligation traditionally paid at the end of fasting in **Ramadan** to poor Muslims, so that they can celebrate the feast of **Eid al-Fitr**.

Zaydis Also known as "Fivers," a branch of **Shia** Islam who believe Zayd ibn Ali, the great-grandson of Ali ibn Abi Talib, to have been a legitimate **Imam**.

Zikr See **Dhikr**.

INDEX

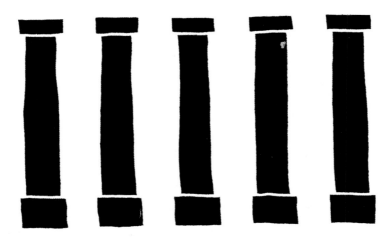

ACKNOWLEDGMENTS

Original styling by
STUDIO 8

Dorling Kindersley would like to thank:

Project Editor Andrew Humphreys
Senior Editors Scarlett O'Hara, Camilla Hallinan
US Editor Karyn Gerhard
Project Designer Amy Child
Project Art Editor Renata Latipova
Illustrations James Graham
Managing Editor Christine Stroyan
Managing Art Editor Anna Hall
Jacket Designer Surabhi Wadhwa
Jacket Design Development Manager Sophia MTT
Senior Jacket Designer Suhita Dharamjit
Jackets Editorial Coordinator Priyanka Sharma
Managing Jackets Editor Saloni Singh
DTP Designer Rakesh Kumar
Senior Pre-producer Andy Hilliard
Print Producer Jude Crozier
Art Director Karen Self
Associate Publishing Director Liz Wheeler
Publishing Director Jonathan Metcalf

Thanks to Jacob Field for the Directory, Neil Hewison for the Glossary, Katie John for proofreading, and Helen Peters for the Index.

PICTURE CREDITS

The publisher would like to thank the following for heir kind permission to reproduce their photographs:

(Key: a-above; b-below/bottom; c-center; f-far; l-left; r-right; t-top)

21 SuperStock: DeAgostini (tr). **24 Alamy Stock Photo:** The History Collection (bl). **SuperStock:** Universal Images (tr). **26 Dreamstime.com:** Alengolas (bl). **27 akg-images:** Gerard Degeorge (tl). **29 Alamy Stock Photo:** Art Collection 2 (tr). **30 Alamy Stock Photo:** age fotostock (tl). **31 Getty Images:** Werner Forman / Universal Images Group (bl). **33 Rex by Shutterstock:** Harper Collins Publishers (bc). **35 Getty Images:** Culture Club / Hulton Archive (tr). **39 Getty Images:** AFP / Haidar Mohammed Ali (br). **40 eyevine:** Alexandra Boulat / VII / Redux (tr). **41 iStockphoto.com:** sitox (bl). **SuperStock:** imageBroker (tl). **43 Getty Images:** Prakash Singh / AFP (tl). **45 Alamy Stock Photo:** Godong (tl). **48 Getty Images:** Moment / Harith Samarawickrama (t). **49 Alamy Stock Photo:** B.O'Kane (tr). **Getty Images:** Noorullah Shirzada / AFP (br). **52 Alamy Stock Photo:** Images & Stories (br). **54 Alamy Stock Photo:** orhandurgut (b). **55 Getty Images:** Mustafa Ozer / AFP (tr). **57 Alamy Stock Photo:** halil ibrahim kurucan (tl); Ahmad Faizal Yahya (bl). **59 Alamy Stock Photo:** Kenan Kaya (tl). **66 akg-images:** Jean-Louis Nou (tr). **68 Alamy Stock Photo:** Rapp Halour (t). **69 Alamy Stock Photo:** Science History Images (tr); The History Collection (bl). **72 Getty Images:** Shah Marai / AFP (br). **74 Bridgeman Images:** © British Library Board. All Rights Reserved (b). **75 Alamy Stock Photo:** Godong (tl). **77 Dreamstime.com:** Amani A (bl).

83 Getty Images: Anadolu Agency / Jefri Tarigan (t). **84 akg-images:** Roland and Sabrina Michaud (tl). **85 Getty Images:** AFP / Stringer / Fadel Senna (tr). **87 Getty Images:** Photo12 / Universal Images Group (tr). **89 Alamy Stock Photo:** özkan özmen (tl). **91 Rex by Shutterstock:** AP / Shutterstock. **92 Rex by Shutterstock:** Cci / Shutterstock (crb). **100 123RF.com:** Ievgenii Fesenko / efesenko84 (bl). **Getty Images:** Remi Benali / The Image Bank (tr). **101 Getty Images:** Edwin Remsberg / VW PICS / Universal Images Group Editorial (br). **103 Alamy Stock Photo:** Allstar Picture Library / ALLSTAR TRAVEL (tr). **105 SuperStock:** Universal Images (tr). **106 Bridgeman Images:** Tallandier (bl). **107 Alamy Stock Photo:** rasoul ali (tl). **111 Rex by Shutterstock:** Str / EPA / Shutterstock (tl). **113 Getty Images:** Education Images / Universal Images Group (r). **115 Getty Images:** age fotostock / Konrad Zelazowski (tr). **117 Getty Images:** Yegor Aleyev / TASS (bl). **121 Getty Images:** Asif Hassan / AFP (bl). **122 Alamy Stock Photo:** Roland Liptak (t). **123 iStockphoto.com:** SoumenNath / E+ (br). **125 Getty Images:** Patti McConville (br). **131 Alamy Stock Photo:** Hemis / Rieger Bertrand / Hemis.fr (br). **133 Getty Images:** Wathiq Khuzaie / Getty Images News (tr). **138 Getty Images:** laura rangel copyright / Moment (t). **139 Alamy Stock Photo:** Science History Images (tr). **142 Alamy Stock Photo:** photosindia (bl). **144 iStockphoto.com:** mustafagull (t). **145 Getty Images:** Jack Vartoogian / Archive Photos (tr). **151 Alamy Stock Photo:** Science History Images / Photo Researchers (tr). **153 akg-images:** Pictures From History (br). **154 Alamy Stock Photo:** Science History Images / Photo Researchers (tr). **155 Alamy Stock Photo:** Science History Images (br). **157 123RF.com:** Olga Popova (tr). **Alamy Stock Photo:** Art Directors & Trip (bl). **159 Alamy Stock Photo:** Melvyn Longhurst (bl). **161 Getty Images:** Dea Picture Library / DeAgostini (t). **163 Alamy Stock Photo:** Photononstop / Philippe Lissac (tr). **164 Alamy Stock Photo:** John Warburton-Lee Photography / Julian Love (br). **168 Alamy Stock Photo:** Ruth Hofshi (tl). **169 Dreamstime.com:** Elevationus (bl). **170 Dreamstime.com:** Sorin Colac (bl). **171 akg-images:** Album / Oronoz (bl). **Alamy Stock Photo:** Granger Historical Picture Archive (t). **172 Getty Images:** Apic / Hulton Archive (bc). **173 Bridgeman Images:** Archives Charmet (tl). **175 Maypop Books:** Coleman Barks (bl). **177 Alamy Stock Photo:** Ian Dagnall (tr). **178 Alamy Stock Photo:** Granger Historical Picture Archive / Granger, NYC (bl). **179 Alamy Stock Photo:** World History Archive (tr). **181 Alamy Stock Photo:** Art Collection (tl). **183 Alamy Stock Photo:** Interfoto / History (tl). **184 Alamy Stock Photo:** Niday Picture Library (tr). **185 Alamy Stock Photo:** The Picture Art Collection (br). **187 SuperStock:** DeAgostini (tr). **188 Getty Images:** Marco Brivio / Photographer's Choice (bl); Heritage Images / Hulton Fine Art Collection (tc). **189 Alamy Stock Photo:** age fotostock / Historical Views (tr). **190 Shutterstock:** emran (bc). **191 The Metropolitan Museum of Art, New York:** Gift of J. Pierpont Morgan, 1917 (tr). **193 Alamy Stock Photo:** dbimages / dbtravel (bl). **Getty Images:** Kyodo News (bl). **196 Alamy Stock Photo:** dov makabaw Israel (b). **197 Alamy Stock Photo:** Prisma Archivo (bc). **Depositphotos Inc:** morrmota (tc, tr). **Dreamstime.com:** Adel Mohamady (tl). **198 Alamy**

Stock Photo: travelpixs (tr). **199 Dreamstime.com:** Daniel M. Cisilino (b). **200 Alamy Stock Photo:** Guillem Lopez (bl). **201 Getty Images:** Colors Hunter - Chasseur de Couleurs / Moment (tr). **203 Alamy Stock Photo:** Terry Mathews (tr). **205 Alamy Stock Photo:** The History Collection (tr). **212 Dreamstime.com:** Peter Hermes Furian (tr). **213 Alamy Stock Photo:** Heritage Image Partnership Ltd / © Fine Art Images (bl, br). **214 Alamy Stock Photo:** MehmetO (bl). **215 Getty Images:** Moment / Natasha Breen (bc); Bernard Roussel (tr). **217 Getty Images:** Anadolu Agency / Enes Kanli (bl). **218 Bridgeman Images:** Gerome, Jean Leon (1824-1904) / French (br). **221 Alamy Stock Photo:** Historic Collection (tr). **Getty Images:** Zöllner / ullstein bild (bl). **223 Alamy Stock Photo:** Classic Image (tr). **225 Alamy Stock Photo:** Niday Picture Library (bc). **226 Getty Images:** Bettmann (tl). **227 Getty Images:** Corbis Historical / Brooks Kraft LLC (br); Getty Images Entertainment / Rachel Murray (tr). **230 Getty Images:** Universal Images Group / Leemage (bl). **231 Getty Images:** AFP / Adem Altan / Stringer (tl). **234 Getty Images:** Aldo Pavan (tl). **235 Getty Images:** Hulton Archive (bc). **236 Getty Images:** EyeEm / Mawardi Bahar (br); The Image Bank / Wayne Eastep (tl). **237 Getty Images:** The Image Bank / Kirklandphotos (tl). **239 Rex by Shutterstock:** AP / Shutterstock (br). **240 Getty Images:** AFP (bl). **241 Getty Images:** Anadolu Agency / Ahmed Ramadan (tl). **245 Getty Images:** Bettmann (tl). **246 Getty Images:** AFP / Sajjad Hussain (bl); ICC / Stu Forster-ICC (tr). **247 Getty Images:** Moment / Aliraza Khatri's Photography (b). **249 Getty Images:** Bettmann (bc). **250 Getty Images:** Gamma-Rapho / Alain Mingam (br). **251 Getty Images:** Bettmann (tr). **257 Shutterstock:** hkhtt hj (tl). **258 Getty Images:** AFP / Stringer / Sam Panthaky (bl). **259 Getty Images:** AFP / Stringer / Haidar Hamdani (tc). **261 Getty Images:** AFP / Luis Tato (br). **263 Getty Images:** The Image Bank / Jorg Greuel (tl). **265 Getty Images:** AFP / Hatem Salhi (br). **267 Getty Images:** AFP (br). **268 Getty Images:** AFP / Fayez Nureldine (br). **269 Getty Images:** AFP / Chaideer Mahyuddin (tr). **271 Getty Images:** AFP / Stringer / Mohammed Al-Shaikh (tc). **274 Getty Images:** Robert Nickelsberg (br). **275 Getty Images:** Hulton Archive / Tom Stoddart Archive (tr). **276 Alamy Stock Photo:** Handout (br). **277 Getty Images:** AFP / Paul Ellis (tr). **279 Getty Images:** AFP / John Wessels (tr). **280 Getty Images:** AFP / Juni Kriswanto (bc). **284 Getty Images:** Clive Brunskill (tr). **285 Getty Images:** AFP / Mandel Ngan (tr). **iStockphoto.com:** E+ / sturti (bc). **287 Getty Images:** Contour / Allison Michael Orenstein (tl). **289 Getty Images:** Stringer / Victor Besa (br). **290 Getty Images:** Aurora Photos / Konstantin Trubavin (crb). **294 Alamy Stock Photo:** Charles O. Cecil (tr); Historic Collection (bl). **295 Getty Images:** Kentaroo Tryman (br). **296 Getty Images:** AFP / Pedro Ugarte (t). **297 Getty Images:** Stringer / Zach Gibson (bl). **298 Getty Images:** AFP / Stringer / Betina Garcia (bl). **299 Getty Images:** Devin Manky (tr). **301 iStockphoto.com:** Lilanakani (tl). **302 Getty Images:** Maskot (tl). **303 Getty Images:** Valeria Ferraro / SOPA Images / LightRocket (tr); Stringer / Matt King (bl).

All other images © Dorling Kindersley.